R.F. Willetts was Professor of Greek and Chairman of the School of Hellenic and Roman Studies at the University of Birmingham. Widely travelled in Mediterranean lands and a regular visitor to Crete, he published on many aspects of Cretan civilization.

Cut-out bronze plaque of two huntsmen, decorated in very low relief with incised details, late seventh century BC

THE CIVILIZATION
OF ANCIENT CRETE

R.F. Willetts

PHOENIX

In Memory of My Father

A PHOENIX PRESS PAPERBACK

First published in Great Britain
by B.T. Batsford Ltd in 1977
This paperback edition published in 2004
by Phoenix Press,
a division of The Orion Publishing Group Ltd,
Orion House, 5 Upper St Martin's Lane,
London WC2H 9EA
Phoenix Press
Sterling Publishing Co Inc
387 Park Avenue South
New York
NY 10016–8810
USA

A CIP catalogue record for this book
is available from the British Library.

Printed and bound in Great Britain by
Butler & Tanner Ltd, Frome and London

ISBN 1 84212 746 2

CONTENTS

TEXT ILLUSTRATIONS

THE PLATES

Frontispiece
Cut-out bronze plaque of two huntsmen, decorated in very low relief with incised details, late seventh century BC

Between pages 160 and 161

ACKNOWLEDGMENTS

The Author and Publishers wish to thank the following for permission to reproduce the illustrations appearing in this book: The Ashmolean Museum, Oxford, pl. 16; Arthur Banks and B.T. Batsford Ltd, fig. 1; the Trustees of the British Museum, London, pl. 12; Cabinet des Médailles, Paris, pl. 22; Clarendon Press, Oxford, pl. 8–9 (from A.J. Evans, *The Palace of Minos*) and 13–14 (from A.J. Evans, *Scripta Minoa*); Peter Clayton, London, pl. 1; Elsevier International Projects Ltd, fig. 3 (from Peter Warren, *The Aegean Civilizations*, 1975); Fotografic, Karlsruhe and Walter de Gruyter Verlag, pl. 23; Alison Frantz, Princeton, pl. 17–18; Evelyn Hagenbeck and Museum für Kunst und Gewerbe, Hamburg, pl. 19–21; Dimitrios Harissiadis and George Rainbird Ltd, pl. 5 and 11; Hirmer Verlag, Munich, pl. 2–4; Iraklion Museum, pl. 10 and 15; Liverpool University Press, fig. 7 (from *Town Planning Review*, xxi, 1950); Methuen & Co. Ltd for figs. 17 and 25 (from J.D.S. Penblebury, *The Archaeology of Crete*, 1939); Musée du Louvre, Paris, jacket illustration and frontispiece; Penguin Books Ltd, figs. 6, 16, 18, and 24 (from R.W. Hutchinson, *Prehistoric Crete*, 1962); Josephine Powell, Rome, pl. 6–7; Princeton University Press, fig. 8 (from J.W. Graham, *The Palaces of Crete*, 1962); Routledge & Kegan Paul Ltd, figs. 2, 13 and 15 (from K. Branigan, *The Foundations of Palatial Crete*, 1970); Thames & Hudson Ltd, figs. 5, 9 and 12 (from Sinclair Hood, *The Minoans*, 1971); Weidenfeld & Nicholson Ltd and MacMillan Publishing Co. Inc., figs. 4 and 14 (from Michael Grant, *Ancient History Atlas*, 1971); Eva Wilson and B.T. Batsford Ltd, figs. 8, 10, 11 and 19–23.

The Author wishes to thank his wife for her assistance in selecting illustrations and their sources; Peter Kemmis Betty for his unfailing advice and care in seeing the book through the press; Walter de Gruyter Verlag for permission to include his translation of the Law Code of Gortyn; and the Trustees of the Leverhulme Trust Fund for the award of a Research Grant which considerably assisted him in the preparation of this book.

CHRONOLOGICAL TABLE

DATE	CRETE	GREECE	EGYPT	
*c.*6000 BC	Neolithic			
*c.*3000 BC				
*c.*2800 BC		Neolithic	Early Dynastic Period	⎰ Dynasty I ⎱ Dynasty II
	Early Minoan I			
*c.*2600 BC				⎧ Dynasty III
*c.*2500 BC	Early Minoan II	Early Helladic I	Old Kingdom	⎨ Dynasty IV, Dynasty V
*c.*2400 BC				
*c.*2300 BC				⎩ Dynasty VI
	Early Minoan III	Early Helladic II		
*c.*2200 BC			First	⎧
*c.*2100 BC	Middle Minoan IA	Early Helladic III	Intermediate	⎨ Dynasties VII to X
			Period	⎩
*c.*2000 BC				
	Middle Minoan IB	Middle Helladic	Middle	⎰ Dynasties
*c.*1900 BC	—————————P		Kingdom	⎱ XI to XIII
	Middle Minoan IIA A			
*c.*1800 BC	—————————L			
	Middle Minoan IIB A		Second	⎧ Dynasties
	C		Intermediate	⎨ XIV to
*c.*1700 BC	—————————E		Period and	XVII
	Middle Minoan IIIA S		Hyksos Kings	⎩
*c.*1600 BC	Middle Minoan IIIB			
	Late Minoan IA P			⎧ Dynasty
*c.*1500 BC	—————————A			XVIII
	Late Minoan IB L			
	—————————A			
	Late Minoan II C			
*c.*1400 BC	—————————E	Mycenaean		
	Late Minoan IIIA S			
*c.*1300 BC				
	Late Minoan IIIB		New	⎨ Dynasty
			Kingdom	XIX
*c.*1200 BC				Dynasty XX
	Late Minoan IIIC			
*c.*1100 BC		Sub-Mycenaean		Dynasty
				⎩ XXI
*c.*1000 BC	Sub-Minoan	Protogeometric		
c. 900 BC				
	Protogeometric	Geometric		
c. 800 BC				
	Geometric			
c. 700 BC				
	Orientalising			
c. 600 BC				
	Archaic Period			
c. 500 BC				
	Classical Period			
330 BC				
	Hellenistic Period			
67 BC	Roman Conquest			
323 AD	Graeco-Roman Period			

INTRODUCTION

Cosmos is a word of Greek origin which, as will be later made clear in this book, has a particular relevance to the island of Crete – at least in its historical period of antiquity as opposed to its even more ample prehistoric or archaeological phases. For us the word now signifies the universe as an ordered whole, or an ordered system of ideas, a kind of sum-total of historical, scientific and intellectual experience. Cosmos connotes vastness, albeit ordered vastness.

It is this concept of order which forms the most substantial link with the original meaning of the term in Greek antiquity, a meaning which had to do, in its most simple and active sense, with the mustering of groups of men. The world in which its various evocations of order developed was, even for an experienced traveller or speculative thinker, essentially the world of the Mediterranean region and of the lands and peoples of its fostering littoral, the coastal regions of the three adjacent continents of Europe, Asia and Africa. Until the very end of antiquity navigation progressed from sailing on rivers to crossing the Mediterranean, or coasting around islands and continents – except for navigating the Indian Ocean by running before the monsoon winds. By comparison, with the aid of the modern rudder and the compass, navigation made more progress between the thirteenth and the fifteenth centuries AD than in the previous four millennia.

John Donne, preaching to the king at court in April 1629 could say, glancing back and looking forward:

That earth, which in some thousands of yeares men could not look over, nor discern what form it had (for neither *Lactantius*, almost three hundred yeares after Christ; nor *S. Augustine*, more than a hundred yeares after him, would beleeve the earth to be round) That earth, which no man in his person is ever said to have compassed till our age: That earth which is too much for man yet, (for as yet a very great part of the earth is unpeopled) That earth, which, if we will cast it all but into a Map, costs many moneths labour to grave it; nay, if we will cast but a piece of an acre of it into a garden, costs many yeares labour to fashion and furnish it; all that earth: and then that heaven, which spreads so farre, as that subtill men have, with some appearance of probabilitie, imagined, that in that heaven, in those manifold Spheres of the Planets and the Starres, there are many earths, many worlds, as big as this which we inhabit: That earth and that heaven, which spent God himself, Almightie God, six dayes in furnishing, Moses sets up in a few syllables, in one line, *In principio, In the beginning God created heaven and earth.* If a *Livie* or a *Guicciardine*, or such extensive and voluminous authors had had this story in hand, God must have made another world, to have made them a library to hold their books, of the making of this world. Into what wire would they have drawn out this earth! Into what leaf-gold would they have beat out these heavens! It may assist our conjecture herein, to consider, that amongst those men, who proceed with a sober modestie and limitation in their writing, and make a conscience not to clog the world with unnecessary books; yet the volumes which are written by them, upon the beginning of Genesis, are scarce less than infinite.

Because of its geographical position in the Mediterranean, Crete has been, several times over, a beginning or genesis of various distinct kinds, whose special characteristics have prompted the attention of writers from antiquity to the present day. Although their accounts can hardly be described as scarce less than infinite, they are nevertheless by this time quite considerable. So much so that a modern scholar, desiring to proceed with sober modesty and not wishing to clog the world with unnecessary books, is obliged to introduce another with some circumspection – especially when it is concerned with the civilization of a relatively tiny portion of a whole world now largely peopled and demanding historical analysis on comparable canvases to a more compelling degree than at any time since Greek historiography created at least the theoretical possibly of world history.

In the course of his remarks upon the development of Greco-Roman historiography in his work *The Idea of History*, R.G. Collingwood pointed out that, after the fifth century BC, the historian's outlook underwent an enlargement in time. In Greek eyes history had been essentially the history of one particular social unit at one particular time; and this particularism had coloured all their historiography before the time of Alexander the Great. Greeks were conscious that this particular social unit was only one among many; in so far as it came into contact with others during the given space of time, these others put in an appearance on the stage of history. Though Herodotos, for instance, had to say something about the Persians, his interest in them was not for their own sake but only as enemies of the Greeks. In the fifth century, and even earlier, Greeks were conscious that there was such a thing as the human world, which was the totality of all particular social units and which they called the *oikoumene* as distinct from the *kosmos*, the natural world. However, their consciousness of this unity of the human world was a geographical and not an historical consciousness, and consequently the idea of oecumenical or world-

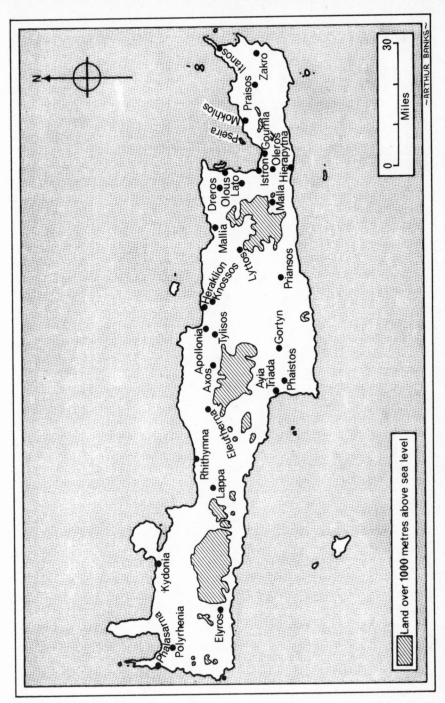

1 Crete

history was still non-existent. They were also conscious that the history of the particular society in which they were interested had been going on for a long time.

The limitations which Collingwood diagnosed in earlier Greek historiography, were, he considered, overcome in the Hellenistic period, with a new kind of history, maturing in the work of Polybios, whose theme was the conquest of the world by Rome, beginning at a point more than 150 years before his time of writing and extending over a field of five generations instead of one. Polybios was modern in the sense that historical inquiry was for him a special type of research needing a special name of its own. With Polybios the Hellenistic tradition of historical thought passed into the hands of Rome. The only original development (for Collingwood) which it received there was from Livy.

It became a familiar fact about the contemporary Hellenistic world that Barbarians could become Greeks. The Greek historical consciousness, which for Herodotus had been primarily the consciousness of hostility between Greeks and Barbarians, became the consciousness of cooperation between them, in which Greeks took the lead and Barbarians, by following their lead, became Greeks, heirs to Greek culture and thus heirs to the Greek historical consciousness. By the conquests of Alexander, the *oikoumene*, or at least a very large part of it, including all the non-Greek peoples in whom the Greeks were specially interested, became a single political unit. The 'world' became not simply a geographical but an historical expression. The empire of Alexander shared a single history of the Greek world; and, potentially, the whole *oikoumene* shared it. Greek history was now a single history that held good from the Adriatic to the Indus and from the Danube to the Sahara.

The idea of the whole world as a single historical unit was a typically Stoic idea and Stoicism was itself a typical product of the Hellenistic period. Hellenism created the idea of oecumenical history. Such world-history could not be written on the strength of testimony from living eye-witnesses and therefore a new method of compilation was required, what Collingwood called the 'scissors-and-paste' historical method, the construction of a patchwork history with materials drawn from authorities, from the works of previous historians who had already written the histories of particular societies at particular times. The oecumenical history of the Hellenistic age (which includes the Roman age) was based on a high estimate of the work done by the particularistic historians of the Hellenic age, especially Herodotos and Thucydides.

To Herodotos and Thucydides, however, as Collingwood had earlier explained, the re-writing of their histories or their incorporation into the history of a longer period, would have seemed an absurdity, because when their generation was dead and gone the work could never be done again. Nowadays, wrote Collingwood, we think of monographs on various subjects as ideally forming parts of a universal history, so that, if their subjects are carefully chosen and their scale and treatment carefully controlled, they might serve as chapters in a single historical work; and this is the way in which a writer like Grote actually treated Herodotos' account of the Persian War and Thucydides' of the Peloponnesian. But if any given history is the autobiography of a generation, it cannot be re-written when that generation has passed away, because the evidence on which it was based will have perished.

There is a special relevance for the historian of Crete in recalling Collingwood's summary of Greco-Roman historiography in terms of transition from particularistic, if majestic, autobiographies of a generation to the threshold of the concept of world history. Crete, like Cyprus, that other great island centre of Aegean civilization, was geographically positioned so as to be continuously influenced by technical and cultural developments of all kinds in those crucial areas of neighbouring continents, Anatolia, Mesopotamia, Egypt, which contributed to the complex texture of the whole history of the ancient Near East. To be influenced is not the same as to be environmentally or economically conditioned. There are aspects of Cretan achievement, conspicuously but by no means exclusively in the Minoan Bronze Age – which must rank as Europe's first major experience of civilization in the sense of sophisticated, ordered living and skilled cultivation of its finer arts – distinctive aspects which demonstrate the vitally original contributions which the island's inhabitants made from early times in assimilating outside influences and bending them to their original purposes. Such contributions oblige recognition of the study of their history as eminently worthy in itself.

In one sense this is to reassert the claims of particularist history in the oldest Hellenic tradition; but only formally and superficially. No particularist history of this kind would now be governed by the limitations of living memory. The scale is enormously prolonged to form the biography of countless generations over the millennia from Neolithic times through the Bronze Age and the Iron Age, from prehistory into historic times. Insofar as its history is a vital part of the history of ancient Greece and of Hellenism, set amid the experience of the older civilizations of the Near East, Cretan history truly participates in universal history.

If we think of particularist history in another sense, as, for instance, the history of writing, or of palace architecture, or of mural painting, or of bronze-working, or of law-making, or of mythology and religion – there are several fields where the record is so arresting that it has compelled a general attention.

Crete is the most southerly province of modern Greece and, next to Cyprus, is the largest island in the Aegean, covering an area of about 8300 sq. km., with a population of nearly half a million, and divided administratively (from west to east) into the four prefectures of Khania, Rethimno, Iraklion and Lassithi. The island was conquered by the Romans in 67 BC and its subsequent history until the present day illustrates its situation from the earliest times as an Aegean lodestone for settler, trader, traveller and rapacious conqueror.

In the last two centuries of Venetian rule, before the arrival of the Turks, there was a considerable renaissance of the arts in Crete, in poetry, drama and in the painting of such masters as Theotokopoulos (El Greco), Dhamaskinos and Klotzas. Despite continuous instability and insecurity, despite the exploitation, the tributes and taxes levied by foreign rulers, the surviving accounts of travellers give revealing insights of the way of life of ordinary people which underwent little basic change, as likewise of an apparently normally prosperous agricultural economy in the sixteenth, seventeenth and eighteenth centuries, with olive oil and grapes as major products. On the basis of such evidence there were, it seems, significant exports of wine and oil; and there is also evidence of the export of wheat, lemons, figs, raisins, almonds, honey, cheese, herbs, silk, wax and cypress wood chests. Such produce was available for local consumption, together with many fruits and vegetables, barley, meat, sugar and cedar wood. Apparently flax had displaced wool for the common manufacture of garments in the early seventeenth century, though flax is no longer grown and wool is commonly produced in the villages. There is mention of silk working in 1739 and in 1834. Though the musket replaced the bow for hunting, there is to this day a flourishing pottery industry which has continued from the earliest times of habitation.

The trade in wine and oil from Crete to England led to the appointment of the first British consul in Candia in 1522. We know of various travellers to Crete in the earlier Venetian period but in the sixteenth century there came such European visitors as Thevet from France in 1549, Ecklin from Germany in 1552, Radziwill from Poland in 1584 and Sommers from Germany in 1590. At the beginning of the century, in 1506, Sir Richard Guylforde and his chaplain visited the church of St Titus at Gortyn in the course of a pilgrimage to the Holy Land. One Roger Bodenham, on a trading voyage in 1550–1, recorded these remarks on contemporary conditions:

> There be in that Iland of Candia many banished men, that live continually in the mountaines, they came down to serve, to the number of foure or five thousand, they are good archers, every one with his bowe and arrowes, a sword and a dagger, with long haire, and bootes that reach up to their grine, and a shirt of male, hanging the one halfe before, and the other halfe behinde, these were sent away againe assoone as the armie was past. They would drinke wine out of all measure.

During the Venetian period it is quite clear that interest in Cretan antiquities had begun to stir. The Florentine priest Buondelmonte travelled there in 1415 and 1418. Much of what he explored and noticed no longer remains. His work was included in the *Creta Sacra* of Cornelius in 1755. Monuments and inscriptions were recorded by Honorio de Belli, historian of Candia, in 1596. Fynes

Moryson, Fellow of Peterhouse, Cambridge, published a book in 1617 about his ten years of travel in many lands from Ireland to Turkey. He landed in Crete in 1596. In Candia he stayed with an English merchant and, on the way there, the Labyrinth of Crete was pointed out to him, as it was no doubt regularly to other travellers.

A Scotsman, William Lithgow, spent fifty-eight days travelling in the western and central parts of Crete round about 1610. He published a book concerning his nineteen years of travel, in Europe, Asia and Africa, in 1632. He tells us something about the dress and habits of the people, gives details about the crops – and he too saw the entry to the Labyrinth. At about the same time, in 1611, came George Sandys, who published a first edition of a book about his travels in 1615. He seems to have been the first British traveller to enter the Labyrinth, which he correctly understood to be nothing more than a quarry at the foot of Mount Ida. He also gives an interesting description of a folk-dance which could well have survived from antiquity:

> The Country people do dance with their Bows ready bent on their arms, their Quivers hanging on their backs, and their swords by their sides, imitating therein their Ancestors (a custom also amongst the Lacedemonians) called by them *Pyrricha*: and as of old, so use they to sing in their dancings, and reply to one another.

Bernard Randolph, who made his visit in 1680, published an account in 1687, which is valuable for his description of conditions in the initial years of Turkish rule. Tournefort, in his *Voyage au Levant* of 1717 described the island as he saw it in his journeys of 1700. Dr Richard Pococke, who arrived in Crete in August 1739, described economic and social conditions and gave interesting details of the Turkish administration, tax collecting and so on in the second volume of his *Description of the East* of 1745.

Meursius in his *Creta*, which was published in Amsterdam in 1675, was concerned with collecting the references from ancient authorities about Crete. Karl Hoeck, who never himself visited Crete, was similarly concerned but his *Kreta* (1823–9) presented the first genuinely scholarly account of the island. This modern scholarly tradition of work on Crete was further enhanced by Robert Pashley, Fellow of Trinity College, Cambridge, who travelled all over Crete in 1834, soon after the Greek War of Independence. His account of the condition of Crete and its language, his accurate identification of most of the important sites, was published in the two volumes of his *Travels in Crete* of 1837. Victor Raulin began his work on Crete in 1845 and his substantial account of the physical features of the island was published in the two volumes of his *Description Physique de l'Isle de Crète* in 1869. Between 1851 and 1853, Captain (later Admiral) T.A.B. Spratt was surveying the coast of Crete for the Admiralty. In the course of his work he also journeyed into the interior of the island on several occasions. His two volumes on *Travels and Researches in Crete*, published in 1865, contain valuable information about the natural history and geology as well as a survey of the archaeology which sometimes supplements or corrects the work of Pashley.

This earlier impressive scholarly work of the nineteenth century was a prelude to the spectacular discoveries of its closing decades, which were to reveal the rich heritage of the Cretan past, the vast inheritance of skill and high achievement of the islanders from Neolithic times, through the two millennia of the Aegean Bronze Age, the transition to the Iron Age and their important role in the historical period of Classical and Hellenistic times. Not only were the archaeological discoveries of the most spectacular kind, but a quantity of epigraphical material was to be discovered, forming an invaluable storehouse of information about the history of the Greek language and the basic social institutions of the Greek city-state.

Already in 1878 the aptly named Minos Kalokairinos had done a preliminary work of excavation on the site of the Palace of Minos at Knossos; so also had Heinrich Schliemann, excavator of Troy, Mycenae and Tiryns. Sir Arthur Evans visited Crete for the first time in 1893 to search for seal-stones and investigate the prehistoric script associated with them. Evans, Federigo Halbherr and Antonio Taramelli described more ancient sites. In 1897 Evans was given permission to excavate part of the Knossos Palace site, and the principal work was done there in the six seasons from 1900 to 1905. Evans continued the work annually until 1914 and again from 1920 until 1932, to be magnificently presented in *The Palace of Minos*, the first volume appearing in 1921 and the fourth in 1935.

Other British archaeologists excavated at Zakro and Palaikastro in the eastern extremity of the island. The American archaeologists, Richard Seager and Harriet Boyd, excavated at Vasiliki, Mochlos and Gournia on the Gulf of Mirabello. Italian archaeologists began to reveal the palace of Phaistos in the south. Joseph Hazzidakis began the excavation of a third palace at Mallia on the north coast, to the east of Knossos, in 1915, work which was continued by French archaeologists after the end of the First World War. Hazzidakis also excavated at other places, including Tylissos, to the west of Knossos. Stephanos Xanthoudides excavated, from 1904 onward, the famous early circular tombs of the plain of Messara. The great work of Hazzidakis and Xanthoudides has been continued by Spyridon Marinatos, Nicolas Platon, Stylianos Alexiou, Costas Davaras, John Sakellarakis and others. A fourth Bronze Age palace was discovered by Platon at Zakro in 1962 and the work of exploration of the Minoan remains on Santorini (Thera) by Marinatos has extended our knowledge of Minoan civilization and added fuel to the fires of speculation about its collapse.

The work of the late J.D.S. Pendlebury in the 1930s is commemorated in his memorable and definitive work *The Archaeology of Crete* of 1939; and that of R.W. Hutchinson is incorporated in his *Prehistoric Crete* of 1962. The research of Evans and Pendlebury has been continued by the exploration and writings of Sinclair Hood and others associated with the British School of Archaeology – Popham, Warren, Branigan, Cadogan. The archaeological exploration of Doro Levi and his Italian colleagues, of Henry Van Effenterre, Pierre Demargne and their French colleagues, continues to contribute new discoveries and valuable analyses; and Paul Faure has notably added a new dimension by his patient investigation of the island's numerous caves. No doubt many new discoveries await archaeological exploration in the future, promoting fresh theory and fresh speculation. This book will concentrate on what seem to be the more permanent achievements of survival and discovery and will give theory its due where it illuminates facts or artefacts which, like some recorded documents, may be without meaning in themselves.

Part 1

THE ENVIRONMENT

1

GEOGRAPHY

Lying roughly at the same distance from the mainland of Greece, the Cyclades, Rhodes and Libya, the island of Crete flanks the southern entrance to the Aegean basin and must always have been a focus for sea-travellers between the coast fringes of Europe, Asia and Africa. Its extreme length from west to east is about 260km., its widest points in the centre are about 60km. apart and its narrowest, near Ierapetra in the east, only about 12km.

Crete is set in an area which is geologically unstable and has consequently been affected by frequent earthquakes, some of which, in the Bronze Age, account for severe destructions of palaces and towns. There have been other environmental changes of a less dramatic kind which have had their influence throughout the island's long history. For example, the Mediterranean being virtually tideless, the evidence of submerged settlements, houses and harbour installations in many places around its shores indicates that the level of the sea has risen since ancient times. At Chersonesos, on the north coast of Crete between Iraklion and Mallia, the sea is now level with the top of the Roman quay. Roman fish-tanks cut in the rock of the foreshore here and also at Mochlos further east are wholly submerged.[1] However, at Sitia, even further east along the north coast, a slipway for a warship seems to be at roughly the same height above water as when it was being used round about 300 BC.[2]

The rise in sea level could have followed from a considerable general increase in the volume of water in the oceans of the world as a result of the melting of the polar ice caps. There are many Bronze Age settlements along the coasts in central and eastern Crete now entirely or partially submerged below the sea or exposed on the shore; and the sea level along the north coast may be a metre or more higher than it was in Roman times.[3] The sea has covered sandy beaches on which ancient ships could be beached. Modern ships must have anchorage, which helps to explain why the principal Cretan ports of Khania, Rethimno and Iraklion are in modern times on the northern coast.

Seaports in Minoan times were often situated on small promontories which provided harbour facilities on either side according to the wind direction. The present small island of Mochlos, opposite Ayios Nikolaos on the Gulf of

Mirabello, which was excavated by Seager in 1908, was probably such a typical promontory with harbours on either side of an isthmus, until the sea level rose to separate it from the coast. Such places were like the Phaiacian port of Scherie in Homer's Odyssey: 'Around the city is a lofty rampart. There is a fine harbour on either side of it, with a narrow approachway. Rounded ships are drawn up along the road; and each man has a berth for himself. Here too is their market-place, on both sides of a fair temple of Poseidon, walled with stone blocks, quarried and dragged to the spot, where they tend the tackle of their black ships, cables and sails, and smooth their oars.'[4]

Another remarkable change in the configuration of the coastline was first observed by Spratt during his surveys of the 1850s, namely the considerable elevation of all the western part of Crete. The results could be observed as successive stages on the cliffs to the north of Souda Bay. In ancient times the Greek city of Phalasarna on the north-west coast used to have an inner harbour which was joined to the sea by a rock-cut canal. The bottom of this canal is now well above the sea level, while the harbour now merely reveals itself in summer as an inland dry depression or in winter as a shallow marsh. The formerly existing level of the sea is apparent in the cliffs of the west as a notch worn by the waves or as holes which were made by rock-boring bivalve shell-fish living on or just below the surface of the water. Its maximum height of 8m. above the present existing level has been traced on the south-west coast between Paleochora and the ancient city of Lissos. This gradual process of elevation could have begun in medieval times, even as late as the ninth century, after the Saracen conquest.[5]

An enormous range of mountains, their peaks thrusting to a height of almost 2500m. in places, is piled along the whole length of the island, with only two extensive breaks to divide the chain into massive blocks. On the southern coast the mountains form a barrier often quite near to the sea and the approaches are difficult with few good harbours. The mountains are formed principally of grey limestone with exposed layers of brown or grey or green schists, quartzites and shales in many places.

The three main groups of mountains are, in the west, the White Mountains, which are separated from the main central block around Mount Ida by lower country of the kind which again intervenes between the Dikte range in the east. The latter culminates in the low and narrow isthmus of Ierapetra with its eastern barrier of the Thriphte mountains and a high stretch of limestone beyond Sitia to the coast. The best sheltered bay is Souda in the north-west and the largest gulf Mirabello in the north-east; and a series of lesser gulfs, bays and capes faces the Greek mainland on this northern coast. There are several small islands off the coasts and the largest inhabited one of them is Gavdos in the south-west. Lying some 20km. to the south in the Libyan Sea, this islet is the southernmost inhabited point of Greece and of Europe. Its lighthouse, built in 1880, aids shipping in the Libyan Sea. Here St Paul stayed for a few days on his way to Rome.[6]

The Cretan limestones on their schist, phyllite or crystalline limestone beds, are traced to various geological periods – Tertiary, Upper Cretaceous, Jurassic, Triassic and Permian to Permian or Carboniferous – with characteristic features and colouring. In general the main mountain groups of the White Mountains, the Ida range and the Dikte range are composed of dark limestones, dolomites and dolomitic limestones. The soft white marly limestone known as *kouskouras* is found in coastal areas, for instance around Knossos and Phaistos, but especially in the north where the principal ancient centres of habitation were situated. In the Bronze Age exposed stretches of *kouskouras* were selected for digging tombs. The soft gypsum stone which the Minoans used extensively in the construction of their palaces appears in outcrops in various places. In fact no less than 165 gypsum quarries and 10 mines have been noted. The hill of Gypsades, to the south of Knossos, provided the source of supply for the palace. Local sources in the plain of Messara were used for quarrying the gypsum blocks for the palaces at Phaistos and Ayia Triada in the south.[7]

In his definitive monograph on Minoan stone vases, Warren has clarified a common confusion in Minoan publications between two materials used in the manufacture of stone vessels from early Minoan times which should be mentioned here. He notes that in 1897 Sir Arthur Evans had published his discovery of 'plentiful beds of steatite of a translucent greenish hue' in the Sarakina valley above Myrtos on the south-east coast of Crete. Evans also referred to 'equally prolific' deposits along the coast near Arvi and further west in the Asterousia range, but he did not visit these deposits. Warren decides that Evans was correct in calling the Sarakina material steatite but also incorrectly gave this name to the ordinary serpentine vases from nearby Arvi. Since then almost any Minoan vase has been called 'steatite' if it is not an exotic stone or some form of limestone, marble or breccia. The term steatite must be restricted to those vases and objects of true steatite, that is talc or soap-stone, and the term serpentine applied to the much greater number which are predominantly of this material, which is an altered basic rock of several varieties, used for about 47 per cent of all Minoan stone vessels. The probable major source of the commonest variety for the lapidaries had recently been determined. Extensive deposits occur on both sides of a narrow valley called Lepria, at a spot immediately south of the road about 2.3 km. west of Gonies in the northern foothills of Mount Ida. A mass of serpentine also forms a hill, occupied by a Minoan site, just west of Spili in the Rethimno province and there is a much larger area south of this in the hills behind and to the west and north of Ardaktos. Yet another source is on the south coast between Myrtos and Arvi just west of the hamlet of Tersa (or Terzi). The distinction now made is important because, as Warren points out, serpentine was used from early Minoan times onward for almost all types of stone vases, the commonest variety occurring with vases all over the island.[8]

The geological composition of the island and the seismic upheavals it has suffered over the ages have caused it to be honeycombed with many hundreds of caves and rock-shelters, some of them small, others vast, not a few of extreme archaeological and religious importance. In very recent times, as so often in the past, caves have been used by the Cretans as places of refuge and focal points of survival and resistance. Many have been associated with the Christian religion; and even today there are said to be over a hundred churches in Cretan caves.

As elsewhere, the use of cave-mouths and rock-shelters as sanctuaries was a consequence of their original occupation as places of habitation. Archaeology has confirmed the Greek tradition that caves were indeed the earliest homes and also shrines of men.[9] The dead were frequently interred in caves used as dwellings, a practice which continued after people had moved to huts and houses; and this practice promoted a custom of burying the dead beneath the floor of a house, which persisted in Greece to late Mycenaean times. The evidence throughout the island in the late and sub-Neolithic periods shows that inhumation in caves and rock-shelters was apparently the common method of burial.[10] The Cretan caves, apart from their intrinsic and often spectacular geological interest, have supplied us with invaluable evidence of their sacred functions from Neolithic through to historical times. The importance of the caves as invaluable sources for our knowledge of the remote past has been abundantly demonstrated in the devoted and exhaustive researches of Faure in recent years.[11]

Roughly two-thirds of the whole surface area of the island consists of the mountainous regions now so conspicuously rugged and barren. Their high peaks and crags must always have been unusable and unproductive; nowadays nearly half the land area is really only suitable for nomadic grazing. There is little forest remaining, half of it in the province of Khania and one-fifth on the southern and eastern slopes of the Ida range. Deforestation has been continuous from early times: trees have been cut down by men for fuel, houses and ships, and the young shoots have been devoured by grazing goats.

In Minoan times, however, the whole area west of Ida was probably virgin forest. Cypress was abundant in Pliny's time; and the Cretan forests were yielding their supplies of cypress wood for the Venetian navy during the middle ages. Indeed the cypress was still conspicuous enough to provoke comment from Moryson and Lithgow, the latter remarking that Ida was 'over-clad even to the toppe with *Cypre* trees'. The diminished cypress is now restricted to limestone areas, with evergreen oak and myrtle most commonly found in schist areas, becoming prickly shrubs on higher ground. As was perhaps also the case in ancient times, the natural vegetation comprises the following categories at different levels. Common lentisk, large seeded juniper, tamarisk, willow, oleanders, almond and quince up to 150m.; terebinth, deciduous oak, myrtle, arbutus, oleander, black mulberry and styrax between 150m. and 600m.; dog rose, plane trees and ivy between about 600m. and 900m.; pines, white mulberry and wild pear grow at levels up to 900m.; oak, maple, cypress and native *salvia cretica* between 900m. and 1200m.; evergreen cypress, Cretan maple and prickly evergreen oak, at the limit of true forest areas, between 1200m. and 1800m.; common juniper, Cretan barberry, creeping plum and buckthorn on subalpine slopes between 1800m. and 2400m. The black mulberry, found at levels up to 600m., was perhaps introduced originally for the silk trade.[12]

The almond and the quince[13] are both probably indigenous. In more recent times they have been supplemented by such fruits as apples, oranges, peaches, apricots and plums. Similarly the peas, chickpeas and beans, which were cultivated in early times, have been supplemented by the addition of such vegetables as potatoes and tomatoes. The superb honey, now produced in apiaries all over the island, was the chief means of sweetening food in antiquity.

The carob-tree, also indigenous in the Levant, still plays an important role in Cretan agricultural economy, with an annual production of up to 30,000 tonnes of carob beans. The fruit of this evergreen leguminous tree, long flat horn-like pods containing numerous hard seeds embedded in pulp, were the locusts eaten by the Baptist and hence called 'Locust-pods' and 'St John's Bread'. The pods are rich in sugar and proteins and were always used as food for men and animals and also for fermented beverages. Gum made from these pods is used in paper manufacture and the curing of tobacco, as a stabilizer in food products and as a celluloid in photographic materials. *Keration*, a Greek diminutive meaning 'small horn', was the fruit of the carob-tree and also a measure of weight – hence the English word 'carat'.

The natural vegetation also includes such wild vegetables as celery, carrot, cabbage, lettuce, asparagus, and a great variety of flowers and plants, many of them apparently indigenous as well as those common to the whole region and its climate. In the hilly areas especially grow the island's famed aromatic herbs, thyme, sage, mint and, in particular, the Cretan dittany, a kind of wild marjoram, still highly regarded for its pharmaceutical properties, especially for women in childbirth. Naturally herbal lore of this kind has an old history in Crete, as may be gathered from a study of the inscriptions of the sanctuary of Asklepios at Lebena, the sea-port of Gortyn. One cure undertaken by the god in the first century BC for continuous coughing and vomiting called for rocket to nibble on an empty stomach; Italian wine flavoured with pepper to drink; starch with hot water; powdered holy ashes; holy water; egg and pine-resin; moist pitch; iris with honey; a quince and wild purslane to be boiled together; and a fig with holy ashes from the sacrificial altar. Another, for the same patient, this time suffering from an acute inflammation of the right shoulder, required the application of a plaster of barley-meal mixed with old wine and a pine-cone ground down with olive-oil, with the addition of a fig and goat's fat, milk with pepper, wax-pitch and olive-oil boiled together. A third, from roughly the same period of time, for an ulcer on a woman's little finger, was promoted by the application of the shell of an oyster, burnt and ground down with rose-ointment, and an anointing with a compound of mallow and olive-oil.[14]

The fauna in very early times may have included deer, wild boar and lions, as well as the ancestor of the more remarkable *agrimi*, or wild goat, which survives in the mountains of the west. Such goats appear frequently in Minoan art, sitting on the roof of a shrine, for example, or drawing chariots,[15] or leaping over rocks, sometimes with huntsmen and hounds in pursuit. Early hunters probably supplemented their diet with such birds as pigeons, partridges or migrant hoopoes. The sea provided such fish as tunny, mullet, bass, bream, lobster, crab, sole, mackerel, octopus and cuttle-fish, as well as shellfish such as mussels, oysters and whelks. Domesticated animals were presumably brought to the island by the first settlers.[16] Though there are no poisonous snakes nowadays, there are vipers, scorpions and the venomous spiders known as rogaliḍhas – dancing is a customary cure for their bite.

Continuous deforestation throughout the centuries has turned Crete, once one of the most fertile and prosperous islands in the Mediterranean, into one of the rockiest and most barren. When there were plenty of trees on the lower mountain slopes, water could be absorbed into the soil and so provide a natural reserve in dry seasons; but now the soil which the trees conserved has been swept away by the rains from the slopes. In this way deforestation has contributed to the present shortage of water.

The island has no navigable rivers, for the streams which can be called rivers are too shallow and rocky. Few rivers in Crete are more than a trickle in summer, while most are dry beds only. Pendlebury mentioned five which have never been known to dry up completely, namely: the Platania, west of Khania, the Gazanos, west of Iraklion, the Metropolitanos in the Messara, the Anapodhiari, flowing from the Messara to the south coast, and the Mylopotamos, flowing out on the north coast, east of Rethimno. Other places which have permanently flowing streams though they may not merit the title of rivers are Amnisos, Sitia, Zakro and Kato Viannos; also springs are fairly common in the mountains and in the coastal plains water is drawn from wells, in the Mallia plain at a depth of only 5m., but at Knossos some 12–14m.

Climatic conditions, probably not markedly different from those prevalent in antiquity, naturally do vary according to altitudes. There is now less water than was the case, so far as we can judge, in the Bronze Age, for instance; but, as we have seen, this is due to deforestation and not to climatic changes. Generally speaking, the climate is marine, temperate and dry, with sunny winters and rare snowfall in the coastal areas, though snow in the high mountains can last through the summer. Nearly all the rainfall occurs between October and March. There is practically no rain at all in the summer months between May and August and the lack of water reserves at this season of drought is then most acute. The summer heat is tempered by the then more frequent prevailing winds from the north or north-west, except when the hot southerly sirocco blows from Africa. The winds are harnessed for irrigation purposes to turn the thousands of windmills which are a feature of the landscape.

Roughly 30 per cent of the land area of Crete is nowadays available for the cultivation of crops and orchard produce, and for permanent grazing, fallow or meadow land. This percentage could not have been higher in antiquity. Only a modest proportion, roughly a quarter, of this area, mostly in the plain of Messara, has really good soil. Deforestation (and the consequent erosion of the hillsides) has resulted in a shifting and changing of the soils since antiquity in ways which naturally cannot be estimated in detail.[17]

The largest plain is the Messara, a fertile stretch of roughly 45km. in length and 10km. wide in the central southern region of what is now the prefecture of Iraklion, between the Ida foothills and the Asterousi mountains on the south coast, with the ancient sites of Phaistos at the western end, Ayia Triada nearby, and Gortyn in its north-east corner. Other such areas of cultivation in the north are the lands around the ancient palace and city of Knossos, near modern Iraklion; those that lie around Souda Bay and Khania, and then, proceeding eastward, around Rethimno, the bay of Mallia, with another Bronze Age palace and city, the Gulf of Mirabello, and Sitia.

In addition to these fertile coastal areas there are a number of upland plains surrounded by mountains and drained by their caverns and swallow-holes. The most fertile and thickly populated is the plain of Lasithi, at a height of about 900m. below Mount Dikte, and irrigated during the summer by water pumped from wells to the surface by a large number of windmills. The plain of Omalos is in the White Mountains at a height of about 1000m., with the entrance to the famous Gorge of Samaria, 18km. long, with its steep walls rising sometimes to a height of 600m. at its western end. A third major upland plain is Nidha, roughly 1500m. high, on the north-east slopes of Mount Ida.

Considering the environmental difficulties already described and bearing in mind that traditional, indeed primitive methods of cultivation are still often prevalent, agricultural yields, especially of certain produce, including exported surpluses, are impressively high. More will have to be said about traditional techniques of cultivation and traditional varieties of crops when the heritage passed on from the early settlers is discussed. Meantime, a few details may be cited concerning those traditional products, the olive and the grape. Though contemporary, such details are relevant to our understanding of conditions in the past if only because so many old techniques have survived into the present. They serve to illustrate how the careful husbandry of its most fertile areas has sustained a vigorous population through the ages and has also, from time to time, in antiquity, in the middle ages and in the present, bestowed upon Crete in its flourishing periods a widespread reputation for its agricultural produce.

Cretan olive trees – there are said to be 13 million of them – averaged a yield of 5 pounds (2.27kg.) of oil per tree before 1939, as compared with an average of 3.7 pounds (1.67kg.) for Greece as a whole and 3.1 pounds (1.4kg.) for Italy and Turkey; and thus the crop represented (as indeed it still apparently does today, with a slight variation) a large percentage – more than a third – of the Greek crop as a whole. Grapes, largely in the form of dried grapes or raisins, are now Crete's largest export, in the region of 10,000 tonnes annually. Cretan wines, however, have always enjoyed a certain reputation from antiquity onward. Wine was a chief export from the island in the middle ages; and, as we have already noticed, the first English consul was appointed in Crete in the time of Henry VIII in the interests of the wine trade. Cretan muscadine and malmsey wines acquired a considerable esteem abroad but this had been lost by the eighteenth century and they were no longer major competitors in the international market.

We have seen that, in present conditions, Crete can sustain a population of nearly half a million. It is impossible to arrive at anything like reasonably accurate estimates of population figures at any time in antiquity, although, for obvious reasons, even plausible approximations would be invaluable for our understanding of social and economic conditions at various periods in earlier or later antiquity. Broad general statements about expansion or decline or fresh influx or migrations of population at different times or in different places can be inferred from such archaeological evidence as the distribution, size or abandonment of sites, pottery distribution, quantity and type of artefacts and so on, as we shall see in succeeding chapters.

Even when we are dealing with written records in much more recent times caution is necessary, as may be illustrated from a careful survey of the evidence by Warren.[18] It is worth citing here both for its intrinsic interest and the light it throws on the upper limits of population figures and the causes of fluctuation over a period of several centuries. Warren begins with a statement made by the English traveller, Bernard Randolph, after he visited Crete in 1680, in his book of 1687 called *The Present State of the Islands in the Archipelago*, at a particularly interesting period of history.

Randolph claimed that the population before the recent Turkish conquest had been one million but was now, in 1669, eleven years later, under 80,000, of whom 30,000 were Turks. The first estimate is likely to be too high and the second too low. The first reliable figure seems to be 271,489, just before Foscarini came to Crete in 1574. In 1524, 24,000 died of plague, suggesting a total in the region of 300,000 just before that year. No accurate estimate before this seems possible, but Pashley[19] says that it may be inferred from Venetian sources that the population at the time of the Venetian acquisition of the island in 1204 was very much greater than in the sixteenth century. But a figure of one million is not credible. Raulin[20] shows that, with its land surface of 7800 sq. km. one million would mean a population density greater than the most populous areas of mid-nineteenth-century France, not even including the fact that much of the 7800 sq. km. was almost uninhabited mountains.

In the later sixteenth century the figure went down rapidly – 219,000 in 1475–8 and about 176,000 in 1588. But Randolph's 80,000 for 1680 is impossibly low. A census a little before the Turkish conquest of 1669 gives 260,000.[21] Pococke[22] said it was not above 300,000 in 1739, the number of Christians being more than double the Turks. Olivier in his *Voyage dans l'Empire Othoman* of 1795 estimated 240,000 and the figure was 260,000 in 1821 before the War of Independence, reduced to 129,000 by 1834, according to Pashley. The figure thereafter fluctuated: 160,000 in 1847, 128,675 in 1855,[23] before rising steadily to Spratt's figure of 210,000 in 1865. It was not until 1900, however, that a figure of 300,000 was again reached.[24] Official census figures for 1951 are 462,124; for 1961, 483,258; and for 1971, 456,208, with a decline of 6 per cent from the 1961 figure.

2

NEIGHBOURS

As we saw, Crete has been successful in maintaining a characteristic and individual identity despite the vicissitudes of its turbulent history since ancient times and its often compulsory absorption of foreign influences. The difficult internal communications have played a major part in preserving the individuality. As these communications rapidly improve, the more necessary it will become not to overlook the influence of such prolonged dominant conditions of life in Crete.

The natural means of communication has always been by mountain paths suitable in many cases only to pedestrians, paths which frequently began as mere game tracks. It was not till the coming of wheeled traffic, and swift-wheeled traffic at that, when gradients had to be considered, that artificial roads were cut; the 'kalderims', or roughly paved roads made by the Romans, Venetians or Turks for military purposes, merely followed the prehistoric paths, and although there are few cases where Minoan banking or Greek bridges survive we are justified in considering that the means of communication between ancient sites was the same as that in use in modern times or rather before the network of car roads was begun.

These observations of Pendlebury were the prelude to a salutary account of routes and topography[1] which began with emphasis upon the importance, when considering the distribution of sites at certain periods, of looking at the means of communication each had with its neighbours; whether easy access from one quarter had caused a site to favour in its style of pottery the technique of another which might lie at a considerable distance from it; through what sections of the country would pass the traffic from Egypt, influencing perhaps one group of sites while another group was in closer touch with the Cyclades.

Only those who have walked the mountains, he went on, can tell how misleading a map may be. Who would think that from Souia on the south coast to Lakkoi south of Khania is as long a day's journey as from Tsoutsouros, the ancient Priansos, on the south coast to Amnisos on the north coast? Distances are useless. Times alone matter. His own times for the routes he detailed were all walking – not riding – times, not allowing for halts, varying according to the weather and the fitness of the pedestrian at the time: which provoked a suggestion that a cross-country runner who would undertake to explore the various ancient routes in Greece before the countryside was ruined by car-roads would collect a lot of interesting material.[2]

Pendlebury concluded these memorable pages, mostly written out of personal experience, by again emphasizing that communications by land had changed little save for the gashing of the countryside by car roads. The communications by sea, however, played an important part. The reference to the gashing of the countryside by car-roads was prophetic; but the reference to the importance of sea communications was perhaps severely understated for a major island with Crete's geographical location.

The philosopher Thales, founder of the Milesian school, took the view that the earth floats on water. This is one of the few things we know about his cosmological doctrines; and commentators, ancient and modern, have speculated about its significance and its source. A modern traveller to the isles of Greece, knowing nothing about Thales, might have the same thought as he observes those sea-girt pieces of earth, large and small, emerging below him from a seat in an aeroplane. Except in the old Cretan myth of the cunning Daidalos, the ancients did not fly in safety over the Aegean. However, it is becoming increasingly clear that they did float in safety, like the earth in the imagination of Thales, from very early times. It follows that, from these very early times, what we now call Greece – the mainland and the islands – had a prodigiously long and navigable coastline. From a narrower focus it is equally true to say that Crete too may be magnified in its natural proportions and the extent of its communications if we think in terms of its coastline, of accessibility from anchorage to anchorage or as goal for the more distant traveller.

The implications will be discussed appropriately in more detail in the next chapter. Yet the point may be emphasized at this stage by mentioning the results of some recent excavations at the Franchthi Cave in southern Greece.[3] This, the largest cave in Greece, was continuously inhabited throughout the Stone Age from 20,000 BC or earlier to 3000 BC. It has Palaeolithic, Mesolithic and Neolithic layers, directly above each other, a sequence unique in any known site in the Old World. Situated on a headland which forms the northern arm of a shallow bay in the Gulf of Argolis, south-east of Nafplion, it has yielded the first proofs of Mesolithic settlement in Greece from c.9000 BC to c.6000 BC.

There is also remarkable and convincing evidence at Franchthi that its inhabitants had started to navigate the deep over a considerable distance long before anyone was previously known to have travelled by sea. The evidence is in the first appearance of obsidian and, simultaneously, of large fish bones in layers identified by radiocarbon dating between 7500 and 7000 BC. The large bones are of deep-sea fish and the obsidian could only have come from Melos, the volcanic island lying 120km. to the south-east.

At the beginning of the Neolithic era, about 6500 BC, excavation has revealed the sudden appearance of domesticated sheep or goats, and of cereals, such as wheat and barley, which did not exist before, even in a wild form. Fishing apparently ceased abruptly and pottery appeared for the first time; and there were new types of tools and implements. All of which, it is inferred, indicates a large-scale change of population about 6500–6000 BC. It was at about this time that Crete, Cyprus, and sites on the east coast of Greece showed the first signs of human occupation. The director of the excavations, Dr Jacobsen, believes these newcomers were immigrants, probably from Asia Minor, who had brought with them their domesticated animals and plants, their arts, crafts and customs. Earlier theories, based on Neolithic sites in Thessaly, that these animals were indigenous to Greece would, in his opinion, have to be revised.

The obsidian used for various purposes in Crete during the Neolithic period also came mainly from Melos, though some apparently came from as far afield as Central Anatolia.[4] If deep-sea navigation began so early and materials could be carried over fair distances between mainland and islands, it is necessary, from the beginning, to think of Crete, in the broadest sense, as forming part of a major complex of development in its neighbouring continental areas.

This complex of the whole Near East and eastern Mediterranean region nourished most of the technological inventions of antiquity. The Mediterranean sea itself was one highway of influence and interchange between communities. So too were the great rivers, the Tigris and Euphrates and the Nile.

Immense climatic changes followed the ending of the last Ice Age, roughly 12,000 years ago. The ice which had covered much of the northern hemisphere had receded approximately to its present confines. Previous areas of tundra became areas of pine forest. The more southerly pine areas changed to deciduous forests and tropical forests took the place of the deciduous forests. Palaeolithic hunters and food-gatherers gave way to Neolithic farmers and stockbreeders. The development of agriculture and its associated techniques, such as the wooden hoe, the sickle of wood or bone set with flint blades, the flail and the quern, culminated in the first great technological revolution in the history of mankind. Nature was becoming a provider in the service of man and his work, as animals were domesticated and plants, grasses and cereals cultivated.

By the eighth millennium BC, in modern Jordan and Iraq, at Jericho and Jarmo, societies with their economy based on agriculture were in being. In the course of the next three millennia such agricultural communities were established in favourable areas of mainland Greece, southern Anatolia, Syria, Palestine, the Mesopotamian valley, Persia as well as Iraq, in Cyprus and in Crete. The Neolithic peoples in these areas had domesticated sheep, goats, cattle and pigs; were provided with milk, meat and grain; and controlled the techniques of pottery, spinning and weaving. Dwellings were made of mud, reeds, logs, stone or withies, plastered with clay. A sun-dried brick was being made in moulds in Crete as in Western Turkey by 5000 BC, the moulds probably bottomless wooden boxes with handles for lifting.[5]

By 4000 BC agriculture had spread as far east as northern India, southward into the lower Nile and the coastal areas of north Africa and also along the Danube into Europe. Neolithic village economy became more widespread as increased areas of land were cleared and prepared for cultivation. Within these village economies special skills were developed by particular persons and we can assume division of labour between the sexes, so that women played a considerable role in the invention and utilization of the technological resources of Neolithic economy. They would continue to play their part in the cultivation of the village plots, the grinding and cooking of grain, spinning and weaving cloth, making textiles into wearing apparel and in the making of ceramics. The manufacture of tools and weapons, hunting and building, clearing land for cultivation and care of the livestock were tasks probably more generally appropriate for the menfolk.

On the basis of village economy and social organization, the way was being prepared for the rise of towns and cities. Jericho can be described as a walled town by the eighth millennium BC. The remarkable site of Çatal Hüyük, 32 miles south-east of Konya in southern Turkey, ranks, in the opinion of its excavator, with Jericho, as one of man's first known essays in the development of town-life.[6] Covering an area of about 32 acres, Çatal Hüyük is the largest known Neolithic site of the Near East.

What the site has already revealed is eloquent testimony to the achievements of mankind in this whole area as settled agricultural economy became consolidated. As the excavator comments:

> Çatal Hüyük has proved to be not only a major Neolithic site, yielding rich evidence of a remarkably advanced civilization that flourished on the Anatolian Plateau in the seventh and early sixth millennium BC, but it was also the centre of art in a period that hitherto had been regarded as inartistic. Çatal Hüyük is remarkable for its wall-paintings and plaster reliefs, its sculpture in stone and clay as well as for its advanced technology in the crafts of weaving, woodwork, metallurgy and obsidian working. Its numerous sanctuaries testify to an advanced religion, complete with symbolism and mythology; its buildings to the birth of architecture and conscious planning; its economy to advanced practices in agriculture and stockbreeding; and its numerous imports to a flourishing trade in raw materials.[7]

The builders of Çatal Hüyük worked methodically. Orderliness and planning are apparent in the size of bricks, the standard plan of houses and shrines, the heights of panels, doorways, hearths and ovens, to a great extent in the size of rooms. Houses, small and large, are invariably of rectangular plan, with straight wall lines; store-rooms and the like are arranged around the main rooms. The cult-rooms are no different from ordinary dwelling-places and are an essential part of the whole architectural complex in the same way as the later palace sanctuary areas of the Near East, Crete and Greece. The main criteria for the recognition of these shrines are, apparently, the presence of elaborate wall-paintings with ritual or religious significance; plaster reliefs showing deities, animals or animal heads; horns of cattle set into benches; rows of bucrania and the presence of groups of cult statues found in the main room; ex-voto figures stuck into the walls; human skulls set up on platforms and the like. There are remarkable resemblances with Crete of a later period, not only in architectural features but markedly in terms of cult and ritual. The most important animal, for example, is the bull, object of worship and symbol of fertility.[8]

Since the bull crania attached to the walls of many shrines represented the whole animal (occasionally found in the same shrine), it is likely that these heads, together with another remarkable feature, at last resolve the disputed question of the origin and significance of the Minoan 'horns of consecration'. Not only the head could represent the whole bull, but also the horn cores, usually mounted in a rectangular, pillar-like structure, or along the sides of a bench seven feet deep. At times all three forms – whole animal, head, and 'bull-pillar' – occurred together in one shrine. The separate horns of the Anatolian shrines were then, it has been argued, the ancestors of the Cretan horns of consecration which had been imported to the island direct from the east; despite the curious stereotype shape they assumed in Cretan hands, giving rise to much speculation concerning their significance, the association with the figure of the bull, as well as the important position they held in cult, is evident from these Anatolian finds.[9]

The economy of Çatal Hüyük could supply such luxury goods as obsidian mirrors, ceremonial daggers, and trinkets of metal. It is highly significant that copper and lead were smelted and worked into beads, tubes and possibly small tools. The beginnings of metallurgy can thus be traced back here into the seventh millennium BC.[10] How the remarkable discovery of copper smelting was made is uncertain, but by the second half of the fifth millennium copper was being used for chisels, axes, needles, pins, awls and daggers.[11] A further great metallurgical advance was made with the controlled production of bronze, a copper-tin alloy, sometimes previously produced by accident from ores containing both of the metals. Important as had been the skilled working of copper, bronze was a radical improvement on copper because it could provide harder and more durable tools, making possible the really fine casting which could not be done with unalloyed copper.[12] The Bronze Age of Anatolia may be dated to the middle of the fourth millennium BC. By the beginning of the third millennium BC there were Bronze Age cultures at Troy, Poliochni, Thermi, and Emporio in north-west Anatolia, Beycesultan in the south-west, and Tarsus in Cilicia, with their large settlements, often defended by thick walls and their treasures and artefacts displaying evidence of wealthy ruling classes.[13] City-states were established in Syria such as Ras Shamra (Ugarit), Byblos and Alalakh and also in Palestine. The older, more egalitarian communities of farmers had given place over a wide area to sharply differentiated class societies, with small groups of kings, nobles, priests and merchants with their bureaucracies and armies depending upon a majority of cultivators, some free, some servile, maintaining themselves at subsistence level and providing a surplus for the rulers.

These societies, by the third millennium BC, were based upon cultivators and artisans and made use of the technical advances which had been developed since the invention of agriculture. Pottery, spinning and weaving, copper-smelting, bronze manufacture, the plough, the wheeled cart, the harness and the sailing ship had been followed by the bellows, the tongs and then the highly skilled *cire-perdue* method of bronze-casting. A wax-model of the required shape was made, coated with clay, placed in a furnace so that the wax could melt and the clay be baked to form a mould. Molten metal could then be poured into the mould and the clay broken away after cooling. After about 2500 BC fundamental advances ceased for a long time and in some techniques, like the harness or spinning, no further progress was made until medieval times. However, the impressive store of Bronze Age skills became more and more widely diffused over many areas of Europe and Asia.[14]

The great Bronze Age states in Mesopotamia and Egypt employed these techniques impressively and their skilled craftsmen produced many and varied articles and tools. They also organized labour on an immense scale to build temples, palaces and pyramids; and also to construct vast irrigation works which enabled them to provide a great agricultural surplus.

Ur became the capital of a Sumerian dynasty – The Third Dynasty of Ur – which controlled the whole of Mesopotamia. After about a century this centralized bureaucratic control collapsed under pressure from the Semitic Amurru or Amorites, and of the Elamites from southern Persia. After this breakdown, followed by the rise of various dynasties in different cities, came the First Dynasty of Babylon (1894–1595 BC), particularly memorable in history for the reign of Hammurabi (1792–1750 BC). Conditions were such that his political and diplomatic skill, administrative and military prowess, raised Babylon to the position of lasting achievement in ancient history. To the north was the kingdom of Assyria, where the Amorite Shamshi-Adad became king in 1814 BC; and there were other centres of Amorite power in North Syria.

Mari,[15] at the site called Tell Hariri on the Middle Euphrates in eastern Syria, had been an outpost of Sumerian civilization, and in the early second millennium BC was the capital of a kingdom extending over 320km. along the river. It had an enormous palace with about 300 rooms extending over something like an area of six acres, with mural paintings, kitchens, baths and pantries, behind a strong defensive wall, with its huge ziggurat and surrounding temples. The palace, pillaged in about 1760 BC by Hammurabi, was royal residence and also administrative centre, containing great quantities of letters, administrative and judicial documents; it was also a business centre, with warehouses for merchants to deposit their wares, and had barracks for a garrison of troops. The king regulated the calendar and appointed governors over the cities, although in practice citizens could supplicate for their own nominees; and he was much concerned with diplomatic affairs and state security. There was a standing army of about 10,000 men which often had to deal with raiding tribesmen. Merchants were an important element of the population, which numbered up to about 100,000 at most. There were slaves and noble families. The basis of the economy of the state was agricultural and industries were carried on in the towns. There were specialized craftsmen such as boatmen, carpenters, leather-workers, fishermen, potters, masons, metal-workers, weavers, fullers, gem-cutters, jewellers, painters and perfume makers. Something like one-fifth of the population was engaged in crafts of various kinds and men, women and children took their part in all kinds of work. Workers were paid in kind, in the form of rations of corn, wool, clothing, wine and oil, or wholly or partly in silver.

The majority of the population outside the towns was occupied with farming, either cultivating crops or rearing flocks of sheep and goats. Cultivation was dependent on irrigation: the irrigated area extended over a depth of several kilometres along the south bank of the Euphrates for most of the extent of the 320km. of the kingdom, with a network of canals, requiring supervisory officials. From time to time townsmen and villagers were called upon to work on the irrigation canals, cleaning channels and strengthening the banks against floods. Staple crops were barley and sesame. Ploughing was done by oxen; sheep and goats were the principal source of meat supplies.

Irrigation was, of course, equally important for the Egyptian economy. In Egypt too much ingenuity of organization went into the building of huge structures like the pyramids. The Great Pyramid of Cheops, for example, was constructed with about 2,300,000 blocks of stone, in all about 5,750,000 tonnes in weight, each block averaging $2\frac{1}{2}$ tonnes but some of them weighing up to 15 tonnes. These had to be quarried and transported, with the help of sledges, sleepers, ropes and levers, from the quarries to the Nile, where they were carried on barges and raised over 30m. to the level of the site. Here a permanent labour force of some 4000 was at work, in addition to unspecified numbers in the quarries. Ramps of earth and brick were built against the rising sides of the pyramid, the blocks dragged on sledges and manhandled by ropes and levers, lubricated by a thin layer of mortar. Surveying was done by sightings of the stars, measuring rods, perhaps the plumb-line, and water for levelling – perhaps derived from irrigation techniques. A watercourse was made around the workings, banked with mud, and measured down from it to the required level at many points. Despite the primitive techniques the margins of error in angles and levels are negligible.[16]

Egypt and the Mesopotamian cities were compelled to expand their influence in order to gain access to supplies of necessary raw materials. Trading routes were developed into Anatolia and with the cities on the coasts of Palestine and Syria, with their good harbours, their accessibility to fertile valleys and the mountain areas which could supply materials such as tin, timber and stone. The economic, cultural and religious traditions of the hinterland of Afro-Asia were thus conveyed to the eastern Aegean. These city-states flourished under this stimulus and there was an intensified industrial production. They naturally themselves could serve as important channels of influence for these older traditions on the developing Bronze Age culture of Cyprus and particularly of Crete.

In a graphic description of the excavation of the palace of Level IV at Alalakh (*c.*1450–*c.*1370 BC) Woolley[17] commented that the building-methods used were traditional to the country and even the details of the plan had much in common with the Yarim-Lim palace of three centuries before. The architecture was native, developed in Asia, and parallels in other lands were due to borrowing from Asia. In his opinion there was a close analogy between Alalakh and Knossos.

However, more is known about the city-state of Ugarit (modern Ras Shamra), on the north Syrian coast, during the two centuries before it was destroyed, sacked and burnt, about 1200 BC, than about any other Syrian city of the second millennium.[18] Several thousands of tablets from private and public buildings supply rich documentary evidence to support the extensive excavations carried out over two-thirds of the site and the adjacent port installation. They include letters and memoranda of merchants and private persons, written in the local dialect and script. There are lists of towns and country districts, which provided contributions to the government in the form of silver, or produce or of *corvée* labour; of bowmen and slingmen, payrolls and tax receipts. There are diplomatic archives written in Akkadian and legal texts mostly in the same language. Ugaritic was a local dialect of North Canaanite, spoken by the largest section of a population of different nationalities. Tablets in Ugaritic contain mythological and liturgical texts, lists of offerings and omen texts for the use of priests; there are glossaries and lexicographical texts for scholarly purposes, and tablets in Hurrian and Cypro-Mycenaean; there are bilingual glossaries for use by the large Hurrian-speaking minority; one lexicographical tablet contains equivalents in Hurrian, Ugaritic, Sumerian and Babylonian. That the population included Minoan and, later, Mycenaean settlers, has been inferred from the quantities of Mycenaean and of some Minoan imported pottery, some of which was imitated. There is also evidence of people from Cyprus for trading purposes, and of Hittite and Egyptian merchants and envoys, of Babylonians and Palestinians from over the Jordan. Travellers and traders from Tyre, Byblos,

Beirut and other neighbouring kingdoms also came to Ugarit.

Although little is known of its earlier history, it is clear that Ugarit was already a flourishing state by the eighteenth century BC. In the early fourteenth century Ugarit came within the Egyptian sphere of influence and was almost certainly bound by treaty to keep its ports – there were at least four of them – open to Egyptian shipping for commercial and strategic reasons. Later there was a treaty imposed by the Hittites, but Ugarit maintained its position as a great centre of the carrying trade between Egypt and the Hittite empire. Its territory included a long stretch of fertile coastal plain, hills with olive groves and vineyards, wooded mountains, and behind there were lands suited to grazing and hunting. A natural link between the Levant and the Aegean area, its ports received cargoes from Beirut, Byblos, Tyre and Crete. Ugarit also controlled the caravan route from the coast through to Aleppo, and on by way of Emar and Carchemish to join the Euphrates route to Babylonia or the road eastward to Assyria; and there was another road which gave eventual access to central Anatolia.

Foundries for metal workers were situated in the port and the city and manufactured excellent bronze weapons and vessels of various kinds.[19] Linen and wool, obtained from the large flocks of sheep and goats on the grazing land, were dyed in the same areas, where quantities of crushed murex-shells have been found, and there made into bales or finished garments for export. Grain and olive-oil, wine, salt, timber, such as box, juniper and pine, were exported; and scented oils and cosmetics were put into locally made containers of ivory and alabaster which were modelled on Egyptian originals.

The administrative districts consisted of a township with dependent suburbs, and they contributed their taxes and dues to the state in silver, in kind, or by labour service. Likewise, payments for public service were paid in silver or in kind; and military and naval manpower was supplied by draft quotas on the communities and guilds. For specialist craftsmen were organized in fraternities and guilds, men being segregated according to their occupations or guilds, which tended to be hereditary. There were different kinds of warriors and priests, craftsmen such as smiths, builders, wainwrights, potters, launderers, sculptors, fowlers, shepherds, grooms and gatekeepers. Scribes and other professional people may have been organized in the same way. Such forms of administrative organization were developed on the basis of an old tribal system, for the population still maintained its tribal traditions. An older form of qualification by tribal name still occurred, though it became more common for names to be qualified by the name of the local township. Since the king as head of state was believed to have divine sanction, members of his clan and other politically important clans were placed in important offices like the priesthood.[20]

In its grandest form, in the fourteenth and thirteenth centuries, the palace of the city extended over about two and a half acres and is considered to have been one of the largest in western Asia, with many rooms, eight entrance staircases with pillared porticoes and nine interior courtyards, a large walled garden with flower beds and a pavilion, and a piped water-supply leading to an ornamental basin in one of the courtyards. The palace was an administrative centre, and official documents were baked in a bell-shaped oven in one of the courtyards, then stored according to category in various archive rooms. The palace also included workshops. Houses of the wealthy were grouped to the east and south of the palace, most of them having a good drainage system with bathrooms and lavatories; and there was a family vault below each of them. Smaller houses were tightly grouped in the north-east and north-west areas of the city on either side of narrow, winding streets. The artisans' quarter was in the south, where the houses of goldsmiths, silversmiths, seal-cutters, sculptors and bronzesmiths were grouped around an open square. There were two main temples, one dedicated to Dagan, the other to Ba'al, whose worship was common throughout Canaan.[21]

Some of the tablets of Ugarit were written in a script different from any known cuneiform system, with a limited number of signs, indicating that the script was alphabetic. They were written in an alphabet consisting of cuneiform signs invented to express the phonemes peculiar to the Semitic dialect of Ugarit. One tablet discovered enumerated the Ugaritic alphabet in the order of its letters, corresponding with the order of the Hebrew and Phoenician alphabets, except for the insertion of eight additional letters of the Ugaritic alphabet, representing sound-values either absent or unexpressed in Phoenician and Hebrew. This alphabet seems also to have approximated to the Arabic, in differentiating between shades of guttural, dental and sibilant sounds. Though its origin is not clear, considerable progress is proved to have been made, from the middle of the second millennium BC, towards the invention of a proper alphabetic system. The history of the alphabet, one of mankind's great achievements, is, as we shall see, of special relevance to Crete, which was one of the first, if not the first, centres of reception of alphabetic writing at a later stage. The eventual failure of this impressive Ugaritic system was perhaps due to the fact that the Phoenician system was already in competition with it, and also because clay was not a natural writing material in the area and because, in any case, the destruction of Ugaritic civilization contributed to its disappearance.[22] The destruction was sudden and complete to the extent that fragments of the large and beautifully written mythological tablets were later used in the construction of small walls by a people who had no reverence for, or understanding of, their contents. Thus the alphabetic script of Ugarit was forgotten and the city abandoned by those who could read it.[23]

The evidence we now possess of deep-sea navigation in very early times persuades us to think of the sea primarily as a means of transport rather than a source of food and justifies an emphasis upon the view that Crete must be set within a context of general development in Near Eastern regions over several millennia in which the direction of influence is from Asia into the west. The achievements of Neolithic culture as so conspicuously exemplified at Catal Hüyük and the prosperous Bronze Age culture of a particular kind developed at such a city as Ugarit, with its prosperity based to a significant extent on an accumulation of merchant capital, illustrate the debt which the island of Crete necessarily owed to its geographical position. At the same time the description of these two areas within their respective periods may serve as a basis of comparison to illustrate the distinctive contribution of the island's population in their adaptation of the heritage of skill and culture received from neighbouring continental achievements.

In the light of this more recently accumulated general evidence it still seems fitting that Sir Arthur Evans, in the same way that he arranged the sequence of Neolithic pottery at Knossos into three periods, Early, Middle and Late, should, by 1905, have announced his division of the Bronze Age of Crete into Early, Middle and Late Minoan, after the legendary King Minos – a dynastic use of the term comparable with the Egyptian use of Pharaoh. As the bearer of a divine title, Cretan Minos could also be compared with the divine 'priest-kings' of Anatolia, who represented a god, wore his dress, wielded his authority and often bore his name.[24] Each of the three main periods was subdivided into three, Early Minoan I, II, III and so on, with further subdivisions where necessary by means of As and Bs. The work of Schliemann and Evans opened the way forward to a new chronology, as Minoan objects were excavated on Egyptian sites and Egyptian on Minoan, and Cretan prehistory was synchronized at many points with Egyptian annals, dated in their turn by the Egyptian calendar. This system of chronology is not without its difficulties as fresh evidence has accumulated from other sites than Knossos and objections have been raised against it. An alternative system of nomenclature is sometimes adopted by calling the earlier part of the Bronze Age Pre-Palatial, the period before the destruction of the first or early palaces Proto-Palatial and the period of the second or later palaces Neo-Palatial.[25]

3

EARLY SETTLERS AND EARLY ACHIEVEMENTS

So far we have been giving some essential preliminary consideration to Crete within a wide context of space and time as a great offshore island of continental areas where fundamental technical and social changes had been taking place as settled habitation fostered great developments of far-reaching consequences. Now we must begin to bring the island itself into sharper focus from the time when there emerges the first clear evidence of human settlement at about 6000 BC up to about 2000 BC. The brevity of this chapter is in marked contrast with the enormous time-span of the 4000 years which it surveys, comprising the 3000 years of the Cretan Neolithic period and the 1000 years of the early Bronze Age terminating with the foundation of the first great palace centres. It is well to bear in mind that this time-span is double that of the whole Christian era; and also double that of the great climactic Bronze Age era of the second millennium BC plus the whole of the archaic, Classical and Hellenistic periods of the Iron Age first millennium BC. Our knowledge of crucial developments over this vast extent of time is necessarily partial and sketchy, since we have to rely upon archaeological data from a few sites to illuminate these developments. Such data acquire considerable significance in relation to the wider context we have been considering; and some detailed archaeological investigation in recent years has produced fresh important evidence about the very early phases of settlement in various parts of the island.

No indication has yet been found that Crete was ever inhabited by Palaeolithic food-gatherers and hunters. One stone implement from Lasithi, superficially Palaeolithic, was not found in a Palaeolithic context and is more likely to be of Neolithic or Bronze Age provenance.[1] During the last Ice Age until about 10,000 years ago, so much water of the oceans was locked in the polar ice caps that the Mediterranean was something like 100m. below its present level.[2] This has led to speculation that hunters from the Peloponnese could have crossed over to Crete in pursuit of game or adventure by swimming or drifting on logs or rafts.[3] If they did, they have left no mark of their visitations, so far as we can tell; and, for all practical purposes, the human prehistory of Crete has a Neolithic origin.[4]

The Neolithic farmers who migrated across the sea to Crete presumably came from the East, from western Anatolia perhaps or from Cilicia or from Syria-Palestine.[5] They must have brought sheep and cattle with them as well as various plants. Their implements, such as axes, chisels, blades, sickles, scrapers, arrow-heads, were made by grinding stone or from the bones of animals. Their wooden clubs sometimes had perforated stone heads.[6] These folk were presumably already adept in the spinning and weaving of cloth, making clay shuttles, spindle whorls and loom weights.

It has long been recognized that Knossos was a highly important early occupation site and excavations in recent years have established no less than ten successive building levels. Like their Anatolian neighbours, these early inhabitants were moulding mud bricks for the walls of their houses which may well have had flat roofs with a thick covering of clay over branches supported by wooden rafters.[7] Whenever these houses had to be levelled for one reason or another, new dwellings were erected over them, eventually forming a great artificial mound. The ten established levels have been divided into four stages, two Early, one Middle and one Late Neolithic, according to variations in shape and style of pottery.[8]

If we rely upon Carbon 14 datings, the ten Neolithic levels at Knossos would cover a period of about 3000 years from *c*.6000 BC, with an average of about 300 years per level.[9] No pottery was found in the small area excavated of level 10 and very little in level 9. It is possible – assuming that the absence of pottery in the first settlement is general – that level 10 at Knossos may correspond with the situation found elsewhere at settlement mounds throughout the Near East inhabited by agriculturalists not yet using pottery.

The first settlers at Knossos could have lived in wooden huts, no traces having been found of solid walls but only post holes, beaten earth floors and evidence of hearths. Houses with walls of mud or mud bricks, some apparently hardened by firing, were being constructed at the time of level 9. In the later Neolithic levels at Knossos, as throughout the Bronze Age there and elsewhere in Crete, bricks were not fire-hardened but dried in the sun. This difference in technique introduces a possibility that the first immigrants of level 10 or a new band of settlers who introduced pottery with the beginning of level 9 could have been accustomed to the use of fire-hardened bricks but subsequently abandoned the practice. These first houses seemingly had rooms of rectangular shape and their walls lacked stone foundations, whereas, in later Neolithic levels, the upper mud or mud-brick walls were usually built on stone foundations, as was indeed to be the practice into Greco-Roman times.

A house of the Middle Neolithic level 3 at Knossos had a room about 5m. square, a door in one corner and a low platform in the corner furthest from the door, similar to the low sleeping platforms occasionally found in the Bronze Age palaces and houses. The walls seem to have been covered with clay plaster. The floor of beaten earth had a hearth sunk in the middle.[10]

Many Neolithic inhabitants of Crete used caves as dwellings, especially in the mountain regions. The dead were often buried in such caves and this practice continued after the people had moved to huts or houses.[11] The practice could, alternatively, prompt the custom of burying the dead beneath the floor of a house, which lasted in Greece to late Mycenaean times.[12] Commenting on the difficulty of explaining the sudden flowering of village life which seems to have taken place at the beginning of the Early Bronze Age in Crete, Branigan[13] points out that the abandonment of a cave and the building of a house by an individual can be explained in terms of the greater flexibility and comfort which a house could offer; but the sudden emergence of village communities cannot. In his opinion this can only be explained by a growing social and commercial awareness.

Branigan goes on to observe that there had been a village of considerable size at Knossos ever since Early Neolithic times, but that this seems to be the only such village in Crete until the end of the Late Neolithic period when there is a village at Phaistos. Elsewhere there are the odd remains of single farmsteads like those at Katsambas and Magasa, the latter with an L-shaped house which could have accommodated a large family. Large families are apparently consistent with the indications from the remains of the Late Neolithic village at Knossos, where one house plan has been completely recovered, but where the evidence also suggests houses of standardized plan. In the plan made by Evans there seem to be the fragments of two other houses, all three joined together to form a block – a system adopted in some areas of the Greek mainland in the Early Bronze Age. The complete house had a living room with a fixed hearth, a small area which might have been open to the sky to provide light, and an L-shaped arrangement of five small, almost square rooms along two sides of a courtyard. Assuming that the house plans were basically the same, Branigan concludes that a 'social awareness' is clearly manifested in this architecture of the Late Neolithic at Knossos, the emergence of a standard house plan testifying to what he calls 'the total acceptance of the idea of community life'.

This may seem slender evidence on which to generalize about 'community life' but it is consistent with other archaeological evidence and with some broad inferences which may be theoretically applied to Crete from the record of comparative ethnography. The basic social unit of Palaeolithic peoples was the clan, based on principles of kinship and of communal usage of resources, membership of the unit being determined by descent from a common ancestor or totem of some kind, animal, plant or material object. The unit formed a circle of blood relations, with intermarriage forbidden among them. The clan unit was exogamous and a number of such intermarrying units would form some kind of tribal grouping. The ties between such basic social units could lead to the development of classificatory systems of relationship, more complex and also more comprehensive than those based on the family as the social unit. This form of social organization, developed in the Palaeolithic past, continued into Neolithic times. There seems to be no good reason for not assuming that the early Neolithic settlers in Crete brought such social institutions with them, including communal land tenure, normal among modern peoples at a comparable stage of economic development.[14]

Inhumation in caves or rock shelters was the normal method of burial in the Late Neolithic and for some time afterwards. Hood observes[15] that Neolithic settlers appear to have passed beyond the stage of burying their dead inside their houses before they arrived in Crete. In the lowest aceramic level 10 at Knossos seven burials were found during the recent excavations, all of young children – a widespread custom in early times; but in Crete during the rest of the Neolithic period and throughout the Bronze Age even children were normally taken outside the settlement for burial. There are eight Carbon 14 dates for the Knossian Neolithic, the earliest for the aceramic level 10 of 6100 BC, the latest of 3730 BC for level 4, the first roughly corresponding with those obtained for the lower levels of Çatal Hüyük.[16] In the light of these early Carbon 14 dates, he thinks, the advanced and sophisticated character of the Neolithic civilization of Crete is curious.[17]

For, at Knossos, even in the aceramic level 10, the adult dead were no longer buried inside their houses as they were at Çatal Hüyük; and the earliest Neolithic pottery, when it appears in level 9, is of an evolved type which looks as if it was the heir of a long tradition. Hood then expresses the hope that, one day, it should be possible to find convincing parallels for this earliest Neolithic pottery of Crete in some other part of the Near East, which would show that the people who made it came from there.

Although we remain uncertain about the origins of the Neolithic population of Crete, it is hardly surprising that, by the beginning of the third millennium BC, they should have become, as it were, 'Cretans' rather than 'Anatolians' or 'Syrians' or any other name that may be applied to the first Early Neolithic settlers.[18] As with many other significant cultural changes in prehistory, it is extremely difficult to assess the balance between indigenous and external influences promoting such change.

For Hood,[19] the transition from the Neolithic to the Minoan Bronze Age is defined in terms of radical changes in pottery fashions, changes which may reflect the presence of immigrants or invaders from overseas; and he points to signs of widespread dislocation and upheaval throughout Crete at the end of the Neolithic period, c.3000 BC. Many people seem to have taken refuge in the caves of the island then, as in other troubled periods of Cretan history, and some of the earliest Bronze Age settlements are on high defensible hills. If invaders reached Crete at this time from some area with a more advanced technology, they might have introduced the art of metal-working to inaugurate a true Bronze Age; but supplies of copper were available in many parts of the island and may have been exploited before the end of the Neolithic period.

Or again, Branigan,[20] also judging from an archaeological standpoint, does not doubt there were outside *influences*. Cycladic connections are clear, and perhaps from this area the Cretans learnt about metallurgy. Connections likewise with the Troad, the Greek mainland, Cilicia, Syria, Palestine and Egypt can be postulated but not proved. If they could be proved, unlikely though it is that they could exist all together at *c.*3000 BC, the problem would remain. He concludes that there may well have been influence, probably indirect in most instances, without an initial influx of people.

As investigation proceeds, we shall learn more about the motivating influences of the Cretan Early Bronze Age in the third millennium BC, with its accompanying economic and social developments. There is general agreement about the great historical importance of the third millennium BC, as trades and crafts were stimulated by the development of metallurgy, in which the islands of the central Aegean had a major share.[21] The phenomena of progress are unfolded in Crete by the appearance of villages and small towns as the normal centres of social life. Architectural changes are of special significance in Crete because of the many great circular tombs which have survived for exploration. Originally simple pits dug in the earth in caves or in the open, they had already attained considerable and impressive proportions in the form of these Early Bronze Age tholoi of Crete.

The exploration of these communal chamber tombs in the Messara plain between 1904 to 1918 was the great achievement of Stephanos Xanthoudides. The definitive account of his excavations was published in 1924.[22] In the course of 14 years Xanthoudides had excavated 15 tombs, with some further partial additions. The lasting importance of his work has been particularly stressed by Branigan in a recent careful study of the Messara tombs.[23] He has no doubt that Xanthoudides' excavations still provide the backbone of our studies of the Messara tholoi; and that Xanthoudides' monograph remains the most important single publication for our study of Pre-Palatial Crete.[24] There was renewed discovery and excavation of Messara tombs between 1954–69. In consequence, if we include the late, the atypical, and the unexcavated and uncertain examples of Early Bronze Age tholoi in the total, there is information about nearly 80 of these tombs, of which about 50 have been excavated.[25]

In the course of his survey Branigan observes that villages and small towns are now, at the beginning of the Early Bronze Age (i.e. Early Minoan I), the norm and isolated farmsteads are no longer found. Whether in the form of a circular tholos, a rectangular built tomb or a burial cave, the communal tomb is widely adopted. The new tombs are used for hundreds rather than dozens of burials; and they are erected for the use either of the whole community or at least a substantial part of it.[26]

Specialized craftsmen have made their appearance, initially perhaps only in metal-working but soon also in pottery manufacture. The circular tombs, whether vaulted or not, were far in advance of any Neolithic structures yet found in Crete. There was further architectural development in the Early Minoan II period, buildings at Vacsiliki and Fournou Korifi (Myrtos) containing many rooms with characteristics hitherto unknown in Crete. Here, according to Branigan, is the first evidence for the emergence of a wealthier class in Cretan society, able to build and maintain a mansion of the size of many contemporary villages. Craft specialization spread to the production of stone vases and the manufacture of seal-stones; and there was increased commercial activity with other parts of the Aegean.[27]

A peaceful environment encouraged an increased general prosperity. In the course of the millennium from the start of the Early Bronze Age to the rise of the palaces, there is no evidence for major destruction or warfare. The early towns, like the later palatial towns, had no defensive walls, such as are found on several Cycladic islands, at Troy, Poliochni, Manika, Raphina, Asketario, Aegina and Lerna during the Aegean Early Bronze Age. Similarly, the other islands of the Aegean and the Greek mainland did not indulge in the widespread trade that the Minoans pursued, and consequently did not reap its benefits in terms of technical and cultural advance. Whilst the mainland of Greece passed through a somewhat troubled and unrewarding Early Bronze Age, and the Cycladic islands never fulfilled their early promise of cultural excellence, Crete moved forward at an increasing tempo towards the brilliant civilization of the palatial age. Five hundred years of palatial splendour were preceded by a thousand of prosperous and peaceful development[28].

In the present state of archaeological knowledge of the third millennium BC, it would therefore appear that the markedly peaceful character of Minoan civilization at its peak was securely based on slowly but firmly matured indigenous traditions. Though it is true that the Early Minoan settlements at Vasiliki and Myrtos were both destroyed by fire in the latter part of Early Minoan II,[29] other Early Minoan II settlement sites have failed to produce evidence of violent destruction at this time; and there seems to be no reason for supposing that the two destroyed Cretan sites should be linked with the widespread destructions in the Argolid at the end of Early Helladic II.

The important site of Vasiliki was substantially excavated in 1904 and 1906.[30] A building here, assigned to the Early Minoan II period, is large enough to be regarded as a mansion or small palace, perhaps, as Hutchinson thought,[31] the prototype in miniature of the splendid buildings later to be erected at Knossos, Phaistos and Mallia. Its orientation, with its corners towards the cardinal points of the compass, a practice normal in Mesopotamia and the Middle East generally, but abnormal in Egypt and the Aegean, led Hutchinson to surmise that this architectural feature was due to the people who introduced Vasiliki pottery, with its Anatolian forms. Although it is not possible to reconstruct the original plan, it seemed to him not unlikely that the various wings were grouped round an open court in the centre.[32] The rectangular rooms of all shapes and sizes, sometimes united internally by long passages, illustrated the typically Minoan labyrinthine, agglutinative architecture which was to culminate in the Palace of Minos.

Our knowledge of Early Bronze Age Crete, until recent years so modest and

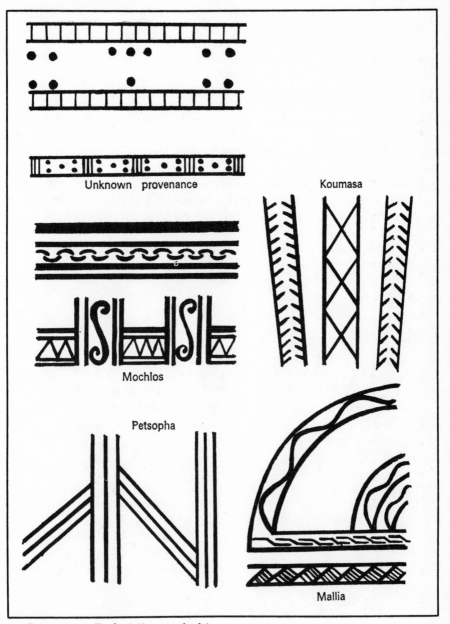

2 Patterns on Early Minoan clothing

partial, has now been supplemented further by the excavation of a complete settlement at Myrtos by Warren in 1967 and 1968. The rich evidence from the site has been carefully described with a detailed documentation worthy of its unique importance.[33]

The Myrtos settlement was destroyed by fire *c.*2200 BC. The work of excavation revealed two periods distinguished by their contexts and ceramic content, Early Minoan IIA and IIB, with a likely total span of about 400 years from *c.*2600 BC.

Myrtos is one of several new settlements established in eastern Crete at the beginning of the Early Minoan II period. Warren suggests that the ultimate cause may have been an expansion of population from the well-developed Early Minoan I groups in the north central or south central regions of the island into an area with many suitable coastal sites and adjacent fertile land, the Myrtos region perhaps being particularly suitable because of an absence of extensive evergreen forest. The actual settlement was sited on the summit of a hill called Fournou Korifi, 66m. high above a narrow shore. Its difficulty of access, with domestic water supply perhaps half a kilometre away from buildings, may be partially accounted for by needs of defence, although the outer wall of the settlement, with its two entrances, is only 0.40–0.50m. thick and

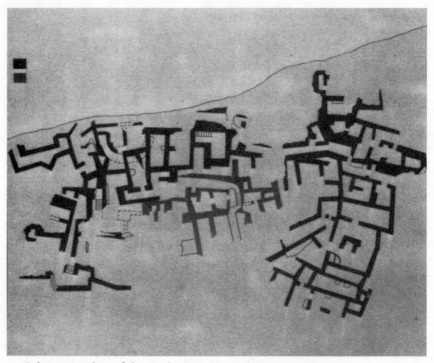

3   Schematic plan of the Early Bronze settlement at Myrtos

does not therefore suggest a real security against serious attack. Or it may have been a suitable area for the production of textiles.[34]

The inhabitants of the settlement practised mixed farming. They grew barley and wheat, cultivated the vine and the olive – there could have been as many as a thousand olive trees – and they kept sheep, goats, pigs and cattle. This evidence firmly supports the view that the economic basis of the subsequent palatial civilization was established in the course of the long Early Bronze Age. The store-rooms of Knossos and Phaistos demonstrate the importance of large-scale olive, vine and cereal production. Compared with cereals, olives and vines require only modest and seasonal amounts of time and manpower, thus liberating most of the population for other work. The discoveries at Myrtos show how the origins of this cultivation were laid by the small farming communities of Early Minoan times, when olive-growing and viticulture were novelties and when the realization of their potential gave a wholly new pattern to life and an impetus to progress.[35]

A population figure of about 100–120 is suggested as likely, with farmers perhaps supporting specialized craftsmen, since pottery production and possibly textile manufacture were flourishing operations.[36]

The settlement plan is of considerable interest and importance. The complex must be considered as a single, large unit where a clan or tribe lived communally and, to quote Warren's own words, 'perhaps not differentiated into individual families, and quite without any apparent chief or ruler'; and Warren goes on to conclude, quite logically, that the contemporary House-on-the-Hill at Vasiliki was certainly another such large, single unit.[37] Archaeological evidence, in itself, can neither prove nor disprove the possibility of some kind of chieftaincy at this stage of social development, but Warren would have been right, on grounds of comparative ethnography, to which he does not appeal, to dismiss more decisively any possibility of differentiation into 'individual families' in the third millennium BC, as will become increasingly clear as the social history of the island is further investigated and more readily capable of scientific analysis in the light of other than purely archaeological records.

However, what is more important than a difference of opinion about the interpretation of archaeological evidence from Vasiliki and Myrtos, in terms of interpretation of possible social trends at this early period, is the amount of common ground that Warren, after his judicious appraisal of the Myrtos and related evidence, is at pains to establish. He points out that a single large unit, a clan or tribe living communally, is just such a social organization as is strongly suggested by the Early Minoan burial evidence, always communal, never with individual graves. As he says, the circular tombs of the Messara imply no differentiation in social structure. Branigan had already suggested that the use of more than one communal tomb at one cemetery at the same time seems to imply more than one clan or large individual group in the relevant settlement. This hypothesis seems thoroughly acceptable to Warren, who would emphasize the communal aspect of the tombs, each used by a clan or group with apparently undifferentiated members all buried together; and he concludes that the settlement architecture of Myrtos seems to provide for such a social organization a good parallel among the living.[38] What is bound to impress the investigator into the origins of the great period of Minoan Bronze Age achievement in the second millennium BC is the evidence now clearly enunciated by both Warren and Branigan of the firm foundations for future development laid by indigenous Cretan achievement in the long, slow course of the Early Bronze second millennium BC.

In this connection it should be noticed that Warren points out two main sources of evidence for religious practices at Myrtos which have their significance for the future.[39] The strongest point in favour of accepting Room 92 as a shrine, he argues, is the similarity to later shrines like that of the Double Axes at Knossos.[40] Both have a low bench or structure against a wall, a female figure (which can have had no practical domestic function) originally on the structure and a number of good-sized vessels on the floor nearby, presumably for offerings. The consequences are that the Minoan household shrine[41] is now known to begin in the Early Bronze Age, earlier than any peak sanctuary, and that this type of building has a continuous history beginning before the Palaces and taken over in them.[42] The Phaistos palace shrine of MM II is the next known example.[43] A further consequence is that the Minoan household goddess is also known continuously from the Early Minoan period. A Myrtos figure is the one example actually from a domestic context, but similar figurines with EM II and EM III contexts from Koumasa, Mallia, Mochlos and the Trapeza Cave probably represent the same divinity or divinities.[44] This Myrtos figure with a jug may have been thought of as a protectress of the water supply (vital for a waterless settlement), as well as domestic crafts and industries which all needed water. For Warren, such attributes recall Athene Evgane, who was especially concerned with spinning and weaving and also had connections with water.[45]

In the same way, tables of offerings are now known, from the Myrtos evidence, to begin in Early Minoan times and are used throughout the whole Minoan period.[46]

In his discussion of domestic architecture at Myrtos, Warren emphasizes that many rooms had no door and were entered from the roofs.[47] The layout of the settlement is in the form of a single, large building complex – except possibly for one separate building – divided by three long, narrow passages, with no suggestion of individual, self-contained houses; and the presence of store-rooms, kitchens, work-rooms and probably living rooms (in the southern area) suggests that the settlement was thought of as a single unit with different parts having different functions.[48] These features are strongly reminiscent of the layout of Çatal Hüyük – an impression which is reinforced by a study of Warren's detailed site plan. Indeed, certain common architectural and religious features of Çatal Hüyük and of Crete some thousands of years later add fascination to the current general problems of Aegean prehistory.[49]

Warren himself points to similarities with the future grand palaces as suggesting that the origins of the palaces are to be sought in settlements such as Myrtos and Vasiliki, architecturally in part and economically in full. The dozens of little rooms and areas separated by three main passages in the plan of Myrtos can be seen as prototypes of the fully developed Late Minoan settlement plan, best exemplified at Gournia and Palaikastro. Within the whole complex particular areas had particular functions, with store-rooms and work-rooms towards the north end, possibly spinning and weaving places in the centre, magazines, kitchen and work-rooms in the south-east part, larger rooms which were probably living places west of the South Entrance Passage, more work-rooms towards the south-west, and a shrine in the south-west corner with a probably shrine treasury next to it, and another possible cult-room adjacent on the east. This whole system of distinct though not too vigorously defined units of use, as he puts it, is basically the same as the functionally distinct areas of the palaces despite the absence of such particular features of the later palaces as the central court; but other apparently deliberate and careful details of planning are indeed reminiscent of the later palaces.[50]

Part 2

THE BRONZE AGE

4

PALACES AND PALACE ECONOMY

The preceding chapters have surveyed the geographical and historical environment which, over four millennia, helped to shape a firm basis for Cretan social life with special characteristics. In the prolonged phases of the whole Neolithic and the early Bronze Ages there were already, as we have seen, some singular achievements specifically belonging to those times; but there had also long emerged two clearly defined dispositions of behaviour. On the one hand there may be inferred an aptitude of the inhabitants, formed by the necessity of geographical position, to absorb cultural influences from neighbouring centres where quite remarkable progress in various fields had been intensively stimulated; and, on the other hand, an ability to absorb these influences in such a way as to mark them with a mould of originality which ripens with unique impact in the course of time. Thus the special features of the palaces which typify the splendours of Minoan Bronze Age civilization of the second millennium can be traced in the exploration of earlier settlements such as Vasiliki and Myrtos. These rested on a deeply rooted and stable basis, as did the later palaces. A prolonged Neolithic development meant that Crete was at the agricultural stage from its beginnings. Agriculture was its staple industry, supplemented by hunting, fishing and stock-raising; and agricultural techniques, it would seem, were blended with handicraft manufacture to form compact structures of simple self-sufficiency.

The Bronze Age urban centres and great palaces of the first half of the second millennium arose out of this solid social framework, with characteristic features of Neolithic economy surviving and supporting major new developments. The surplus produce from the farming communities contributed to the maintenance of highly skilled and specialized craftsmen such as coppersmiths, goldsmiths, potters, carpenters and masons. The vigorous advance of skilled metallurgy testifies to an obvious increase in wealth accompanied by an increase in population and an expanded food supply.

The golden age of Minoan civilization lasted for about 600 years, from approximately 2000 BC. In broad terms, the Bronze Age in Greek lands lasted for the best part of two millennia, from about 2800 BC to about 1100 BC. The Early and Middle Bronze Age civilizations of mainland Greece, the Cyclades

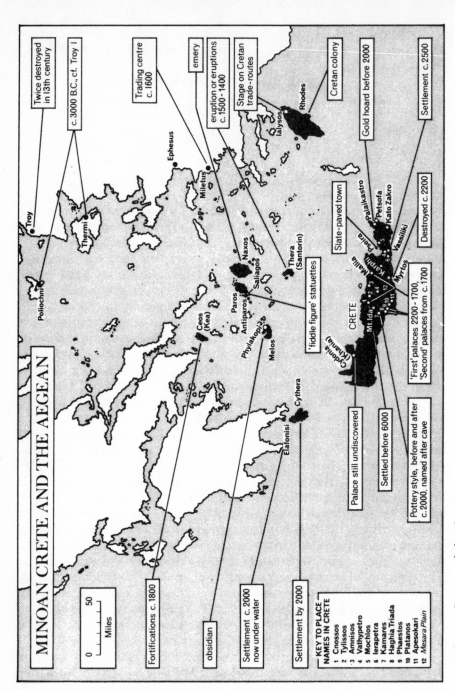

4   Minoan Crete and the Aegean

and Crete were succeeded by the Creto-Mycenaean civilization of Late Bronze Age Crete and Greece, from approximately the mid-second millennium until about 1100 BC. This latter period had a chronological span similar to the Middle Minoan Bronze Age at its zenith, both shorter by several centuries than the Early Bronze Age. If, by using a terminology perhaps more architectural than strictly archaeological, we describe the Cretan Early Bronze Age as Pre-Palatial Minoan, then the Middle Minoan period up to 1700 BC may well be and sometimes is, described as Old-Palace Minoan; and that from 1700 BC to about 1450 BC as New-Palace Minoan.

The Old Palaces suffered repeated damage and were eventually so violently destroyed, perhaps by earthquake, that it was apparently impossible to rebuild them on their original plan. The consequence is that those palaces which have been excavated are, naturally, the New Palaces (apparently constructed according to a similar design), although it has been possible to explore parts of the older remains at Knossos and Phaistos.

Until recent years, three palatial centres were conceived as being the focal points of Minoan achievement. The Palace of Minos at Knossos in the north, lavishly restored by Evans, and monumentally published on a scale which is a lasting tribute to the inspiration which can be derived from the study of a great past achievement of human endeavour,[1] has naturally tended to occupy a central position in the minds of archaeologists and prehistorians. There are good reasons why an exaggerated emphasis on the role of Knossos in the Cretan Bronze Age needs to be modified – among them, and not least, the indigenous social and economic foundations laid in the Neolithic and Early Bronze Age centuries.

When Evans had begun his work at Knossos in the north, other archaeologists had begun their explorations elsewhere on Cretan soil. Halbherr started his work in 1900 on the palace site of Phaistos on the eastern end of the ridge which closes the opening to the plain of Messara from the sea, and in a place of great natural beauty. Luigi Pernier took control of these invaluable excavations in the following year.

The third great palace was at Mallia in the north. The site was first discovered and partially excavated by Hazzidakis. In more recent years, it has been systematically and thoroughly explored by the French Archaeological School. At all three major sites, the patient work of excavation, restoration and preservation has been continued year by year. However, in comparison with Knossos, the restorations at Phaistos and Mallia have been more discreetly established.

The three principal palaces had all been pillaged to a greater or lesser extent before archaeological excavation at the sites could begin. In recent years a fourth palace has been undergoing exploration at Zakro in the eastern extremity of Crete. Here preliminary work at the beginning of this century had already revealed Minoan buildings, pottery, tools and clay seals. The more

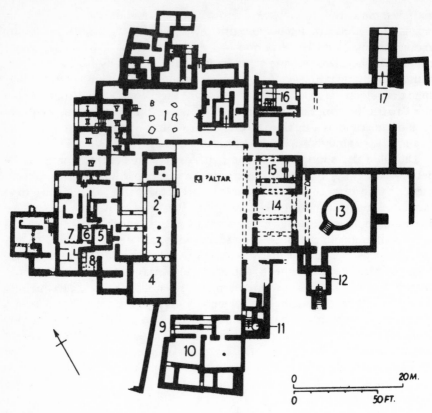

5 Plan of the palace at Zakro

recent excavations have shown evidence of a palace similar to the palaces of Knossos, Phaistos and Mallia, to judge from the impressive material of various kinds so far discovered. These large palaces were central features of sizable cities, with streets leading to them from the periphery. Apparently they were also administrative and religious centres of self-supporting regions of the island.

Though it seems unlikely that palaces of comparable size will be uncovered, there are grounds for supposing that there was a large palace in the north-west, in the fertile coastal plain at Khania, and quite near to the modern town. There may well have been smaller palaces and villas at smaller urban centres in various parts during the Bronze Age, in addition to those few which have already been discovered and excavated. Ayia Triada, near Phaistos, has yielded artistic masterpieces though the documentation of this important site is still incomplete. West of the Ida massif, near Monasteraki in the plain of Amari, what could have been another small palace has been discovered, though some of the rooms assigned to the palace building may perhaps have belonged to houses in the surrounding town.[2] The only quite substantially excavated town of the Bronze Age is Gournia on the Ierapetra Isthmus in the east, where there was also a modest palace, with an open square in front and houses built along narrow paved streets. A pathway from the main street leads up to a small temple to the north of the palace. The houses are small, with five or six rooms on the ground floor, some of them with staircases which could have given access to a second storey.

Bearing in mind what has been said previously about house-building in excavated settlements in earlier times, we are justified in supposing that most houses throughout the Bronze Age in the villages and hamlets had a single storey, just as they do in many parts of Crete to this day. Such a house was excavated in 1965 at Ayia Varvara on the outskirts of the city of Mallia.[3] Of rectangular shape, about 9m. across from north to south, longer from east to west, the house had an open court and six main rooms. The longest, apparently used for cooking and eating, may have served as bedroom for the men. Wooden steps in the corner of one room could have led into the women's quarters – a large room with a wooden floor supported by a cross wall above the surface of the ground. A stone against one wall could have served as base for a wooden loom, for many clay loom weights were found nearby. A storage room beyond contained clay jars, some with seeds of vetch and grain, and stone weights for fishing nets. Yet another room could have been a small open well for light and air. Such 'light wells' were common features of urban houses and palaces.

This house at Ayia Varvara was destroyed by fire at the time of the general disasters of *c.*1450 BC.[4] So was a large town house (House A) at Tylissos, west of Knossos.[5] At least two storeys high, with three staircases, its living room opened through three doors on to a colonnade flanking a small open court or light well. On one side of this living room was a sunken bathroom, presumably an ordinary house bathroom which had clay or metal containers for the water. Such rooms, with steps leading down into them, like the one adjacent to the 'Throne Room' at Knossos, and thought to have served ritual purposes in the palaces, were called by Evans Lustral Basins.[6]

Another room on the outside wall of the living room had a drain and could have been a lavatory, as regularly elsewhere in such houses and in palaces. Several other adjacent small rooms could have been men's bedrooms; and another block in the south-west corner of the house could have been the women's quarters, with a staircase giving access to their part of the upper storey. A room with a square pillar, reminiscent of pillar rooms at Knossos, looks like a house shrine. There were two store-rooms, one with a window opening on to a light well. Two other rooms with storage jars seemingly for food, were placed below what could have been a dining-hall, such an arrangement being familiar in the palaces, more particularly at Zakro.

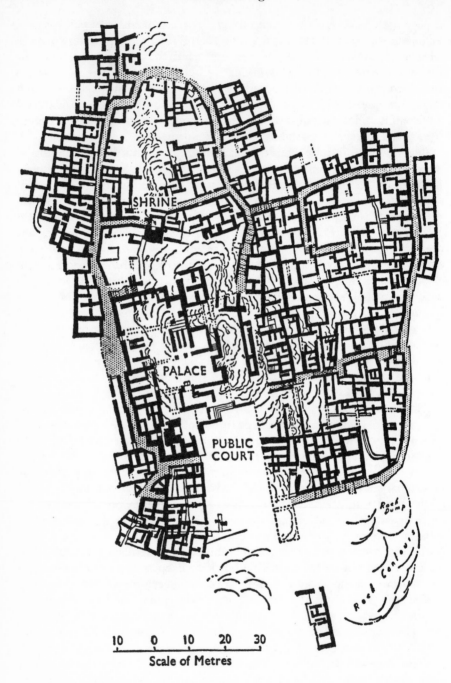

6   Plan of Gournia

The 'agglutinative' architecture of these structures, larger or smaller palaces, villas, houses, seems to reflect the continuing influence of a collective form of social organization. In layout and function the Minoan palace is symbolic of a large, close-knit household, reminiscent of those divine households of Sumer and other focal points of early adjacent civilizations.[7] The kinds of work formerly performed on a collective basis by Neolithic households were increasingly differentiated and so more perfected skills were divided among specialist craftsmen and artisans, who were maintained from a surplus food supply stored within the temple granaries and drawing upon the household store for their raw materials.

Elsewhere, in the older centres of Bronze Age civilization, this kind of dependence on the specialists seems to have resulted in a marked loss of freedom and of prestige which had accrued to them in the earlier and less centralized economies. The increasing diversity of specialist production under the economic and commercial stimulus of the Minoan palace centres may well, on the contrary, have resulted rather in an extension of such freedom and social prestige. The tenacious collective traditions of the past still appear to have exercised an enormous influence in the flourishing high period of palatial Minoan Crete.

It is within this context and perspective that we should probably place the rise of the Minoan palaces as architectural, social, economic and religious monuments. Resemblances have been noted between the Cretan palaces and those, for instance at ancient Alalakh (Tel Atchana) or at Beycesultan in western Turkey or, again, with Egyptian architecture.[8] Until we have far more firm evidence to draw upon concerning the prehistory of the ancient Near East it is perhaps advisable to resist the allure of adventitious prototypes and to accept, as consistent with past traditions, an emphasis upon essentially Cretan originality in architecture.[9]

Even before more recent excavations enlarged our knowledge, it was considered likely that Cretan houses developed in plan from a 'but-and-ben' two-compartment structure, with a single entrance, into rectangular houses, shallow, wide and with terraced flat roofs. With more complex planning by the early second millennium BC, rooms were being grouped around central courts and light-wells.[10] Earlier structural development, supported by the analogy of house architecture at Çatal Hüyük, lend substance to the view that the palaces developed from elaboration of the contemporary house-plan, with fundamental differences of arrangement between those of Crete and mainland Mycenae.[11]

Cretan palaces, unlike Mycenaean, bear no resemblance to castles. There are no defensive walls or fortifications around any of the palaces. The enclosure wall at Knossos, for instance, is the retaining wall of the western forecourt. Such walls were stout enough, up to a certain height built of ashlar masonry with layers of clay between courses and backed by rubble, held firm by a framework of timber beams. Cretan preferences for flat roofs and terraces suited the steep slope of the Knossos site, whose planning also took account of varying climatic conditions. Main living-rooms had a minimum of outside exposure, tending to be grouped around rectangular light-wells, reflecting sunlight through columned peristyles. There was access to main halls through ranges of doorways with deep reveals, into which doors could be folded back in summer.[12] The terracing, combined with an upper storey as a *piano mobile*, for the first time in history contributed to a marked emphasis upon staircases as conspicuous features of domestic architecture. The staircase in the so-called 'King's Suite', for example, is 1.8m. wide with a central newel-post 90cm. square. Its treads of 45cm. were cut from single slabs of gypsum, built 18cm. into the flanking walls, dressed on the underside to form a stone ceiling to the lower flight. A quite novel element was also introduced into column design. Pillars of cypress wood, which tapered sharply downward from the top, originally had fairly tall stone bases of various sorts, with preference in the Late Minoan period for flat disks of limestone.

Unfortified townships had tended to develop, where there were good harbour facilities, growing out of village communities centred around a market-place as focus of its social and religious life as well as for the exchange of commodities. The more heterogeneous settlements of the third millennium apparently managed to survive peacefully; and in the Middle Minoan period, with its probable increased emphasis upon commercial enterprise, there was a continued peaceful development. The main areas, presumably independent and centred upon their palaces, seem to have progressed fairly evenly. It is significant that the use of caves for habitation is hardly known in either the earlier or the later palace periods.[13] A flourishing Bronze Age economy was apparently achieved with absence of internal strife and without inviting aggressive attention from overseas.

It has been maintained that such outside influences as can be recognized do not alter the essentially indigenous qualities of Cretan architecture, whose distinctive characteristics were not derived from elsewhere.[14] These characteristics include the typically 'Cretan Hall', the pier-and-door partition, the light-well, the use of alabaster veneering, the sunken bathroom or lustral chamber, the downward-tapering column, the column oval in cross-section, the porticoed Central Courts, the alternating pier-and-column scheme, the columned propylon, the terraced and porticoed gardens of the residential quarters, the use of monumental stairways, and the system of putting the main public rooms on upper floors.

The large rectangular Central Courts are conspicuous features of the palaces. They were roughly orientated from north to south, perhaps to catch the winter sun, perhaps for ritual reasons; the small square stone surround in the north-west corner of the Court at Zakro may have been the base of an altar.[15] This feature was also common in the temples and palaces of the Near

East where outer walls bounded the structures, built in straight lines at right angles; hence their rectangular inner rooms and their Central Courts took their shape from the outer walls. The Cretan palaces, however, radiated outwards from their Central Courts to groups of rooms and apartments at varying heights and in several storeys.

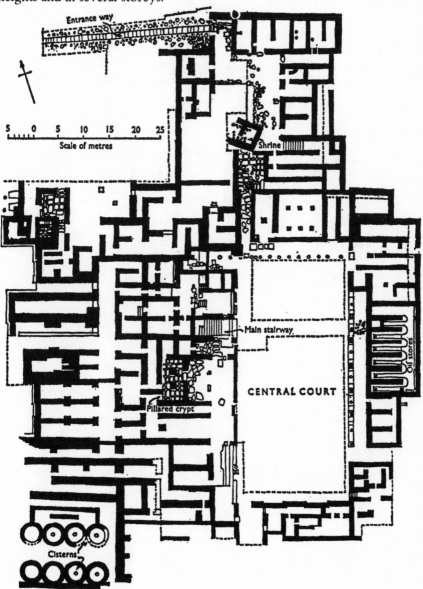

7   Middle Minoan palace at Mallia

Despite their individual differences, the Knossos palace could have served as a sort of prototype for those at Phaistos, Mallia and Zakro. Thus the large pillared hall beyond the north end of the Central Court of Knossos seems to

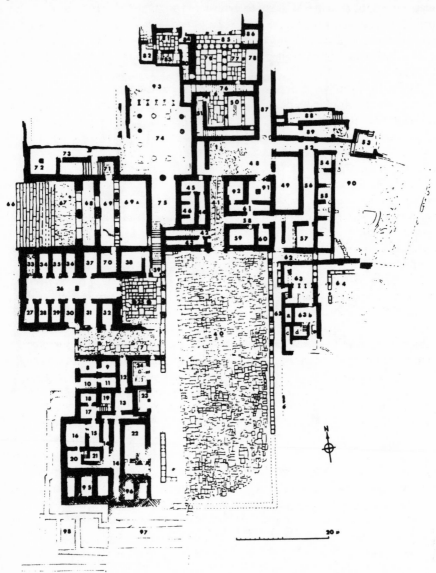

8   The later palace at Phaistos

have had a dining-room above it like that above the kitchen at Zakro. Much of the area to the east and the south of this pillared hall has been destroyed by erosion and also by quarrying for stone in later times; but quantities of cooking pots have been discovered in the North-east Magazines.[16] The Knossos palace had store-rooms on the western side; cult-rooms west of the Central Court; work-rooms and storerooms to the north-east; a residential quarter to the south-east; and public rooms chiefly above the rooms to the west of the Central Court.

At Phaistos too the ground plan cannot be completely envisaged, because rooms which might have existed along the south end and the southern part of the east side of the Central Court would have been destroyed by erosion. Nevertheless what is left can be defined into such areas as: guest-rooms and cult-rooms; magazines and entrance way; service-rooms; a main residential quarter; the Central Court; main public rooms above certain of these areas.

At Mallia the layout reveals: cult-rooms west of the Central Court; store-rooms along the western front; rooms, perhaps for guests, at the south-western corner; store-rooms to the east of the Central Court; a residential quarter at the north-western corner; store-rooms and work-rooms at the north-end; the Central Court; and the main public rooms above some store-rooms on the western side and to the north of the Central Court.

It is thus clear that the Cretan palaces were designed to serve a variety of different purposes as did the temples of the Near East. Large administrative centres, dwellings for rulers and their retinues, they were also warehouses and manufacturing centres. Again we are reminded of the earlier settlements which serve as indigenous prototypes for future economic developments and help to explain why magazines and workshops at Knossos and Phaistos, for instance, are proportionately more conspicuous and occupy a relatively larger area than in the temples of Erech or Lagash.[17] If it was indeed the case that a smaller proportion of the palace contents and products was absorbed for household needs, the balance being used for trade, the consequence might well have been that the economy centred upon the palace must have relied largely upon secondary industry and commerce as compared with agricultural production which was likely to have been not subject to anything like the same degree of centralized control. Village communities and lesser households would have preserved their traditional autonomy and social traditions.[18]

What Evans called at Knossos the Domestic Quarter, reserved for the ruling family, constituted a relatively modest proportion of the total area of the palaces. At Knossos this part of the palace lay to the east of the Central Court, the lowest storey having a large hall, the so-called Hall of the Double Axes, where signs of the double axe were inscribed on the walls of the light-well. This is similar to the Men's Halls elsewhere, with access to wide terraces. There was also a Queen's Hall or Women's Hall, with a bathroom (as indicated by the remains of a clay tub). Other private rooms included a lavatory, connected to the sewage and drainage system of the Domestic Quarter. For, even in the earlier palaces, the system of public works, including drainage, was astonishingly sophisticated.[19]

After the destruction of the old palace centres, presumably by earthquake, round about 1700 BC, they were built again on an even more impressive scale. The new palace at Knossos covered an area of about 22,000 square metres, with three storeys on the west side, four, or perhaps even five, on the east side. There must have been more than 1500 rooms altogether, including living quarters, reception rooms, workshops, store-rooms and so on.[20] The west wing of the palace had narrow store-rooms opening from a long corridor, with stone-lined boxes or cists let down into the floors of rooms and corridor. These, together with the huge jars known as pithoi (which are still made to this day by the potters of Crete), were used for storage purposes. When the palace was finally destroyed round about 1450 BC, the cists and pithoi were in use as containers for olive oil; and their capacity has been estimated at more than 240,000 gallons.[21] In comparison with Knossos the area of the Zakro palace was between 7000–8000 square metres, and at Phaistos and Mallia 900 square metres.[22]

The work-rooms for such craftsmen as potters, lapidaries and metal-workers can sometimes be recognized from the remains of the materials they used in their work. Such workshops and store-rooms took up a fair proportion of the total area. At Mallia, for instance, store-rooms occupied about a third of the room space of the ground floor. Here, as elsewhere, this part of the palace was devoted to such purposes because it was easy of access and because upper storeys would have needed more constructional support if they had been so employed.

There can, however, be no doubt that most of the west wing of the Minoan palaces was reserved for purposes of cult. Pillar-crypts and the columned rooms over them, together with the treasuries often associated with them, served as cult-rooms. Just as archives were under divine protection, so much of the palace industry served to produce ritual objects of great splendour.[23]

These cult-rooms needed water for lustral purposes. There is a stone-lined pit at the bottom of a short stairway, opposite the throne in the Throne Room at Knossos which was found in its original position against the north wall of the room. Made of stone, with high back and hollowed seat, it was fashioned on the model of a wooden throne or elaborate chair. Here sat the presiding ritual functionary, playing some indispensable part in a religious palace ceremonial vital to the life and functioning of the community. Was this person the Minoan 'priest-king' himself, as is often supposed, or perhaps rather a high priestess? To this highly important question we shall have to return.[24]

For the present, we may note that Platon, writing on public and private life in the period of the old palaces, cites certain kinds of evidence which support the hypothesis of a theocratic administration. It is very difficult to explain, he argues, how such vast and complex palace buildings ever came to be constructed unless with the voluntary participation of the whole popula-- tion. The only sufficiently strong motive to account for such an outlay of capital and labour would have been the belief that they were building a home for the goddess, in which the king would live as her representative. It seems impossible to believe that those incomparable edifices were built by an en- slaved people working under a tyrant's lash. It is clear that Crete enjoyed good government from the Old-Palace period onwards, and indeed the memory of it remained undiminished right through to Hellenic times. Good government of a quality to account for Crete's unique internal balance of power would have been difficult to achieve unless it rested on a theocratic organization.[25]

On the subject of the sanctuary of the deity in the New Palace complex at Knossos, Platon further argues that the arrangement of the west wing makes it clear that the sanctuary and its auxiliary apartments were the main elements of the palace; which shows that the political organization at Knossos still retained the theocratic basis which had been so evident in the Old-Palace Period. The sanctuary stood in the centre of the west wing, facing the Central Court. Its pillared facade was divided into three parts, the middle and highest one crowned with pairs of horns. Though only the base of the facade remains, its original appearance is known from palace frescoes. The sanctuary comprised the priests' vestibule; pillar crypts with engravings of sacred axes on the pillars and special arrangements for the reception of votive offerings; the three-columned sanctuary of the divinity on the upper floor, above the pillar crypts; the archive rooms; the temple repositories, which contained valuable ritual vessels and cult objects stored carefully away in special containers and fine faience figurines of the various deities; the 'sacristy', where there were shallow basins used in preparations for the sacrificial ceremony; and the long row of 21 magazines, linked by a corridor, equipped with special underground cists and vats to hold various offerings and containing rows of jars stored with produce of every kind, since the Minoans offered their deity the first fruits of each harvest. The upper storeys of the sanctuary were reached by the wide stairway of the propylaia, enclosed by columned wings, and the central stair case leading directly to the sanctuary rooms from the Central Court. These stretched northwards beyond the staircase, centred around the Throne Room. The complex of rooms comprising the sanctuary and covering the whole western wing had a separate entrance close to the harbour gate. The reason for building a special entrance so close to the monumental north gate becomes clear when we remember that the sanctuary was regarded as a separate entity of a closed character within the palace, which also accounts for the unusual construction of the sanctuary entrance. Next to the door and the two-columned porch was an open-air enclosure containing a lustral basin similar to the one in the Throne Room; and Platon recalls that Evans had called this open space

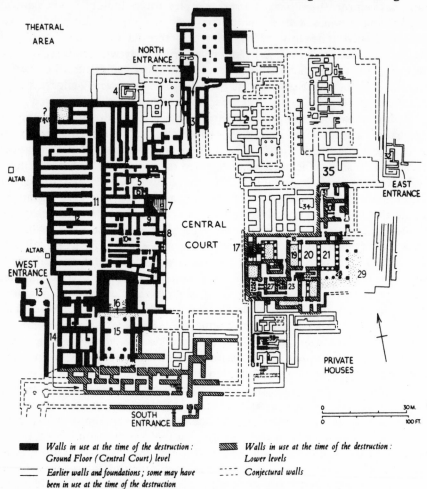

9 The palace of Minos at Knossos in fourteenth century BC

the initiation area and proposed the theory that the lustral basin was used for the purification of the votaries who wished to enter the sanctuary.[26]

The development of the Bronze Age palace-based economies led not only to the construction for commercial purposes of harbours, bridges and roads, but as elsewhere in the Bronze Age involved other important consequences. The copper ingots which have been found at Ayia Triada, Tylissos, Mochlos and Knossos[27] indicate that a rudimentary form of money was needed, for weighing out against other commodities. Exchange transactions needed measurement by weights.[28] Written scripts also came into use, divided by Evans as they were discovered in the course of archaeological investigation into pictographic and linear scripts.[29]

Commodity production, if mainly of luxury goods, had already therefore become fairly extensive by Middle Minoan times. As commodities were required for the market, for internal exchange as well as for export, so craftsmen skilled in special techniques became more numerous, depending on the economy of the palaces but perhaps enjoying considerable power of initiative and freedom.

Trade between Crete and the Aegean islands and with such countries as Egypt, for which a good deal of evidence now exists, must have led to the increase in numbers and in influence of a class of merchants such as also existed in Egypt and other Levantine countries in these times. It is likely that a great deal of exports from Crete comprised raw materials and such perishable goods as foodstuffs and cloth, and also the superb Cretan painted pottery of various kinds. For their own basic needs the islanders were fairly self-supporting, having no need to import food or timber and stone for ships and buildings. There may have been imports of copper to supplement local resources. The tin needed to mix with copper for the manufacture of bronze would have been imported, perhaps from central Europe or from the western coast of Italy. Such luxury materials as gold and silver could have been imported from the Aegean islands or from western Anatolia; emery from Naxos, to be used as an abrasive in the making of stone bowls; fine stones from the south Peloponnese; obsidian from Anatolia or from Yiali near Cos; alabaster from Egypt; ivory from Syria; ostrich eggs – to be turned into libation vases – and ostrich plumes, from Egypt or North Africa.[30]

In addition to the large palace centres, there were smaller palaces of the type best known perhaps at Ayia Triada, three kilometres away from the major palace at Phaistos. This is often described as a 'summer palace', and it contains miniature versions of the different sorts of rooms found in the great palaces – sanctuaries, magazines, treasuries and workshops. Large villas or farmsteads have now been discovered in various parts of Crete, mostly dating from the times of the later palaces. They include the villas at Sklavokampos and Nirou Khani, large farmsteads at Vathypetro, Vitsilia in the area of Lykastos, Mitropolis at Gortyn and Plate in Lasithi, all in central Crete; in the eastern part, there are the farmsteads at Sitia, Zou, Achladia, Prophetes Elias and Ayios Konstantinos in the area of Praisos, and Epano Zakro. Most of them have sanctuaries and other rooms similar to those of the palaces. Nearly all were two storeys or more high, containing at least 30 and sometimes more than 50 rooms. The farmsteads had wine presses, vats for treading grapes, containers for the must and drainage for waste. There were not so many olive presses but there are proofs of workshops with grinding stones, graters, mortars, pestles and hand mills. The pottery workshop at Zou had troughs for kneading clay, pottery kilns and other appropriate amenities. To judge from the quantities of loom weights, much weaving was done by the women; and there were sometimes special basins for dyeing textiles.[31]

It is clear that the siting of these buildings was carefully chosen, since they often command highly picturesque views and they were constructed with appropriate appurtenances such as balconies, verandahs and porticoes. Their workshops invite comparison with the country houses of Roman Britain.[32]

Cities and towns near the great palaces, the farmsteads and villas, as well as the presumably numerous villages and hamlets all testify to a considerable density of population in the high period of the Cretan Bronze Age until the massive destructions of *c.*1450 BC. Until there has been far more detailed investigation of the various settlements in the island at this period, it is impossible to be precise about population densities and economic details.[33] It may have been the case, however, that traditional systems of communal land tenure were still preserved in the countryside, but modified to the extent that a system of tributary relations, involving the collection of a certain fixed quantity of produce from cultivators, had been developing. The expansion of the economy and the construction of vast buildings and engineering works compels us to ask also if the peasantry might have been expected to contribute their labour services at specific times for the work on palaces, roads, aqueducts, bridges, harbours and so on. We may also ask to what extent some form of household slavery might have developed, sooner or later; and whether the cultivators exchanged produce against wares supplied by merchants over and above any tribute in kind formally imposed by palace officials. To these speculations we must return at a later stage.[34]

5

TECHNOLOGY AND THE ARTS

A high level of architectural skill is already apparent from the fragmentary evidence of the ruins of the older palaces, particularly perhaps in the ingenious adaptation of a complexity of forms within a harmonious total structure which turned the features of natural sites to artistic and functional advantages. Different levels of hillsides suggested terracing as a basic architectural design for a multi-storey structure, radiating from Central Courts by means of corridors and stairways to outer courts and rooms of various kinds and various dimensions grouped for different purposes.

Conscious purpose and detailed planning developed from such basic principles are naturally more easily apprehended from examination of the more ample evidence of the ruins of the later palaces. Thus Platon[1] observes that the characteristic trend towards the picturesque, the variegated, the charming is immediately evident. There is a sense of centrifugal movement away from the Central Court as gravitational centre of the palace. The light-wells, interior courts and exterior porticoes create a chiaroscuro effect, while the deliberate avoidance of symmetry in the arrangement of buildings and façades adds even greater variety to the overall composition. Long corridors lead unexpectedly into spacious well-lit rooms with splendid fresco decoration, the picturesque effect increased by liberal use of bright colours, especially on timber sections and downward-tapering columns, and by the striking interior decoration. Compared with the architectural monuments of Egypt, the Minoan palace has no air of the indestructible and the eternal about it, nothing to proclaim the grandeur of the kings, like the palaces of the East, even in its most monumental sections. The main residential quarter and ceremonial halls were on the upper floors, while the rows of small rooms, seemingly inappropriate to a larger palace, were designed for cult and service purposes at ground level.

It is scarcely surprising, adds Platon,[2] that the Palace of Minos was remembered as a labyrinth in later legends connected with Crete. Minoan architecture more than any other (except perhaps Japanese, which sprang from a similar conception of the sacred quality of nature) preserved the closest possible links between man and the natural world and there seems no reason to doubt that this unique style of palace architecture in fact originated in Crete. The only exception, Platon agrees,[3] is the palace at Ugarit, but in it he finds many elements attesting Minoan influence. In the palaces of the East, the basic principle is an analytic arrangement of buildings in an enclosed area, while in Minoan palaces the buildings spread out in a synthetic arrangement around a central open area. Minoan architecture, he concludes, was certainly influenced by the architectural styles which prevailed in other countries at that period; on the other hand, the architecture of the East and Egypt also betray considerable Minoan influence, especially in the field of interior decoration.

Typical of the technical skill combined with aesthetic sensitivity of Minoan architecture is the stairway which formed the approach to the Grand Propylaeum and the state apartments of the Palace at Phaistos. Open to the sky, though within the palace, it was made of twelve limestone steps with sloping treads only 12.7cm. high and 71.12cm. deep and with a width of 13.715m. This stairway, as Graham[4] has observed, exhibits an architectural subtlety which emphasizes the remarkable aesthetic sensitivity of the Cretans, namely the distinct 'crowning' or upward curvature of each step toward the centre. This would appear to have been intended, as in the case of the well known convexity of the steps of the Parthenon and other Greek buildings, which it anticipates by over a thousand years, to produce a certain feeling of elasticity and life, as well as to offset any tendency for the long horizontal lines to appear to sag in the middle due to an optical illusion.

Minoan knowledge of engineering, drainage and hydraulics was similarly advanced.[5] In fact the drainage system at Knossos, for example, was quite complex and, although it cannot be reconstructed in its details, was, for the times, highly sophisticated. It was established practice for waste water to be collected in stone gutters set at a gradient and run off into a main drain, which became deeper as it descended the slope. Junctions are found, with three or four gutters meeting. Or we find channels which emptied into a main drain whose function was to collect storm water from unroofed areas. Cisterns and spring chambers were lined with water-resistant plaster by the Late Minoan period and even earlier. As at Zakro these were often circular with steps leading into them and some, it is suggested, may have been domed like the later spring chambers of Sardinia. Covered drains and open channels of clay and stone carried rain water and waste. Lavatories, which were usually set against outside walls, were common features of palaces and houses. A small room at Knossos had a low platform which could have been for the bed of an attendant; and in a small compartment against one of the walls of this room was a lavatory with a seat, as in Egypt, set over a drain. This was but a portion of an elaborate system of stone-lined drains, big enough for a man to crawl through, which ran below the ground floor rooms of the residential quarter and which were fed from upper floors by means of vertical chutes.

Elaborate systems of water supply certainly indicate a high degree of comfort but there was also pressing necessity for their construction. Palaces had bedrooms, guest rooms and work-rooms. Their cult rooms required water for lustral purposes, of which the conspicuous example is the lustral chamber which consists of a stone-lined pit at the bottom of the short stairway opposite the throne in the Throne Room at Knossos. The assumption is that the Minoan priest-king (or queen, or high priestess) was seated here during the celebration of some important ritual.[6]

Different systems of water supply were used in different places. The palace at Knossos apparently did not depend on well-water alone, since terracotta pipes below the floors suggest a constant supply of running water. These pipes, between 60 and 75cm. long, were cemented at their joints and it is not improbable that water flowed through them under some kind of pressure system. There was perhaps an aqueduct to bring water from a spring about ten kilometres away on the slopes of Mount Juktas in earthenware pipes that traversed the countryside and were brought on narrow stone bridges across gulleys. The apparent remains of this aqueduct have been found in the palace precincts, in the East Wing, and also on the southern slopes of the hillside. The pipe sections were so designed as to allow the water to gain momentum at repeated intervals, and so prevent the supply system from blocking. Each section tapered to a narrow neck at one end, which was cemented to the next section; and there were curved clamps to secure the joints in place. The spring which was the source of supply was high on the mountain and this made practicable the task of bringing the water to the hill of Kephala on which the palace was constructed. Similar water-channels have been discovered at such places as Tylissos and Vathypetro. Though the details of the water-supply system at other palaces are deficient, there is evidence to suggest the use of large cisterns.[7]

The stone-lined pits like broad wells were called by the workmen in the excavations at Knossos *kouloures* and Evans adopted the name. Filled with potsherds and broken stone vases, it is considered likely that they were used for ritual purposes. They have come to be described as *hieroi apothetai*, they may have been sacred repositories, and they are found at the old palaces. At Mallia, there were found eight *kouloures* of this kind, which were arranged in two rows of four. Their walls were lined with plaster and the existence of central pillars suggests that the circular pits were roofed over. Some think that they were used as cisterns, others as granaries. They were more likely to have been used as cisterns, since the palace had areas of store-rooms, where grain and liquids could be stored in pithoi.[8]

The walls of palaces, houses and villas – and sometimes even their floors – were painted with frescoes, most certainly at the time of the later palaces from about 1700 BC.[9] Normally the frescoes were painted on damp plaster, either on a flat surface or by modelling figures in light relief and then applying the colours.[10] An inlay technique was also used in some wall paintings, the surface requiring more detailed treatment being cut away and refilled with plaster of finer quality. During the earlier Middle Minoan period, a dark Pompeian red was a quite usual colouring for walls, and remains of plaster painted in red have been found, of apparent Early Minoan dating, both at Knossos and Vasiliki and also at the settlement of Myrtos. Walls and floors were sometimes decorated with simple geometric designs in red and white at the beginning of Middle Minoan times, perhaps even earlier. The vivid colours of the paintings were mainly derived from mineral substances, haematite, yellow ochre, black perhaps from carbonaceous shale or charred bones, blue that seems to be a silicate of copper and soda – though the blue paint of the Ayia Triada sarcophagus was apparently made by grinding expensive lapis lazuli from Afghanistan.[11]

Just as in contemporary examples from Egypt and Mesopotamia, men, women and animals were normally sideways portrayed in a single plane and without perspective. In landscape scenes rocks and plants project from the sides and top of the picture as well as from the bottom, as if the scene were viewed from the air.[12] Many scenes convey the vivid impression of movement momentarily stilled which makes plausible the description of Minoan frescopainting as naturalist. However, although subjects may be drawn from the natural world, the rendering of the figures and the shapes is as a rule conventionally decorative.[13] Green is seldom used for vegetation, rocks and animals are painted in improbable colours – all of which conflicts with a naturalist definition.

As in Egypt, men were conventionally painted brown and women white, though there are exceptions;[14] and figures were painted as freely moving silhouettes. Crowd scenes were impressionistically rendered, heads and bodies suggested by a single stroke of the brush, the red and white bodies shown in large spots of paint. There was careful attention to detail in the reproduction of the veins in coloured rocks or decorative features in clothing or the wings of birds. Animals were astonishingly life-like against a natural background, often just a thicket. Blue apes in gardens, partridges flying in pairs or hiding near water, octopuses, sponges and coral on the sea-bed, dolphins surfacing, flying fish above the waves – these scenes witness to an almost intoxicating delight in the world of natural beauty. In fact the world of nature and the ceremonies of religious ritual were the major subjects of the paintings, rather than the glorification of grand persons or the celebrations of historical events.[15]

The wall paintings were by no means of any standard size, for they sometimes filled a complete wall surface above a narrow dado or were restricted to quite small panels, as in bull-leaping scenes from Knossos, where the human figures are less than half a metre in height. Or there could be long narrow friezes, like the charming scene of hoopoes and partridges against a natural background of rocks, bushes and water, which apparently ran around the top of the walls south of the palace at Knossos. From one dwelling at Amnisos, harbour town of Knossos, the reconstructed fragments show formal flower-gardens with clumps of red and white lilies. Other memorable scenes were portrayed in the palace at Ayia Triada, where fragments include the scene of a wild cat stalking an unsuspecting pheasant; or another of a deer which is leaping away through a scene of rocks and flowers. From the so-called 'House of the Frescoes' near Knossos, came fragments which also portray wild life in a natural setting, with rocky landscapes and clumps of flowers, wild roses, lilies, irises, crocuses, shoots of young myrtle, even an artificial fountain in a white background. A central column of water rises from a forked base, the falling drops on either side in deep blue contrasting with the white drops in front of the main jet. Blue monkeys play in the vegetation and a blue bird, perhaps a roller, with red-spotted breast, rises from behind a rock as if on the point of taking wing.

The majority of the paintings which have survived come from the Palace of Minos and the palace of Ayia Triada. It may be that one of the earliest of the surviving wall pictures is that of the Saffron Gatherer from Knossos. With its background of Pompeian red it could have been painted in the seventeenth century BC (Middle Minoan IIIA). There was then a fashion for clay vases with red bands and white spots like those portrayed here with flowers in them – apparently saffron crocuses which were used for making yellow dye. Though the head of the figure in the picture is missing, Evans concluded that it was that of a boy, because of the red lines on the body suggesting dress. However, the figure is more likely to have been a monkey than a boy. Blue was the conventional colour for monkeys in Crete as in Egypt, and a tail and the nose of another monkey have been identified on fragments of the painting. The animal was presumably a pet and it wears a red leather harness. Assuming that this more recent interpretation of the scene portrayed is correct, the pet monkey might have been pulling flowers out of pots in the palace gardens and its earlier title therefore misleading.[16]

The large relief decoration of a charging bull on the colonnade above the north entrance of the Palace of Minos at Knossos was reconstructed from fragments of the head, breast, lower feet, a tree, pieces of human figures and of rocky soil. The head, except for the horns, was well preserved, standing forth as one of the noblest revelations of Minoan art, as Evans said. Perhaps we are witnessing the capture of a bull in nets set between olive-trees or some representation of the Minoan bull-sport. A fresco panel from the Court of the Stone Spout from the Palace of Minos shows us a bull-leaping scene in three phases. The athlete waits for the charging bull and grasps it by the horns. As the bull tosses its head the athlete somersaults over the horns and the back of the bull and then lands on his feet behind the bull. Figures painted white may be women dressed as men.[17] These bull-games no doubt had religious significance,[18] and the same is true of the heraldic frieze of griffins flanking the throne in the Throne Room of the Palace of Minos. The fragments of the Dolphin Fresco were found scattered in the area of the bedroom in the

Residential Quarter at Knossos. Playing in the sea among other fishes, the dolphins have the upper part as well as their fins and tails painted deep blue, a double band of orange yellow ran along their sides and their bellies were creamy white. Evans thought the fresco belonged to an earlier scheme of wall decoration in the bedroom, but it is possible that it was an adornment of the floor of an upper room in this part of the palace at the time of its final destruction.[19]

One of the most remarkable and important of all Minoan pictures was found at the end of the Corridor of the Procession leading to the Central Court of the Palace of Minos. This figure in plaster relief, restored by Gilliéron, is known as the Priest-King Relief or Prince of the Lilies. Except for footgear and loincloth, the dignified, youthful figure is nude, its head, thighs and legs in profile, but the upper part of the body turned outwards. Locks of hair fall down in front of the left breast and beneath the clenched hand. There is some suggestion that he is leading a sacred animal by a rope. He wears a crown of lilies with long peacock plumes falling behind and a necklace of lilies hangs round his neck. Evans considered this picture to be the impersonation of a semi-divine youthful Priest-King of Knossos, moving in Elysian fields of exotic flowers and butterflies.[20] It has been suggested that the figure had been painted white and might have represented a princess in bull-leaping costume, perhaps leading a bull.[21] The elaborate headdress is of a type worn by sphinxes, always female, and by a priestess on the Ayia Triada sarcophagus.[22] If the restoration as a single figure is correct, its height of 2.10m. (well over life-size) might suggest that the figure was divine.[23]

The female figure known as 'La Parisienne' belongs to a larger composition known as the 'Camp Stool Fresco', consisting of pairs of young persons in long robes, seated facing each other and passing a goblet. The girl, with bright lips, expressive eye, perky nose and elegant hair curling down over her brow, received her name when she was discovered. It is not inept and also suggests the impressionistic style of her representation, with suppression of details not immediately apparent and a vivid concentration on characteristic essentials.[24] The composition adorned an upper room in the north-west corner of the Palace of Knossos at the time of its destruction. Since (as Cameron has shown) 'La Parisienne' was one of a pair of twin figures considerably larger than the rest, it has been inferred that these represented a pair of goddesses presiding over religious rites.[25]

Another well-known fragment of miniature fresco is the 'Captain of the Blacks' from the area of the House of the Frescoes west of the Palace of Minos. There seems here to be a portrayal of a smart officer leading a file of black soldiers at the double. He wears a helmet with two small horns, is dressed in a short yellow tunic and carries two spears. Perhaps we have in this scene some proof for the use of black troops as mercenaries in Late Minoan times, which would certainly support other indications of increasing militarism during the final phases of Minoan civilization.[26] The painting is assignable, on stylistic grounds, to Late Minoan II–III, i.e. well after the disasters of *c.*1450 BC.[27]

The most elaborate fresco was painted on the walls of the Corridor of the Procession and in the Great Propylaeum of the Palace of Minos at Knossos. Originally it may well have been composed of hundreds of figures, going in a processional file from two directions. They would have been bare-headed, with long, wavy hair and wearing silver ear-rings, necklaces, bracelets and anklets, in tunics or long skirts, and carrying presents in vases or musical instruments. The central figure, with a ceremonial veil falling to her feet, was either a goddess or a priestess. The most complete figure is called the 'Cup-Bearer'.[28]

The frescoes are important from another point of view in that they bear witness to the prominence of women in Minoan society, for example in the crowded miniature frescoes. Women are painted on a larger scale than anyone else and with elaborate detail. Women in the crowd are on the same scale as the men, indicating that it was not their sex but their function that made the larger-scale ladies so special, the desired end of the ritual invocation portrayed being a divine epiphany.[29]

The paintings on the limestone sarcophagos from Ayia Triada, frequently reproduced and discussed, have an obvious relationship with the frescoes.[30] Their style seems to place them near the beginning of the Late Minoan III period. The limestone was coated with a plaster surface for the brightly coloured panelled paintings whose meaning is still enigmatic. On one side there is an animal tied up for sacrifice on an altar table, its blood dripping into a bucket on the ground below and two goats sit waiting for their turn to come. Three women in long robes approach from the left with a musician playing on the double pipes to pass behind the altar. A female figure, perhaps a priestess, dressed in the skin of a sacrificial animal, places her hands on an altar reserved for offerings of fruit and libations, as may be inferred from the dish of fruit and the jug above. There is a tall pole surmounted by an elaborate double axe with a bird perched on it and even farther to the right there is a shrine with a sacred tree and horns of consecration.

On the other side of the sarcophagos a dead man or his mummy is apparently standing in front of his tomb to receive offerings from three priests(?) dressed in animal skins. The offerings appear to be two calves (or models of them) and a model boat, which may have symbolized the means of crossing the waters between the living and the dead. To the left, and with the accompaniment of a seven-stringed lyre, two women, one dressed in a long robe and wearing a crown on her head, the other wearing a skin, are pouring libations into a vessel which is set between two stepped bases holding poles for double axes with birds on them.

At each end of the sarcophagos there is a chariot, each one containing two female figures, one of them perhaps a goddess, the other a priestess, riding in it. One of the chariots is drawn by goats and the other by winged griffins.

The excavations in recent years, from 1967 onward, on the island of Thera (Santorini) at Akrotiri have produced some remarkable results, including a spectacular series of Minoan frescoes which have substantially supplemented our knowledge of the technique and range of content of the art form.[31]

The excavations on Thera have given evidence that the inhabitants constructed houses of two or three storeys which were decorated with frescoes. Timber ties familiar from other Minoan architectural contexts were used, and doors and windows of similar design have been found, with stone jambs and lintels. Some of the doors of upper storeys have survived and floors of several upper rooms had regular slab paving. The settlement at Akrotiri was divided into two by a paved road which has been named Telchinon Street (Coppersmiths' Street); and one group of buildings presents palatial features. Telchinon Street runs from north to south and runs into a little square with the most substantial houses around at intervals of about 22–27m.

The first square (the Mill Square) has a room which revealed frescoes of the Antelopes and the Boxing Children, both now in the National Archaeological Museum in Athens. There are six antelopes, vividly portrayed, in the one fresco. In the other one perhaps, it is suggested, we have a brother and sister, aged between six and seven, with a first artistic representation of boxing-gloves. Another room nearby contained a fresco (now in the Archaeological Museum in Athens) of Flying Monkeys, with a background of mountain rocks, in a design which ran around the corners on all the walls of the room. It is unlikely that either antelopes or monkeys lived on Thera and the landscape appears to be sub-tropical.

Then there is the Triangle Square with its façade of the West House and just beyond the House of the Ladies, with a painting of a group of three women, one of them perhaps a seated goddess, with a peplos and other offerings being made to her.

Another small room, which seems to have been a house sanctuary, had frescoes entirely preserved on its walls. Here was found (now transferred to the Archaeological Museum in Athens) the so-called Springtime Fresco, which (it is suggested) adorned the shrine of the Earth-Mother. Clefted volcanic rocks have their sides covered in lilies, some in full bloom, and swallows, singly or in pairs, are flying about the landscape.

The fresco of the Fishermen, now in the Archaeological Museum in Athens, from a room in the West House at Akrotiri, shows the first completely nude figure in this kind of painting. He was excellently preserved, stands one metre high, has a shaven head with only a few locks of hair and he is holding two strings of mackerel in his hands. A second fresco of a fisherman, less well-preserved, was discovered in the same place.

Along the north, east and south walls of a room of the West House was a frieze of miniature style, of which a length of more than six metres has survived. Of considerable artistic merit, its historical importance may also be highly significant. According to Marinatos, the frieze narrates the story of an expedition in a sub-tropical landscape, presumably Libya. (This interpretation may provide a clue to the supposed location of the Antelopes and Flying Monkeys.)

A fleet of seven warships and several smaller ships and boats, three towns, cattle, wild beasts and eighty people participate. At the beginning of the frieze there is a steep hill on the shore and several people on the top. There follows the scene of a sea-battle, with realistic silhouettes of drowning men. Warriors armed with body-shields, boar's tusk helmets, swords and large spears are being landed. The first 'town' may be no more than a hamlet with sheep-folds, for there are herds and herdsmen apparently depicted.

Along the east wall is a sub-tropical landscape, showing a stream of water bordered by palm-trees, and there can be seen ducks, flamingoes (or ibises), panthers, a roe-deer and a flying griffin.

The south wall contained the main subject of the frieze. The second town is on the left. In the mountains above, a lion pursues a herd of stags. The town presents a peaceful aspect, with people gathered on the roofs or walking about in the streets. A man and a woman are talking beside a stream. There is some kind of promontory to the right of the town and the fleet is sailing past. Seven ships, in two parallel columns, are sailing towards the right. One of them has sails, the others are being poled along in the shallows, and what is apparently the flagship is in full colours. The first ships have already reached the third town, whose boats are coming out to meet them; ladies await their arrival from the towers of the town and children are running about excitedly.

This remarkable painting, now in the Archaeological Museum in Athens, may represent a scene of friendly relations between the Aegean and some part of Libya, if we assume there were Minoanized settlements there just as there may have been Libyan settlers in the Aegean area.

Pottery in Neolithic times was made by hand, presumably by women, mostly with a darkish surface, smaller domestic vessels being burnished. Incised decoration of various kinds was common; and by the middle Neolithic rippling of the surface had become an established alternative form of decoration. The painted Vasiliki and Ayios Onouphrios wares were already distinctive by early Minoan times. Indeed the latter has been singled out as of such quality and of such relative uniformity in style and type as to indicate the possibility that pottery had already become a specialized industry by the E.M. I period.[32]

Pottery manufacture was a main industry at the Early Minoan settlement at Myrtos; and a potter's workshop was uncovered there, dating from Period I of the site (c.2600–2400 BC). The eight turn-tables found still lying on the floor can be assigned to this period. They were simple hand-turned disks. There is, however, evidence to suggest that an incipient stage of the freely-revolving wheel was later achieved.[33] In the opinion of the excavator, the pottery of Myrtos had technically reached the summit of what can be accomplished without a freely revolving wheel. Though slight irregularities of shape are often apparent, some types have incredibly thin walls in relation to the size of the vases; and a real mastery of ceramic techniques was needed to produce such pots on hand-turned disks. Decoratively the achievements seem meagre in comparison with the glories of Middle Minoan design.[34]

The fast potter's wheel, used in Egypt since the Pyramid Age and long before in Mesopotamia could have reached Crete by the Middle Minoan IA period; and it was in common use by Middle Minoan IB. Larger vases, however, continued to be normally hand-made until the beginning of the Late Minoan period.[35]

With a long craft tradition already well established, the general introduction of the wheel led to that generally appreciated superb achievement of pottery manufacture and decoration in the peak periods of Minoan civilization of the second millennium BC.[36] Great quantities of pottery have been discovered from the palaces at Knossos and Phaistos especially. The justly celebrated polychrome Kamares ware received its name from a cave on Mount Ida where it was first noted about 1890. The shiny glaze, dark in hue and often black, formed the background for designs in white, combined or dotted with shades of red and occasionally other colours, such as brown or yellow. There is rich formal variety and such delicacy in manufacture that this 'egg-shell' ware could often imitate metal shapes and ornamentation. Spiral designs and rosette patterns were common and a decorative naturalism which incorporates representation of octopuses, fish, shells, lilies, crocuses and palm-trees. Besides the palace pottery, which included ritual vessels, we have examples of such ordinary utensils as cheese-graters, lamps, funnels, sieves and charcoal-pans.

There also developed a monochrome style of decoration, using white paint on a darker ground. In the time of the later palaces, naturalistic motifs were rendered in dark hues on a light background and two principal naturalistic styles became dominant. A complete surface might be covered with a continuous 'marine design' of octopuses, argonauts, starfish, rock and seaweed. This 'marine design' style of ware combined with the 'plant style' of floral motifs. Marine-style pottery may have been produced in the palace workshops at Knossos, their designs adapted from wall-paintings or relief vases of stone or metal. Vessels of this kind, usually ritualistic, were sent to all parts of Crete and even to the mainland of Greece.

By the beginning of the period of the first Cretan palaces, round about the beginning of the second millennium BC, bronze was generally being used for tools and weapons in the Aegean. Metal-workers had discovered the alloy bronze presumably by trial and error methods; and, by smelting small quantities of tin ore with the copper ores they had made available a harder and more useful metal than copper because it could be more easily worked. Since the

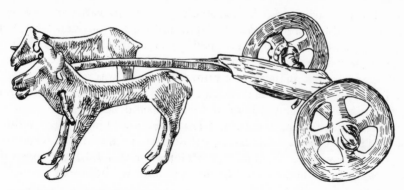

10   Late Minoan yoked oxen

melting point was reduced by mixing small quantities of tin with copper, the temperatures required for casting copper could produce a metal more fluid and easier to cast.[37]

Tinstone was probably never very common in Near Eastern lands. In Crete, as elsewhere in the Aegean, there could have been small amounts of tin at an early date, but it must have been chiefly imported from elsewhere, Anatolia or Syria, perhaps from as far afield as Bohemia, Etruria or southern Spain. Copper could have been imported from Cyprus and elsewhere, though it was available in parts of Crete.[38] Sources in the Asterousi mountains bordering the plain of Messara in the south could well have been tapped during the third millennium BC. It is perhaps significant that all the known Early Bronze Age settlements of the Messara are within ten kilometres of a source of copper, and in the adjacent tombs there is clear evidence of a developed metallurgy from the nature of the deposits – daggers, spearheads, chisels, awls, tweezers, scrapers, razors as well as pieces of jewellery.[39]

Pillaging of major sites throughout the centuries must have resulted in the loss of many masterpieces of metal work, but enough has survived to indicate that the Minoan craftsman in this sphere had developed a refinement matching other arts. In fact tools, weapons and vessels made of bronze reached a level of technical and aesthetic quality that does not suffer by comparison with later archaic and classical masterpieces. Once again a prolonged Minoan tradition lay behind achievements of many centuries later; and the tradition helps to account for the continuing remarkable excellence of bronze work which was done in Crete.[40]

Bronze was fashioned into a variety of products in the workshops of Minoan times. Tools and weapons from Ayia Triada, for instance, include a pickaxe, a crowbar, saws, axes, razors, small wheels and daggers. The largest of several massive cauldrons from Tylissos is more than a metre in diameter and weighs over fifty kilograms. Its bowl was made of four sheets, one for the bottom, three for the sides, and the rim of three sheets, with three handles. The parts of the cauldron were riveted together. All these cauldrons were in fact decorated with rivet heads. So were some jugs from Knossos, one of which, made out of two riveted pieces, had a top decorated with a braided pattern, while a projecting band covered the seam between the body and the neck.

Metalwork was apparently so admired that fine clay vases were manufactured which imitated a variety of metal shapes; even the riveting was sometimes imitated.[41] Large swords were produced by laminating and hammering; and a ceremonial sword from Mallia has a crystal pommel. Such swords do not seem to have been at all common before the twelfth century BC. However, the well-known inlaid daggers from the Mycenae shaft-graves which date from 400 years earlier were probably of Cretan manufacture. Their blades were of cast and hammered bronze, with an inlaid decoration of gold, silver and niello.

These pieces include a dagger-blade portraying a lion-hunt. The scene shows four men carrying spears and an archer who are attacking a pride of lions. One of the lions has dragged down one of the hunters. The technique used in the manufacture is interesting. For the silhouettes were cut out of the bronze and these were then filled with gold and silver leaf which was hammered in and then polished. A paler filling was used for the bodies of the warriors and the lion, a reddish gold, perhaps mixed with copper, for the lances. Another fine example of a Mycenaean dagger-blade has a portrayal of leopards hunting wild duck beside a papyrus swamp. The silver band which marks the water

11   Bronze vessels from one of the Zafer Papoura tombs at Knossos

on this blade was oxidized so as to make the fish and the ducks' wings of pure silver revealed more conspicuously against a darker background.

Increasing refinement of copper and bronze tools in everyday use had beneficial effects on other craft industries such as carpentry and leather-working. Saws and chisels, awls and punches have survived for our inspection, but, in the nature of things, wooden furniture and objects made of leather have not. Local supplies of timber were no doubt used in the building of houses, wagons and ships, as well as for the beams and columns of villas and palaces. All such tasks required skills to which the perfection of the tools can testify.[42]

Minoan craftsmen were highly skilled in the manufacture of stone vases, for funerary, ritual, palatial and domestic purposes. This manufacture developed rapidly from early in the Bronze Age and has evoked a detailed study worthy of its importance.[43] Some 3500 artefacts have survived from a long period, that is to say, from about 2600 to 1100 BC. Quite apart from the considerable artistic merit of some of these pieces, the stone vases form a valuable source of evidence for Minoan civilization in a number of ways. The stone vases with relief scenes especially add to our appreciation of the freshness of Minoan interest in the actions of human beings and animals, in marine life and in nature generally.

Already, within the period from about 2200 BC to the time of the destruction of the first palaces round about 1700 BC, the evidence shows that the export of stone vases was part of an initial widespread economic development as the island began to play a quite significant role in overseas trade. Between 1700 and 1400 BC the export of stone vases was extensive and mainly directed, as in earlier times, towards the Argolid, the Cyclades, and the southern Peloponnese; and some pieces found their way to more distant places such as Atchana, Byblos and Troy.

The local stone from which stone vases were made included breccia, calcite, chlorite or chlorite schist, dolomitic marble, gabbro, gypsum, various kinds of limestone, marble, serpentine and steatite.[44] Imported stone was also used and included Egyptian alabaster, and obsidian.[45] Study of the artefacts, including unfinished works, bore cores and so on, has enabled the history and processes of manufacture to be recovered.[46] The piece of stone was first roughly shaped with a chipping hammer or chisel and then the inside was drilled out, the actual cutting being done by abrasive powder fed into the hole. Finishing and polishing of the exterior was done, probably with a little oil, after incised or relief decoration, if required, had been applied. For the earliest vases, of chlorite and chlorite schist, made in EM II–III, a flat-edged chisel was used inside as well as outside. A tubular drill, probably a hollow reed, came into regular use in Early Minoan III/Middle Minoan I. It could be that by Middle Minoan III–Late Minoan I (or perhaps earlier) a form of metal drill or cutter was also brought into use, since many vases of this dating have diameters of about 10cm.; and it is not likely that reeds large enough existed to produce holes of this size. Such vases could have been rotated under a fixed drill, or were fixed to a rotating wheel or the vase was fixed and a large weighted drill was turned with the hand by means of a bar or crank. In any case it is clear that from MM III onwards a remarkable degree of highly skilled craftsmanship had been achieved.

One supreme masterpiece, recovered in recent years and now in the Iraklion Museum, is a rhyton of rock crystal which was found in the repository of the sanctuary at the Zakro Palace along with other ritual vessels, dated 1500–1450 BC.[47] This rhyton was carved in one piece and the interior undercutting of the shoulder was done diagonally with a pointed tool of emery. The separate turned ring of the neck was formed of crystal pieces joined by intermediate foils of astonishingly thin gilded faience. The crystal beads of the handle were threaded on to a bronze wire. This work has been aptly described as the greatest *tour de force* of the Minoan lapidaries, since it required such intricate small-scale work in the hardest material used for stone vessels.[48]

The famous bull's head rhyton, carved in black serpentine, which was used for pouring libations, was found in the so-called 'Little Palace', a large city house to the north-west of the great Palace at Knossos. It is one of the several such rhytons of Cretan manufacture of the period Middle Minoan III and Late Minoan I. Its golden wooden horns and the ears, left eye and part of the left cheek have been plausibly restored. The genuine right eye has a border of red jasper surrounding a crystal lens on the back of which the pupil and iris are painted in red and black. There is an inlay of white shell around the nostrils. The libation liquid was inserted into the rhyton through a hole at the top and was poured through the mouth on to the altar.[49] Another rhyton in the shape of the head of a lioness was fashioned in a creamy-white, translucent, marble-like limestone, with libation holes in the top of the head, the nose and the mouth. Perhaps of the same date as the bull's head-rhyton, it was found, together with other stone vases of the same period in a room of the west wing of the Knossos Palace which was apparently in use at the time of the final destruction in the fourteenth century BC.[50]

The Minoan stone vases with relief scenes[51] belong to the period of the later palaces and were mainly designed for ritual purposes. Most of them – 20 out of 28 – come from Knossos; and the distribution and the stylistic uniformity in the representation of human figures and objects suggest that the whole group was in fact produced at Knossos, a few being sent out to other centres. Four of them deserve special mention here for their general importance and interest. These are the Harvester Vase, the Boxer Vase and the Chieftain Cup, all three from Ayia Triada, and the Peak Sanctuary Rhyton from Zakro.

The Harvester Vase, an acknowledged masterpiece, of which only the top part has survived, was made of black steatite or serpentine. The scene in relief was interpreted by Sir John Forsdyke[52] as a procession at the time of ploughing and sowing, rather than a harvest celebration, as is sometimes (not without good reason) supposed. No less than 27 figures compose the festive throng which sweeps continuously all around the vase. The marchers carry what may be hoes with long shoots of willow attached. Bags presumably filled with seed corn are slung from their belts. A long-haired priest in the centre who wears a scaly ritual cloak or cuirass is leader of the procession, and a sistrum player accompanies the singing. A slight depth of field of a few millimetres enables a kind of perspective to be suggested, figures farthest away not being made smaller but sometimes shown in relief and merging into the background. The different positions of the sistrum player, of the man who has stooped or fallen and of one man who has turned around are vividly caught in their suspended motion and vary the basic uniformity of the other figures.

The Boxer Vase is a conical rhyton of serpentine, decorated with four bands of reliefs. One has a scene of bull-leaping; a man has been impaled on a bull's horns. In the two lowest bands long-haired men, wearing necklaces and short kilts, are boxing, armed with knuckle-dusters and those in the upper row have bronze helmets. A pillar at the back may be the base of a flag-pole and thus indicate the ritual nature of the sports, taking place before a shrine.[53]

The Chieftain Cup, also of serpentine, has a relief scene on one side which has been variously interpreted as a king before a god, or a subordinate officer before a young king or prince (or 'priest-king'?). The reverse, which is damaged, apparently showed three men behind objects which might be bulls' hides, presumably to be presented to the king or god.[54]

The Peak Sanctuary Rhyton from Zakro is of chlorite, brown in parts from the effects of destruction fire, with seven fragments of gold leaf still remaining. The relief scene shows a sanctuary built of isodomic masonry on several levels. In the centre is an elaborate doorway with linked relief spiral decoration. Over the doorway sit four heraldically placed *agrimis*. Horns of consecration crown the walls in several places. Below the spiral-decorated central part of the shrine is a small altar with incurving sides, which was a standard Cretan shape for small stone altars suitable for offerings of incense, vegetables or fruits. Tall poles with rectangular 'boxes' flank the doorway and their similarity to the bases on the Boxer Vase may help to explain the ritual nature of the scene these portrayed. The sanctuary has a rocky landscape for its setting, which occupies much of the lower part of the vase. There are flowers and plants among the rocks, which include crocuses. A wild goat leaps in full flight across the rocks.[55]

Minoan craftsmen excelled in the production of miniature works of art; and their miniature stone-carving especially has yielded numerous examples of fine seal-engravings of microscopic shapes on hard semi-precious or precious stones. Pictorial representation of this kind first developed in Crete to a high level during the period of the first palaces. The consequences were to be of the utmost importance, as elsewhere, in the early history of writing. For seals were originally owners' marks, required for identification purposes before there were proper written scripts or any kind of general widespread literacy. A piece of wet clay could be placed on articles fastened with string and stamped with the owner's seal. This concept of personal identification can be inferred from the practice of burying the dead with their seals in the vaulted tombs of the Messara. Some have heads of animals or whole animals; one portrays a dove, its young under its wing, another a man trampling a lion. It may be that the lions, scorpions and spiders commonly portrayed on early Cretan seals were intended to serve as magical deterrents.

Cylinder seals such as were common in Mesopotamia, Syrian and Levantine stamp seals, Egyptian scarabs, were all bead seals which could be worn on necklaces, just as lentoid seals of the later Bronze Age could be worn like wrist-watches. In Early Minoan times a Cretan standard shape was in the form of a stamp or button which appears to have derived from Syria. The cylinder seal was modified for local purposes; and a lentoid shape remained standard throughout Late Minoan times. Almond-shaped (amygdaloid) seals appear towards the end of Middle Minoan times. The signet ring, normally made of gold, silver or bronze, but also of stone, was common in Late Minoan times. Other kinds of seal were also made of metal but were mostly of stone.

At first softer materials such as soapstone or serpentine or imported ivory and similar substances like bone or animal teeth were used in the manufacture. Later, as the drill and the cutter's wheel came into use, harder stones like rock-crystal, jasper, amethyst, black haematite, cornelian and obsidian could be effectively worked upon. Serpentine remained the common material for ordinary seals. It is possible that magnifiers could have helped the craftsmen in their delicate and detailed work; and crystal lenses that could have been used as magnifiers have been found in a Middle Minoan tomb at Knossos.[56]

The shapes and designs reveal great variety. Subjects included naturalistic portrayals of human beings and animals, and also of cult practices. These precise, imaginative and sensitively rendered miniatures are an invaluable source of information about habits of dress, marine life, animals and insects, as well as for their documentation of certain aspects of the history and practices of Minoan religion.

Ivory-working probably had its origins in the Near Eastern countries, carving in the round having been practised from early times by the craftsmen of Phoenicia, Syria and Palestine. The craft had its own long traditions in Crete, where the ivory sculpturing of figurines already appears evident from Early Minoan times; and there are fine carvings of figured handles to ivory stamp seals. The ivory itself was probably imported from Syria or Egypt.

From the time of the later palace at Knossos we have considerable deposits of ivory figurines, one of a bull-leaper being especially remarkable for its superb rendering of active concentration of a beautifully proportioned figure.

Such statuettes were made in separate pieces which were fitted together by means of pins and dowels. The tiny holes in the head of the bull-leaper show where the hair was fitted; and another head from the same quarter had hair which was formed from bronze wire plated with gold.

Also from Knossos came an inlaid gaming board, measuring about a metre by over half a metre. Its framework of gold-plated ivory was presumably supported by a panel of wood; an outer border had daisies in relief with central bosses of rock crystal; inside the border, around the central and lower part of the board, there was a second band of plaster which had a coating of blue paste; in the top two corners there were argonaut reliefs on a blue background, once again with a central crystal boss; then came a group of four large medallions set in crystal bars backed with silver plates whose curving *cloisons* were made of ribbed ivory. The centre of this elaborate piece was formed of six ribbed bars of crystal backed by silver plates alternating with five of gold-plated ivory; and below the centre were ten smaller medallions. On either side of this grouping and between the two wings were further crystal bars which were separated by bands of ivory. The gaming board, the 'Royal Draught Board', was dated by Evans to the end of the Middle Minoan period. The four ivory objects found nearby, although in a rather earlier deposit, may have been draughtsmen for the board.[57]

Already in the Early Bronze Age Crete was producing pieces of gold jewellery that match the high standards of the palace periods. Some of the best of Minoan jewellery comes from exploration of the communal tombs at Mochlos and the tholos tombs of the plain of Messara, which date to the period of the first palaces. Techniques of the goldsmith included soldering and casting, filigree and granulation, perhaps due to Syrian or Egyptian influences. The bee (or wasp) pendant from Mallia, perhaps to be dated between 1700 and 1600 BC is a famous specimen of Minoan jewellery which superbly exemplifies the technique of granulation. The insects were soldered together at the heads and tips of their abdomens and their legs of gold wire hold what seems to be a honeycomb which, like the eyes and abdomens, were decorated with granulations. The sitting toad from Koumasa has its body spotted with granulations. Rings, necklaces, amulets and ear-rings, pendants and beads were also manufactured in quantity.[58]

12   Bee pendant from Mallia

The treasure of gold jewellery acquired by the British Museum in 1892 from sponge-fishers from Aigina, thought by Evans to have been from a Late Bronze Age Aigina tomb, could well have been Cretan of the seventeenth and sixteenth centuries BC; and it is thought possible that it could have been plundered from the tomb at Mallia where the gold bee pendant was found by French excavators in 1930.[59] The Aigina treasure includes earrings and pendants that could have been worn as pectorals on the chest, their backs being made of flat sheets of gold. One piece, either a pendant or the head of a large pin shows a male figure, perhaps a god, wearing a kilt with a tassel of beads. Others portray animals. These finds appear to indicate that gold was more plentiful than silver in Crete of the Bronze Age. Certainly it was put to good use by the goldsmiths who had acquired an enviable command of intricate techniques by the end of Middle Minoan times.

6

CRETAN WRITING IN THE BRONZE AGE

Sir Arthur Evans went to Crete with the intention of finding an early system of writing; and it was he who first gave serious attention to the Bronze Age scripts of Crete and of mainland Greece.[1] Quite soon after beginning his excavation at Knossos he found a hoard of clay documents and by the end of the first season more than a thousand inscribed tablets, either complete or fragmentary, had been brought to light. The various Minoan archives subsequently discovered in the course of archaeological investigation, of immense importance in themselves, are also highly relevant to the study of the larger problems of the origins and types of writing of the Ancient Near East in general. The bibliography of the subject is already immense and it is likely to expand continuously as fresh discoveries are made and as more refined analyses of existing evidence are published. All that can be attempted here is a summary account of the range of investigation. As background to this account it is as well to have in mind that, before alphabetic writing began to develop at the end of the Bronze Age,[2] there are various stages in the formation and evolution of pre-alphabetic forms of writing which are normally acknowledged. In pictographic writing, the written unit is a pictogram, a picture of the object which the unit signifies. In ideographic writing, which may be derived from pictograms in simplified, stylized or modified forms which are no longer simple pictures but have meaningful concepts, the unit is the ideogram, symbolic of the idea of an object without expressing its name. Phonographic writing is composed of phonograms as units, these units now denoting particular sounds or groups of sounds.

The growth of cities in Mesopotamia brought about the need for administrators to keep records, so that pictures drawn on lumps of clay represent the earliest examples of the beginning of writing round about 3000 BC. Perhaps the stamp seals pressed into clay as means of identification formed the first rudiments of written records. However that may be, it is quite possible that pictures drawn on wet clay may have derived from some earlier stage of pictographic writing in some other material such as palm leaves, of which of course no trace remains. Although the earliest writing discovered in this region cannot yet be read, it is assumed to be a form of the language which is called Sumerian.

Such writing apparently developed in response to the need of recording economic data such as receipts and issues of articles by temple authorities. It was subsequently extended to the recording of other economic data and also to information about religion. In addition to lists of animals and household possessions, the scribes were making catalogues of the names of deities by the second quarter of the third millennium BC. The Sumerian scribes rapidly simplified the forms of the original pictograms and, instead of writing down more or less realistic representations of objects, had turned pictures into ideograms. However, writing was not at all widely used for literary purposes until about a thousand years after it had been invented, when the Sumerian language was passing out. Now that its literature could no longer be orally transmitted, the texts had to be written down. This accounts for the sudden appearance of considerable quantities of Sumerian literary tablets soon after the beginning of the second millennium BC. By this time the Semitic language called Akkadian was being so readily written down in syllabic cuneiform that documents of various kinds, law-codes, literature, official and private letters have survived. The Babylonian cuneiform script is so called because its signs were composed of wedge-shaped strokes, and owed its form to the clay on which it was written, though it was also used for inscriptions on stone. The script became systematized as a syllabary, each syllable being represented by a separate phonetic sign.

Although writing makes its appearance in Egypt roughly at the same time as in Mesopotamia, and when Egypt was under strong Mesopotamian influence, nevertheless the use of a different writing material produced a different system; and the Egyptian script was never systematized like the Babylonian but continued as a combination of pictograms, ideograms and phonograms, even adopting a few alphabetical signs. Linear scripts, also apparently originating round about 3000 BC, are found on the periphery of the cuneiform areas, later tending to become regional survivals as cuneiform became more dominant. Commenting on the advance shown by cuneiform and hieroglyphic writing, Evans observed that we see here an artificial selection – in the primitive Babylonian system a very restricted one – from the almost limitless field of primitive picture-signs. We see, he continued, the results of organized convention and that great step is made towards the ultimate goal of alphabetic writing by which once solely ideographic signs can be used as phonograms without reference to their original sense, and one finally abbreviated into syllables or letters. Such an elaborate selection and systematization of primitive elements necessarily presupposes a highly centralized social and political organization.[3]

Evans had also noted resemblances between the signs of the earliest Cretan script, which he called Hieroglyphic or Pictographic, and the earliest Egyptian writing of the Predynastic and Protodynastic periods.[4] Though Egyptian influence is apparent and some of the signs may have been copied from Egyptian originals, direct imitation can be ruled out. A few of the signs are reminiscent of the earliest pre-cuneiform writing of Mesopotamia. Similarities between the Cretan scripts and those of Cyprus and the Hittite hieroglyphic script of Anatolia in much later times are probably most readily explained in terms of the possibility that earlier scripts had existed in that region from which they had all borrowed.[5]

In suggesting the probability that the hieroglyphic signs, originally derived from natural shapes, received a stereotyped form through a talismanic use at the end of the Early Minoan age, V.E.G. Kenna has pointed out that our regard for, or approach to, seals and script is in the reverse order to the estimation of ancient times. For in the Bronze Age, since seals were invented before script, they received due precedence, the other qualities with which they were believed to be invested also ensuring this position.[6] The germs of a hieroglyphic script with pictorial characters that can be classified as ideographic are found on

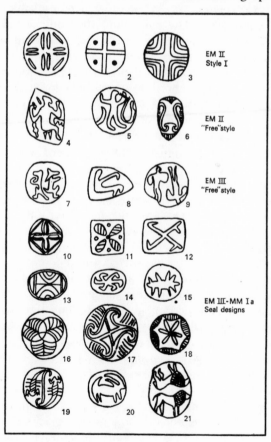

13   Early Minoan seal-stone designs

pre-Palatial seals at the end of the third millennium BC. However, since these pictorial signs represent objects connected with the occupation of the owner of the seal, it is not always certain that they were truly ideographic.[7] Seals were still being made with inscriptions in the Cretan hieroglyphic script at the end of the Middle Minoan period, and a few sealings impressed by such hiero-glyphic seals have been found in buildings destroyed in the disasters of *c.*1450 BC.[8] Simplified linear versions of the hieroglyphic system were in use for incising inscriptions on clay labels, tablets and bars and stone ritual bowls. Graffiti were painted or scratched on the walls of houses and palaces at Knossos and Ayia Triada.[9] Perhaps, as in Egypt, such a simplified script could have been used early on for writing in ink, on papyrus or on palm leaves. The only ink inscriptions available, however, are on two clay cups from Knossos of about 1600 BC; and the earliest clay tablets with a linear form of hieroglyphic script are from Phaistos, of perhaps *c.*1700 BC.

The subjects represented in the hieroglyphic script were classified by Evans, on the basis of 135 examples, under the following headings: the human body and its parts (11); arms, implements and instruments (24); cult objects and symbols (5); houses and enclosures (6); utensils, stores and treasure (10); ships and marine objects (4); animals and their parts (24); insects (2); plants and trees (20); sky and earth (8); uncertain objects and simple geometrical signs (21). He emphasized that the main characteristics of the script are essentially of glyptic origin. The earliest evidence of this form of script is found on the seals: it is on these that we see the once purely pictorial types transformed into the more conventional and abbreviated forms that answer to the 'hieroglyphic' stage.[10]

Evans was firmly of the opinion that, on the whole, the Minoan hieroglyphic system was essentially of home growth, forming an epitome of the early civilization of the island as it existed about the end of the third millennium before our era, with its indications of a mercantile and industrial as well as of a pastoral and agricultural community.[11] Arms and implements are passed in review and we see the tools, some of them (he thought) obviously of Egyptian origin, used by the masons, carpenters and decorators of the great Cretan palaces. One of the signs indicated that the eight-stringed lyre had already reached the same stage of development as that of the Classical Age of Greece, over a thousand years before the days of Terpander. The recurrence of the ship sign suggested commercial activity. The ingot, he said, illustrated the medium of currency otherwise recorded by the clay tablets of the linear class and by the actual deposit of bronze ingots in the palace of Ayia Triada. Varieties of vases and other domestic utensils were numerous. The spider and the bee appeared to represent spinning and bee-keeping. Domesticated animals included the ox, goat, swine, horned sheep and dog. Species of wild animals were illustrated by the lion's mask and wolf's head and one can see in another sign the cat already acclimatized in the European area. Agriculture was well to the fore, for the plough was of constant recurrence and there were evidently a great number of plants and trees under cultivation. We have the grain of a cereal in flower in one sign, another probably shows an ear of barley, another apparently a gourd, others the olive branch and the fig. Yet another seemed to indicate that an important branch of cultivation had been of the saffron crocus which supplied the brilliant dyes for the Minoan ladies' robes.

Although the hieratic element was not by any means so prominent as in the Egyptian hieroglyphic series, such signs as the double axe and the altar horns, as well as the bucranium, had an obvious reference to the cult of the great Minoan divinities. Having thus concluded this general survey and the broad inferences to be derived, Evans went on to consider the characteristics of the hieroglyphic script by posing what he thought the most important question regarding these conventionalized pictographic signs: namely, how far we have to do with simple ideograms or 'word signs', and how far the system had reached the phonographic stage in which the signs have the value of syllables or even of single letters.

This important question remains on the agenda of Minoan writing problems. Indeed the question was, if anything, made more complicated by the discovery of the famous Phaistos Disk in 1908. It was found by Pernier in a room apparently destroyed towards the end of the Middle Minoan III period. The Disk is about 16cm. in diameter and is completely covered on both sides with an inscription in picture-like signs, each of which seems to have been separately impressed on the clay while still soft by some kind of stamp. This intriguing document not only indicated that various local scripts or scripts designed for special purposes might have been in contemporary usage. It always serves as a first example of printing insofar as printing is based on the practice of impressing movable signs on to a suitable surface. The signs are arranged on the Disk in groups between curving lines and divided from each other by perpendicular lines.

The signs of the Disk differ from the normal signs of the hieroglyphic script. Many of them represent human figures, parts of the body, weapons, tools, utensils, animals and plants, buildings and ships. Since, at the time of its discovery, these signs had no known parallel, it was generally believed to have been of foreign origin. However other spiral inscriptions of a religious or magical kind are now known to be undoubtedly Cretan. Similar signs were incised on a stone offering table from Mallia and on a bronze double axe from a sacred cave at Arkalokhori.[12]

Evans devoted a preliminary chapter of his *Scripta Minoa* to a survey of the antiquity and European diffusion of the Pictographs and Linear signs. He likened to the early figures on rock carvings in various areas the linear signs that make their appearance on primitive pottery.[13] The best collection of such signs on primitive European pottery, except for the Aegean area, had been found at Broos in Transylvania – on the borders of the great Thracian province whose primitive culture showed so many points of affinity with that of Western Asia Minor. Signs on the whorls and vessels from this site displayed a remarkable parallelism with those found by Schliemann on similar materials at Hissarlik. So far as they might be regarded as signs, it seemed safest to interpret these rude linear figures on the Neolithic and Early Metal Age pottery of Hissarlik and Broos as simple ideographs rather than as syllables or letters.[14]

During excavations in 1961 at the prehistoric settlement of Tartaria in the valley of the Maros (Múres) in Rumania, three prehistoric clay tablets were discovered by the excavator Dr N. Vlassa of the Historical Museum at Cluj and were subsequently published. Their discovery and publication led to a highly interesting and informative discussion of the similarities between them and early writing in Mesopotamia and Crete by Sinclair Hood in 1967.[15] Certain of his remarks and conclusions which are particularly relevant to the wider implications of the study of the Cretan writing systems may be conveniently mentioned at this stage. As a preliminary, we should bear in mind that what Evans and others referred to as Broos lies to the east of Tordos, which now replaces Broos as a key place-name in the literature.[16] Tartaria lies some 20km. east of Tordos. In 1927 the late Gordon Childe drew attention to the similarities between signs found on pottery from the prehistoric tells or settlement mounds of Vinča in Jugoslavia and Tordos in Rumania and signs in Predynastic Egypt and at Troy.[17]

The settlement at Vinča was on the south bank of the Danube near Belgrade, Tordos beside the river Maros (Múres) which flows into the river Tisza (Theiss), a northern tributary of the Danube. Tordos was thus situated in the gold-bearing parts of Transylvania, to which the valleys of the Tisza and the Maros provide the easiest route of access from the Danube region round Vinča, from which Tordos is some 200km. distant in a direct line. Settlers at Vinča and Tordos shared a common culture and they spread from an apparently original area of settlement in the Morava valley and on the Danube round Vinča north and east into Transylvania. Excavations of a kind were begun at Tordos in 1874, Vinča was first excavated in 1908. Many fragments of pottery with incised signs were found at Tordos and similar signs were later observed on pottery from Vinča and neighbouring sites. Similarities between the Tordos and Trojan signs were noted; and comparable marks were found on vases of the late Predynastic and Protodynastic periods in Egypt, and from 1896 onwards on pottery at Phylakopi, capital of the obsidian-exporting island of Melos. The signs on the pottery from Tordos, like those at Troy and elsewhere, can be interpreted as potters' or owners' marks; but their variety and their similarity to the signs associated with writing in Crete and Egypt, together with their occasional appearance in groups like the comparable Trojan signs, made it reasonable to suppose that they might reflect the existence of some primitive system of writing. Hence the interest shown by Evans in the

Tordos signs in his *Scripta Minoa*. Thereafter in this country there was a waning of interest in these signs, though Childe had still remembered their relevance to writing in 1929.[18] There was more excavating at Tordos in 1910 which resulted in the discovery of many fragments of vases with signs on them, duly reported in the eventual publication of these excavations in 1941.

Excavations were started at Tartaria in 1942–3 and resumed by Dr Vlassa in 1961. The three clay tablets were found at the bottom of a small pit along with 26 burnt clay idols; and they may have survived because they were baked by the fire into which they had been put together with the idols. Signs on the tablets were considered comparable with those of the script of the Late Predynastic (Uruk III–Jemdet Nasr) period in Mesopotamia, though it seems unlikely that they were drafted by a Sumerian hand or in the Sumerian language of early Mesopotamia; but the signs are so comparable with the early tablets from Uruk and Jemdet Nasr as to make it virtually certain that they are somehow connected. Several of the signs apparently derive from Mesopotamian signs for numerals.

The closest parallels for the Tartaria signs are Mesopotamian, but some of the signs of the Cretan scripts, especially those of the earliest, called by Evans the Hieroglyphic or Pictographic, can also be compared. Indeed the Cretan parallels for the signs would appear to be closer than the Mesopotamian in one or two cases. There is also a remarkable similarity in shape between the Tartaria tablets and some of the earliest clay tablets yet recovered in Crete, especially those from the so-called Hieroglyphic Deposit in the Knossos Palace.[19] Two of the Tartaria tablets have string-holes of a kind foreign to the early tablets of Mesopotamia but which are a regular feature of the tablets from the Hieroglyphic Deposit and which occur on other early tablets from Crete. Most of the tablets from the Hieroglyphic Deposit were long bars, square or almost square in section. A few were rectangular and similar in shape and section to two from Tartaria. Tablets of similar shape were found in a rather earlier deposit at Phaistos and others at Mallia. The roundel tablet from Tartaria resembles those from Mallia and from the Hieroglyphic Deposit at Knossos, except that the top edge of the Cretan roundels is scalloped on each side of the string-hole; and one or two of the roundels and tablets from the Hieroglyphic Deposit show the same system of dividing the sign groups into compartments as on the Tartaria and Mesopotamian tablets. These could be late examples of a practice once standard in Crete. The Cretan tablets on the conventional dating must be a thousand years or more later than those of Uruk III and Jemdet Nasr in Mesopotamia, and they are almost certainly a good deal later than the Tartaria tablets.

In the course of more detailed examination of problems of comparison and dating, Hood observes that not only the technique of writing on clay tablets, but many of the signs of the Cretan scripts may derive from the early pre-cuneiform script of Mesopotamia. Syria is likely to have been the intermediary for their transmission to Crete. Some of the earliest Cretan seals are remarkably similar to the stamp seals which have been found in Syria from a very remote period, perhaps even sixth millennium BC.[20] The ivory of which many of the earliest Cretan seals are made again points to Syria, where elephants lived and provided ivory until they became extinct in Assyrian times. If seals and seal usage reached Crete from Syria, it is very possible that writing did also; though no clay tablets of a date before *c.*2000 BC have yet been found in Syria. Yet the idea of writing on clay tablets might have been introduced to Crete from Syria along with new styles in pottery at the beginning of Early Minoan II, *c.*2600 BC or earlier; but the oldest clay tablets of Crete are assignable at the earliest to Middle Minoan IIA or IB and can hardly be dated before 2000 BC and may be as late as *c.*1750 BC. The Knossos Hieroglyphic Deposit, containing tablets comparable in some respects with the Tartaria tablets, appears to belong to Middle Minoan IIB, *c.*1700 BC; and the similar tablets from Mallia may be even later.

In conclusion of his survey Hood makes the following points which seem valid in the light of the evidence adduced. The discovery of comparable signs on pottery at Tordos in Rumania, at Troy, on Melos and in Egypt had already at the beginning of this century produced a widespread belief that a single system of writing had developed at an early period throughout this area. It now begins to look as if this belief, apparently fantastic, might not be entirely unfounded. The most likely centre from which either ideas about writing or the signs used for writing may have spread is likely to have been Mesopotamia or some adjacent region rather than Egypt. Signs similar to those of Melos, Tordos and Troy have now been supplemented from the Greek mainland, in the Peloponnese and as far north as Thessaly. Most of the Peloponnesian signs date from the Early Bronze Age or later and could reflect an acquaintance with, if not the use of writing. Signs on the underneath of the bases of two pots from a horizon of the local Neolithic at Tsangli in Thessaly are reminiscent of Tordos; and from the same level came a rectangular four-footed dish comparable with the 'altars' of the Tordos-Vinča and earlier Starcevo cultures. Burial pithoi with stamps, or in some cases with incised designs composed of sign-like pictures, come from a cemetery assignable to the period of Troy I and early Troy II at Karataş-Semayük in Lycia. Some of the signs are like the signs on Trojan pots and whorls; and beehive-like huts on stilts have been compared with a sign on the Phaistos Disk.[21] The Lycian pithoi call to mind the stamped pithoi used for burials at Byblos (in Eneolithic B). The 'libation-formula' on some early Cretan Hieroglyphic seals may have some funerary connexion. It could be that in Western Anatolia and in Rumania, if not in Crete, the first spread of writing or of signs derived from writing may have been in a strictly religious or magical context.

It could also be that the signs on the Tartaria tablets do not represent true writing. If that should prove to be the case, the signs must then have been copied for magical purposes, without understanding of their meaning, from the actual written documents of a civilized people somewhere in the Levant. Similarities between the Tartaria tablets and the earliest known clay tablets of Crete suggest that the source of these documents could have been in Cilicia or Syria, whence it is likely that the art of writing reached Crete.[22] Even if the Tartaria tablets should not be examples of true writing, they do argue the existence of remarkably close connexions between Rumania and the East in early times, which must have been through Troy, perhaps established by sea around the south coast of Anatolia with Cilicia and Syria rather than overland. Evidence exists for close connexions between Early Bronze Cilicia and Troy II, which had the use of the fast potter's wheel from the East before it was adopted on the central Anatolian plateau. One reason for the establishment of these connexions was no doubt the Oriental demand for metals – and above all for the gold of Transylvania in the heart of which lies Tartaria.[23]

There are plausible reasons for the continued use of hieroglyphic script in the early part of the New Palace period even though a linear syllabic script, known in its early form as protolinear, had already been introduced alongside it at the close of the Old Palace period. The new script could have developed as a stylized, simplified version of the older hieroglyphic signs, being adapted to include abbreviations, combinations of syllabic signs, and more determinative elements. Ideographs would have continued in use to render concrete meanings in pictorial terms, these being of enormous help to the first students of the Minoan script in their efforts to guess the subjects of the texts. Some of these texts, like those incised on some of the Knossian frescoes, on some jars, and on ritual stone utensils of the kind found at Apodoulou in the Rethimno district are closer to protolinear, meaning that Linear Script A must have developed directly out of the protolinear script. Unlike Linear Script B, used in Crete only at Knossos, Linear A was in use over a wider area, although examples of it outside Crete are comparatively rare. In Cyprus, the early Cypro-Minoan script seems to have developed out of Linear A, but then followed a completely independent course. Many local variants of Script A can be distinguished, but in general they all bear great resemblance to one another. Among the best-known are the 'magic' texts, written spirally on the insides of the two conical cups found in the house of the monolithic pillars near the Knossos Palace. These texts were written in cuttlefish ink, which shows that writing in ink on a suitable material was quite usual. There can be no doubt about the religious nature of the texts carved on the vessels used in sacred rituals, tables of offering, stone ladles, ritual cups and so on.[24]

About 1500 BC a system of writing which differs from that of the Minoans appeared in Cyprus, and is called the Cypriot syllabic script. Its signs are linear, combinations of straight and curved lines, incised on clay tablets, and either incised or painted on vessels. Towards the end of the second millennium BC, the signs were also engraved on bronze surfaces. The first definite example of

Cypriot writing is on part of a rectangular clay tablet of about 1500 BC found at Enkomi in 1955, the writing being incised on one face of the tablet in three rows separated by lines. The signs, fairly large and complex, are in many respects similar to the signs of Cretan Linear A. There are examples of writing from the period between 1400–1150 BC on vessels and tablets. A famous clay cylinder from Enkomi, of thirteenth or twelfth century BC dating, has its whole surface covered by writing on 27 rows with divisions between the words. An example of an Aegean script of a Cypro-Minoan character has been found at Ugarit, with signs similar to those on the Enkomi tablets. This discovery of Cypro-Minoan writing on the Syrian coast is not surprising since a community of Cypriot merchants was probably established in the commercial centre of Ugarit.

From the last phase of the Late Bronze Age (1150–1050 BC) there is a great variety of objects with writing inscribed on them, including bronze bowls, tools, farming equipment, votive rods, Eastern-type cylinder seals, loom weights, and inscribed tablets from Enkomi, supplemented by inscriptions on clay vessels. Although knowledge of the script of this period is sketchy, the great number and variety of inscribed objects and the spread of the script to many parts of the island show that it was in general use towards the end of the Bronze Age. Successful decipherment of the Cypriot syllabic script of the Classical period during the latter half of the nineteenth century encouraged philologists to formulate theories about the earlier script. The Cypriot syllabic script which appeared around the end of the eighth century BC, to be replaced in part by the Greek alphabetic script in the fourth century BC was the last form of the Minoan linear system of writing. Sayce (in 1905) showed that there was a second script in Cyprus similar to the Classical script but earlier and it was this second script which had evidently been in use during the Bronze Age. About the origin and evolution of this script two theories have been proposed.

According to the first theory, the Minoan Linear A script was the forerunner of the Cypriot Bronze Age script. The Cypro-Minoan, or Cypro-Mycenaean script, as Evans called it, was then succeeded by the Cypriot syllabic script of the Classical period. According to the second theory, the script was introduced into Cyprus from mainland Greece during the period of Achaean colonization after 1200 BC. The archaeological evidence, however, for example the sixteenth century tablet from Enkomi with its writing similar to that of Cretan Linear A, proves that the Cypriot script must be earlier than the Mycenaean colonization. Since there is no archaeological evidence for direct links between Cyprus and Crete at the time, the possibility has been suggested that the Cypriots must have learnt the script from Minoan merchants who had settled in the commercial centres on the Syro-Palestinian coast.[25]

The term 'Linear Class A' was applied by Evans to distinguish earlier Cretan scripts from the 'Linear Class B' script used at Knossos when the Palace was finally destroyed in the fourteenth century BC; and fragments of more than

3000 clay tablets inscribed in Linear B have been recovered from the ruins of the Palace and other buildings destroyed at the same time, which is a total about ten times greater than the total of Linear A inscriptions so far discovered. Heavy winter rains in Crete render unlikely the possibility of survival of clay tablets unless they were deposited in some building destroyed by fire which had baked the clay. Clay tablets with linear inscriptions have thus been recovered from houses and palaces burnt down at the time of the disasters round about 1450 BC, mostly from Ayia Triada and from Zakro. Despite local differences the scripts are apparently closely related and are classed as Linear A together with the linear scripts which were current in the Middle Minoan III period.

In 1939 tablets with writing in the Linear B script were recovered on the mainland of Greece near Messenian Pylos. Since 1945 more were found at Mycenae, Tiryns and Thebes. So far as Crete is concerned the only Linear B tablets so far assignable to a period after the disasters of round about 1450 BC are those from Knossos. Vases with signs or short inscriptions painted or scratched on them from Khania and elsewhere in the west and centre of the island suggest that the practice of writing was not then restricted to Knossos; and vases with similar painted signs are known from several mainland sites. Many of the Linear B signs differ from those of the Linear A scripts, the signs for numerals being dissimilar and the system used for fractions changed from one corresponding with the Egyptian system to one apparently based on the Mesopotamian.[26]

Linear B texts were normally written on small clay tablets. Scribes evidently ruled a series of parallel lines on the moist surface of the clay and subsequently inserted the signs from left to right between the ruled lines and from top to bottom of the tablets. Short groups of signs, forming words, were divided from each other by short, vertical strokes. The tablets mainly, if not all, are lists of persons, animals and a variety of commodities. The writing is composed of words, singly or in short sequences, sometimes in longer sequences, and also of ideograms which apparently represent commodities, quantities, values and numerals. The signs are virtually the same in number and in form and the same words recur. Therefore, it seems, a single language was current in all localities. However, the tablets which Evans found at Knossos he ascribed to the Late Minoan II period terminating at roughly 1400 BC, while the mainland tablets in the main belong to the time of the destruction of Pylos and Mycenae at roughly 1200 BC. Since the writing is virtually the same, despite the interval of about two centuries between the Knossos and mainland examples, it has been suggested that a redating is necessary for the final phases of the Knossos Palace.[27]

There have been suggested decipherments of the various prehistoric Aegean scripts as forms of Greek for nigh on a century. That which is now best known and widely accepted is the decipherment of the late Michael Ventris in association with Dr. John Chadwick. An account of this decipherment was first published in the *Journal of Hellenic Studies* in 1953. The language of the Linear B tablets was understood as an early kind of Greek, pre-Dorian, and allied to the Classical Arcadian and Cypriot scripts. As already mentioned, the relevant Cypriot inscriptions are written in a special syllabary; the Linear B script is likewise mainly a syllabary. By studying the way in which the syllabic signs are used and in part inferring the meaning of the documents from signs which are ideographic and not syllabic, the possibility of discovering the phonetic value of the syllabic signs was maintained. This decipherment of Linear B as a form of Greek has not been universally accepted and there is still division of opinion in the scholarly world.[28]

Under the stimulus of the Ventris–Chadwick decipherment and subsequent sustained discussion and elaboration, renewed attempts have been made to decipher the Linear A script; and these include decipherments of this script as akin to Hittite by Davis and as a form of North-west Semitic by Gordon.[29]

The decipherment of the Linear B script as a form of early Greek announced in 1953 has not only served as a stimulus to further linguistic and archaeological researches. It has led to the publication of a vast amount of material, in learned journals and in books, much of which is naturally formulated in highly technical terms. For the serious student of the tablets, whether as documents in their own right or in their relation to other (and sometimes conflicting) classes of evidence, the fundamental and indispensable guide is *Documents in Mycenaean Greek* (Ventris and Chadwick, 1956; 2nd edition, by Chadwick, 1973). More recently, Dr Chadwick has presented us in *The Mycenaean World* (1976) with his picture of Mycenaean Greece reconstructed from the documentary evidence and complementary to the archaeological sources. As an illustration of the varied interpretations that can be wrested from the complex evidence, the arguments of this recent book may profitably be compared with those developed, from a historical viewpoint, in J.T. Hooker's *Mycenaean Greece* (1977).

The final chapter of *The Mycenaean World* deals with the vexed and controversial theme of the end of that world. In his concluding remarks to this chapter, Dr Chadwick makes certain observations which are relevant to some of the major themes I have discussed in this book. It used to be, as he says, fashionable to cast the Dorians for the role of villains in the Mycenaean tragedy. The Dorians were in later times the dominant people of the southern and western mainland of Greece, and they retained a traditional hostility to the Ionians, the dominant people of the central Aegean, which culminated in the twenty-seven years of war in the fifth century. He continues: 'Since they undoubtedly profited by the Mycenaean collapse, it was natural to blame them for it. But the major difficulty has always been the absence of any archaeological evidence of the series of Dorian invasions necessary to account for the change of dialect. One by one the material innovations ascribed to the Dorians have been shown to be unconnected: there is no common element which distinguishes the linguistically Dorian areas and only these.

'It is traditionally believed that the Dorians moved south to occupy their classical homes, and there is no doubt that there were major shifts in population at this period. But where were all the Dorians during the Mycenaean period? And why were they content to wait in the wings until the time was ripe for their intervention? The period from the eleventh to the eighth century is deservedly called the Dark Age of Greece, for we have very little information about it except from the miserable contents of simple tombs.'

In a later chapter (Chapter 11) I shall focus attention on examples of the kind of linguistic evidence which I think may well be increasingly important for those who seek to cast light upon the Greek Dark Age and to find firm links of survival and continuity – albeit in changed forms – enduring from prehistoric times.

For rather different reasons I have, in the summary sketch of this chapter, laid considerable emphasis upon those earlier phases in the development of writing which tend to receive more cursory attention. For Crete, as Evans recognized, was an important centre in these early phases; and, as the Tartaria and more recent discoveries demonstrate, this particular Cretan material is likely to attract further investigation within the wider context of the history of one of mankind's more remarkable achievements.

7

MYTHS AND LEGENDS

On the most conservative estimate, the Greek language has the longest and most complete historical record of all the European languages. Which means not only that it has been a spoken language for at least 3000 years but also carries within its surviving records an unparalleled store of human experience in terms of precise statement of facts and events of various kinds and also in terms of history, philosophy or creative literature. Greek historians, philosophers, dramatists and poets have made an abiding impact on the consciousness of European mankind. The original sources of this impact, their perpetuation and modification in the vernacular literatures of Europe can be understood and appreciated in broad terms without either thorough knowledge of or even some familiarity with the language, ancient or modern.

Nothing better illustrates this point than the way in which the steady attempt to turn myth and legend into reality has succeeded in our own times to the point where Bronze Age Crete is now Minoan Crete. Equally remarkable, if not more so, is the way in which the culminating period of the Helladic Bronze Age has become known as the Mycenaean Age after Schliemann had uncovered its primary centre. Schliemann was a devoted believer in the authenticity of legend, but even he might be surprised at the extent to which Minoan civilization and the Minoans, Mycenaean civilization and the Mycenaeans, have been conjured into massive existence with the progress of archaeology out of a legendary king and a place-name.

The transformation wrought in the terminology of Aegean pre-history in the course of the last hundred years seems to require a brief account in this chapter of an important stratum of Cretan myth and legend in ancient sources as a preliminary to the account of Minoan cults in the following chapter. It is normally difficult and often impossible to separate mythology from cult, which together form the flesh and bone of ancient Greek religion. Myth and legend often tend to be as closely associated in terms of traditional lore. Traditional lore is part of the stuff of history and can indeed, as in the present context, help to formulate its terminology and its concepts. It may then be profitable to dissociate myth and legend from religion temporarily so far as possible in order to appreciate what was once the force of their combination as traditional lore.

Cretan Knossos, unlike mainland Mycenae, continued to be a city of considerable importance long after the Bronze Age in historical Greek and Roman times. Strabo,[1] for example, considered that the greatest and most famous of the Cretan cities were Knossos, Gortyn and Kydonia. Minos had gained the mastery of the sea, divided the island into three parts and founded a city in each part, Knossos and Kydonia lying to the north. Knossos and Gortyn had to cooperate in order to ensure the subjection of the remainder, so much so that there was strife throughout the island whenever they quarrelled. Naturally the city of Minos, of the Minotaur and the Labyrinth was consolidated as a centre of myth and legend.

The authority of the Homeric poems aided this process of consolidation throughout the Greek world. The Cretan contribution to the Greek expedition against Troy as recorded in the Catalogue of Ships in the second book of the *Iliad* is impressively large.[2] A famous spearman called Idomeneus, we are told, led the Cretans who came from those fair cities of Knossos, Gortyn, Lyktos, Miletos, Lykastos, Phaistos and Rhytion, and others who lived elsewhere in Crete, island of a hundred cities. Idomeneus and Meriones were in command of these troops and their 80 ships. This fleet of 80 ships may be compared with the 100 ships under the command of Agamemnon himself, the 90 under Nestor, the 60 under Menelaos and the modest 12 under Odysseus and 12 also under Aias.[3] The seven cities of Crete specifically named were all in the centre of the island, presumably the principal area of occupation by Achaean Greeks from the mainland – if such an occupation had taken place in the later Bronze Age.[4]

Elsewhere in the *Iliad*,[5] Idomeneus triumphantly boasts of a divine descent which is Minoan and Olympian combined. Zeus had made his son Minos the guardian or watcher (*epiouros*) over Crete. Minos had been the father of Deukalion. Idomeneus himself was the son of Deukalion and so became the lord (*wanax*) over many people in that spacious land. Zeus explains to Hera that the illustrious daughter of Phoinix bore to him Minos and also godlike Rhadamanthys.[6]

The illustrious daughter of Phoinix was Europa, conspicuous in Cretan legend as in cult. Her cult aspects will be considered later.[7] For the present we may recall that, according to another familiar mythological pedigree, Belos and Agenor were the sons of Poseidon and Libya. While Belos became king of Egypt, Agenor settled in Phoenicia and his children were Europa, Phoinix, Kilix and Kadmos. Zeus, disguised as a bull, carried off Europa to Crete, where she became the mother of Minos. Kilix and Kadmos searched for their sister, a search which took Kadmos to Delphi by way of Rhodes and Thasos. The oracle at Delphi told him to abandon the search and follow a cow to the place where it sat down. The place became the site of Thebes.[8]

Herodotus, at the beginning of his history, reaches back into the legendary past to find causes for an abiding hostility, and explains that, according to Persian sources, the Phoenicians committed the first trespass by carrying off Io to Egypt from Argos. Later on, certain Greeks, probably Cretans, landed at Tyre on the Phoenician coast and retaliated by carrying off the king's daughter Europa.[9] It was possible, though the derivation of the name is really unknown, that Europe was so called after the Tyrian Europa, having been nameless before her time. It was certain, however, that Europa was an Asiatic who never even set foot upon what the Greeks now called Europe, only sailing from Phoenicia to Crete and from Crete to Lycia.[10] This legendary link between Asia Minor and Crete was perpetuated in the coinage of the two Phoenician cities of Tyre and Sidon and the Cretan cities of Gortyn and Phaistos.

Sidon was the ancient metropolis of Phoenicia and it issued the most important coinage of its region down to the time of Alexander, from about the end of the fifth century BC. Between 202–111 BC there was a small autonomous bronze coinage which included Europa on a bull among its types. A similar type was issued during the autonomous era of Sidon from 111 BC to Imperial times and from the time of Augustus to Severus Alexander. The Phoenician standard coins of Tyre, as late as c.126–5 BC to AD 195–6 include types showing Zeus as a bull approaching Europa.[11] The earliest coins of Gortyn and Phaistos, of the fifth century BC, portray an archaic Europa, riding on a bull;[12] and the type persists in Gortynian coinage throughout the fifth century. The pictorial nature of these coins has suggested a derivation from local frescoes, even more pronounced in types of the following century from Gortyn and from Phaistos, where one type has Europa sitting on a rock and welcoming with raised hand the approaching bull. A contemporary Gortyn series illustrates the sacred marriage of Zeus and Europa.[13] As Seltman explained, Europa at first sits pensively in her willow tree; the bull, on the reverse, is licking his flank. Then Zeus has changed into an eagle on a branch beside her and she lifts her veil with the gesture of a bride; and on the reverse, since the god is now an eagle, the bull is once more mortal, startled by a teasing gad-fly. Next there is the embrace, with Europa and the eagle grouped like a Leda and swan, while the bull is maddened by the gad-fly. This is surely, argued Seltman, the story told by some painter and translated to a series of coins, a weird myth full of lost or faintly discerned links with the beliefs of Minoan Crete, its sacred trees and birds and bulls, and its all-powerful goddess, sunk now to the rank of a nymph though bearing the name of a continent.[14]

The disguised Odysseus, returned to Ithaca, claims to be a native of Crete, described as the place of Minos's folk.[15] More specifically of Knossos Homer says that Daidalos had there once designed a dancing-floor for Ariadne of the lovely hair.[16] Perhaps here we have a reference to the Knossian Labyrinth, recognized in antiquity as an imitation of the Egyptian Labyrinth (generally believed to be sacred to the sun).[17] The actual Labyrinth, it has been suggested, may have been the so-called Theatral Area at the north-west corner of the Knossos Palace, an *orchestra* or arena fashioned for the performance of a mimetic dance.[18] Pasiphae, the wife of Minos, was supposed to have entertained a passion for a bull, sent in answer to the prayers of Minos and which he had promised to sacrifice. Instead he put it among his herds and sacrificed another. His wife's irrational obsession was his punishment. Daidalos made for Pasiphae a wooden cow on wheels, hollowed it out, sewed it up in the hide of a cow which he had skinned, and put it in the meadow where the bull grazed. He then put Pasiphae inside this effigy and the bull coupled with it. Pasiphae in due course gave birth to Asterios ('Starry One') who was called the Minotaur (or 'Minos bull'). Though he had a bull's face, he was otherwise human. Obeying oracles, Minos shut him up under guard in the Labyrinth – which was also made by Daidalos – a building which led astray by its intricate windings those who sought to escape from it.[19]

The scholiast on the *Iliad* passage explains that Theseus, after escaping from the Labyrinth with the aid of Ariadne's clue, together with the youths and maidens he rescued, instructed by Daidalos, wove a circling dance for the gods which resembled his own entrance into and exit from the Labyrinth.[20] A similar kind of dance was known in Delos and Plutarch associates this dance with the same traditions. When Theseus had sailed away from Crete, he put in at Delos, sacrificed to the god, dedicated the image of Aphrodite that he had received from Ariadne, and danced a dance with the young men which evidently still survived among the Delians. It imitated the circuits and exits of the Labyrinth by a certain measure which involved turnings and returnings. The dance was called the Crane Dance and it was danced by Theseus round the Horned Altar; and it was also said that Theseus instituted a contest in Delos and was the first to award a palm to the victors.[21]

The story about the journey of Theseus to kill the Cretan Minotaur was familiar at Athens. The purpose was to free the Athenians from an obligation to send to Minos a sacrificial tribute of seven boys and seven girls every eight years. The probable date of the Crane Dance at Delos which was associated with the myth of Theseus and the Minotaur was the 7th of the month Thargelion, during a festival which celebrated the birth of Apollo and Artemis. The date would certainly coincide with the number of sacrificial victims, seven for Apollo and seven for Artemis. On the day before, the Athenians celebrated their deliverance from the old Minoan tribute by a pilgrimage to Delos, as the festival known as the Thargelia began. Tradition said that a custom of putting to death two human victims, one on behalf of the men, one on behalf of the women, had been established in this festival as an expiation for the death of Androgeos, a son of Minos.[22]

Odysseus, on his visit to the underworld of Hades had seen a traditional beneficent Minos, whom Homer calls here a 'splendid son of Zeus, seated, holding a golden sceptre, ordaining righteousness among the dead, who were sitting or standing around the lord (*wanax*), questioning him about their rights, within the wide gates of the House of Hades'.[23] Earlier, however, in the same book, Homer tells us that, among the heroines seen by Odysseus in Hades were 'Phaidra, Prokris and fair Ariadne, the daughter of ill-designing (*oloophron*) Minos, whom Theseus once upon a time tried to carry off from Crete to the fruitful land of sacred Athens, though he had no joy of her. For, before that could happen, Artemis killed her in sea-girt Dia, on the testimony of Dionysos'.[24] Thus Homer sharply presents us with a double aspect of Minos by now all too familiar as the result of repeated discussion and comment.

In historical antiquity memory of the great Cretan Bronze Age past was concentrated in this diverse tradition of Minos. With good reason therefore, and with general approval, Sir Arthur Evans named this civilization 'Minoan'.[25] On the one side, as he explained, we gain a vision of a beneficent ruler, patron of the arts, founder of palaces, establisher of civilized dominion. On the other was depicted a tyrant and destroyer. Athenian chauvinism, he considered, was to blame for exaggerating the tyrannical aspect of the early sea-dominion. Archaeology had demonstrated that the palace envisaged as an ogre's den had been in reality the peaceful abode of 'priest-kings', even though Minos 'the destroyer' may have existed from the standpoint of subject peoples. The application of the term by the Greeks to traditional settlements from prehistoric Crete showed that they were accustomed to conceive of the word 'Minoan' in an ethnic or dynastic as well as a personal sense. This dynastic use of the term could be compared with the Egyptian use of Pharaoh. (Aristotle made a similar point when he explained that the 'caste'-system still in existence in Egypt and Crete in his own day was first established in Egypt by the legislation of Sesostris and in Crete by that of Minos).[26]

As the bearer of a divine title, in Evans's view the Cretan Minos could be compared with the divine 'priest-kings' of the religious centres of Anatolia, who represented a god, wore his dress, wielded his authority and often bore his name. The almost universal divine nature of primitive kingship was well exemplified in the case of Egypt. In Egypt, however, the temple overshadowed the palace; whereas, in the Anatolian centres, royal and sacerdotal dwellings were combined. Hence the conditions of Minoan Crete were more like those of Anatolia than of Egypt, for the Knossian palace was permeated with religious elements. The sign of the sacred double-axe or *labrys* appears constantly on its stone blocks, on stucco and painted pottery, on seals, on the altar of a shrine. Wall-paintings have direct or indirect religious associations. Large parts of the palace consisted of small shrines for ritual use. The so-called 'Room of the Throne' was clearly designed for religious functions. The arrangement of the throne, of the surrounding stone benches, and of the tank opposite the throne, suggested close comparison with the 'Hall of Initiation' in the sanctuary of Mên Askaënos and a Mother-goddess, near the Pisidion Antioch,[27] which led to the presumption that the much earlier 'Room of the

Throne' at Knossos was intended for similar rites of initiation and purification, presided over by a Minoan 'priest-king', adopted son on earth of a Cretan Great Mother.

When Evans, at the beginning of this century, formulated the comparison between the Cretan Minos and the divine 'priest-kings' elsewhere, there were compelling reasons in favour of its acceptance at the time, so compelling indeed that the whole conception has become a familiar feature of the Minoan background. A series of place-names and personal names, apparently derived from an early linguistic substratum which was common to Crete and to those regions in Asia where 'priest-kings' were a normal institution, include the words Knossos, Minos and *basileus* ('king' or 'prince').[28]

Nilsson, in his great work on Minoan-Mycenaean religion, agreed that Evans correctly described the king of Knossos as a 'priest-king'.[29] The palace was a sacred house in which cults were practised. At Mycenae and in two other important Mycenaean towns, Athens and perhaps Tiryns, the temple of the divine protectress of the Greek city-state, Athene or Hera, is built upon the ruins of the palace of the Mycenaean king. Even after the abolition of the kingship in Greece, republican sacral officials continued to hold the title of *basileus*.[30] At Athens the Council used to meet in the King's Porch under the presidency of the *archon basileus* (the 'king archon'), who was responsible for the care of the Eleusinian Mysteries, for lawsuits about sacrilege and impiety, priesthoods and murder.[31] It can therefore be inferred that this important republican magistrate assumed the sacral functions of the old king. The name of 'king', attached to the highest sacral officials, was especially common in Ionian towns, and the Ionians, of all the Greek peoples, came first and most permanently into contact with Minoan culture.[32]

In an earlier survey of the subject of the 'priest-king'[33] I drew the conclusion that the Minoan 'priest-king' was apparently a young man whose tenure of office depended upon the periodically granted sanction of the Minoan goddess, for whom the male deity, Zeus, was substituted in Homeric and later Greek tradition. Since the nature of this tenure could have been closely associated with cult practices, further discussion of the possible implications may be postponed to the next chapter. The direct evidence from the monuments, I pointed out,[34] was slight; and Evans himself had exhausted the possibilities of inference from the materials available to him, both of a direct and indirect nature, in establishing his conception of a 'priest-king' analogous to Oriental prototypes.[35] The two representations which could more definitely be accepted as those of a ruler or 'priest-king' were the 'Chieftain Vase' from Ayia Triada[36] and the fresco described by Evans as 'The Priest-King Relief'.[37]

Although Evans did not himself place the hides carried by the troop of men on the Vase in a religious context, his identification had provided Forsdyke with the clue to a new interpretation of the Vase scene.[38] For various detailed reasons we need not hesitate to accept a youthful representative of the king.

The Minos referred to by Homer was not the great king of Knossos but the grandfather of Idomeneus. This king would have been an Achaean conqueror who, if he called himself Minos, would have assumed the name and the honours of his Cretan predecessors.[39] Greek folk-memory, Forsdyke argued, is too heavily contaminated by literary interference to be acceptable in its details. Though containing a record of pre-historic events, times and persons associated with these events tend to be confused or invented. The self-contradictory Greek traditions consequently have to be assessed against the facts of archaeology or contemporary statements in the history of other countries. The contradictory accounts of Minos in Herodotus and Thucydides were cited as an example of this kind of confusion.

Herodotus reports a Cretan tradition that, in ancient times, the Carians had been subjects of Minos.[40] They were called Leleges, occupied the islands, and they paid no tribute. Herodotos expressly states that he had checked, to the best of his ability, the tradition that they paid no tribute. The implication is that other peoples were subjected to tribute and that the Carians were exempt because of their service as sailors.[41] However, they manned the ships of Minos whenever he required them to do so. Because Minos subdued an extensive territory and prospered in war, the Carians were by far the most considerable of the peoples of that time. Thucydides states[42] that Minos was the first person known by tradition to have established a navy. He made himself the master of what was known in the time of Thucydides as the Hellenic sea, ruled over the Cyclades, into most of which he sent the first colonies, expelled the Carians, appointed his own sons governors and so did his best to suppress piracy as a means of securing the revenues for his own use.

Herodotos and Thucydides agree that Minos was a powerful ruler, possessing a navy and overseas dominions; but whereas, according to Herodotos, the Carians manned his ships, according to Thucydides he drove them out of the islands. It appears that they are attributing the activities of different times and tendencies to a single person. A different solution was adopted by the Parian chronicler, who reconciled these conflicting traditions by assuming that there were two kings of the name Minos.[43] The Cretan command of the sea, however, must have lasted from about 1600 BC until the fall of Knossos, about 1400 BC; and it cannot be restricted to the life-span of a single king. This power may have reached its culminating point at the time (about 1500 BC) of the first Minoan embassies to Egypt in the reigns of Hatshepsut and Thothmes III.[44] The grandfather of Idomeneus, on the dating of Eratosthenes, must have lived at about 1250 BC, and it was he who may have driven the Carians out of the islands.[45] Though conceding the possibility that there may have been a king of Crete, about the middle of the eighteenth Egyptian dynasty, who bore the name of Minos and impressed it upon posterity to the exclusion of other names, Forsdyke followed Evans in supposing that the title was dynastic. He also argued that, since the figures on the Vase wear very short kilts, they can be taken to represent a transitional stage from the loin-cloth to the kilt, to be dated, on the Egyptian evidence, to about 1470 BC. This date would fall within the generation ascribed by the Parian Marble to the earlier Minos.[46]

As the result of fresh discoveries and re-examination of previous evidence, the concept of male superioty in Minoan affairs, particularly in the person of the 'priest-king', has encountered criticism on various grounds which must lead to considerable modification. Particularly is this likely to be true of the energetically peaceful heyday of Minoan civilization, to which the beneficent Minos of later Greek tradition, already juxtaposed by Homer with the other more malevolent autocrat, may possibly have ultimately derived.

An impressive examination of the evidence about the Throne Room at Knossos by Helga Reusch leads to the conclusion that the symbolic altars and griffins heraldically featured on either side of the throne mean that its occupant must have been divine in the sense of being the priestess as goddess when she mimed her epiphany.[47] Or, as Sinclair Hood interprets, the Throne Room was evidently used for ritual, and the Queen as representative of the goddess may have sat upon the throne here.[48] Emmett L. Bennett, reviewing the reasons for the adoption of the idea of a Minoan 'Priest-King', argued that its continued use and elaboration, although perhaps not Evans's own conception of what he intended, had thoroughly distorted our view of Minoan religion and its relation to Minoan government and economy.[49] Henri Van Effenterre found the Knossian concept of royalty inadequate on the political side and incompatible with recent discoveries at Mallia of important Middle Minoan installations such as the 'agora', a road-system and hypostyle crypt, apparently independent of the Palace.[50] F.J. Tritsch found little evidence for Minos the Priest-King but more for Minos the Judge, in harmony with many subsequent Greek traditions.[51]

These critical views have been cited and persuasively supplemented more recently by Helen Waterhouse[52] with the purpose of establishing the following arguments: that the existence before the Late Minoan II period of a king, let alone a 'priest-king', is not supported by the majority of the surviving monuments; that Greek traditions about Minos and the Minoan thalassocracy refer to the period immediately before the destruction of the Palace at Knossos in the fourteenth century BC; that other Greek traditions about the Cretan past were either derived from ritual or other religious practices or, if secular in content, were distorted in transmission by Greek political and social ways of thought; and that Minoan culture was in essence unlike its contemporaries, and especially that of mainland Greece, and so it is reasonable to suppose that its social structure was equally *sui generis*.

Furthermore, this concept of 'priest-king', adopted during the excavation of Knossos, is not necessarily valid for Minoan culture as a whole, since Knossos is atypical by reason of its Late Minoan II–IIIA occupation. For Evans's ideas about kingship and aggressive Minoan imperialism were distorted by having encountered first, by stratigraphical necessity, the evidence of this semi-alien period.

The arguments and conclusions were based on certain assumptions, which have a bearing on matters to be discussed in more detail in a following chapter.[53] Firstly, that the widespread destruction of Middle Minoan I, Middle Minoan IIIB and the lesser one of Late Minoan IA were the result of earthquakes. Secondly, that the destructions at the end of Late Minoan IB were caused by enemy action.[54] Thirdly, that in Late Minoan II and Late Minoan IIIA kings of mainland origin ruled over Crete with Knossos as their capital until its destruction and their expulsion.

Possible pictorial evidence for Priest-kings[55] was considered inconclusive, because, although scenes of ceremony are common in Minoan art, no kingly figure takes part in or presides over any of them. In contrast, there is massive pictorial evidence, from the Miniature Frescoes onwards, for the predominant position of women in such scenes and in Minoan culture as a whole. Evans's own awareness of this is expressed in many places,[56] although these are contradicted by the general tenor of the *Palace of Minos*; and Helga Reusch had demonstrated that the throne at Knossos can only have been occupied by the goddess in the person of her priestess – a possibility also considered by Evans himself.[57]

The predominantly religious character of Minoan Palaces, recognized by Evans and implied by his frequent use of papal analogies, would suggest that they were rather temples, or religious houses, and that the hierarchy living in them consisted chiefly of priestesses, for they alone could enact the epiphany of the goddess.[58] An extension from religious to civil leadership would follow from their sole ability to speak for the divine, and thus to guide the state in all its actions.[59] The precedent of the Sumerian cities illustrates that temples as well as palaces did fulfil economic redistributive functions. However, no parallels could be adduced for a theocratic state run by women: kingship was the normal and traditional form of government in the Bronze Age, as at many times and places.

However, there is evidence to suggest that in Minoan Crete aggressive instincts were channelled into the conquest of the environment, in which indeed the Cretans early outdistanced the other Aegean peoples. The cooperative settlement at Early Minoan Myrtos, the long-continued practice of communal burial, the apparently even development of the several palace regions, combine with a general, though not total, absence of fortifications to indicate at least a high degree of mutual tolerance; and the scattered country houses and undefended towns of the later palace period speak clearly of internal peace and external confidence. This contrasts strongly with the internecine rivalries of later Greek states in any comparable area. Though arms and armour were early developed, and Cretan swords were the best in the Aegean, there is little evidence from Crete itself for their use in human combat (in contrast with, for example, the Mycenae Shaft Graves). Before Late Minoan II there are just two sealings each from Kato Zakro and Ayia Triada with sword battles.[60] Shields, daggers, bows and spears were all used for hunting and may have been largely developed for that purpose.

Greek traditions of the thalassocracy have been used as evidence for Minoan imperialism, especially during Middle Minoan IIIB–Late Minoan IA, when foreign contacts and artistic influence were at their peak. Chester Starr had argued that 'thalassocracy' was a concept created in fifth-century Athens; Renfrew and Buck criticized the idea of a Minoan sea-empire as exaggerated, and Buck saw no place for it later than Middle Minoan III.[61] There is no firm evidence that the Minoans set out to dominate even in places where they can be shown to have settled, like Ayia Irini or Phylakopi; and Marinatos had lately argued strongly for the independence of Thera and other small states in the Aegean in the 'Minoan' period.[62] Widespread Cretan artistic and religious influence was a natural consequence of the superior achievements of Minoan culture. The establishment at Nirou Khani suggested that religion, not empire, was in fact the primary concern of those at the head of Cretan affairs.

No doubt male hierarchies had co-existed with the palace priestesses, some in charge perhaps of trade and maritime affairs, others serving as priests, of native Minoan deities as well as of the oriental gods whose cults are thought to have been adopted in Crete by Late Minoan IA. Among these was perhaps to be sought the original holder of the title Minos at Knossos. He would have held his office for an eight-year cycle (*enneoros*) as perhaps the chief priestess had always done. In general, the predominance of the priestesses seems to have been in decline through Late Minoan I. Successive earthquake destructions may well have called into question the effectiveness of the hierarchy's relations with the divine, and the shift in emphasis from communal to individual well-being, noted at Mallia,[63] like the encroachment of private houses on the palace precinct at Knossos, may show a general weakening of religious influence. Close contacts with more usual regimes in Egypt, Syria, and the rest of the Aegean may already have sapped the power of the priestesses before the Late Minoan IB catastrophe. Its partial survival is indicated, however, by the 'royal' burial of a priestess at Arkhanes in Late Minoan IIIA.[64]

It is a commonplace that the Minos of Greek legend has two incompatible characters, the just law-giver and the oppressor. The first, it was suggested, could have been a typical Greek personalization of the long sacerdotal line which guided the life of Knossos in its great days into a single male ruler, a king. The second really was a king, the last Achaean ruler at Knossos of the whole of Crete, who used the wealth and naval resources of the island to exact tribute from the rest of the Aegean, and establish a thalassocracy of fear which earned the epithet *oloophron* as recorded in the eleventh book of the *Odyssey*. The Knossos sword, arrow and chariot tablets perhaps record his preparations for attacks on the mainland. With a Minos of this date and character the Theseus story falls into place, his short-lived alliance with Ariadne symbolizing the Cretan support for his eviction of the alien ruler who then, as Herodotos and Diodoros record, sailed off westwards and came to a bad end in Sicily. It may have been in defence against his depredations that the other Mycenaean powers first built up the fleets that were the necessary prelude to their own overseas expansion in the later fourteenth century.

Some of the conclusions drawn from this fresh and stimulating approach to the problem of the concepts of Priest-king rule are similar to those reached, from different premises, in my own earlier treatment of the subject.[65] A certain similarity of emphasis and some different details of interpretation will also emerge in the following chapter.

8

CULTS

The material remains which can be studied as essential features of Minoan religion are vast in their quantity and variety. They include the great palaces, the shrines and sanctuaries, cult rooms and cult objects, tombs, caves, rock shelters and pillar crypts, idols and votive offerings, frescoes and sealings, sacred trees and columns, symbols such as the horns of consecration, the double-axe or the sacred knot so often found in association with it, representations of processions, dancing and bull-leaping. All that is lacking is a text to assist and control interpretation. Whereas archaeologists and prehistorians may recognize and establish breaks in a cultural sequence, invasions or natural catastrophes, religion, from its nature, more often exhibits signs of compromise or continuity. It is true, as E.R. Dodds has observed,[1] that the study of ritual is essential for an understanding of the basic elements of Greek religion as it affected the everyday life of ordinary people. For, while myths are liable to change their form every time they are retold, the astonishing thing about ritual is its fixity, its stubborn conservatism. Although the Aegean world has passed through two great religious changes, from Minoan to Classical Greek religion and from Classical Greek religion to Christianity, there are actually cult practices which have survived *both* these changes.

Nevertheless it is possible to distinguish specific features of Minoan religion in relation to its earlier Cretan background; and also to establish differences between Minoan and Mycenaean, in the sense that one is dominated by female, the other by male conceptions of deity. This male conception does appear to become more obtrusive in the later Minoan phases and must have been stimulated into further expansion when Crete became involved with mainland influences, especially if some part was indeed played in this process by Greek-speaking people from the mainland.[2]

There would be a large measure of agreement about certain major characteristics of Greek religion in general in relation to its more distant past. It is certain that the official and popular religion of historical times, dominated, in varying degrees in various localities by principal deities of the Olympian pantheon, retained many singular features from the Bronze Age and earlier times. This applies particularly to the whole sphere of nature – religion and

ertility – cults. The use of caves and rock-shelters as centres of cult was a
primary blend of Cretan religion from very early times until late antiquity.
Cretan religion, as part of the complex of Greek religion in general, had
become by Classical times an amalgam of indigenous Aegean elements,
especially fertility cults, and of increasingly intrusive 'Indo-European'
features, directly associated with peoples whose language was Greek, as part
of the Indo-European family of languages. Study of evidence from representations on sealings, rings and the like, does suggest a tradition of vegetation-
worship, a dominant goddess in association with a young male, ecstatic dancing and sometimes mourning rites, animal and bird cult figures, a sacred
conception of trees and plants connected with axes, stones and pillars. Any
kind of clearly defined polytheism is difficult to recognize and the strong
mystical strains of Cretan religion are bound up with the concept of a 'Mother-
goddess' and a god who is born, lives as a child and youth and who then (in
contrast with the Olympians) also dies, and who is closely connected with
the bull.

Cretan Zeus, who dies and is born again, is different from the Zeus of the
traditional Greek pantheon, who was nevertheless in historical times also
worshipped in Crete under varying epithets.[3] This Cretan Zeus was in fact
much more akin to the familiar Greek Dionysos, also a bull-god and a dying
god.

It is possible, with Nilsson, to regard Minoan-Mycenaean religion as, for
practical purposes, a unity. Yet Herodotos tells us[4] that Homer and Hesiod
were the first to compose theogonies, to give the gods their epithets, allot them
offices and occupations and describe their forms. From this it is reasonable to
infer that these traditional Greek theogonies derived from epic poetry, which
was rooted in the Mycenaean period. Further, the two conceptions of Zeus so
marked in the Cretan context invite us to establish a distinction between what
may be termed Minoan and Mycenaean phases in Cretan religion. The
Minoan phase, lacking in polytheistic definition, was dominated by a goddess
cult in various forms, while the Mycenaean phase initiated a domination of
male deity, a tendency which, however, certainly begins to be more obtrusive
in the later Minoan phase.

The name Zeus is undoubtedly Indo-European and we must suppose that
it was applied to a Minoan deity whose role and function can be discerned
from an enduring store of legend, myth and cult practice. At present, we can
do no more than make plausible guesses about the original name or names of
his male figure. It has been suggested, for example, as one possibility, that an
originally Oriental name which travelled to Crete via Phoenicia became
Hellenized into Zagreus.[5] Or again that it could have been Welkhanos
(Velkhanos) virtually the same as Vulcan, the Etruscan god adopted by the
Romans and equated by them with the Greek Hephaistos.[6] Coins of Phaistos
in historical times portray him as a youthful, beardless god sitting on the

branches of a leafless tree, his right hand caressing a cock, and on the reverse is a bull.[7]

The metal signet rings which may be assigned to the sixteenth and fifteenth centuries BC, engraved with ritualistic or mythical scenes are difficult of interpretation. It is quite likely, however, that the death and resurrection of the god, consort of the goddess, was prominent in the myth and enacted ritual of Bronze Age Crete as elsewhere in the Levant; and a number of these metal signet rings could portray scenes with this theme.[8] On a bronze signet from Knossos a goddess stands outside a shrine or enclosure of squared masonry with a sacred tree in or behind it. A female attendant seems to have climbed the wall of the enclosure and is pulling down a bough of the tree. Behind the goddess, stooping as if in sorrow, is an object shaped like a jar of the sort used for burials in many parts of Crete during the Middle Minoan period from c.2000 BC onward. A gold signet ring of similar theme from a tomb at Arkhanes shows a goddess in the middle with an elaborately flounced dress. A man on the right attacks a tree in or behind a shrine. Another man on the left clasps an object like a large storage jar upside down in the way that burial jars were often set in tombs. The question is whether such scenes represent a rite of mourning for a dead god, while a search is made for a magic bough or fruit to restore him to life. Some such ritual could account for the legend of Glaukos, son of Minos, drowned in a jar of honey, but restored to life with a herb revealed by a snake.[9] On another gold signet ring from Mochlos a goddess sits in a boat with the head of an animal at one end and an object like a plant at the other. There is a shrine with a tree in or behind the boat; and on land to the right stands another shrine or enclosure. Since boats were a regular part of funerary apparatus in Egypt, models of which are sometimes found in Bronze Age tombs in Crete, it could be that this scene portrays a journey of the goddess over the water in search of her dead consort.

The idea of an Elysion, or Isles of the Blessed, as opposed to the Hades of the Homeric poems, is thought to be a legacy from Bronze Age Crete.[10] The way in which the Cretans tended their dead suggests that, like the Egyptians, they believed in an after-life of some kind. It is of course likely that any religious ideas which derive from a primitive cycle of birth and death, depending on totemistic beliefs and fertility-cult, is bound to induce a reverence for the dead and a confidence in the probability of their reincarnation. Hood finds significance in a clay model assigned to the end of the Middle Minoan period, c.1600 BC, from the large circular tomb at Kamilari near Phaistos, showing two couples with altars or tables in front of them upon which offerings of food and drink are being placed. For the couples who receive the offerings may be the deceased, unless they are meant for gods.[11]

The scene on the Ayia Triada Sarcophagus[12] of the fourteenth century BC allows of a similar but more certain interpretation. For the dead man here stands in front of his tomb while two women pour libations into a large vase set between a pair of pillars surmounted by elaborate double axes with birds on top of them. The three men dressed in skins bring the dead man a pair of bulls or models of them, along with a boat which he may need for his voyage to the Isles of the Blessed.

The burial complex known as the Temple Tomb discovered by Evans in 1931 at Knossos, with an upper storey and a pillar crypt, could date towards the end of the Middle Minoan period. Decorated clay vases found on the floor of the pillar crypt and in the open outside the entrance to the tomb indicate that a cult of the dead continued here at least until the final destruction of the palace at Knossos.[13] No other certain example of a royal or princely tomb of the period before *c*.1450 BC has been identified.[14]

The usual rite of burial apparently practised throughout Crete during the Late Neolithic and Early Minoan I phases was inhumation in caves or rock shelters. Cremation is infrequent before the end of the Bronze Age. It is suggested that isolated cremation burials in tombs of the Ailias cemetery at Knossos dating from the end of the Middle Minoan period, *c*.1600 BC, may be those of foreigners who had married into local clans.[15] During the early Bronze Age the Cretans normally buried their dead in collective tombs, used by clans over a long period of time and often containing hundreds of burials. This custom of collective burial lasted in some areas until the end of the fifteenth century BC or later, and a few of the old communal tombs continued to be used, notably at Kamilari near Phaistos.

On the assumption that the many circular tombs of the Messara, containing hundreds of successive burials, were tribal tombs, it has been inferred that a vigorous tribal life extended from Early Minoan times until the old tribal ties weakened and a tendency emerges to construct smaller tombs.[16] At Knossos early collective tombs were carved out of the local soft limestone (*kouskouras*) and some were still in use in the area at the beginning of the Late Minoan period. One recently excavated at Poros had a large pillared chamber and rich contents assigned to Middle Minoan III and Late Minoan I.[17] In areas of hard rock, caves were used for burial as they had been in Neolithic times or tombs were constructed above the ground. A burial complex discovered in 1966 at Arkhanes, south of Knossos, had replaced an earlier collective tomb and it could have been in continuous use for more than five hundred years until the fourteenth century BC or later.[18]

After the middle of the fifteenth century BC burial was mainly in small tombs holding a group of three or four immediate relatives, or a couple, or even a single individual.[19] Built tombs at Knossos, perhaps of rulers immediately after *c*.1450 BC, include a tholos with circular chamber deep on the ground at Kefala on the Isopata ridge north of the Bronze Age city and the Isopata Royal Tomb on the north end of the ridge.[20] Other similar stone-built tombs of the Late Minoan III period are known from other areas. What could have been the tomb of the royal clan of Mallia during the Middle Minoan period and perhaps even until the palace was destroyed in the disaster of *c*.1450 BC lay on the north-east edge of the city. A large rectangular building with a colonnade on the east side and a complex of rooms within, this tomb perhaps once housed the 'Aigina treasure' mentioned earlier.[21]

This archaeological evidence from burial customs and tomb architecture, which emphasizes the tenacity of collective customs inherent in tribal organization, testifies to the firm foundations of Cretan economy and social structure laid by the Neolithic inhabitants of the island.[22] Presumably the first settlers had brought with them their tribal and clan structures derived from their own Palaeolithic ancestors. Transplanted to a Cretan setting, these social institutions, including communal land tenure in their villages and communal burial customs, also would influence the survival of totemistic features in Cretan religion. The figurines which are so common a feature of Neolithic and Chalcolithic sites from Central Europe, the Mediterranean area and the Near East are generically similar to Palaeolithic types. The Cretan type of figurine, found with clay birds and animals in the Neolithic strata of Knossos, were discussed by Evans.[23] Though fragments of male figures were recognized, the majority of images of human shape were female; and of two main types. The rarer type was flat and broad. The more regular type was short, stumpy, steatopygous, either squatting with the legs bent under the body or sitting with knees drawn up and feet drawn together. Both were assumed to have a common origin with close Anatolian parallels. Though direct descent from Palaeolithic prototypes may not be directly established, they must have been part of the inheritance of the first inhabitants, together with a changing pattern of magical custom.[24] The people who made the figurines were now settled food-producers. The earlier magical rituals of their ancestors can partially be understood through interpretation of the mural art of Palaeolithic hunters still surviving in caves and rock shelters. Rituals of this kind seem to have linked the life and death cycle of animals and human beings in forms of totemic imagery, symbolic of ancestry and of rebirth. Later these rituals were transformed into the fertility cults of settled farming communities, now envisaging nature and their own social structure as depending upon the earth and her fruits, rather than the animals who roved upon the earth. The bond between them long endured as a female fertility principle. It is hardly surprising that votive images from sanctuaries, idols from shrines, graves and tombs portray various concepts and functions. Of the numerous terracotta and bronze figurines of Minoan times, early examples have postures suggestive of childbirth and a variety of later types indicates magical efficacy in association with death, accounting for their presence in graves and tombs; or they might serve as votive offerings to the goddess for succour in sickness or childbirth or at critical times of initiation or marriage or bereavement; or they could be images of the goddess herself, gifts of thanksgiving for patronage.

Evans decided that it was not possible to dissociate the Neolithic female figurines from those which later occur in shrines and sanctuaries of the deity he termed the 'Great Minoan Goddess'.[15] How the goddess was named, or if she had several names, during the time she became so prominent in Middle Minoan times, is an unprofitable question. We can, however, easily detect her pervasive influence from a great variety of cult associations and symbols. She is represented with animals, birds and snakes, with the baetylic pillar and sacred trees, with poppies and lilies, with swords and double-axes. Huntress and goddess of sports, armed or presiding over ritual dancing, with apparent dominion over mountain, sky, earth and sea, over life and death, she is at once a household-goddess, a palace goddess, vegetation and fertility goddess, a Mother and a Maid. The palace divinity attended by priestesses reveals her Neolithic origins in the magical fetishes and totem symbols often present beside her. Through them we may imagine that the ancestral spirits of the clans had been earlier realized, perpetuated and renewed in association with a vegetation cycle of fertility. Perhaps the axe was sacred from its use in cutting timber, work done by women in early societies – and the double-axe is certainly connected with the goddess.[26] Because it casts its slough and renews itself, the snake signifies immortality; and snakes are also incarnations of the dead. As a fertility symbol accompanying the goddess in her role as protectress of the household, the snake is associated with Minoan just as with later Greek domestic cult.

The concepts of moon-goddess and fertility goddess were closely allied. Moon-worship is involved with primitive time-keeping systems in agricultural communities and the moon tends to be regarded as a fertility stimulus in plants and vegetation. Sacrificial animals offered by women to the moon are normally small creatures such as hares, goats, pigs, doves and also cats. The Cretan goddess is found with goats and doves; pigs and cats are variously represented in Minoan contexts. Traditions of herbal magic may account for the connection of the Minoan goddess with such plants as lilies and poppies.[27] Many of these traditional ties were preserved in the cults and functions of goddesses whom we can specify as having distinctive Cretan attributes, though sometimes they have wandered away from the confines of the island.

The cult of the goddess Britomartis is of particular interest for several reasons. It seems certain that this goddess bears a Minoan name which we can understand as 'Sweet Maid'.[28] Her name and cult persisted well into historical times at various places in Crete, for example at Dreros, where she was known as Britomarpis, which was apparently the specifically Cretan form of her name. The surviving epigraphic evidence shows that her cult survived from early times in central Crete and especially along the north coast. At Khersonesos, the port of Lyttos, Britomartis had a temple and her head, represented on coins of the period 370–300 BC, may perhaps be a copy of a cult-statue. This persistence of cult ensured that Britomartis did not become a simple epithet of Artemis.[29] In mythology she is associated with Minos and is being assimilated to Artemis, represented as a marriageable girl who suffers transformation and a change of name when she is pursued by Minos. She is said to have escaped his attentions by hiding in a grove at Aigina where she was worshipped as Aphaia – who is Artemis or Diktynna.[30] Or she was the companion of Artemis, and hid away from Minos in some oak-groves in the meadows; she was then pursued by Minos for nine months, escaped by throwing herself into the sea. Saved by the nets of some fishermen, she was afterwards known as Diktynna (because *diktyon* = 'net').[31]

Diktynna was, like Artemis, a deity of the countryside and the mountains, a huntress. Her cult was widespread outside Crete, including Athens and Sparta. Coins of Crete as late as the time of Trajan represent her seated on rocks between two Kouretes, nursing an infant Zeus. She thus retains her ancient aspect of a mountain-mother, a guardian of the young, a maid become a mother, a mature Britomartis. Her continuing worship is attested at a number of other places in Crete, including the principal centre of the Diktynnaion, on the promontory between Phalasarna and Kydonia, both of which cities exercised a control over it at various times. The temple seems to have flourished, with increasing wealth and influence. In Roman times its revenues were considered as the property of the public treasury and provided the resources for such public works as roads for the whole of Crete.[32]

Even a casual acquaintance with Greek mythology will associate Ariadne, through Theseus, with Knossos, with Minos and the Minotaur. However, when Nilsson observed[33] that no other heroine suffered death in so many ways as Ariadne, and that these different versions can only be explained as originating in a cult in which her death was celebrated, it may be that he was beginning to turn folklore and fairy-tale along a path of productive scientific enquiry. Nilsson was impressed by the historical fact that, at Naxos, Ariadne had two festivals, perhaps two parts of the same festival.[34] One of them was a festival of rejoicing in honour of Ariadne as bride of Dionysos, and the other was a festival of mourning for Ariadne who dies in Naxos, when she was forsaken by Theseus. So Nilsson thought that the Naxian rite gave the clue, in the sense that it closely resembled a type of vegetation-festival, well known from the Oriental religions but foreign to the true Greek religion. Death of the god of vegetation was celebrated with sorrow and lamentations, his resurrection with joy and exultation. In these cults it is a god who is worshipped: but in this case it is a goddess, which seems to make certain the originality of the cult. The death of such a goddess is unique, although it may seem that the idea of the death of vegetation might be applied not only to the god but also to the goddess of fertility. Yet the idea that the goddess of fertility also dies might be understood. Her death was celebrated annually for she dies every year. The idea is nevertheless un-Greek; and it does not occur in Asia in this form. Therefore it has to be considered as an original product of Minoan religious genius.[35]

It does seem valid to conclude that Ariadne was a real vegetation-goddess of

Minoan origin, a form of the Minoan goddess like Britomartis. For, just as Britomartis can be interpreted as 'Sweet Maid', so Ariadne (or Ariagne) seems to mean 'Very Holy Maid' – just like the epithet of Panayia applied to Mary the mother of Jesus in the Greek world of today.[36] Like Pasiphae too, she had associations with the moon, and so with fertility cult.[37] Argument has been advanced to suggest that the seat in the Throne Room at Knossos was occupied not by Minos, but by Ariadne and so used in a ritual by a queen representing the goddess.[38]

In the course of his exhaustive exploration of the caves of Crete, Faure surveyed the peninsula of Akrotiri, north-east of Khania (the ancient Kydonia). Considerable remains in caves and elsewhere led to a confident conclusion that the area was densely populated at least by the end of the Bronze Age; and at Kydonia remains extend at least as far back as the middle of the second millennium BC. According to tradition, Zeus was here suckled by a bitch, metamorphosed into a bear. Coins of Roman Imperial times even show Diktynna holding a young Zeus, and at Kydonia, as elsewhere in western Crete, Diktynna was associated with Cretan-born Zeus. Several heads of Artemis, of Classical and Hellenistic times, were found in a cave on Akrotiri called Arkoudia ('Cave of the She-Bear'). The cave is consecrated to the Purification of the Virgin, with the local name of Panayia Arkoudiotissa, and there is an annual festival. It seems that a cult of a divine Mother has been perpetuated here at least from Minoan times and it may be that a great central stalagmite in the cave, shaped like a bear or a bitch, could be associated with local traditions of the birth and childhood of Zeus.[39]

Eileithyia was a goddess of childbirth, described by Homer as *mogostokos* or 'goddess of the pains of birth'; and he tells how she attended at the birth of Apollo when Lato bore him in Delos, together with other goddesses who bathed the child and wrapped him in swaddling-clothes.[40] The cave of Eileithyia at Amnisos, a harbour town of Knossos, is mentioned in the *Odyssey*, which may signify that the Homeric tradition is derived from the Minoan Age.[41] The cave was identified in the last century and its exploration has established proof of continuity of cult from Neolithic times, with indications even of a revival in Roman times. This goddess had a widespread cult in the Greek world but this was particularly the case in Crete. Her name is apparently not Indo-European, and this makes it more likely that she was indeed descended from a Minoan goddess in her aspect as divinity of childbirth.[42]

The name of the goddess Leto (Doric Lato, as in the name of the Cretan city which derives from that of the goddess), may be connected with a Carian word *lada*, meaning simply 'woman' or 'lady'.[43] The evidence reveals that a cult of this goddess endured in Crete, especially in the central and eastern areas of the island. Of particular interest in the context of survival of primitive cults is the festival known as the Ekdysia which survived in the city of Phaistos, where we would naturally expect the survival of Minoan traditions. The festival was associated with a local cult of Lato Phytia – Lato 'the productive' – and it was an occasion for the young men of the city to cast aside boyish clothes and dress themselves as men. The myth associated with this festival concerns one Leukippos, who was changed from a girl to a boy. In the myth, Galatea, daughter of Eurytos and wife of Lampros, gave birth to a daughter; and she persuaded Lato to let the girl change her sex when she grew up. The people of Phaistos celebrated the Ekdysia festival to commemorate this transformation, and, when they married, they lay down beside the statue of Leukippos – presumably situated in the sanctuary of Lato.

Festival and myth clearly reveal strong traces of fertility, initiation and marriage ritual, with more than a hint of a change from a female to a male cult. The youth of Phaistos, in historical times, were apparently still initiated into manhood, citizenship and marriage at the same crucial time of life. The divine Phytia, like her counterpart Physkoa at Olympia, and perhaps also another counterpart called Orthia at Sparta – since the three names bear the same sort of meaning – is she who stimulates growth, which includes growth of fertility in the young. Once this growth is accomplished, the youth dies as a boy and is re-born as a man. The change is celebrated with the abandonment of boys' clothes and the assumption of adult costume.[44]

According to the Homeric Hymn to Demeter, that goddess arrived in Greece from Crete and in the *Odyssey* we have the earliest attested form of the sacred marriage.[45] For Demeter is said to have been embraced by Iasion in a thrice-ploughed field, or in other words, in a field prepared for sowing, confirming that the sacred marriage is bound up with the vegetation cycle of death and renewal, the fertility of crops. Hence Cretan Demeter shared common characteristics with Oriental cults such as Magna Mater and Attis, Aphrodite and Adonis, Ishtar and Tammuz.[46] It was Demeter who gave seed-corn and a plough to Triptolemos and despatched him over the world to instruct mankind in the arts of agriculture.[47] Triptolemos emerges in myth when a more active part is being played by men, presumably associated with the use of the cattle-drawn plough.[48]

In historical times the cult of Demeter was established in various cities of Crete.[49] Of particular interest is the evidence about her worship at Knossos, now available as a result of the excavation of her sanctuary in recent years.[50] The sanctity of this site certainly goes back as far as the second half of the eighth century BC. Under the sanctuary, ubiquitous Minoan house walls show that the area had been thickly populated in the Late Bronze Age, when the lower slopes of Gypsadhes formed the southern quarter of the town. Apparently the cult was most probably formed by a fusion of Minoan and Dorian elements. The Classical temple, built shortly before 400 BC, seems to have had no predecessor; and we are to suppose that the worship of Demeter was conducted in the open air before its construction.[51]

The name of the goddess is inscribed in the Doric form on a silver ring from the sanctuary of the third century BC. Some two hundred years earlier, shortly before the temple was built, one Nothokartes offered a ring to the goddess as the Mother. The inscription on the ring seems to indicate that Nothokartes was the victor on six occasions in some kind of contest at Knossos in honour of the goddess.[52] At Knossos, as late as the first or second century AD, Persephone is referred to as the Maid.[53] At Hierapytna, in eastern Crete, after some disaster, in the first century BC or first century AD, a dedication was made by a girl to Demeter and Persephone, who is called the Maid.[54] It is not possible to be certain whether Demeter or Persephone is portrayed on coins of Knossos (*c*.400–350 BC), of Kydonia (*c*.400–300 BC) and of Rhaukos (*c*.300–*c*.165 BC).[55] This continuing close association of Demeter and Persephone, of Mother and Maid, serves as a reminder of the double aspect of the Minoan goddess as Mother and Maid. Coins of Priansos (*c*.430–200 BC) portray a goddess enthroned beneath a palm-tree, caressing the head of a snake with her hand. Though her identity cannot be positively established – perhaps she was Persephone, perhaps Hygieia – her association with the snake is a clue that she was akin to the Minoan snake-goddess. Similarly, Demeter's attributes of snakes, trees, poppies and small animals bear witness to her ultimate origin.[56]

The familiar myth of the rape of Persephone may have been symbolic of the practice of storing the seed-corn from harvest-time to sowing-time in underground pits, so that it could be fertilized by contact with the dead.[57] Persephone as spirit of the corn, like the corn-seed, dies and is born again. Ravished away by Hades, she was mourned by her mother and restored to life again on condition that she joined Hades again below the earth for a third part of each year.

The Eleusinian Mysteries were performed in honour of Demeter and Persephone. Whatever their ultimate origin, the Homeric Hymn to Demeter testifies that they came to mainland Greece from Crete; and Diodoros has these significant remarks:[58]

As what they consider to be the chief proof of their contention that divine honours, sacrifices and rites involved in the Mysteries were transmitted from Crete to other peoples, the Cretans advance the following argument. The rite celebrated by the Athenians at Eleusis, perhaps the most remarkable of all, the one in Samothraike, and that in Thrace among the Kikones, whence came Orpheus who introduced them – these were all transmitted in secret forms: at Knossos in Crete, however, it was customary, from ancient times, for these rites to be transmitted to all quite openly; and such things as are elsewhere transmitted in secret are there not concealed from anyone who wishes to know about them. They declare that most of the gods proceeded from Crete to many parts of the inhabited world conferring benefits upon the races of men and sharing among each of them the advantages of their own discoveries. Thus Demeter passed over into Attica and from there to Sicily and, later on, to Egypt. In these places especially she received great honours among those she benefited in transmitting the fruit of the corn and in teaching them about the sowing of the seed.

In 36 BC a colony of Campanians was settled at Knossos by Octavian and their arrival roughly coincides with the beginnings of a new phase in the history of the cult of Demeter. As in the earlier period, once again the festivities seem to have taken place in the open air. Perhaps, it is suggested,[59] it was the open-air character of the celebrations, in contrast with the heavily enclosed Telesterion at Eleusis with its carefully guarded approach, which moved Diodoros to write as he did about the Mysteries at Knossos.

Since Persephone, like Demeter, was originally fatherless, it has been maintained that the mythological background was matriarchal and that the kernel of the Mysteries was probably a matriarchal palace-cult.[60] With such a background in mind, the cult of Cretan Zeus, Zeus Kretagenes, so unlike the patriarchal Olympian of traditional Greek mythology and religion, assumes a particular significance and importance. The late appearance and subordinate status of a male Minoan deity emphasizes in its own way the paramount importance of the Cretan goddess of the Bronze Age, although there is a clear tendency by the end of Minoan times to elevate him to superior status.[61] The legends which centre upon the birth of Cretan Zeus were responsible for the epithet Kretagenes which appears in the epigraphic evidence of historical times.[62] The mythological evidence is closely associated with the Diktaian Cave. The epithet Diktaios derives from Dikte and the same (presumably pre-Greek) root is common to the mountain Dikte, the goddess Diktynna and to the epithet.[63]

Hesiod tells the story of the birth of Cretan Zeus in this way. Before the times of Olympian supremacy, the children of Ouranos and Gaia (Heaven and Earth), the Titans, occupied a position of paramount importance. Kronos, the youngest of the Titans, married Rhea. Afraid that he would lose his kingship through one of them, Kronos swallowed their first children – Hestia, Demeter, Hera, Hades and Poseidon. When she was about to give birth to Zeus, Rhea took the precaution of seeking the advice of Ouranos and Gaia about the possibilities of concealing the birth. As a result she was brought to Lyttos in Crete and Gaia took the baby Zeus from Rhea to rear him. She hid him in a deep cave on the wooded mountain Aigaion ('Goat-mountain') and then substituted for the baby a stone wrapped in swaddling-clothes. Kronos swallowed the stone and later vomited this up together with the children whom he had swallowed before. The legends which tell how the infant Zeus was nurtured in the cave by bees or doves or a goat or pig seem to be associated with totemistic survivals from early religious strata.[64] This is markedly so in the case of the pig. Explaining how the Cretans continued to have a taboo on sow's flesh, Athenaios cites[65] the report that the sanctity of swine was due to the myth of the birth of Zeus on Mount Dikte, where a sacrifice that was not to be mentioned occurred. A sow was supposed to have suckled Zeus and made its whimpers inaudible by grunting as it trotted around the baby. Hence the sow was regarded as especially sacred and its flesh was not eaten. The Praisians of eastern Crete in fact made offerings to a pig and this was their normal sacrifice before marriage. This story is consistent with other indications that the people of Praisos tenaciously preserved Minoan traditions.[66]

According to an alternative and more generally familiar legend the baby Zeus was entrusted to the Kouretes (or the Korybantes, later identified with them) who danced around the baby, beating their drums and clashing their shields and spears to prevent its cries from being heard by Kronos. These Kouretes have associations with the Mother-goddess and with traditional tribal initiation rites.[67]

Just as there are legends of the birth, so there are also legends of the death of Cretan Zeus. In fact a tradition about the tomb of Zeus has continued from ancient times, located by Ennius at Knossos, Mount Ida by Varro and Porphyrios and on Mount Dikte by Nonnus.[68] The Cretans were censured for their belief in a dying Zeus as liars and worse by Kallimachos, the censure being repeated by St Paul and other Christian writers. There were different versions of an inscription on the tomb of Zeus, but they imply that the old name Zan for Zeus was familiar in Crete; and also that, if it did not actually grow out of an earlier cult of Minos, the cult of Zeus was certainly at least associated, linked by an annual festival in honour of a god like Adonis or Tammuz, at which the god was eaten in the form of a bull. Though the evidence for tomb and epitaph is late, it shows how Cretan Zeus was thought of as a dying god, a god who, at least originally, died annually and was born again.

The Zeus of Crete married with Europa. The marriage occurred in or under an evergreen plane-tree near a stream at Gortyn. Fifth-century coins of the city show a goddess in a tree, generally identified as Europa, possessed by Zeus in the form of an eagle; and a bull's head is often apparently fixed to the trunk of the tree. This sacred marriage of Zeus and Europa fused Neolithic and Minoan with Mycenaean cult traditions, as seems to be clear from the art, the literature and the numismatic evidence of historical times.[69]

Homer describes Minos as a nine-year king (*enneoros*), familiar of Zeus.[70] *Enneoros* means literally 'for nine years'. However, since the Greeks, in reckoning intervals of time numerically, included both the terms separated by the interval, *enneoros* really means at 'intervals of eight years'. In the same way, the word *enneaeteris* meaning literally 'a period of nine years', was used to signify the octennium or eight-year cycle. Though the passage was interpreted in various ways even in antiquity,[71] Plato, Strabo and most modern writers, understand it to mean that Minos consulted with Zeus 'every ninth year' – that is to say, at each octennium. Much evidence from literary, mythological and archaeological sources indicates a connection between the octennium and ancient Bronze Age kingship. In Greek antiquity the year was divided into 12 months alternating between 29 and 30 days, the deficit of eleven days being made good by intercalating a thirteen month in three years out of every eight. There is also much evidence in support of the view that this lunisolar calendar, based on an octennial cycle, goes back into the Minoan period.[72] Zeus is a relatively late-comer on the religious scene, at least under that name, and the tradition of regular consultation by Minos in the cave of Zeus could indicate that a youthful Minos, whether consort, king or priest-king held tenure of office subject to a periodically renewed sanction; and it could also be that this sanction was originally bestowed by the Minoan goddess, later supplanted by Zeus, with Minos as his familiar, in Homeric and subsequent Greek tradition. The duties of the person who received periodic divine sanction would have included supervision and regulation of the calendar. The periodic tenure would thus be explained in terms of calendrical ritual, essential for an advanced society dependent on agricultural resources, where sun and bull were combined in cult and associated with royal rule.[73]

9

CLIMAX AND TRANSITION

An advanced civilization centred upon the great Minoan palaces developed and matured over a period of roughly 600 years. At the zenith of its achievements in the arts and in technology, and when its general overseas influences were most extensive, its unique career was fairly abruptly terminated. The palaces were destroyed and were never built again.

The old palace centres had suffered calamity even before the widespread destructions of c.1700 BC. It is unlikely that the disastrous end of the early palaces was brought about by foreign invaders – whether early Greek settlers, Hyksos from Egypt or Luwians from southern Anatolia.[1] The new palaces were soon built on a grander scale and on a similar plan. Nor does it seem necessary to suppose that these destructions were due to wars between the different states of Crete.[2] The siting of the three major palaces in the centre of the island is inconsistent with any assumption of political rivalry and their defensive features are quite rudimentary. Even the ring wall at the residential area of the palace at Mallia can be adequately explained by its proximity to the shore.[3] Though it may be inferred from archaeological evidence that Crete had been drawn into an area of contemporary political and economic rivalry extending from the Nile valley to Mesopotamia, Syria and Anatolia, there was no rival of equal standing on the sea routes, since other states were land powers. Egypt, for instance, was only interested in the sea route to Syria, which provided Crete with a good basis for economic and cultural exchange; and the Asia Minor states were more concerned with the interior and the East rather than the sea. As the Aegean area became Crete's sphere of interest the cultural balance shifted in favour of the Minoans to give them a leading place. The consequence was that Crete advanced in wealth and prosperity and drew Aegean neighbours into the orbit of this advance; and as Minoan civilization reached its maturity, so Aegean hegemony had begun to pass to the Mycenaean mainland.

If then the development of Minoan society from Early Minoan until Late Minoan times was interrupted at times only by natural disasters, such as earthquakes, without disturbance from invasion or migration, its unique features become even more remarkable. Most remarkable of all is the apparently quite peaceful nature of this development over many centuries, testifying to a highly stable social system, confident, dynamic and flexible. In the period of the later palaces from *c.*1700 BC the island was densely populated, which may help to account for Cretan settlements overseas in such places as Thera, Melos, Kea and Rhodes, apparently without aggressive intent. Social organization, based on tenacious collective traditions, to which the settlement at Early Minoan Myrtos and the enduring habit of communal burial bear witness, enabled the Cretans to adapt their energies to the conquest of their environment earlier, and more successfully than other Aegean peoples. It has already been suitably emphasized that the apparently even development of the various palace regions combine with the general, though not total absence of fortifications to suggest at least a high degree of mutual tolerance. In marked contrast with the internecine rivalries of later Greek states in any comparable area, the scattered country houses and undefended towns of the later palace period speak clearly of internal peace and external confidence.[5]

It is generally agreed that the important part played by women in art is characteristic of Minoan life in general. Their appearance in cult scenes matches the dominant position of the mother-goddess. No kingly figure participates in or presides over the many ceremonial scenes in Minoan art. On the other hand the privileged role of women is illustrated in the very considerable pictorial evidence from the time of the Miniature Frescoes onward. Though inferences derived from the monuments do not constitute clear proof, this class of evidence strongly supports the theory of a matriarchal basis for Minoan society.[6] Discussing the honourable position reserved for the women of the Temple Fresco, Evans thought it seemed natural to connect it with a matriarchal stage of society.[7] Women took the higher rank in society, corresponding to the position of the Great Goddess.[8] It was certain that, however much the male element had asserted itself in the domain of government by the great days of Minoan civilization, the religion still continued to reflect the older matriarchal stage of social development.[9] Evans was not consistent in this attitude and indeed such passages of his work are contradicted by its general tenor.[10] Some scholars have more consistently supported and supplemented the arguments for the persistence of matriarchal custom.[11] Although the part played by collective social units like tribe, clan and household from the Neolithic period onward cannot be precisely described, there are certain factors, including the evidence of Minoan art and late sociological and religious survivals into the historical period, which indicate the survival of matriarchal custom within their fabric. An initially dominant part could have been played by women in maintaining clan and household cults. The Minoan palaces were also households. It is within the palaces that the development of the great goddess attended by her priestesses – and perhaps also queens? – can most readily be imagined.[12]

By about 1200 BC the Bronze Age cultures of the Mediterranean were in a

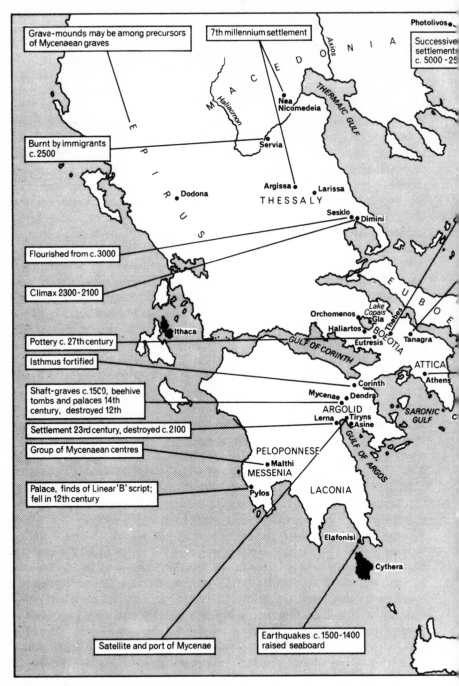

Grave-mounds may be among precursors of Mycenaean graves

7th millennium settlement

Successive settlements c. 5000 - 25

Photolivos

MACEDONIA

Axios

Haliacmon

Nea Nicomedeia

THERMAIC GULF

Burnt by immigrants c. 2500

Servia

EPIRUS

Dodona

Argissa

Larissa

THESSALY

Sesklo

Dimini

Flourished from c. 3000

Climax 2300-2100

EUBOE

Lake Copais

Orchomenos

Gla

Thebes

Haliartos

BOEOTIA

Pottery c. 27th century

Ithaca

GULF OF CORINTH

Eutresis

Tanagra

Isthmus fortified

ATTICA

Athens

Shaft-graves c.1500, beehive tombs and palaces 14th century, destroyed 12th

Corinth

Mycenae

Dendra

Settlement 23rd century, destroyed c.2100

ARGOLID

Lerna

Tiryns

Asine

SARONIC GULF

Group of Mycenaean centres

PELOPONNESE

Malthi

MESSENIA

GULF OF ARGOS

Palace, finds of Linear 'B' script; fell in 12th century

Pylos

LACONIA

Elafonisi

Cythera

Satellite and port of Mycenae

Earthquakes c. 1500-1400 raised seaboard

14   Mycenaean Greece *c.*1450–1150 BC

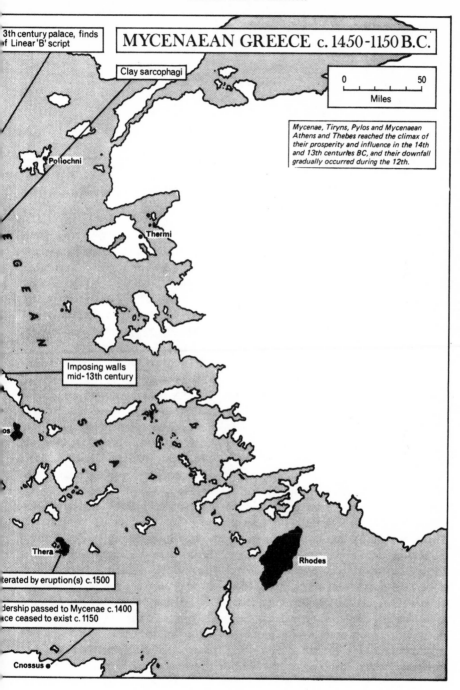

MYCENAEAN GREECE c. 1450-1150 B.C.

3th century palace, finds
f Linear 'B' script

Clay sarcophagi

0   50
Miles

*Mycenae, Tiryns, Pylos and Mycenaean
Athens and Thebes reached the climax of
their prosperity and influence in the 14th
and 13th centuries BC, and their downfall
gradually occurred during the 12th.*

Poliochni

Thermi

E
G
E
A
N

Imposing walls
mid-13th century

os

Thera

terated by eruption(s) c.1500

Jership passed to Mycenae c.1400
ice ceased to exist c. 1150

Rhodes

Cnossus

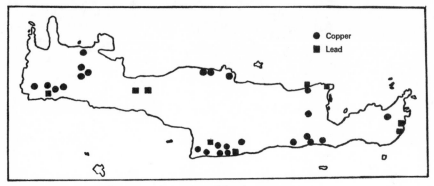

15   Distribution of Cretan copper and lead sources

state of upheaval, crisis and decay. I have maintained elsewhere[13] that these forms of Bronze Age economy of the second millennium BC exhibit certain common characteristics, not only among Hittites, Egyptians and Achaeans, but also among the Chinese. These characteristics include: militarization; social inequalities now fairly based on rigid divisions of labour; forms of service to a central authority; the maintenance of royal, military, administrative and priestly hierarchies through the appropriation of agricultural surplus and the development of a major class of tribute-paying cultivators; and the extension of this general system to other territories through conquest, coercion or dynastic alliances. Ruling classes had monopoly control of bronze, expensive but essential for the manufacture of products by craftsmen which chiefly benefited the wealthy. Intensified search for further wealth resulted from a one-sided economic relationship whereby an agrarian surplus provided for specialist craftsmen who produced mainly luxury goods and weapons for merchants, soldiers, priests and administrators. Communal relations among the peasantry, still maintained in varying degrees, contrasted with the unequal distribution of wealth. As tribute and services became obligatory, the area from which they were exacted was forcibly expanded to concentrate greater wealth at one pole of society.

There are indications that Cretan society was independently developing some analogous characteristics in the Late Minoan period before there was any possible close fusion with Mycenaean or Achaean culture. From what has been said above about the development of Minoan society, on the basis of inferences to be drawn from the monuments, it seems clear that we should be wary of seeking marked traces of these characteristics at too early a date. In formulating his historical conclusions about the Early Palace Period, from *c.*2000 to 1700 BC, Matz[14] emphasizes that the peaceful character of Minoan civilization is astonishing even in the Pre-Palatial Period. The repeated destructions of the palaces, he agrees, were caused not by enemy hands but by earthquakes. Although the coasts of Crete are long and exposed, the Cretans showed surprisingly little interest in the art of fortification which was highly developed elsewhere, as we know from important remains in the Aegean islands, on the Anatolian coast and in Greece itself. However, it is for Matz clear enough that the political links, which had certainly been loose hitherto, were tightened into a strongly centralized monarchy at the foundation of the palaces. The large number of store-rooms and storage vessels in the palaces suggests the existence of a highly organized administrative service with many branches, even if we suppose that the supplies of grain, oil and wine were intended only to serve the needs of the royal household. These supplies, together with the valuables which lay in the treasuries, seem to have formed the wealth of the prince and not to have been destined ultimately for export. The insight into the archive system of the period afforded by the great find of sealings at Phaistos has shown us that even then the administration was carried out in accordance with a system which had been known previously only from the later palaces of Crete and from the citadels of the Mycenaean period.

The seals, he continues, provide an insight also into the structure of society. It can be seen from the archives at Phaistos that the administration considered it important to control the suppliers and that they for their part required documentary proof that they had fulfilled their obligations. The general resemblance of the seals to those in the tholoi of the Messara shows that the goods delivered to the palace came from the landowners whose family vaults were the tholoi. These relations, however, can be interpreted only in a general sense, because the impressions from Phaistos represent an advanced stage of gem-cutting and the seals in the tholoi are mainly earlier in date. It is evident that now, if not earlier, the farmers had become vassals, as we may infer from the later seals such as those from the Hieroglyphic Deposit. The magnificent development in the art of seal-cutting, which had reached its peak when the older palaces had been destroyed, enables us to arrive at some conclusions about the owners of the seals. A nobility had arisen round the court of the rulers and drew its members from the class of those who had probably been free landowners. There is evidence of a pause in the development of gem-cutting at the time when the palaces were founded, and this pause may reflect the changing status of the landowners upon the rise of the central power.

In commenting upon the zenith of Minoan civilization in the Late Palace Period, from *c.*1700–1380 BC, Matz[15] begins by stating that our ideas about the Minoan state and especially the Minoan monarchy of this epoch are at best vague. Yet, he goes on, the only certain fact is that the development of a centralized system with a prince at its head continues. It may be conjectured that the prince was also a priest, but the conjecture cannot be substantiated. Though surprising in view of the abundance of Minoan pictures, the character of Minoan religion is such that portraits of the king were not necessary, whereas they were in Egypt and the Near East. The ecstatic religion of the Minoans was not concerned to confer immortality on the king himself by means of his portrait, as was done in Egypt, nor to magnify his connexions with the gods, as was done in the Near East. The peculiarity of Minoan pictures lies in the ability to conjure up an appearance of life, a vision, and not in an attempt to recreate existence. This quality marks a fundamental difference between the character of the Minoans and that of the Orient, so that it is possible to understand the absence or at least the unobtrusiveness of the king in monuments of art.

Sources of the Early Palace Period had already enabled the inference to be drawn that the king exercised his government with the support of a nobility. Clear traces of this class have been found outside the palaces as well as within them during the Early Palace Period, for the round tombs of the Messara can be seen as the resting-place of landowning families. In the Late Palace Period they had largely changed into a court nobility, whose luxurious dwellings were grouped round the palace both at Knossos and Mallia and to whom belonged the chamber tombs of Mavro Spilio and Ayios Elias on the east slope of the Kairatos ravine facing the palace of Knossos and of Ayios Ioannes and Gypsadhes to the north and south. Though we have no means of judging whether they exercised their power in the name of the king or as free lords possessing free estates and owing only certain services to the court, we must imagine that the noble lords also resided in the villas scattered up and down the country, for example at Tylissos and Vathypetro. The relationship between city and palace at Gournia could be taken as typical. The lords of these small palaces can have discharged their duties only in the name of the king.

Marked changes in Cretan society in the direction of these harsher characteristics of later Bronze Age societies mentioned above[16] can be more firmly adduced from a wider range of evidence in the Late Minoan period and especially after the disastrous events of *c.*1450 BC. Some of them are discussed by Matz, for whom the Linear B documents show that the Achaeans of the mainland had taken over the control of Knossos in the course of the fifteenth century BC.[17] He stresses, surely correctly, that the importance attached to commerce may indicate a fundamental difference of the Minoan palace in its organization from its Near Eastern and Egyptian counterparts. Even the size and the number of the store-rooms in Crete are symptomatic, and so is the fact that they are grouped together in the basement. At Mari, Ugarit, Beyce-sultan and El-Amarna they are unobtrusive in comparison. A commercial purpose also was served by the highways which were constructed at the latest in the Late Palace Period. Lack of interest in pictures of battles and of warriors generally is remarkable. Weapons are rarely found in Cretan tombs before the Late Minoan II level, but common on the Mycenaean mainland. The introduction of the horse[18] into the island in the Late Minoan I period, brought with it new methods of warfare and new arms. The small shield, curved at the top but otherwise rectangular, which still occurred on seals of the Temple Repositories, was replaced by the figure-of-eight tower shield, which was a

Minoan invention,[19] and which presupposes that the warrior carrying it was brought to the battlefield by chariot. The boar's tusk helmet with cheek protector and plume came into use at the same time and the sword blade was refined and lengthened to form a rapier. The finest pieces from the Shaft Graves of Mycenae are considered to be Cretan products.[20]

Originally without cult images, Minoan religion underwent significant changes in the Late Palace Period, becoming, in the opinion of Matz, strongly influenced by the Oriental representations of gods. There were still no cult images, however, and no idols until after the destruction of the palaces.[21] The Mother Goddess was differently represented, appearing naked or clothed, with lions, griffins, birds or snakes accompanying her, and she sometimes carried a large shield. A male partner joined her, whose inspiration and prototypes are found in Syria and Asia Minor.

Matz insists on the assumption that peaceful relations between Crete and the mainland lasted throughout the seventeenth and sixteenth centuries BC, despite the cultural advance and growing strength of the Helladic powers. The wealth in gold apparent in the Shaft Graves at Mycenae cannot be explained as the result of looting in Crete, unless there is a clear reflection of such looting in the Minoan palaces. Nor can Minoan overlordship on the mainland be assumed.

Discussing the changes apparent in Crete after the disastrous events of c.1450 BC, Hood[22] writes that these changes suggest the presence of conquerors from the Greek mainland, which does not appear to have suffered at this time. The largest of the new houses built at Gournia, and a palace that arose on the ruins of the old one at Ayia Triada, may have been planned according to mainland ideas. New pottery shapes found at Knossos during the Late Minoan II period also seem to be derived from the mainland, while the contemporary 'Palace Style' is so different in spirit from what went before it that it could reflect the presence of foreign conquerors even if it was not actually introduced by them. A new type of tomb carved deep in the rock and approached by a long, narrow passage (or *dromos*) with inward sloping sides is first attested at Knossos in Late Minoan II and may have been evolved there under the influence of Egyptian or Cypriote models. The despatch of captive architects and artists to the mainland after the conquest could have been responsible for the rapid spread of this type of tomb and of other Cretan fashions there. The underground *tholos* tomb for royal burials was probably introduced from the mainland to Crete now. That on the Kefala ridge at Knossos has been assigned to an earlier period, but the Palace Style jars of which fragments were recovered in it suggest that it was first used for burials in Late Minoan II times. Graves of warriors accompanied by whole armouries of superb weapons are found during Late Minoan II in the region of Knossos and also on the Greek mainland. Although none of these warrior graves at Knossos can be assigned to a period before the conquest, it is just possible that the conquerors were of colonial or mixed origin, descendants of Cretans who had carved territories for themselves on the mainland. Against this view is the very prevalent assumption that the conquerors spoke and wrote a different language from the Cretans, and that this language was Greek.

Though the palaces in the east of Crete were not rebuilt, the palace of Knossos survived and was apparently modified to adapt it to foreign tastes and ritual. There may have been another centre of power in the south, where a new palace was built at Ayia Triada, and there was reoccupation at Phaistos, though whether as a palace or no is uncertain. There could have been a third palatial centre in the west at Khania, which could even have escaped the conquest of the rest of Crete. The fine decorated pottery here and throughout Crete during the Late Minoan IIIA period reflects Knossian fashions and may imply centralized government from a capital at Knossos. Colonies overseas apparently suffered disaster at the end of Late Minoan IB. The settlement at Kastri on Kythera was abandoned, that at Ayia Irini on Kea destroyed by fire.

Hood concludes that the centre and east of Crete, if not the whole island, could have been under direct Knossian rule after the disaster of c.1450 BC. Warrior graves, and military scenes painted on the walls of the palace at Knossos, imply, as Evans saw, the presence of a new and war-like dynasty. Great vases decorated in the 'Palace Style' suggest the wealth and splendour of the capital and the decline of taste. What he describes as an era of chill military grandeur at Knossos ended in catastrophe, since the palace was destroyed by fire (probably about 1375–1350 BC rather than later, in his opinion) and it was not rebuilt. This final destruction of the palace at Knossos, whatever its date, is likely to have been the work of enemies. The warrior graves and princely tombs in the Knossian region all appear to belong to a period before the destruction. It looks as if the destroyers came from abroad, and were probably once again from the mainland of Greece. They could have ravaged Crete and afterwards subjected it to their rule. Evidence suggests that the so-called Palace of Kadmos at Thebes on the mainland was destroyed about the same time as that at Knossos. Possibly both these great centres, one in the north and the other in the south, fell victims to the aggrandisement of Mycenae, which during the thirteenth century BC appears to have been the capital of an empire in control of most of the Aegean area.

For those who believe in a historical reality behind the Homeric poems it has not been difficult to believe that there were Greek-speaking people (whether they be called Achaeans, in Homeric terms, or Mycenaeans, perhaps more dubiously, in archaeological terms) in Crete in the late Bronze Age. A substantial portion of the second half of the *Odyssey* has a recurrent Cretan background. Odysseus explains to Penelope[23] that the Cretans have a mixture of languages, since there are Achaeans, Eteocretans, Kydonians, Dorians and Pelasgians in the land. There is also Knossos, a mighty city, where Minos used to be king for nine years, a familiar of mighty Zeus. Evans[24] considered that the name of Idomeneus, the Achaean leader, seems to point to early settlement

in the land round Ida. The account of the Achaean domination over central
Crete, according to the Catalogue of Ships in the *Iliad*[25] (which need not
exclude the participation of other Hellenic elements such as the Dorian) seems
to offer a real glimpse of historic conditions in Crete at the beginning of the
Iron Age. On the other hand, the endeavour to annex Minos and to thrust
back Achaean or Dorian dominion in Crete into the glorious days of Minoan
history was but part of a process of which other traces are perceptible. Following Beloch,[26] Evans found one such trace to be supplied by an interpolation
in the above cited passage of the *Odyssey*, arguing that the interpolator –
regardless of the order of composition or even of the most obvious grammatical
requirements – had broken into the sentence 'Ninety cities and among them
Knossos' to insert a brief summary of the later ethnography of the island –
including an allusion to the three Dorian tribes.

Lorimer,[27] however, considered that the Cretan entry in the Catalogue
contains nothing which suggests interpolation and found the Crete mirrored
in the Catalogue's selection from her hundred towns to be, as she thought, the
Crete of the Achaean occupation in Late Helladic III. The situation of these
seven towns of central Crete is the region which contains the road linking the
ports of her northern and southern coasts. That it was occupied by the
Achaeans is plain from the lines in the *Odyssey* (mentioning Achaeans, Eteocretans and Kydonians) which give the main division into centre, east and
west.[28] They are not necessarily interpolated as line 177 (which contains the
reference to Dorians and Pelasgians) certainly is, but even if they are, their
evidence is none the worse for that. The interpolation which Evans thought
had been recently exposed by Beloch, now commends less general recognition
than he thought inevitable once attention had been called to it, owing to later
advances in our knowledge. Though the mention of the Dorians does still
cause most difficulty, it would even so be wiser to withhold even partial
recognition of the supposed interpolation.[29] In any case no difficulty is presented now by the mention of the Achaeans and their dominion over central
Crete, whether or no the decipherment of Linear B as Greek is accepted.

Since 1939, intensive linguistic work on the linear scripts, renewed and
equally intensive archaeological exploration on the mainland and in Crete, the
discovery of another important Minoan palace at Zakro, the excavations on
the island of Thera (Santorini) conducted by Professor Marinatos, have all
combined to complicate and refine our knowledge of events in the last
centuries of the Bronze Age and of the possible causes for the collapse of
Minoan civilization. In the recent period the exploration of Bronze Age
Thera has produced spectacular results and spectacular theories.

When Pendlebury published his classic work on *The Archaeology of Crete* in
1939, he described what he called the downfall of the Minoan power in the
following terms.[30] The catastrophe which overtook the Cretan cities at the
end of Late Minoan IB (or Late Minoan II at Knossos) was practically universal.

Knossos, Phaistos, Ayia Triada, Gournia, Mochlos, Mallia and Zakro all showed traces of violent destruction accompanied by burning. At Palaikastro, Pseira, Nirou Khani, Tylissos and Plate there was distinct break in the habitation, though no trace of burning was found. This overwhelming disaster must have taken place at one and the same time and it had been attributed to a severe earthquake.[31] He objected that earthquakes in ancient times were not liable to cause fires, which are the result of gas and electricity. Moreover, woodwork had been more sparingly used at this time than before, and previous earthquakes, strong enough to fling great blocks of the Knossos Palace into the houses below, had neither caused fires, though the woodwork was more extensive, nor such a complete break and set-back in the culture. Instead, they had spurred fresh endeavours. At Knossos, the first damage an earthquake of such magnitude would have done would be to shake down the Domestic Quarters and particularly the Grand Staircase, where four floors at least were supported on wooden columns. A very mild earthquake in 1931 had snapped and shifted the upper part of a reinforced concrete column no less than 6cm.; but the Grand Staircase had remained complete and practically undamaged long enough for it to be silted up with debris and earth which preserved the landing on a level with the Central Court to within $1\frac{1}{2}$m. of its original position. The marks of fire are most obvious on the Western or official wing.

Pendlebury concluded that everything pointed to a deliberate sacking on the part of enemies of the most powerful cities in Crete. Considering the prosperity of the period, it was obvious that no mere Viking raid could have accomplished such destruction. It must have been a highly organized expedition with an avowed purpose. It was clear that this purpose was not to invade and colonize the island from the way in which the Minoan culture continues, albeit in a very minor key and without mainland influence until the very end of Late Minoan III. The object of this thorough and relentless destruction must have been purely political.

Two diametrically opposed theories to account for this were then discussed by Pendlebury. According to the first theory, brought to his notice by Professor Wace, the Minoan domination over the mainland had been grossly exaggerated. The mainland and Crete were separate, independent powers, the former merely adopting the outward trappings of a higher civilization. In Late Minoan II, however, the mainland was strong enough to establish control over Crete; and this would account for the emphatically mainland character of the 'Palace Style'. The destruction of the Cretan cities was in that case due to a nationalist revolt against the foreign 'harmosts'; and supporting evidence is that in the succeeding, Late Minoan III period, the civilization of Crete has little connexion with that of the mainland and indeed is rather markedly Minoan.

The second theory, adhered to by Pendlebury himself, would regard the Minoanization of the mainland as too pronounced to be the result of mere influence. The archaeological results supported legend, which admittedly only referred to the Saronic Gulf, that Crete had by the end of Late Minoan I–II established a considerable dominion over the rest of the Aegean, main dealings abroad being with Egypt and the Egyptian empire in Syria. Egyptian objects and influence were so rare on the mainland that it would seem as if that part of the Minoan empire was barred from direct traffic with Egypt. The presence of mainland vessels in Egypt was easily explained by the fact that they were more suitable for travelling and that therefore the tribute of the mainland to the Cretan overlord was sent direct to Egypt in payment of goods instead of being unloaded in Crete and reshipped thence. Though superficially Minoanized, the mainland still kept a good deal of its native culture and taste. The richest market in the world was barred and we might perhaps catch an echo of the attempt to find fresh markets in the story of Jason's voyage to the Black Sea. At all events, it was not hard to imagine the rebellious feelings of the dominions, and we might well imagine things getting to the pitch of a concerted effort on their part to smash the capital state of the empire.

The name of Theseus had always been associated, if not with the sack of Knossos, at least with the liberation of its subjects. As he had already suggested, the seven youths and seven maidens might have been the mainland quota for the bull-ring at Knossos – just the type of detail that would be remembered, the more so in that it might well have been the sentimental reason without which no purely commercial war can ever take place. No doubt the rape of Helen was a very good rallying cry when the Mycenaean Empire wished to break through to the Black Sea trade which Troy was keeping for itself.

And in the last decade of the fifteenth century on a spring day, when a strong south wind was blowing which carried the flames of the burning beams almost horizontally northwards, Knossos fell. The final scene took place in the most dramatic room ever excavated – the Throne Room – which had been found in a state of complete confusion. A great oil jar lay overturned in one corner, ritual vessels were in the act of being used when the disaster came. It looked as if the king had been hurried there to undergo too late some last ceremony in the hopes of saving the people. Crete had fallen and henceforward she was to · be a mere satellite of the world centring round Greece, gradually drawing nearer until she was absorbed in the general Hellenic culture which she herself had done so much to found.

Some sites such as Pseira, Mochlos and Nirou Khani remained deserted. Other sites were re-occupied but on a much smaller scale. With the destruction of the great centres and palaces the concentration of power ceased and perhaps the ruling caste was wiped out.

As we have seen, during his excavation of the Palace of Minos from 1900–05, Evans had discovered a vast quantity of Linear B clay tablets and seal impressions, preserved by hardening in the fires of destruction dated by him to *c.*1400 BC. A few examples of the same script were also found at Thebes and elsewhere in mainland Greece. In 1939 during excavations at Messenian Pylos Blegen discovered over 500 inscribed Linear B tablets in a room of the Mycenaean palace, destroyed *c.*1200 BC. Since 1945 similar tablets have been found elsewhere on the mainland, at Mycenae, Tiryns and Thebes. Discrepancy in the dating of the destructions at Knossos and Pylos gave rise to doubts whether the excavators had made mistakes in their stratigraphy. In 1960 Palmer offered the suggestion that the Knossos palace was finally destroyed *c.*1150 BC, on the assumption that the Greek emerging by the decipherment from the Linear B tablets at Knossos showed later forms than the Greek of those from Pylos on the mainland *c.*1200 BC. Other scholars who accepted the decipherment nevertheless disagreed with this assumption.

By 1971 Sinclair Hood argued, despite much controversy as to what pottery Evans found with the tablets and disagreement about the date of some of it, that it should be possible to date the final destruction of the palace at Knossos by means of the pottery.[32] The three main groups of pottery involved included: (a) a small group of fine decorated vases from the southern edge of the palace area, assignable to Late Minoan IIIB (*c.*1300–1200 BC); (b) a quantity of fine decorated ware, studied by Popham and assignable to Late Minoan IIIA2, and perhaps to an early phase of it *c.*1375 BC, or not much later; (c) a mass of plain ware, and a number of vases (notably large storage stirrup-jars) with comparatively simple decoration – the pottery of this last group being crucial. This had been assigned by Evans to a period of reoccupation of the palace site after the final destruction of the palace as such. However, Palmer, after his investigations, had argued that this pottery was actually found with the clay tablets and seal impressions in the burnt ruins of the final destruction of the palace. Though persuaded that Palmer was right in this conclusion, he disagreed with the usually accepted date of Late Minoan IIIB for this group of pottery and believed it to be earlier and contemporary with the fine decorated ware assignable to Late Minoan IIIA2. On this view the vases of Group (c) were mainly the plain and coarse wares which were in use alongside the fine decorated table wares of group (b) in the Knossos palace at the time of its final destruction in Late Minoan IIIA2, *c.*1375 BC or not much later. In agreement with Boardman he would assign the vases of group (a), admittedly Late Minoan IIIB in date, to some kind of reoccupation in a limited area on the southern edge of the palace site after the final destruction of the palace, the reoccupation perhaps reflecting a religious cult which continued into Classical Greek times.

The discoveries made on Thera under Marinatos since 1967 promoted speculation of a different kind,[33] for a time preoccupied with possible connections between three major topics. Firstly, the violent destruction of the Minoan civilization; secondly, an equally violent eruption of the volcanic island of Thera (Santorini); thirdly, the subsequent chance of discovering new reality behind the legend of the lost civilization of Atlantis.

The first clear proof of Bronze Age settlements on Thera emerged in the 1860s as the result of quarrying operations caused by the building of the Suez Canal. Pumice dust mixed with lime in the proportion of 3 to 1 made a durable cement, resistant to seawater, for harbour installations at Port Said. Great quantities of pumice were removed by the Suez Canal Company from Thera's inexhaustible supply at points on the interior of the bay north of Akrotiri, near Cape Tinos on north-east Therasia, and over almost all the extent of the cliffs on the south of Therasia. In places on the south face of Therasia the lower limit of the pumice was indicated by numerous stone blocks, in fact the tops of ancient walls.

A volcanic eruption which started in January 1866 drew the attention of the scientific world to Thera in rather a different way. Some indications of pre-historic dwellings were noticed below the deposits of an ancient eruption and serious excavations here started in 1867. The results of these excavations were published (in the form of a treatise in Latin) in 1874 by the French archaeologist Mammet. Two years earlier, Louis Figuier expressed the opinion that Plato's Atlantis was an island in the Aegean archipelago submerged by geological convulsion, an island which could only be Santorini, part of it sunk into the sea and the remainder covered with a thick layer of pumice. He further suggested that towns and villages were buried under this layer just as Pompeii and Herculaneum had been buried in the volcanic ash from the eruption of Vesuvius in AD 79. The speculations were overshadowed by the dramatic excavations by Schliemann at Mycenae and his claim to have found the graves of King Agamemnon and his companions, done to death by Klytemnestra on their return from the Trojan War.

Then, on 19 February 1909, writing anonymously in *The Times*, K.T. Frost published a first report of his theory that Plato's Atlantis story was an account of the destruction of Minoan Crete preserved in Egyptian records. A similar suggestion was made in 1917 by D.A. Mackenzie; and the American geographer E.S. Balch advanced arguments on the same lines before the American Geographical Society. Apart from a short campaign by Zahn, however, no further work was done to increase our factual knowledge of Bronze Age Thera until 1967. The immense catastrophe of the volcanic explosion could have formed the basis of truth behind the story which (if not invented by Plato) the Athenian Solon was told by priests in Egypt some 800 years later about the lost Atlantis. However that may be, it is certainly true, as Luce pointed out in his scholarly and judicious account of the subject, that the suggestion that Atlantis reflected Minoan Crete was not made, and could not have been made, until the archaeological discoveries of this century revealed once more the achievements of Minoan art and technology.

The eruption of Thera has been frequently compared with the eruption of the island of Krakatoa, between Java and Sumatra, in 1883. As a result of the eruption the discharge of pumice caused the formation of the existing sea-filled crater. The great rush of water would have stirred up great waves (*tsunamis*) to spread outward and burst down upon the neighbouring coasts – and Crete is only some 120km. distant to the south. The single island of Thera became a group of three, subsequently increased to five as the result of further volcanic explosion in Roman and more recent times.

It has been argued by Pomerance[34] that this explosion took place around 1200 BC, which would explain the wide areas of disaster around the Aegean and eastern Mediterranean at the time. This dating and explanation, however, is contrary to the views of most archaeologists concerned with the problem. It seems rather[35] that the explosion occurred *c.*1500 BC and buried the Cretan settlements on Thera in huge mounds of pumice. Apparently the settlements were wrecked by an earthquake shortly before the eruption, when most of the inhabitants had time to escape into the open, if not from the island, taking their most valuable possessions with them. The evidence suggests three stages of the eruption in the course of a few weeks or months. Great damage could have been inflicted on towns and settlements in Crete. However, Hood has argued that Crete survived the shock of the eruption, damage to towns, palaces and country houses being quickly repaired. Though there are symptoms that all was not well, Cretan influence in the Aegean islands and on the mainland was at its zenith. In his view, which confirms that of the early excavations of various sites in Crete, the island was devastated by war in the Late Minoan IB period, a generation or so after the eruption of Thera. All the flourishing towns, in the east, centre and south of the island were destroyed. Some, including Zakro, Mochlos and Pseira, were never re-occupied. Most were ravaged by fire. Only at Knossos was the damage limited, perhaps because the city and palace were spared by conquerors anxious to use them.

Part 3

DORIAN ARISTOCRACY

10

PRELUDE TO THE IRON AGE

The centuries between 1100 and 800 BC are conventionally known as the Greek Dark Age. The term 'dark age' should not really be the subject of learned debate. It ought to mean quite simply that we know little or nothing about events throughout its duration. A sceptic might reasonably claim to wonder why, for various reasons, the term continues to be used without qualification with reference to the centuries which mark the termination of the Bronze Age and the beginnings of recorded Greek history in the proper sense. For there are immensely long earlier periods in Greek prehistory, the Neolithic for example, which are equally dark or, from another point of view, continuously less obscure, in terms of the quantity and the interpretation of their surviving artefacts and monuments.

Of course the artefacts and monuments of the Bronze Age are, by comparison with the periods which precede and follow it, remarkable and often quite spectacular. We also possess invaluable written records from the Bronze Age, whose meaning remains in part unknown, in part obscure or debatable. On the other hand, the centuries of the Greek Dark Age are devoid, so far as we at present know, of contemporary written records. Archaeologists, however, do not hesitate to describe these centuries, on the fundamental basis of pottery classification, as Protogeometric and Geometric, in broad terms: and archaeologists are continually refining their techniques and sharpening their definitions. The recovery of the Bronze Age is entirely due to archaeological endeavour, in different degrees learned, lucky or inspired. It is true that the Bronze Age was there waiting to be recovered. So is the so-called Greek Dark Age, whose duration, by comparison with earlier massive periods of once supposed total darkness, is relatively brief. This consideration encourages optimism. A dark age is a challenge to the investigator to throw light into obscure places; and those few vital and baffling centuries are now less obscure than they were even a few years ago, as the result of detailed and cautious archaeological investigation.[1] Such investigation has to take account of great quantities of new and diverse evidence.[2]

The Mycenaean or Achaean supremacy, after the decline of Minoan civilization, was relatively short-lived. Recalled for posterity in the epics of

Homer, a constant source of lore for later Greek mythology and literature, the brief culmination and decline of this age too must be regarded as part of the general upheaval which terminated the Aegean Bronze Age in the later centuries of the second millennium BC. We are here concerned only with the repercussions of these momentous but still obscure events so far as they can be detected in Crete. Once more Crete becomes significant and in a peculiar kind of way as much a focus of attention for the modern archaeologist as for the brilliant pioneers of Greek historiography.

Close and careful study of a collection of pottery stored in the Iraklion Museum by M.R. Popham admirably exemplifies the methods by which cautious advances towards some partial knowledge of the period has to be recovered.[3] Though there was insufficient material as yet to attempt a convincing historical reconstruction of events generally in Crete in the latter part of the Late Minoan III period, two suggestive facts were established as a result of the examination of this material.[4] Firstly, Crete was under some serious threat towards the end of the Late Minoan IIIB period, which led to the abandonment of settlements at Gournia, Palaikastro, Knossos and Mallia, the last of which may have been destroyed by fire. Though it is not clear what was happening at other major centres such as Episkopi in east Crete, and Phaistos and Ayia Triada, several cemeteries of the island do not continue beyond the IIIB period. It is difficult to avoid associating these events in some general way with happenings elsewhere in the Mediterranean, such as the preparations for siege and defence, the destruction of several centres in Greece and the destruction of towns in Cyprus, the overrunning of Syria and Palestine and the attacks on Egypt.

Secondly, a new and strong Mycenaean influence of early IIIc character later becomes evident in the pottery of Crete. Though much remains Minoan, this pottery is in some cases a direct imitation of Mycenaean wares. The most likely meaning is that there had been a settlement of Mycenaeans in the island, possibly peaceful, with resulting formation of mixed communities. About this time or soon afterwards settlements appear on sites unoccupied during the previous period, at Kastri, Vrokastro, Erganos, Mouliana, and elsewhere. It is not certain when Phaistos and Ayia Triada were reoccupied but pottery from the palace at Phaistos indicates occupation by squatters; and mainland type figurines on both sites are strong indications of the presence of Mycenaeans among the inhabitants. It is reasonable to connect this evidence of Mycenaean arrivals in Crete with the arrival of settlers at various places in Cyprus who used pottery of Mycenaean sub IIIB and early IIIc style. There is also a marked Cretan influence on Rhodian and mainland pottery in the early IIIc period. There was continuing Mycenaean influence in Crete during the later stages of IIIc and probably one more influx of Mycenaeans at least, occurring after the period of the sherd material which formed the basis of this particular study.[5]

Popham's detailed analysis is a rewarding example of the kind of work that has to be done in order to gain further insights into the possible course of events in the later Bronze Age, work which can only be done by means of cautious and skilled archaeological investigation. Yet, no matter how refined and sophisticated its techniques, archaeology must operate within the limitations imposed by the nature of its operations – the discovery, excavation and ordered classification of sites, artefacts and monuments – functioning as an auxiliary science of history in the broadest sense.

In this connection it should be borne in mind that the term Mycenaean (with the associated concepts of a 'Mycenaean civilization' or even a 'Mycenaean empire'), has to be treated with considerable reserve, except in strictly archaeological contexts. With regard to the hierarchical stratification of this society, ruled by a warrior class under chieftains or kings, accompanied, after 1400 (in most places not until about 1300), by a dramatic shift from concentration on impressive burial-chambers to the erection of a number of palace-fortresses, M.I. Finley has rightly made the following observations. Such places as Tiryns and Mycenae in the western Peloponnese, the Acropolis in Athens, Thebes and Gla in Boeotia, Iolkos in Thessaly, now looked more like medieval fortress-towns than like the open, agglutinative Cretan complexes. Though there was still cell-like growth, the nucleus was the so-called *megaron* type of house, consisting of a columned fore-porch or vestibule, a long main room and usually a store-room behind. Mycenaean Greece was divided into a number of petty bureaucratic states, with a warrior aristocracy, a high level of craftsmanship, extensive foreign trade in necessities (metals) and luxuries, and a permanent condition of armed neutrality at best in their relations with each other, and perhaps at times with their subjects. Nothing points to an overall authority on the part of Mycenae. That notion, he adds, rests wholly on the Homeric poems, in which Agamemnon is commander-in-chief of a coalition army on an expedition against Troy, in which his authority is easily flouted. The contemporary evidence argues that, whatever the authority of the ruler of Mycenae over the Argolid may have been, Pylos owed him nothing, nor Thebes or Iolkos.[6]

If that notion does rest wholly on the Homeric poems, it is patently false in the sense that the members of the coalition army which went to Troy have three names in the epic poems, namely, Achaioi, Danaoi and Argeioi. The name Argeioi (Argives) obviously applies to the people of Argos or of the Argolid, which was heavily populated in the Late Bronze Age. The Danaoi (Danaans) were called after Danaos, who came to Argos from Egypt. The name of the Achaioi (Achaeans) is fairly certainly historical. For there is a large measure of scholarly agreement that the kingdom of Achchiyawa, referred to in Hittite documents of the late fourteenth and thirteenth centuries BC, belonged to the Achaeans. These Achaeans were probably not mainlanders, but inhabitants of an independent kingdom nearer Hittite lands, perhaps, as some believe, in Rhodes. It is also quite likely that the Achaeans were known as such to the contemporary Egyptians, on the evidence of a document from the reign of the pharaoh Merneptah, in the late thirteenth century BC.

In the *Iliad*, the Achaeans are conventionally 'well-greaved', a description which is appropriate to the actual bronze body-armour of Greek warriors in the fourteenth and thirteenth centuries BC, but not between *c*.1100 and the eighth century BC.[7] For the Achaeans of the *Iliad* are even more frequently described by the conventional epithet of 'bronze-shirted'. This same epithet is applied twice to the Argives and once to the Cretans under Idomeneus[8] – the leader of that impressive contingent of 80 ships in a passage of the *Iliad* which lends support to the view of an occupation of central Crete by Achaeans who could have introduced Greek speech.[9] The Doric speech of Argolis and Laconia, areas once occupied by Achaeans, had Arcadic forms similar to those which underlie the Doric of Crete, Rhodes and Pamphylia, where Achaeans had also preceded Dorians; and the Greek of Cyprus, not settled by Dorians, is very much the same dialect as Arcadic. This was presumably the pre-Doric spoken language of most of the Peloponnese in later prehistoric times.[10]

The second half of the *Odyssey* has a recurrent theme of a wandering Cretan which may be based on something more substantial than mere fiction.[11] Though the details of this story vary, the essentials remain the same. Odysseus, arrived home in Ithaca, in disguise, pretends to be a prominent Cretan chieftain, in some kind of relationship with, though subordinate to, Idomeneus. It can be gathered from this tale that raiding and piracy are normal methods of supplementing wealth derived from landed estates. Conditions in Crete are generally unsettled, and the island is a prey to dissensions. An adventurer overseas can be kidnapped and enslaved, or he may be lucky and make his fortune. The hero of the tale has had a lot of practice in raiding before the Trojan War. He may have been quite typical of the sort of determined adventurer we may envisage as common enough of the period of the Aegean-sea-raiders who were attacking Egypt and other places roughly round about the time of the Trojan War.

In its first version[12] the story is told by Odysseus to Eumaios the swineherd, who had himself been kidnapped from his father's palace and subsequently been sold to Laertes, father of Odysseus.[13] Odysseus says that he is a Cretan, son of a rich man and a concubine. Kastor, son of Hylax, was his father and held him in the same esteem as his many other, legitimate, sons. After the father's death, the sons divided up the estate by lot among themselves and gave only a modest portion to the illegitimate son. However, he married into a well-endowed family by reason of his courage and intelligence. He had not been fond of work nor of the home-life that fosters a fine family. His real prowess revealed itself in warfare. His real love was for ships and battles, javelins and arrows – the baneful things that made others tremble. He had commanded no less than nine overseas expeditions even before the Achaeans went to Troy; and his estate profited from the large amount of booty he acquired in this way. Feared and respected among the Cretans, when the Trojan War occurred, he was persuaded, along with Idomeneus, to lead the Cretan contingent. After Troy was sacked, he returned to Crete, but after a brief month of domestic pleasures, he equipped a fleet to sail to Egypt. When he arrived, his men began to plunder the farms, kill the men and carry off the women and children before he could make his planned reconnaissance. As a result, the alarm was raised in the neighbouring city and his force was over-come, many of his men killed, the others enslaved. He himself surrendered and his life was spared. He stayed for seven years among the Egyptians and gained much wealth from them. He then became acquainted with a Phoen-ician who persuaded him to sail home with him.

After a year in Phoenicia, his companion took him on a ship for Libya, ostensibly in partnership but in reality with the intention of selling him for a good sum. The plot was spoilt by a storm which wrecked the ship after they had passed by Crete. The Cretan was the sole survivor and was cast up on the coast of Thesprotia, where he was given hospitality by the king who later sent him off in a ship for Doulikhion, with instructions to the crew to care for him and escort him to the king of Doulikhion. However, the crew planned to enslave him and, arriving at Ithaca, they tied up their prisoner while they left the ship to eat a meal on the beach. He managed to get free, swim ashore and lie hidden until the crew abandoned their search for him.

The essential features are presented at greater length when Penelope urges her still disguised husband to explain about himself in more detail.[14] He begins this version by explaining how Crete is 'fair and fertile, sea-girt. Therein are many men, countless men, and 90 cities. They have a mixture of languages. For there are Achaeans, stout-hearted Eteocretans, Kydonians, Dorians with their three tribes, god-like Pelasgians.'[15] The passage helps us to establish a case for supposing that the mixed population of Crete could have included, by the onset of the twelfth century BC, Achaeans, Eteocretans, Kydonians and Pelasgians.[16] The Homeric poems present us with a view of pre-Dorian Greece and Dorians exist alongside Achaeans only in Crete. If we suppose that they are named in this passage as the result of interpolation in the text in the course of later transmission, we can remove a difficulty in the cause of simple con-sistency. However, there is independent ancient authority for supposing that a group of Dorians had followed Achaeans into Crete a century or so before they spread over the mainland areas in large numbers.[17]

If this passage of the *Odyssey* is relevant to the ethnography of Crete in the closing phases of the Bronze Age (rather than to a later period of the Iron Age), it may support the impression conveyed in a tradition preserved by Herodo-tos[18] that the period was indeed one of disturbance and of an intermingling of peoples, resulting in the dominance over other elements of the population of Greek-speakers who had formerly constituted a minority in Mycenaean times as that form of the language known as Doric became widespread throughout the island.[19] According to this tradition, Minos went off to Sicily in search of Daidalos and consequently died a violent death. After a time, warned by some god or other, the Cretans, with the exception of the Polichnites and the Praisians, made a great expedition to Sicily, besieged Kamikos for five years, then gave up the attempt and returned homeward. When they reached Iapygia their fleet was wrecked by a storm and, unable to reach Crete, they settled in the Italian mainland, founded the town of Hyria and changed their name to Messapian Iapygians. According to Praisian (that is to say Eteocretan) tradition, people of various nations now flocked to Crete, which had been stripped of its inhabitants, none in such numbers as the Greeks. Three generations after Minos died the Trojan War occurred, in which the Cretans were not the least distinguished of the supporters of Menelaos. When they did return from Troy, they were smitten by famine and pestilence which destroyed men and cattle. Crete was stripped of inhabitants for a second time. A remnant who survived formed, along with fresh settlers, the third Cretan population of the island. By this third population Herodotos presumably had the Dorians in mind.

Some insight into unsettled conditions in the twelfth century BC is obtained from the so-called cities of refuge built on commanding heights such as Vrokastro, Kavousi and especially Karphi founded round about 1150 BC, in a desolate spot high away from the plain of Lasithi.[20] After about 800 BC such places had been abandoned if they were inaccessible, or developed into city-states if their situation was more congenial. In this latter category belongs a city which is known by the name of the modern village of Prinias, which is

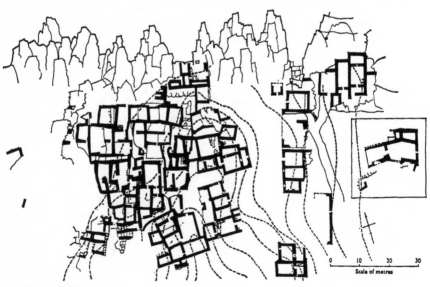

16   Plan of Karphi

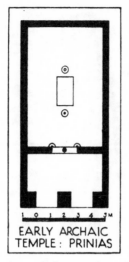

EARLY ARCHAIC
TEMPLE : PRINIAS

17   Early archaic temple at Prinias

near to the ancient site. The centre of this site was a hill first occupied, perhaps as a typical refuge area, in Late Minoan III times. Other such important cities are Lato and Axos.

The hill on which Prinias was sited overlooks the road from Iraklion to the plain of Messara. The site was not abandoned in the archaic period. One of the two temples excavated there dates to round about the middle of the seventh century BC, and it has characteristics rather more reminiscent of the small shrines of the Late Minoan III period than of the archaic Greek temple. The site of Lato in east Crete exhibits interesting features of an early Iron Age city. The site presumably commanded the nearby plain of Lakonia and the coastal routes by the eighth century BC; and it had a secondary harbour town, Lato pros Kamara ('Lato-at-the-Arch'), modern Ayios Nikolaos. This town had a steep double acropolis, an *agora* (market-place) and a *prytaneion* (town-hall) approached by a flight of steps, a temple and other public buildings. These formed albeit on a limited scale the centre of the city. Not far to the north of Lato was Dreros, yet another city of the archaic period, with the same typical features of *agora, prytaneion* and temple, its remains dating as far back as the eighth century BC.[21]

More settled conditions had begun to prevail in Crete by the eighth century BC. The new political form of organization was the city-state, associated with the spread of Dorian aristocratic ordering of society and the replacement of bronze by iron as the typical metal of the historical age for tools and weapons. Nevertheless fine metallurgical work continued to be executed in bronze and artistic achievement in bronze of the archaic period, perpetuating the legacy of an old tradition, is outstanding. In economic terms the new metal was of

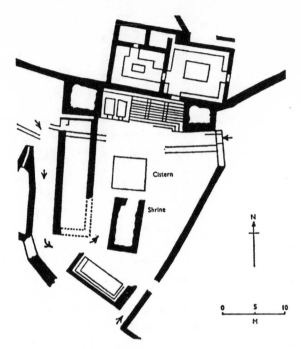

18   Town centre of Lato

much more general practical value in the form of axes, hammers, knives, sickles and ploughshares. Domestic industry, closely associated with agricultural work, enabled craftsmen's products to benefit far more. A balanced relation between industry and agriculture could have promoted more self-sufficiency among village producers. As the city-state economy became more stable, a wider market was re-established but in a new form, corresponding with the new stage of commodity production based on the techniques of iron-working.[22]

There had been a fairly rapid development of iron-working in Iran, Transcaucasia, Syria and Palestine between 1200 and 1000 BC, and it was then adopted in Cyprus, Caucasia and Crete. The introduction of iron-working, as Desborough has properly emphasized in his survey of metals in the Dark Ages[23] was a metallurgical event of the first magnitude, not only for Greece and the Aegean but for the world as a whole. Iron, as he points out, was a precious metal until about 1200 BC, because knowledge of iron-working had hitherto been a closely-guarded secret, confined to the smiths of the region of Kizzuwatna, a province of the Hittite empire probably situated in the southeast corner of Asia Minor; and it was the collapse of the Hittite empire that led to the general diffusion of iron-working. The diffusion was bound to take time. The techniques were unfamiliar, involving skills beyond those of the bronzesmith, though the first stage of the process, heating the ore to a certain temperature, would present no difficulty. What was new was the next vital stage of carburization, by which the metal was hardened. So too were the processes of quenching the carburized metal and of tempering it by reheating and cooling. Both of these processes required much experience of selecting the correct temperature. The technique once mastered, a plentiful supply of iron ore, accompanied by hardness of the finished article, meant that iron became a utilitarian metal, an alternative or an addition to bronze. This does not imply that iron was necessarily superior to bronze, for some bronze tools and weapons were harder than those made of iron.

Iron-working was introduced into the Aegean from the east, with Cyprus as the immediate source. Here iron objects have been found which have been dated to the thirteenth century and later. Iron weapons, knives and ornaments, made in the east Mediterranean, were exported to the Aegean in the latter part of the twelfth century and the early part of the eleventh century BC. What Desborough describes as the momentous stage involving the actual trans-mission of the technique, and also involving the recognition of iron deposits in Greece itself, did not take place until near the end of the early Dark Ages. It was limited to Crete for a while, presumably also the inhabited regions of the Dodecanese and the central Aegean, certainly the Argolid, Athens and Lef-kandi in Euboea. The establishment of an iron industry in these areas was the dominant feature of the eleventh century BC so far as useful metals were concerned; and locally accessible iron deposits would have been of particular advantage.

In the following stage, which may continue into the second half of the tenth century BC, the manufacture of iron artefacts was further extended, in bulk and slightly in area, but what now catches the attention is the rarity of objects made of bronze. This rarity is so pronounced that Snodgrass[24] was led to conclude that there had been a serious shortage of bronze over most of Greece and the Aegean. If proved, this interesting hypothesis would mean that most areas would have been isolated from Cyprus, the source of bronze.

What is of interest for the purposes of this chapter is that Crete seems definitely to have been a centre, to a degree perhaps hitherto unacknowledged, of development of the new metallurgical techniques. It also seems safe to conclude that, if there were temporary shortage of bronze, the new technique was developed by Cretan craftsmen to supplement older techniques, including bronze working, which certainly did later continue to flourish. The implica-tions for the development of the Cretan city-states on a new economic basis cannot be more accurately assessed until we know more about Cretan iron working in the earlier Dark Ages.

11

LANGUAGE AND THE ALPHABET

The passage of the *Odyssey* discussed in the last chapter,[1] describing Crete as an island of 90 cities and with a mixture of tongues, certainly so far as Crete is concerned, indicates that Greek was not the only language prevalent in Mycenaean times. Commenting on this passage, Strabo cited the authority of the historian Staphylos of Naukratis for saying that the Dorians occupied the part of Crete towards the east, the Kydonians the western part, the Eteocretans the southern; and that to the Eteocretans belonged the town of Praisos, where there was the temple of Diktaian Zeus. The other peoples, since they were more powerful, dwelt in the plains. It was likely that the Eteocretans and the Kydonians were autochthonous, that is to say, indigenous peoples and that the others, that is to say, the Dorians, were foreigners who, according to Andron (a fourth-century BC writer on genealogical relationships between Greek tribes and cities), came from Thessaly, from the country which in earlier times was called Doris.[2] From this citation of Andron, it may be inferred that there was a tradition of a Dorian community or communities, perhaps quite small, in the extreme east of the island, beyond Praisos.

We may also infer from Strabo's commentary that the Eteocretans represented surviving elements of earlier pre-Greek inhabitants. The town of Praisos, in the centre of the eastern tip of the island, which belonged to them, preserved an ancient language at least until the third century BC. In fact, six or seven inscriptions have survived from Praisos in three of which at least – one of the sixth, one of the fourth, and one of the third century BC – this 'Eteocretan' language is written in the Greek alphabet.[3] Some traces of this still undeciphered language have been detected in two other places on the island. A decipherment of these texts would give us valuable information of a non-Greek language perhaps by no means restricted to Crete. Herodotos makes it clear that the Praisians had close connections with the old Minoan population;[4] and they could represent a surviving testimony into historical times of a Cretan affinity with Asia Minor so characteristic of Cretan Bronze Age institutions.[5]

When overseas contacts were renewed in the early archaic period, the establishment of the town and trading centre of Al Mina, at the mouth of the

Orontes in North Syria, probably in the later ninth century BC, apparently played a major part in Greek intercourse with the Eastern Mediterranean.[6] There is evidence that Crete was early to the fore in receiving technical innovations suggesting instruction by immigrant craftsmen. Boardman observes that the late ninth century saw the arrival in Knossos of metalsmiths skilled in working gold filigree and granulation, and in cutting hard stones – techniques forgotten in Greece since the Bronze Age. North Syrian metalworkers reached Crete perhaps as early as the Knossos goldsmiths and established a strong tradition for beaten metal work, which in its beginnings is quite oriental but becomes progressively more hellenized.[7]

Later, during the first half of the seventh century, sites in south central Crete (notably Afrati) yield several objects in clay which imitate North Syrian objects in other materials. The possibility that such finds indicate the arrival of foreigners who were to some extent able to impose their taste on local studios may be supported by the fact that many cremation burials at Afrati are subsequently of a distinctive type, with urns set on dishes and covered by inverted pots, matched closely only in the Iron Age cemetery of Carchemish on the Euphrates. Boardman suggests further that it is perhaps right to associate with this immigration the evidence of authors and epigraphy which places the first codification of laws in Greece in Crete and in this period, since written laws were regular in the east and there is much in Greek law which recalls the east.[8]

This remarkable early development of Cretan epigraphy and of the codification of law depended upon another technical borrowing from the east which must be counted among the supreme achievements of civilized man. Alphabetic writing has taken different forms in different parts of the world, but has not significantly changed in its essentials. The various scripts which have used the alphabet owe their ultimate origin to a group of Semitic alphabets current in the Near East in the latter half of the second millennium BC. The European alphabets derived from the Greek, whose model was the North Semitic script. Phoenician origin is indicated by the names of the letters in the Greek alphabet, which derive from Phoenician names, and also by the letter-forms which often

19   The Greek alphabet as represented in the Gortyn Code

resemble Phoenician originals. Some Greek letters indeed correspond with Phoenician letters of the tenth century BC or earlier, but some do not appear in Phoenician inscriptions until the ninth century. Semitic languages make extensive use of vowel gradation (cf. English *sing, sang, sung, song*) enabling a reader readily to supply vowels from the context. Since Greek needed vowel signs, some Phoenician signs which represented consonants not existing in Greek were used for vowels.

Quite the darkest mystery of the Dark Ages is the absence of written records between the latest Bronze Age linear script evidence and the earliest examples of alphabetic writing in the eighth century BC. We cannot exclude the possibility that writing continued to be done on such perishable materials as leather, wood or papyrus, but this is a matter of conjecture. The habit of inscribing a clumsy syllabary on clay tablets should, in theory, be a suggestive aid to the habit of painting simple letters on clay pots. Yet this not very difficult technical innovation appears, in the present state of the evidence, to have taken several centuries to accomplish. The earliest surviving Greek inscription appears to be on an Attic vase of *c.*720 BC attesting that this shall be 'the prize of the dancer who dances more gaily than others' – at least a most auspicious proclamation of a civilized technique of communication. This is not an isolated instance of the practice, for we now have various examples of graffiti on pots from the late eighth century BC; and there is a verse inscription, which could be even a little earlier in its date than the Attic vase, from the Euboean colony of Pithekoussai on the island of Ischia.[9] Crete, Rhodes and Al Mina have all been suggested as candidates for the birth place of the Greek alphabet. This was being used by the Phrygians before the end of the eighth century BC, and it may be that they found it in use at Al Mina or some other place on the Syrian or Cilician coast.[10] The important archaic inscription from Crete published in 1970[11] does perhaps to some extent improve the claim for a Cretan origin.

However that may be, the new Greek alphabet, as it became established during the course of the Greek colonial expansion of the eighth and seventh centuries BC, acquired a variety of forms in different places,[12] falling into the two principal groups of East and West Greek; and the subsequent standard form was derived from the Attic, included in the East Greek group. The Greeks of Cyprus were exceptional in the sense that they continued to make use of a pre-alphabetic script, known as the Cypriot syllabary, until as late as the third century BC. This peculiarity may be compared with the interesting survival of the Eteocretan language in Greek letters which has been noticed already.

In the borrowing from the East which is manifested in Crete in the early period of the new Iron Age, Cyprus played a vital part. Commenting on this intermediary role, Boardman has pointed out that all the 'orientalizing' objects or ideas which Crete accepted during the Dark Ages are either derived directly from Cyprus, or involve the type of object which was as much at home in Cyprus as on the eastern mainland. Even in what he describes as the depressed period following the end of the Bronze Age, when iron was still barely known and the artist was still working in a Minoan-Mycenaean tradition, there are signs of continued relations between these two islands, which had been among the most important centres of the Late Mycenaean world. The evidence lies mainly in the choice of pottery decoration and some vase shapes, but iron spits of a Cypriot type appear in a tenth century BC burial at Knossos, and the most important bronze objects were openwork vase stands, largely composed of rods bent into volute patterns.[12]

There are interesting links of another kind, more directly arising from linguistic evidence and also serving to remind us that the palace age of main-land Greece in the later Bronze Age was a period of overseas trading and settlement, in Cyprus as well as Egypt and Rhodes. We have seen that in the Cretan entry in the Catalogue of Ships in the *Iliad* which gives the impressive total of 80 ships under Idomeneus and Meriones, seven Cretan towns are specifically mentioned – Knossos, Gortyn, Lyktos, Miletos, Lykastos, Phaistos and Rhytion – all from the centre of the island, chief area, presumably, of Achaean occupation and of early Greek speech.[13]

The Cretan Zeus Welkhanos was apparently a survival, as the male partner in a sacred marriage with a Mother-goddess, of a Minoan youth-god of fertility.[14] The temple of Zeus Welkhanos was built upon the ruins of the palace of Ayia Triada.[15] The month-name and spring festival of the god, the Welkhania, is known to us from inscriptions at Gortyn, Lyttos and Knossos.[16] The cult was also conceivably known in Cyprus.[17] The priest-kings of Cyprus, the Kinyradai, claimed descent in the male line from Teukros, the Achaean chieftain, and legend said that he married a daughter of Kinyras, priest of Aphrodite.[18] The Achaean connections of the family are recalled by Homer; and their palace was at Paphos, the home of Aphrodite and the site of one of her chief temples.[19] The royal tombs were nearby and the family had a pre-rogative right to the priesthood.[20] The cults of Aphrodite are relatively few and her history is by no means easy to recover. However, it may be assumed that she probably originated as an Oriental fertility-goddess. Significantly the dove is an attribute common to the Minoan goddess and to Aphrodite;[21] but if we look for evidence of her westward transmission through Crete, there is no really firm evidence among the cities of western Crete,[22] and even in eastern Crete there is evidence relating only to Hierapytna in Hellenistic times.[23] Once more, the cities of central Crete provide us with firmer indica-tions. At Knossos, for example, there was apparently a cult of Ares and Aphrodite in the mid-fifth century BC, and Aphrodite is mentioned in the Drerian oath of the late third or early second century BC.[24] The city of Istron, like Knossos, perhaps had a cult of Ares and Aphrodite.[25] At Lato, Aphrodite had an old temple on the borders of Lato and Olous, and a new temple was built in Hellenistic times.[26] Several statues of Aphrodite have been discovered at Gortyn, and there is an invocation (perhaps along with Ares) in oaths appended to the treaty of the Gortynians and Hierapytnians with the Priansians in the second century BC.[27] At Phaistos Aphrodite was known as Skotia ('The Dark One').[28]

The Greek traditions which concern Achaean settlements overseas in the eastern Mediterranean are confused. This confusion, however, should not provoke undue scepticism because, in itself, this testifies to the independence of the traditions, which do point to a genuine affinity between the scattered Teukroi of Troy, Attica, Salamis, Cilicia, Crete and Cyprus.[29] In the Caucasus too, as in Cilicia and Cyprus, they were associated with the Achaeans; and the Caucasian Heniochoi and Zygioi remembered their Achaean origin throughout antiquity.[30] In Rhodes, the acropolis of Ialysos was known as Achaia, whence came Achaeans who participated in the founding of Soloi in Cilicia.[31] The Cilicians (Kilikes), as Herodotos explains, had once been called Hypachaioi – Mixed Achaeans.[32] There were Cilicians settled near Troy.[33] The Cilician town of Olbe was founded by Aias, son of Teukros, who was a native of Salamis and went to Cyprus at the end of the Trojan War. He landed at Achaion Akte, the Achaean Shore, and founded the Cyprian Salamis, still ruled by his descendants as late as the fourth century BC.[34]

These old traditions in cult and mythology serve to illustrate why Arcado-Cypriot is the name applied to the assumed dialectal prototype of the virtually identical Greek dialects of the widely separated areas of Arcadia and Cyprus in historical times. Because Arcado-Cypriot dialectal elements have been traced in the Doric dialect of all parts, the conclusion is that Doric was super-imposed on Arcado-Cypriot; and also, because of the close association between Arcado-Cypriot and Aeolic, it is inferred that these were developed from the Greek of the Achaeans.[35] It follows that these old traditions underline the probability that Arcado-Cypriot traces in the ancient Cretan dialect were genuine pre-Doric survivals. Not surprisingly, they have been found in the surviving epigraphic evidence from cities of central Crete.[36] Such traces have been more often observed than they have been discussed in relation to their immediate contexts. Bearing in mind what had frequently happened to older populations in so-called Dorian communities by historical times, it is rewarding to look at such of these contexts as are sufficiently complete to invite an examination.

The usage of ἰν for ἐν (preposition = *in*) at Cretan Axos and Eleutherna, as also at the Achaean colony of Metapontum, are probable pre-Doric survivals.[37] Presumably the same is true of the usage ὄνυ for ὅδε (demonstrative = *this, that*) at Axos and Eleutherna. An early legal fragment from Axos[38] yields enough sense for us to be able to conclude that its purpose was to lay down conditions between the authorities of the city and some artisans who might have come in or been brought in from outside. Apparently they were to be fed at public expense and given immunity from certain tributes. There is a relationship between the purport here and that of some contemporary regulations from Gortyn and from Eleutherna.[39] The free artisans mentioned in these documents could have been under compulsion to perform forced labour of some kind; or they might have been free persons – at least in the economic sense, if not in the political sense of free citizens – who had made a kind of temporary work contract for a specific project.

Another early legal fragment from Eleutherna contains the word ἀπαμία, apparently relating to serfs or rather to the land worked by them, and to be connected with the word ἀφαμιῶται, more familiar from the later literature.[40]

An important, though poorly preserved, inscription from Eleutherna of the third or second century BC[41] appears to indicate that the *kosmoi* (magistrates) of the city exercised jurisdiction over the *Artemitai*, who formed some kind of civic community, perhaps a township, or a village, even a group of villages, in the neighbourhood of Eleutherna, and who were presumably connected with the local cult of Artemis. We cannot be certain that the word *kosmos*, in the fourth line of the inscription, indicates the chief magistrate or all the body of magistrates; nor is it clear what had to be done at his or their bidding, under a penalty of a fine of five staters for failure to comply. However, it does seem likely from what follows that the *Artemitai* were subject to restrictions on their movements; and also that failure to inform the *kosmoi* of an intention to leave did entail a sort of excommunication. The *Artemitai* of Eleutherna can be compared with the *Latosioi* of Gortyn, who lived in a special region of that city, called *Latosion*, reserved for metics and freedmen.[42] Though the *Latosioi* were in a subordinate status compared with the free Dorian citizen class, they were relatively privileged perhaps by reason of their artisan status. Another region of Gortyn was called the *Hermaion* up to the first centuries of the Christian era.[43] Nomenclature of this kind reflected the presence of older inhabitants than the existing rulers of the aristocratic city-states. For they formed part of the social system and their influence is reflected in religion as well as in fragmentary dialectal survivals. When placed in a general framework of other survivals from earlier times, religious, mythological and social, these dialectal fragments can assume a rather wider interest when examined within their precise contexts, puzzling though these may often be if studied in isolation.

A survey of the evidence relating to the pre-Greek place-name Ἀμύκλαι (Amyklai) and its common correlatives in the three different areas of Cyprus, Crete and the Peloponnese will illustrate this principle in more detail and in a geographical context as ample as the dialectal term Arcado-Cypriot implies in historical times. It is generally recognized that few Cretan place-names are Doric, with the result that many local place-names survived, including a very high proportion of pre-Hellenic city-names. As it happens, the Cretan evidence about Amyklai is as commonly ignored as the mainland evidence is cited for comparison with the Cypriot. Yet in all three areas it is not merely nomenclature that takes us back to the Bronze Age.

In the Catalogue of Ships in the *Iliad* Amyklai is included in the domain of Menelaos.[44] It is the only one of the several places mentioned in this domain that can certainly be identified, though approximate locations of the others are mostly well attested.[45] It has been argued that if Pharis, one of these others, is to be located at Ayios Vasilios, it seems likely that Allen was right to consider the prehistoric sites at the Amyklaion and at Vaphio as going together, particularly since the classical Amyklai seems to have occupied much of the same area. The site at Vaphio is the largest Mycenaean site yet discovered in Lakonia and the famous gold cups from the tholos tomb nearby are sufficient evidence for its wealth and importance.[46]

Herodotos[47] tells us that the Lacedaemonians once sent to Sardis to buy gold for Apollo (i.e. Pythian Apollo) at Thornax, but Kroisos offered the gold as a present to the god. According to Pausanias,[48] because the Amyklaian Apollo held a higher position in Lakonia, this present of gold was in fact used to decorate his statue. This statue of the god was about 45m. high, crudely fashioned in the sense that, apart from face and tips of feet and hands, it looked just like a bronze pillar. There was a helmet on its head and a lance and bow in its hands.[49] The base of the statue was shaped like an altar and Hyakinthos was said to be buried in it.[50]

Hyakinthos is markedly prehistoric and pre-Greek but he is nevertheless by no means entirely obscured by the cult of Apollo who, according to the familiar myth, both loved Hyakinthos and accidentally killed him with a discus. The Amyklaion itself and several other sites in the area have yielded much evidence of prehistoric occupation, the early pottery from the Amyklaion being mostly late or very late Mycenaean, with the exception of some fragments of palace-style jars; continuity of finds is unbroken from Mycenaean times until late antiquity; and the site was reoccupied comparatively soon after the end of the Mycenaean period.[51] There was also a tomb, variously attributed to Apollo Hyakinthos or to Hyakinthos, at Taras,[52] which was colonized by the Partheniai (Maidens' Sons) of Sparta, rebellious offspring of unmarried women, who, detected in a conspiracy, were sent out to colonize Taras. It has been observed that they planned their *coup* at the festival of the Hyakinthia at Amyklai, which raises the possibility that many of the Partheniai were Amyklaians, since the pre-Dorian cult of Apollo Hyakinthos flourished also at Taras.[53] Women took a prominent part in the Hyakinthia and the Partheniai doubtless had the backing of their wives and mothers.[54]

The festival of the Hyakinthia continued to be one of the most important of all Spartan festivals, celebrated annually and lasting for at least three days. It began with solemnity on the first day, followed by rejoicing and general celebration on the second day. Before the regular burnt sacrifice was offered to Olympian Apollo, the worshippers gave underworld offerings to Hyakinthos through a bronze door beside the altar of Apollo.[55] A compromise

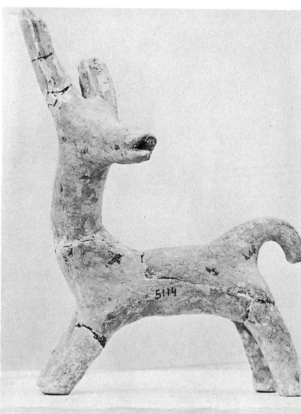

1. above,
Middle Neo-
lithic terracotta
from Knossos
Iraklion Museum

2. above, right,
Terracotta
figure of a deer,
Middle Minoan
Iraklion Museum

3. right,
Bull-shaped
rhyton from
Pseira, Late
Minoan
Iraklion Museum

4. Poppy-goddess
from Gazi, Late Minoan
Iraklion Museum

5. right,
Mycenae : The Lion Gate

6. Knossos : The Royal Road

7. Knossos : Corridor of the West Magazines

8. Knossos : miniature fresco of sacred grave and dance

9. Knossos : miniature fresco of seated ladies in a grandstand
From A. J. Evans, 'The Palace of Minos'

10. The Revellers : detail from the 'Harvester Vase'
Iraklion Museum

16. Relief plaque with sphinx, from late seventh century BC
Ashmolean Museum

17. & 18. Bronze
statuette from
Dreros, seventh
century BC,
showing
sphyrelaton
technique
Iraklion Museum

19. Statuette of seventh century BC, from Aphrati

20. & 21. Corslet in
Cretan style,
seventh century BC
*Museum für Kunst und
Gewerbe, Hamburg*

22. Woman wearing *peplos* of Athene, fifth/fourth century BC
Cabinet des Medailles, Paris

23. The Law Code of Gortyn

between the Olympian and the prehistoric youthful god was thus ritually honoured. The name of the youthful god also denotes a flower, the wild hyacinth or iris. The implication is that Hyakinthos was an annually dying and reborn god of vegetation, akin to Adonis, Attis and Osiris and to his Cretan counterpart, Zeus Kretagenes. Like the Cretan Zeus, Hyakinthos was not reared by his mother. His nurse was the leading nymph and mistress of animals, pre-Greek Artemis.[56] As in Sparta and other Dorian areas where the cult of Hyakinthos was common, there was a month called after his name in Crete.[57]

The epithet Amyklaios, important in the Cretan evidence, derives from the place-name Amyklai. Various traditions connect the mainland settlers of Gortyn in Crete or of some region nearby with the mainland Arcadian area where the Achaean dialect survived or with Achaean Amyklai.

According to Stephanos, the city of Gortyn in Crete had had four names.[58] The first of these names, he explains, was Hellotis, which was how Europa was known among the Cretans. It was then called Larisa, then Kremnia and then Gortys. Gortys was traditionally the name of a hero-founder. We find him mentioned in an inscription from Gortyn of the first half of the first century BC,[59] and also at Lebena, the port of Gortyn, at approximately the same date.[60] The Tegeans of mainland Arcadia claimed that the founder had migrated thence to Crete and gave his name to Gortyn; though the Cretans themselves denied the truth of this legend and favoured a Minoan origin of the founder in the sense of supposing that Gortys was the son, not of Tegeates, but of Rhadamanthys.[61] However, it is true that the Cretan Arcadians of historical times were settled not far to the east of Gortyn.

Another tradition[62] has it that some emigrants from Amyklai who broke with the Dorian Spartans and settled in Melos also occupied Gortyn with the help of neighbouring Cretans. Amyklai had remained Achaean for some time after the Dorian supremacy[63] and it is plausible to suppose that some relationship between Peloponnesian and Cretan Amyklai or Amyklaians might well antedate a Dorian domination at Gortyn.

The 'walled' city of Gortyn mentioned in the Homeric Catalogue of Ships has naturally to be associated with the Achaean settlers of central Crete.[64] Achaean pedigrees, cults, cult-names and modifications which appear in later Gortynian tradition may reasonably be assigned approximately to the same period. The name Gortys or Gortyna, apparently pre-Greek,[65] with Etruscan, Thessalian and Macedonian connections, is most significantly paralleled by the Arcadian Gortyn (or Gortys, Gortyna) and Gortynios, tributary of the Alpheus.[66] The name could have been brought by Achaean settlers from Arcadia, but Minoan tradition, linking Gortyn with Phoenician Europa, despite repeated modification, Achaean or Dorian, was long persistent.[67] This persistence over so many centuries was not based on obstinate fiction.[68]

The evidence for a Cretan Amyklai, though relatively late, is firm enough and confirms these early associations with similar names elsewhere and Stephanos again may be called to witness.[69] A cult of Apollo Amyklaios can be inferred from a section of the Law Code of Gortyn.[70] This passage fairly certainly indicates that there was a cult and temple of Amyklaios in the earlier fifth century BC at Gortyn; and it can presumably be assumed that this deity, like his counterpart on the mainland, was an armed god, equipped with helmet, spear and bow.[71] In the Gortynian calendar there was, in the earlier second century BC, a month called Amyklaios.[72] This important fact is confirmed, with some degree of probability, by a somewhat earlier inscription.[73] Finally, a surviving portion of another valuable document[74] is apparently concerned also with Gortynian Amyklaion and indicates that its inhabitants, *Amyklaioi*, had (presumably long before then – third–second century BC) been reduced to a status of perioecic subjection, as was customary with pre-Dorian communities in Crete, as elsewhere.

The various Greek traditions, supported by the epigraphic and archaeological evidence, certainly demonstrate the likelihood of an association between Peloponnesian and Cretan Amyklai and Amyklaians, ethnic, religious and linguistic. These traditions may be confused about the means by which the association was established, its original focus and its direction of diffusion; but they collectively and tenaciously assert the antiquity of the association. It is easier to conclude than to prove that it was primarily established by settlers from the mainland.[75] It is less easy to conclude and more difficult to prove, in the present state of our knowledge, that the flow of influence was in the reverse direction.[76]

In conjunction with the Peloponnesian and the Cretan evidence, the Cyprus evidence assumes particular interest in directing our attention to non-Greek influences in the ethnic, religious and linguistic context.

The bilingual inscription, with Phoenician and Cypriot text (both plausibly restored), discovered in 1869 and now in the British Museum, dated 388 BC or a little earlier, belonged to the temple of Apollo at Idalion. This document has been published, with detailed commentary, by Masson.[77] It establishes that Cypriot to-a-po-lo-ni to-a-mu-ko-lo-i (τῷ ᾽Απόλ(λ)ωνυι τῷ ᾽Αμύκλωι) = Phoenician *lršpmkl*. Masson explains: 'Dédicace d'une statuette au dieu phénicien Reshef Mikal, assimilé dans le texte chypriote à un Apollon Amyklos, par le prince phénicien Baalrôm, fils d'Abdimilk, dans la quatrième année du règne de Milkyaton, roi de Kition et d'Idalion.'

Masson rightly points out that the document poses a problem in the history of religions and briefly formulates it, emphasizing the importance of the discovery (in 1927) of the Beth Shan (*Beisān*) inscription, dated to the fifteenth century BC, mentioning a Canaanite Baal (*m k l*). His conclusion is positive: 'En tout cas, il convient d'abandonner définitivement l'hypothèse de l'adoption par les Phéniciens de Chypre du culte et du nom d'un Apollon Amyklaios de Laconie, d'où l'on tirait des conséquences pour l'origine péloponnésienne des Achéens qui ont colonisé Chypre: il s'agit au contraire d'une divinité sémitique, dont le nom a été grécisé dans un milieu de Phéniciens plus ou moins hellénisés, avec une influence possible, du point de vue de la forme, de l'épithète grecque 'Αμυκλαῖος'.'

Thus the place-name Amyklai, with its ethnic and religious associations, raises problems of origin and influence shared equally by the Peloponnese, Crete and Cyprus. As more detailed investigation is carried out, these problems will no doubt be clarified.

12

LAW AND CUSTOM

Early Greek society has been impregnated with heroic legends from antiquity onward. Some of these have helped in the furtherance of truth and others have not. Archaic or pre-Classical Greece was the era of the foundation of the city-states, the lyric age[1] of transition from illiteracy to alphabetic literacy in the Iron Age, accompanied by the emergence of rational thought in law as in philosophy. This lengthy era of transition differed in its temporal boundaries in different places, where there is never any risk that we shall know too much about what people did in these distant times but rather a constant regret that we are obliged to know so little. The purpose of this chapter is to suggest that we do have the means of knowing more than is sometimes supposed possible by drawing some parallels and suggesting some connections from certain main features which emerge from a study of Cretan law and especially from the Law Code of Gortyn (see Appendix, p. 216).[2]

The Great Code – more accurately to be defined as a tabulation of statutory enactments amending prior written law on various topics and also modifying even earlier customs – is the first European law-code and the only complete code to have survived from ancient Greece. The discovery of this immensely important document amid the ruins of the ancient city began in 1857 when Thenon found an inscribed stone (Col. XI) built into the walls of a mill beside a stream and purchased it for the Louvre. It was quite difficult to extract proper meaning from this archaic document and it was as late as 1878 before Bréal could prove that the fragment was concerned with the adoption of children. In the following year, 1879, a similar fragment (Cols. VIII–X), detected in a house near the mill and concerned with the rights of heiresses, was copied by Haussoullier. In July 1884, the site was visited by Halbherr and it chanced that the water was drawn off from the mill. A channel of the stream ran over a wall at a short distance below the mill and some letters near the top of this wall were shown to Halbherr. He made a trench along the inside of the wall and found four inscribed columns, the last on the left not completely inscribed at the bottom, so indicating that it formed the end of the whole inscription in that direction.

That part of the inscription so far discovered had been cut upon the layers of stone in the wall with detailed precision. Halbherr copied the four columns and, returning to Iraklion, was able to tell Ernst Fabricius about his new find. Fabricius went to the site towards the end of October and persuaded the owner of the field into which the inscription continued to allow him to dig a trench along the wall to the limit of the inscription. The consequence was that eight more columns were revealed, in a finely preserved condition. It was now apparent that the wall on which the twelve columns of the document had been inscribed was circular; and also, if the circle had been complete, that the wall would have had a diameter of almost 30m. This circular wall had been used to support the auditorium of a theatre perhaps built in the first century BC; but it must earlier have formed part of the structure of a much earlier building, perhaps a law-court. The massive document, over 600 lines long, is quite the best example to have survived of the publication of laws on the walls of public buildings in ancient times. A so-called Second Code, of which only parts survive, completes a corpus sometimes referred to as the Gortyn Codes. This ample title could be loosely used to embrace a whole number of legal docu-ments from the site, some earlier and some perhaps more nearly contemporary. The precise dating of these legal texts is by no means certain, but there is little doubt that the Great Code itself belongs to the fifth century BC, perhaps to the first half.[3] Since Fabricius (in 1884) and Comparetti (in 1885) published their first versions, other editions, translations and commentaries have followed.[4]

Others than legal historians can find valuable, often unique information from the historical jurisprudence or the sociology of the law in those areas of the past they want to explore, especially when other kinds of knowledge are deficient and the legal evidence is itself compulsively significant. Insofar as all things have a history all things change, including the history itself of our awareness of the interrelationship between things. The reason why the lower animals are thought not to have opinion, said Aristotle, is that they do not possess that form of imagination which comes from inference, while the latter implies the former.[5] However, it must be remembered that Greek law, as compared with Roman law, is undefinitive and untidy. It has been properly observed[6] that the philosophers of Greece did not deem law – as distinct from government – to be worthy of their study, nor did it ever become a science nor its rules a system. Little was promulgated or recorded in writing. Democ-racy demanded that the judges should be untrained laymen and therefore the advocates flourished by their eloquence and not by learning. Scribes of specialized experience drafted commercial documents with well-recognized forms and clauses, but the profession of lawyer did not exist even in the Classical age.

In Babylonia, and perhaps in Judah and Israel, the drafting of a code of laws was both a literary exercise of the learned layman and a suggestion of ways of justice for the judge. But long before the Roman law attained its prime in the early third century AD, its features had become those of modern law; a rule was law or was not law; it was a principle, extracted from a number of decisions, which must be applied to the new facts; law was a technical conception in the minds of lawyers, and its rules contained technicalities – it even lived to some extent a life of its own, separate from its changing surroundings and subject only to the power of a legislature to amend it. While the Roman law attained a degree of development and a change in character not previously witnessed in the world's history, it perhaps raised the legal art to a standard never since surpassed.[7]

We have begun to set phenomena in the context of the world's history in a way that was not possible for the ancients. We are also heirs of the Romans and hence modern in our legal concepts in an un-Greek way, heirs too of the concepts which followed on after the collapse of the Romans, the concepts of divine law and of the laws of nature continuously refined by modern scientific theory. We are predisposed to look for change, for general features which can become defined as principles and sometimes as laws. Archaeology, anthropology and sociology have compelled us to be broader witnesses, while philology is still rigorously compulsive in imposing truths and dispelling fictions.

The late Milman Parry was a significant scholar in the field of comparative epic, with his arresting, if debatable conclusion that literature falls into two great parts, not so much because there are two kinds of culture, but because there are two kinds of form – the one part of literature being oral, the other written. Until this is grasped, he argued, we cannot hope for any sound method whereby we could use *Beowulf*, for example, for the better understanding of the *Iliad*. The 'primitive', the 'popular', the 'natural' and the 'heroic' definitions all hang upon a poetry's being oral.[8] Some pertinent observations of a parallel index figure in the field of comparative law have been referred to above.[9] Dr A.S. Diamond's *Primitive Law, Past and Present* began as a third edition of his *Primitive Law*, first published in 1935, of which the second edition, in 1950, was little more than a copy of the first. The chief differences are in the volume of the evidence presented of the legal usages of peoples of recent times and the more detailed references to authorities, especially the skilled monographs of social anthropologists, of a quality which was still new in 1935. So the new work was divided into two sections, one examining the evidence afforded only by the legal remains of the past, and the other the legal usages of present and recent peoples and the light they throw on past laws and legal systems.

The word 'primitive' was retained, Diamond explained, partly because the work was known by this name and partly for lack of a satisfactory substitute, despite Professor Max Gluckman's definition (in his *Politics, Law and Ritual in Tribal Society*) of 'tribal society' as meaning the kind of community which was once described by the term 'primitive society', a term (for him) now rightly rejected. Dr Diamond, on the other hand, ventured to doubt whether there are any expressions used by social anthropologists more inconsistently or with vaguer meaning than 'tribe' or 'tribal' and to think that if the term 'primitive' was now under a cloud, the same cloud had extended itself to those expressions.[10]

He himself used the word 'primitive' precisely in the sense of a study of the stages of legal development from the first rudimentary rules of conduct to the codes of the legal systems, its scope extending from both cultures and legal systems known to us from the ancient and medieval past, including Babylonians and Assyrians, Hittites, Hebrews, Romans, Hindus, English and other German peoples and those of the undeveloped systems of present and recent times in Africa, Australia and America. The attempt to correlate economic with legal development is consolidated and it is demonstrated that laws change with the development of material culture on a time-scale that is economic in the widest sense of the progression of development of visible, measurable, material culture.[11] The primary exemplar of the state of law of the Late Codes and a terminal point in the development of primitive law as compared with mature law is still seen to be the Code of Hammurabi of about 1750 BC, which has its parallels with other systems in other places in medieval and in modern times, including the Hebrew Code, the scanty Greek material which is little more than the remaining traces of Drakon's legislation (of about 620 BC) and the Roman Twelve Tables.[12]

Forty years ago, Dr Diamond viewed the surviving legislation of Gortyn as marking, by its stages of legal as well as economic development, the end of the period of primitive law and the commencement of mature law;[13] and his viewpoint has not changed.[14] For Diamond then (surely quite correctly) this legislation is valuable because it lies betwixt and between, embodying the past and looking to the future. It is a monument of change luckily surviving on the stone on which it was published. Along with the other fragmentary material which also survives from early Crete, it forms a kind of legal epic, certainly in the sense of being objective, persistently expressive in its third person usage, but also significantly in another way. The writing down of early Greek law, especially of Cretan law, has its analogies with the writing down of epic poetry, in the sense that, when we study it and try to understand its implications in perspective, we move in a comparable climate of intellectual history. Literacy is spreading, behaviour is being documented, but memory is still powerful, as are the traditions dependent on memory.

On the evidence of the Gortyn Code, it seems that no written records of the court were maintained. Writing is not made compulsory in any transaction in the Code. However, in some cases, notice is required to be given of certain facts in the presence of witnesses who have to be called, if there is a trial, to prove the notice. An official, a *mnamon* (a 'remembrancer') was attached to the court to assist the judge in procedure. As his name implies, he recorded in his memory facts relevant to the conduct of cases before the practice of writing had become widespread.[15]

A new archaic Cretan text,[16] discovered and published in recent years, perhaps about half a century earlier than the Code, is of general significance in this connection. It is the earliest full record, from any Greek city, of the creation of a high technical office of Scribe and Recorder. He is called *poinikastas*; and his main duty probably was to formulate properly those decisions by the *polis* or a committee of the *polis*, on all matters, sacred and secular, which were to have the force of laws.

The editors of this text did not see this official as a lawgiver in the class of Zaleukos or Solon, but as ranking with those others who had presumably served thus in the past at Dreros, Gortyn and other Cretan cities. The definition of the office is ποινικάζεν καὶ μναμονεῦϝεν, which must mean something like 'record and remember'. In the establishment of this new office it looks as if μναμονεῦϝεν represents the traditional, while ποινικάζεν represents the novel element in the function of the new official. The novelty of the function is marked by the use of ποινικάζεν, meaning 'to do φοινικήια, to write', to do something more novel than the traditional *mnamon*.

Legal enactment was then becoming the province of humbler persons than those imposing, almost heroic characters often normally associated with the beginnings of Greek law. A general trend towards codification was stimulated in the course of the seventh century BC. This profoundly important innovation of the city-states did not first occur on the mainland of Greece but in the colonies and in the more distant and less accessible western colonies – which lends some substance to the view that one motive for the development may very well have been a need to provide single legal codes to colonists originating from different cities with different systems of customary law. Tradition flourishes with settled habitation. Far-flung pioneers needed a different, a more artificial kind of authority, consciously formulated. This legislative movement was responsible for a whole series of famous lawgivers like Zaleukos in Achaean Lokris, Charondas in Ionian Catana, Diokles in Dorian Syracuse. The laws of Zaleukos and Charondas were generally reputed to be the oldest written laws in Greece and they probably belong to the first half of the seventh century BC. Some western codes were introduced into eastern Greece – for example that of Charondas in the island of Kos. In other cities of Asia Minor and the islands there were native legislators like Pittakos of Mytilene. Others, such as Lykourgos of Sparta, Drakon of Athens, Philolaos of Corinth, produced codes – unwritten, of course, in the case of Sparta – for the mainland.[17]

These early lawgivers are invested with the dignified mystery proper to ancestral founding fathers, inspired instruments of legal wisdom which was sacrosanct, even divine. Reluctance to alter or criticize such laws was clearly associated with a general belief in their divine origin.[18]

Yet Crete is not typical, it does not fit in with this general pattern, so far as we can tell from the existing evidence. As Plato puts it, the Cretans call Zeus their lawgiver and Minos, like his brother Rhadamanthys, was inspired by Zeus[19] – the Cretan Zeus who is older and different from Olympian Zeus. Aristotle reaches for the substance behind this philosophic myth-making when he says that the laws of Minos were still observed among the subject population of Crete,[20] though we can only guess what is meant exactly by this observation. It does seem to confirm the survival from Minoan times of some framework of law still powerful enough to influence the Dorian legislation. We cannot, in the circumstances, say how sophisticated this framework might have been, but if we simply assess it as the customary law of tribal or primitive institutions, there it was to play its part in the social life of the servile cultivators descended from the old Minoan population.[21] Occasionally it breaks through strongly enough to show that such a framework is not just plausible conjecture but that a serf family had real social and legal status on the evidence of the Gortyn Code.

A serf could marry and divorce; and his wife could possess her own property – movables, including livestock – which reverted to her in the event of divorce. When she married, she changed masters; when divorced, she either returned to her former master or to his relatives. The right is assumed of a master to a child whose parents were both his serfs. If a serf bore a child after divorce, she was obliged to take it to the master of her former husband. If he did not want the child, it then became the concern of her master; but the husband's master was guaranteed the right to the serf child if the divorced couple re-married within a year.[22]

More remarkable, though the initial portion of the relevant section of the text is not certain, are the provisions concerning children of mixed marriages.[23] The status of the children of such marriages was decided according as the marriage was matrilocal or not. There seems little doubt that a legal kind of relationship was envisaged or at least a relationship sanctioned by custom, since the word which describes it, ὀπύιεν, is regularly used elsewhere of legal marriage. It is not likely that this word would be used to describe a relationship between a free woman and a chattel slave, and so the δôλος of this section is likely to mean a serf and not a chattel slave.[24]

The section of the text has three provisions. Firstly, if a person (who was specified in the initial missing portion) goes to a free woman and marries her, their children are free; secondly, if a free woman goes to the serf, their children are unfree. These two provisions were apparently intended to counterbalance and the restoration of ὁ δôλος in the missing portion is justified. It would then be a logical consequence that a free woman who married twice would become the mother of both free and unfree children. This is in fact the consequence covered by the third provision of this particular section, which rules that, in such cases, where the mother dies, the free children are to have any property.

Such remarkable features as these have an older basis than the legislation of other places in archaic times sanctified by inspired contemporary lawgivers. No lawgiver is associated with the Gortyn Code. The same is true of the earlier legal fragments from Gortyn itself and from such other Cretan cities as Axos, Dreros and Eleutherna. This is conscious legislation, precisely fashioned by minority groups forming the governing classes of the city-states, composed of aristocratic landholders who were free citizens. Respect for Crete as a home of good laws, implicit in the tradition that legislators like Zaleukos and Lykourgos visited Crete, among other places,[25] hardly derives from such historical sources. In Crete the old customs had longer traditions behind them and the innovations are less dramatically announced; but they are real enough.

They are real and not wrapped in mystery because they are so purposive and conscious. When we take into account the other fragmentary documents, the Gortyn Code becomes less of a unique document than it first appears, in its sheer magnitude, its careful precision, its rigorous intention to order so many facets of ordinary social life under the formulations of written law. Other small states were doing the same sort of thing with similar intentions, to erect deliberately a set of institutions initially novel and city-based out of a background with many layers of older tradition, which later became stable models for political theory. We are fortunate to have such a unique survival as the Gortyn Code, if only we remember that it was really unique in the proper sense of belonging to one city, and, although we may quite properly assume similar intentions elsewhere, we may not, without risk, follow the habits of Plato and Aristotle in regarding Crete as a single entity like Sparta, unless we make clear how and why we do so.[26] Old habits die hard. No doubt there are still those who believe, on the authority of Ephoros and Aristotle, that there were ten *kosmoi* in the Cretan city-states.[27] Aristotle normally generalizes on a sound basis about Crete; but this is his most suspect factual statement. With the exception of a single inscription from Hierapytna,[28] and perhaps another from Gortyn,[29] of the second century BC, the epigraphic evidence does not support his statement. However, the relevant inscriptions all belong to the Hellenistic period; and, since Ephoros agrees with Aristotle, we have to be careful. There are no recorded facts to refute the possibility that there were ten *kosmoi* in the fourth century. Composition of the magistracy could have changed in later times, maybe as a result of declining population. No matter how inventive we may like to be in looking for excuses, it is surely better to be surprised at the possibility that there were ever at any one time ten *kosmoi* in all the many cities of Crete; but it is not, of course, impossible. Best to concede, perhaps, that the sources of information available to Ephoros and Aristotle on this aspect of constitutional history were inaccurate, or based upon the practice in a number of cities but not all of them; or (rather desperately) that ten represented a maximum at the time when Aristotle decided to be, for once at any rate, misleadingly authoritative.

To return to the relative uniqueness of the Code, which so revealingly embodies many traces of older practices than its actual date of publication.[30] There are also references to prior written legislation, amendments to older sanctions and regulations that are quite novel, so novel that we may suppose that the whole document was published at a time when – and perhaps really because – somewhat older practices were under pressure from the expanding authority of the state. At any rate we cannot evade the impression of conflict between the old and the new, of a situation of partly rejecting, partly adapting, temporarily resolved as compromise presumably between pressure groups concerned to preserve the status quo or to bring about a change. The stresses are apparent in several ways.

Lawgivers in ancient Greece normally came from the middle classes, though there are examples from all classes of society. There is an acknowledged connection between the practice of the codification of law and the requirements of trade. However, in Crete the aristocracies sustained their power for several centuries and produced no awesome lawgiver whom we can associate even with the Gortyn Code. Yet the connection between legislation and trading is there to be recognized. Such indications as the flourishing and relatively early development of alphabetic writing or the special features in the art of the period from the mid-eighth to the mid-seventh centuries confirm that the commercial expansion of the early Iron Age stirred the Cretan aristocracies to make their contribution in a period of change, the foundation period of the city-state, that most typical of all Aegean institutions of antiquity. We have to assume that trading was controlled in Crete by the aristocracies and kept within safe limits. There was to be no merchant class anywhere of any significance so far as the evidence goes for a long time to come. Centuries passed before Polybios[31] compared the Cretans so adversely with the Spartans, their exact opposites in all respects, including their laws of land tenure and their attitude to money-making. Their laws, he declares, allow the Cretans to possess as much land as they can possibly acquire; and money is held in such esteem that its acquisition is regarded not as merely a necessity, but as a highly reputable pursuit. Ephoros particularly is rebuked for describing the Spartan and Cretan systems in almost identical terms.

I have given my reasons elsewhere[32] for supposing that the basic agricultural economy of Crete remained, despite formal changes in land tenure, into Roman times, and that the undoubtedly increasing role of moneyed wealth as compared with landed wealth is connected with the incessant warfare between the states, with mercenary service and piracy and the expansion of the slave trade.

The onset of the new kind of wealth and the resistant strength of traditional landed wealth can be assessed in various ways which confirm the picture of old and new as conflicting forces in the legal evidence.

Coinage eased the ways of commerce and trade, replacing barter or the use of articles of iron, gold and silver as medium of exchange of commodities. Archaeology confirms the tradition that the first coins were invented by kings of Lydia, whence the innovation spread to the Ionian cities, across to Aigina,

Euboia, Corinth, Athens and on to the Greek cities in Italy and Sicily. Cretan coinage is not apparently developed until the beginning of the fifth century, more than a century after the first European state, the island of Aigina, adopted the coinage. The Spartans were slower still, having no coinage of their own, apart from their traditional iron money, until metal coins began to be struck in the third century. They were similarly reluctant to codify law, or to encourage trade and private property.

Gortyn was one of the first Cretan cities to have its coinage and its introduction antedates, so far as any kind of precision is possible in these matters, in our present state of knowledge, the publication of the Gortyn Code by one or two generations. The close connection between trade, coinage and written legislation is implicit; and we are able to discern some of the consequences of the new kind of moneyed wealth in the regulations of the Code as elsewhere.

Having seen what seem to be firm survivals of an older framework of custom, we may now turn to more controversial examples of survival which emerge from the evidence within the context of these radical general changes outlined above. The evidence is clear enough for three different social classes typified: (a) by a minority of free citizens; (b) a distinct class, about whose composition we are ill-informed, called *apetairoi*, because they were excluded from membership of a *hetaireia*, a closed group, rather like the Athenian phratry, who took their communal meals (*syssitia*) in the *andreion*: they were presumably free persons insofar as they were not servile, though excluded from political rights; (c) a large servile class which included the cultivators presumably descended from the pre-Dorian inhabitants. We can form an estimate of the relative status of these three groupings of the social hierarchy from the wide discrepancies in the scales of fines for certain offences which are announced in the Gortyn Code; and the amount of evidence required for conviction was also disproportionate between the classes.

The legal and literary evidence shows the continued existence of a class of bondsmen or serfs, tied to the soil, an integral part of the estates of the citizen landlords, the origin of whose status may lie in the Bronze Age, but with certain clearly defined rights which distinguish them from chattel slaves, proper, of a status – or lack of status – familiar in the history of later antiquity.

Apart from those rights of marriage and divorce which I have referred to, serfs possessed other rights which must have distinguished their status from the status of chattel slaves. They had right of tenure of the houses in which they lived and the contents of those houses, regarded as part of the estate, like the serfs themselves; and they could possess cattle in their own right.[33] Aristotle tells us that the Cretans allowed their servile population the same rights as they had themselves with the exception of gymnastic exercises and the possession of arms[34] – which helps one to infer, from a disputed passage of the Code, that, in certain rare circumstances, the serfs of an ancestral estate might even assume tenure of that estate.[35] Serfs must also have possessed money to be able to pay the fines assessed for offences in the Code.[36]

The Gortyn Code uses two servile terms, Ϝοικέυς and δôλος, which some (including myself) render as *serf* and *slave* respectively. However, the two words are not strictly used to define two different statuses, although it may be maintained that there are two different statuses of servitude specified in the Code. The word δôλος is apparently sometimes synonymous with Ϝοικέυς and sometimes denotes a chattel slave as is made clear, or so it seems to me, in two places.

One passage refers to the buying of slaves in the market place and responsibility for damages done by such slaves.[37] The passage coincides with the Roman rule: *noxa caput sequitur*. Liability for *noxa* attached to the present owner of a slave and, in a case of sale after damage was done, to the purchaser and not the seller, because the slave could be returned to the seller by the buyer. The regulation applies strictly to sales in the slave-market. We know from other Greek sources that market-sales were subject to official control so as to ensure that a defective slave, particularly a slave suffering from a disease, could be returned to the vendor and the buyer be indemnified by a public procedure. Though clerks or supervisors of the market are not mentioned in the epigraphic evidence from Gortyn until the first century BC, they must have existed there and elsewhere in Crete much earlier. It is obvious from this particular regulation that some such officials must have existed in the early fifth century, no matter what their name. Among the activities of Cretan pirates in Hellenistic times was wholesale kidnapping of persons for ransom and the slave trade. We can infer from this market-regulation of the Code that there was an organized slave-trade under official state control early in the fifth century. There is no evidence for dating the emergence of slave-markets in Cretan cities, but Herodotos tells us a story about the foundation of Kydonia by Samian emigrants which seems to show that Cretans were engaged in the slave-trade in the previous century.[38] The Samians came to Kydonia in 524 BC, stayed and flourished there for five years before they were attacked by a force of Aeginetans and Cretans and reduced to slavery.

This passage then serves as a reminder that the bought slave was a mere commodity, subject to the rules of the market. Consequently, when it is ordained that, in case a master dies and the heirs cannot agree about their proper shares, then the property shall be sold and the proceeds divided among them, we are to understand that the slaves are to be sold as part of the property.[39] When the heiress is allowed to take possession of a town-house and everything in the house, the furniture and the slaves are meant.[40] Other documentary evidence from Gortyn at the beginning of the fifth century implies that resident aliens and freedmen lived in a special quarter of the city called Latosion.[41] Freedmen presuppose the prior existence of slaves, which is confirmed by the existence of a slave-market with established rules. So early fifth century Gortyn had a mixed form of slave economy, with serfdom still paramount, though chattel slavery must at least have been as well developed as anywhere else in Crete, though naturally most of the relevant provisions of the Code have to be interpreted as referring to serfs.

There is, however, a second passage which distinguishes chattel slave from serf. A penalty is laid down for rape against a domestic,[42] with the consequence that we have one rule applying to a serf, another to a slave; and, in fact, cases are therefore examined in order where the victim of rape is (a) a free citizen: (b) an *apetairos*: (c) a serf: and (d) a slave.[43] Fines scheduled for these offences illustrate sharp differences in social status, being respectively assessed at (a) 1200 obols; (b) 120 obols; (c) 30 obols; and (d) 24 (or 2) obols, depending on circumstances. It is likely that, in the fourth case, the offence was committed not by the master of the slave but by some other person and that the master received the fine.[44]

Generally speaking, with one single exception which illustrates new trends, Cretan terms of servitude seem to derive their significance from original application to that class of peasant bondsmen or serfs who lived and worked on the estates of their Dorian masters. The exception is the word χρυσώνητος, *a person bought for gold*, which Kallistratos[45] uses of Cretan city-slaves, in contrast with servile countrymen whom he describes, as others do, as *aphamiotai*,[46] seemingly connected with the word ἀπαμία[47] found in an early legal fragment from the city of Eleutherna, apparently relating to serfs or to the land worked by them.[48]

The Cretan legislation as exemplified by the Gortyn Code is particularly valuable in demonstrating that close relationship so characteristic generally of ancient Greece between property, marriage and kinship – but at a different level from what we find, say, in Classical Athens, a level that is still markedly tribal if not primitive. For here too some marked changes are under way, changes consciously formulated in legal terms to restrict the old rights of the clan in favour of narrower family groupings certainly among the governing classes of the developing city-state. I have dealt in some detail with this complex subject in my edition of the Gortyn Code and elsewhere[49] and here shall select only one very significant and crucial example of change of custom regulated by law to illustrate my emphasis upon the stress and change brought about by conscious law-making.

Broadly speaking, the system of inheritance at Gortyn, as detailed in the Code, demonstrates: (a) that so far as Dorian citizens were concerned, the social system was now essentially patriarchal and centred upon the growth of the *oikos* ('household'), a more restricted kinship group within the wider circle of the clan, as happened elsewhere; and (b) that this smaller unit of the *oikos* was closely related to the tenure of the ancestral *klaros*, with its land and attached bondsmen. Land tenure and inheritance were in their turn related to marriage customs, changes in one sphere causing changes in another. Tribal kinship, despite pressures for change, was still very important, and marriage customs differed from those with which we are familiar, though paralleled elsewhere in other places at other times, including recent times.

There is general agreement that those special regulations which govern the marriage of the heiress and the disposition of her property[50] are of considerable interest and historical importance. They have sometimes been interpreted as indicating an enlightened outlook because they show more concern for the rights of women than was the case, for example, in Classical Athens. However, it does seem that Gortynian custom was now under pressure to diminish these rights.

Women were still looked upon as tribal kinsfolk, but the marriage of the heiress was governed by special rules. When these rules could not apply even in the case of the heiress a customary rule of tribal endogamy was then allowed to apply. The heiress apart, we must then assume that such a rule was normally operative in Gortyn in the early fifth century The rule can be detected as applying elsewhere in Crete 300 years later, in a treaty made between Hierapytna and Priansos at the beginning of the second century, where the right of *epigamia* is granted to all who are tribal kinsfolk.[51]

A passage in Strabo, who quotes Ephoros, illustrates how custom might normally have operated.[52] He explains that all those who graduated from the *agela* of the youth were obliged to marry at the same time, which implies that those of the same age-grade took part in an annual festival of marriage, an implication confirmed by other sources who show how such festivals continued to be important.

An heiress is defined as a daughter who had no father and no brother of the same father and she inherited all her father's property but was under the obligation to marry the next of kin. The order of priority of claimants is clearly set out. Her paternal uncle came first, and the oldest of them if there were several. If there were several heiresses and several paternal uncles, they were to marry in order of age. If there were no paternal uncles, the heiress was then to marry her paternal cousin, and the oldest of them if there were more than one. If there were several heiresses and several paternal cousins, they had to marry in order of age of the brothers. The order of priority agrees with the order of inheritance as detailed elsewhere,[53] where the brothers of the dead man and their offspring are named next in succession to the children and grandchildren. However, so far as a claim to marriage with the heiress is concerned, only the paternal uncles and their sons were thought to be eligible. Grandchildren are not here mentioned, and we must assume the reason to have been that they would be too young to be eligible – nor were their sisters' sons taken into account.

A daughter inherited in her own right, although her share was smaller than a son's and the heiress could refuse to marry the next of kin by surrendering part of her inheritance to him. But there are two very special features about the rules for marriage of the heiress. In the first place, if the *epiballon*, the groom-elect, did not want to marry the heiress, although they were both old enough to marry, on the grounds that he was still a minor, an *apodromos*, then all the property and the produce were to be at the disposal of the heiress until he married her. This implies that the minor who had not yet graduated from the *agela* was *allowed* to marry an heiress, despite a general custom that all those promoted from the *agela* married at the same time. The minor was now granted a legal right to marry an heiress contrary to the normal custom. In the second place, the heiress could be married at the age of 12. A necessity to provide for succession in the male line seems to account for these two special regulations, of which the second naturally rendered immature girls legal appendages of an estate – compare the Athenian term *epikleros* with Gortynian *patroiokos*.

The sections on the heiress illustrate how the patriarchal system of the *oikos* was more and more concerned to limit ownership to a more restricted circle of relationship; and, consequently, how it had now begun to make fundamental changes in the custom of general marriage following graduation from the *agela*. In other words, an old rule of exogamy, by which husband and wife came from different clans, could now be broken. In place of what I consider to have been a system of cross-cousin marriage of two exogamous groups,[54] the possibility now emerged of another system of cousin-marriage, the marriage of ortho-cousins as opposed to cross-cousins.[55] The possibility was exceptional, but it was now quite firmly established if there were heiresses but no fathers' brothers to marry them. So the legal existence of ortho-cousin marriage, now sanctioned within the limits of the patriarchal household, was set against an earlier and more general system of cross-cousin marriage, to which of course it does bear some formal resemblance. However, there is constant re-assertion of the rights of clansmen or kinsmen whenever the new rule of patriarchal ortho-cousin marriage could be deemed non-operative; and this shows how the new rules were to be allowed to function within restricted limits; and also that old customs were still strong enough to make some compromises necessary from time to time.

However, there is a reminder at the end of the Code that this monumental document has no definitive finality about it. For there is a regulation[56] which complicates the whole question of the administration of the estate of the young heiress, apparently already quite satisfactorily settled in an earlier passage.[57] This amendment has the effect of introducing further limitation in favour of the nearer male kinsfolk.[58] The document ends on a note of change.

13

SOCIETY AND GOVERNMENT

As E.R. Dodds has said,[1] the problem, so familiar to us, of reconciling the claims of the individual with the interests of the community was for the first time consciously recognized as a problem in the fifth century BC. But it presented itself to the Greeks in a peculiar way, as one aspect of a still wider issue, the issue between *nomos* and *physis*, law and nature. When a Greek of the archaic period spoke of 'law', and even when he spoke of 'the laws' in the plural, he usually meant not the contents of a statute-book but the entire body of traditional usage which governed the whole of his civic conduct, political, social and religious. He thought of it, not as something which was liable to be altered next year, but as an accepted inheritance which formed the permanent background of his life. The laws represented the collective wisdom of the past; perhaps they had been codified by some great man, a Lykourgos or a Solon, but they were felt to rest ultimately on an authority higher than that of any individual statesman.

There is no denying that in the course of the fifth century two things happened which between them upset the unquestioned authority of *nomos*.[2] One was the growing complexity of the social and economic structure, which compelled the introduction of a multitude of new laws. These had no sanction of antiquity, and at Athens at least they were continually being changed – a situation personified by Aristophanes in the figure of the 'Decree-merchant' who is so roughly handled in the *Birds*. Or again: 'How', asks Hippias in the *Memorabilia*, 'can one take seriously laws which are constantly being repealed by the very same people who passed them?' And again, as early as 441 BC, Sophocles could already (in the *Antigone*) contrast such ephemeral man-made laws, to their disadvantage, with the timeless prescriptions of tradition, 'the statutes of Heaven, unwritten and unshakeable'. The other unsettling factor was a widening of intellectual horizons making possible the beginnings of a comparative anthropology and a recognition of the relativity of *nomos*.

Even so, drastic novel forces of this kind were not uniformly operative at the same time in all parts of the Greek world. Certainly not in Crete, even though we can recognize some changes in the social and economic structure which do begin to be reflected in the introduction of new laws. It is generally true, says Aristotle, that the old is less perfected than the new, when he reports in the *Politics*³ the tradition that Spartan institutions are not Dorian but pre-Dorian, established in Crete originally by Minos, received from the previous inhabitants by the Spartan colony of Lyttos and thence passed to Lykourgos when he visited Crete; which also explains why the laws of Minos are still in force among the subject population of Crete. After some further discussion of the Cretan constitution, he goes on to say that its geographical position is Crete's salvation, distance producing the same results as alien-acts. The serf-population in Crete is undisturbed, while the helots of Sparta often revolt. The Cretans have no foreign dominions; and also the island has but lately been invaded by warfare from abroad – which has made clear the weakness of the existing laws.⁴ Modern historians date the reference to warfare from abroad either to 343 or 333 BC.⁵

Before the mid-fifth century and perhaps for some time afterwards a Cretan, one suspects, might have felt a natural sympathy with the sentiment expressed by Herakleitos⁶ when he declares that 'all human laws are sustained by one law, which is divine'. The word θιοί (Gods!) is written out of alignment in the margin above the first line proper of the Gortyn Code. This imprecation, perhaps added after all the columns had been inscribed, was presumably intended as an appeal for divine blessing on the legislation. Near-contemporary Gortynian parallels indicate that this practice was not unusual in such public documents.

In Crete at this time we are still moving in an earlier climate of opinion where it is indeed meaningful to envisage the possibility – as compared with what was happening in contemporary Athens – that when a Greek of the archaic period spoke of 'law' or 'the laws', he meant not the contents of a statute-book but the entire body of traditional usage which governed the whole of his civic conduct, political, social and religious and which represented the collective wisdom of the past. In Crete the accepted inheritance which formed the permanent background of his life went a long way back, as did the great men and great deities like Minos and Rhadamanthys, Cretan Zeus and Britomartis. Hence the need to emphasize that the Code of Gortyn is an ordered collection of statutes embodying revision of prior written and unwritten law and custom.

Periods of peace in Crete were of short duration, from the end of the fourth century until the Roman conquest and warfare between the various city-states of the island became endemic. In Hellenistic times it was quite common for Greek states to form federations; and, despite the strife between her cities, such a federation (*koinon*, 'community') also existed in Crete in the Hellenistic period. It had some features which suggest that the concept of a Cretan unity which it theoretically embodied did have the sanction of an ancient traditional authority, which perhaps makes the Cretan *koinon* rather different from other federations of the times. However, the relevant inscriptions, 13 in all,⁷ do show that the Cretan Koinon did share common features with contemporary federal unions elsewhere.

Towards the end of the third century BC, *asylia* ('inviolability' or 'safety') for the sanctuary of Poseidon and Amphritite at Tenos was recognized by several cities of the Cretan Koinon.[8] In 207/6 BC in a decree of the Epidamnians concerning the *asylia* of Magnesia on the Maeander and the festival of Artemis Leukophryene, the Magnesians were praised for service to the Cretan Koinon in putting an end to internal war.[9] About the same time there was a fictitious decree concerned with the foundation of Magnesia on the Maeander, presented as if by the Cretan Koinon, to confirm the legend that the city had been founded by Cretans.[10] Early in the following century there was published a proxeny decree of the Cretan Koinon in favour of a Megalopolitan.[11] From some time in that century we have a mutilated fragment of a decree of the Cretan Koinon.[12] Round about 165 BC a proxeny decree of the Cretan Koinon in favour of Kassandros was published.[13] From between 158 and 150 BC there survives a decree of the Cretan mercenaries in the service of Ptolemy VI Philometor, king of Egypt, who had been sent to Alexandria by the Cretan Koinon, though it is likely that each member state had to send troops by terms of a treaty between the Koinon and Ptolemy. Embassies are mentioned from the states to which the troops belonged to Aglaos of Kos, an important official in Ptolemy's service.[14] About 151 BC there was published a decree of the Knossians and the Cretan Koinon in honour of Hegesandros of Athens;[15] and also from the same authorities a decree in honour of some unknown person.[16] There is dispute about the date of a decree of Aptera in honour of Attalos of Pergamon for his solicitude towards the Cretan Koinon and particularly to Aptera.[17] A judgment of the Magnesians in 112/111 BC in a dispute between Itanos and Hierapytna made reference to the Ptolemaic control of Itanos approved by the Cretan Koinon towards the middle of the second century.[18] In the same century there was a decree of the Councillors and Assembly of the Cretans concerning the *asylia* of Anaphe;[19] and also a decree of the Cretan Koinon in honour of Samian Epikles and the Samians.[20]

It is quite probable that sources which make use of some such formula as πάντες Κρηταιεῖς ('all the Cretans') referred to the Koinon.[21] These include an Athenian decree for Eumaridas of Kydonia;[22] some fragments of decrees of Mylasa about Crete;[23] the Gortyn-Magnesian agreement of 196/5 BC;[24] details of the pacification of Crete by Aratos in 216 BC;[25] and about the Rhodian embassy in 168 BC;[26] a decree of Aptera in honour of Polykles of Paros;[27] the decree of the Cretan mercenaries about Aglaos of Kos;[28] and the Magnesian arbitration between Itanos and Hierapytna.[29] The existence of the Koinon has been plausibly inferred in other sources,[30] concerning, for instance, the Cretan-Roman negotiations of 170 BC;[31] the embassy of Antiphatas to the Achaeans in the second Creto-Rhodian war;[32] or negotiations with Rome in 70 BC.[33]

All this evidence suggests the following conclusions.[34] The Cretan Koinon of the Hellenistic period was a loose federal union dominated (and this is what we might expect) by Gortyn and Knossos. Its Council consisted of delegates from the various member states, called *synedroi*. Its popular Assembly, composed of the citizens of member states, was called τὸ κοινὸν or τὸ πλῆθος τῶν Κρηταιέων. Its decrees issued jointly from the *synedroi* and the Assembly. It seems to have met in various places such as Knossos or Axos or Priansos or Lappa. The Koinon differed, however, in certain respects from such contemporary federal organizations as the Achaean League. It could grant *asylia* and honours to foreigners, but there is no evidence in the documents of Cretan citizenship, of a federal army[35] or federal magistrates to carry on diplomatic relations, since documents were dated by reference to *protokosmoi* ('presidents of *kosmoi*') of Gortyn and Knossos. Individual member states apparently had much independence in their foreign relations and were not bound by federal policy. For in the decree of the Cretan mercenaries[36] in the service of Ptolemy VI Philometor, the embassies to Aglaos were mentioned as from the states to which the troops belonged and not from the Koinon. In 183 BC Eumenes II made a treaty separately with each member state of the Koinon,[37] and the Rhodians acted similarly in the course of their negotiations in 168 BC.[38]

The tradition that the Cretans dropped their incessant internecine strife when they were threatened by a common enemy was expressed in the word *synkretismos*, meaning, as Plutarch explains,[39] a union or federation of their communities. Van der Mijnsbrugge considered that the origin of the Cretan Koinon probably was to be sought in the *synkretismos* in ancient times when the independence of Crete was threatened by foreign enemies; but he felt obliged to differentiate between this ancient *synkretismos* and the Koinon of the historical period on the grounds that this latter was restored at times when no foreign enemy threatened the independence of Crete. He himself dated the first certain restoration of the Koinon to 221 BC.[40] Kirchner preferred 216 BC.[41] Muttelsee placed its foundation between 250 and 225 BC.[42] Van Effenterre also preferred the third quarter of the third century.[43] In a previous review of the evidence,[44] I myself argued that the motive of the original institution as based on menace from abroad might be no more than later guesswork to account for the tradition of an early confederacy of some kind; and also that this was in marked contrast with the emphasis of Aristotle on the recent phenomenon of an invasion of warfare from abroad.[45] Hence the need to seek elsewhere for an explanation of the tradition; and I looked for it in a tribal confederacy of the Dorians formed during their migration into Greece and perpetuated, through necessity and precedent, during their migration over Crete.

Some novel features of the Cretan Koinon do tend to confirm its dependence on archaic, rather than on contemporary Hellenistic precedents. A *koinodikion* is mentioned in two Cretan Hellenistic inscriptions and Polybios also mentions a Cretan *Koinodikaion*.[46] Such a 'common court' might be explained in terms of mutually agreed federal custom, traditionally based upon an ancient practice of submitting disputes to the arbitration of a tribal confederacy. According to the first of the two relevant inscriptions, a treaty between Hierapytna and Priansos, outstanding disputes were to be settled in a court agreed by both states, when they could not be submitted to *koinodikion*.[47] It is in any case clear from the evidence that the authority of *koinodikion* could still be invoked. This is supported by the evidence relating to the *diagramma* ('ordinance', 'regulation') of the Cretans, which has been associated with the concept of *koinodikion*.

The *diagramma* is mentioned in a treaty between Lato and Gortyn at the end of the third century BC;[48] in a treaty between Hierapytna and Priansos in the early part of the following century;[49] in a treaty between Gortyn and Hierapytna with the Priansians, of roughly similar date;[50] and in the decree of the Koinon concerning Anaphe.[51] It seems clear that the application of the *diagramma* was regulated by arbitration treaties.[52] Although it does not specifically allude to the *diagramma*, the treaty between Knossos and Tylissos arranged under the arbitration of Argos[53] affords a real analogy with the operation of *koinodikion* and *diagramma* – if we may assume that these depended on traditional bonds of kinship consolidated in a kind of Dorian tribal league, later recalled as the *synkretismos*, which still exerted its influence on the Koinon of Hellenistic times. This treaty is an early document, dated to about 450 BC. It is of the utmost importance and similar to the many later treaties between Cretan cities. Its regulations concern the calendar, the right to hold real property, seizure of land for debt, frontiers, religious practices, disposal of war booty, mutual help in diplomatic negotiations and mutual rights of hospitality.[54]

This early treaty may have a significance for Cretan history in the sense that the authority of common traditional bonds is exerted from without. We know, from the evidence now available from archaeology and epigraphy, how correct Homer was in describing Crete as an island of many cities. There is a different sort of emphasis in the writings of philosophers and historians, from whom – and especially from Aristotle in the *Politics* – we readily receive an impression of common unity, of Cretan institutions, indeed of a specific Cretan constitution to be compared and contrasted with the Spartan.[55] The history of the Cretan Koinon illustrates how a concept of unity and solidarity conflicted with the separatist tendencies and the inter-city struggles of the Hellenistic period. It is clear from this history that the concept was based on strong internal traditions. It may be that these traditions reached back even beyond a common Dorian heritage to earlier times.

When Plato is discussing the psychology of the tyrannical man in the ninth book of his *Republic*, he tells how, if the city will not submit to him, the tyrant will then try to chastise his fatherland, as he once chastised his father and mother. He will bring in a new band of followers and so will have and hold his once loved fatherland – or motherland, as the Cretans call it.[56] This significant introduction of a specifically Cretan expression is dramatically emphatic in the context. It is as if Plato had been aware, as Aristotle also warned,[57] that the old aristocracies they had both tended to idealize, though rooted in age-old traditions, could also be undermined by selfishness and greed just as other states had been.[58]

Plato, in his old age, thought that the most vexed problem of Hellas was the helot-system of Sparta and analogous forms of servitude.[59] Aristotle thought it to be generally agreed that a characteristic of good government is leisure from the necessary cares of life, though it was not easy to find out how this leisure was to be provided. The *penesteia*, the serfs, of Thessaly, repeatedly rose against the Thessalians, in the same way as the helots of Sparta, who lay in wait like an enemy watching for the misfortunes of the Spartans. But nothing of the kind had ever yet occurred in Crete. The reason was, perhaps, that neighbouring cities, even when at war with one another, never allied themselves with rebellious elements, because this would not have been in their own interests, since they themselves also possessed a serf class; whereas the Spartans were surrounded by hostile neighbours, Argives, Messenians and Arcadians. Likewise, serf-risings against the Thessalians had their origin in the wars of the Thessalians with their neighbours, Achaeans, Perraiboi and Magnesians. Apart from other weaknesses, it was tiresome to have to look after a serf class and establish a satisfactory system of relations. If control was relaxed, serfs became insolent and claimed equality of rights with their masters, and if their lives were made toilsome, they hated and conspired against them. It was clear that those whose serf-system worked out in this way did not find the best means of dealing with the problem.[60]

And elsewhere in the *Politics* Aristotle points out that it is no original or recent discovery of political philosophy that the state should be divided into classes, and that the fighting men should be distinct from the farmers. Such a system had continued to the present time in Egypt and in Crete, having been established in Egypt, according to tradition, by the legislation of Sesostris, and in Crete by Minos. He again emphasized that the land ought to belong to those who possessed arms and shared in the government; and that those who worked the land should be a class distinct from them. The ideal system would be for those who worked the land to be slaves, not all of the same kin and not men of spirit, since they would thus be adapted for their work and unlikely to make a revolution. The next best arrangement was that they should be alien serfs of a similar disposition.[61]

The servile system of ancient Dorian Crete and the status of its *klarotai* or serfs of the ancestral estates, as of the Spartan helots and Thessalian *penestai* were thus early established as important topics for political philosophy. These topics have been much discussed anew in the last twenty years or so by modern historians who have concerned themselves with the development of slavery in antiquity and in particular with the illustration of differences between 'earlier' and 'later' forms of servitude – or patriarchal and chattel slavery, or serfs and slaves. The nomenclature itself is disputed but the essential historical problem is clear.

The problem and the relevant literature have been usefully surveyed by Pierre Vidal-Naquet in a paper which incorporates a summary of some of his own earlier pertinent contributions and goes on to give an account of the ancient historiography on the subject.[62] He begins by citing a passage from Theopompos,[63] reported by Athenaios, which he considers to be at the heart of discussion about slavery over recent years. This passage runs as follows:

> The Chians were the first Greeks after the Thessalians and Lacedaimonians, to use slaves, but they did not acquire them in the same way. For the Lacedaimonians and Thessalians, as will be seen, constituted their servile class (*douleia*) out of the Greeks who had earlier inhabited the territories which they themselves possess today, the Lacedaimonians taking the land of the Achaeans, the Thessalians that of the Perraibians and Magnesians. The people reduced to slavery were in the first instance called helots, in the second *penestai*. But the slaves whom the Chians own are derived from non-Greek peoples and they pay a price for them.

Vidal-Naquet then refers to a well-known statement of M.I. Finley: 'One aspect of Greek history, in short, is the advance, hand in hand, of ancient democracy *and* chattel slavery.'[64] He goes on to say that the text of Theopompos opposes perfectly clearly the two kinds of slavery known to the Greeks, helot-slavery on the one hand and *l'esclavage-marchandise* (what Anglo-Saxon authors describe as *chattel-slavery*) on the other hand. He adds that, since the publication in 1959 of Lotze's book Μεταξὺ ἐλευθέρων καὶ δούλων (*Between Freedom and Slavery*) a good part of the discussion on slavery has consisted in weighing the implications of the distinction made by Theopompos between the two kinds of slavery. He thinks that to speak of two kinds of slavery is an abuse of language, because, while one of the two, chattel-slavery, has a perfectly clear status, the other resists clear, distinct definition. He agrees that I myself am right to distinguish the earlier kind as radically different from *l'esclavage classique* but rebukes me for using the term 'serfs' of the earlier status because this creates a confusion with the period of the European Middle Ages. There is obvious good sense in this criticism but I would only plead in self-defence that the cause is neither lack of thought nor want of effort. A more exact descriptive term would be extremely useful, but it may be that much more discussion on comparative lines of such topics will be required before a greater precision in terminology is possible.

It is against this general background of ancient testimony and modern analysis of a major historical problem that the ample social terminology from Crete has to be studied. What is here attempted is a brief recapitulation of the main evidence, with an indication of where there is controversy, as a prelude to discussion of topics which have been amplified, partly classified, partly further complicated, by some fairly recent contributions to our knowledge.[65]

As was indicated earlier (pp. 172–4), it is still my opinion that four groupings of the population of Crete in historical times should be distinguished, viz. free citizens, *apetairoi*, serfs and slaves, because, although the word *dolos* in the Gortyn Code is ambiguous in meaning, as elsewhere in ancient literature, there are two passages of the Code where specific reference appears to be made to chattel slaves. Other supporting evidence persuades me that the term χρυσώνητος = 'a person who is bought for gold', used by Kallistratos, marks a division between serfdom and the chattel slavery of a slave trade depending on a money economy.[66]

The age-grades specified in the Code are revealing. The *dromeus* ('runner') was an adult, as compared with the minor (the *apodromos*), so-called because he was a young man still excluded from the public athletic exercises (*dromoi*).[67] A youth probably became a *dromeus* at about the age of twenty, though it is impossible to be more precise. When he did become a *dromeus*, the young man was then a citizen; and the Code gives some indication of his legal responsibilities as a witness and as regards property, since free *dromeis* are specified as being competent witnesses in certain cases. Children must be *dromeis* who consent to sale and mortgage of certain family property; and when a groom-elect who is a *dromeus* refuses to marry the heiress, special regulations are ordained concerning the property. The words *anoros* and *anebos* specify the boy or girl below the age of puberty, while the words *ebion, ebionsa* and *orima* specify the boy or girl after the age of puberty. Organization of the youth and their education in *agelai* depended upon the system of age-grades. After formal initiation into manhood and citizenship upon their graduation from the *agela*, the young men could become members of the *andreion* (men's house) as male citizen adults belonging to the *hetaireia*, analogous to the Athenian phratry, a closed organization of male citizens who, attended by their male children, took their communal meals (*syssitia*) in the *andreion*.

The *pyla* ('tribe') remained politically important and women were therein enumerated. The clan appears to be designated as *startos* and Aristotle tells us that the chief magistrates, the *kosmoi*, were drawn from 'certain clans'.[68] The existence of the *oikos* (household) presupposes, as I consider, the growth of smaller units within the clan. These units would tend to become more and more independent of the basic tribal structure, with the growth of family institutions based on a private property system. Since tribal endogamy was still prevalent at Gortyn, it can be inferred that the *epiballontes* of the Gortyn Code, as one exogamous clan grouping within the tribe, inter-married with their *kadestai*, who formed another exogamous clan grouping. Close ties of social obligation would exist between these intermarrying groups. The *epiballontes* and the *kadestai* would thus have been complementary terms which denoted the bonds established by kinship and marriage.

It is still difficult to decide precisely about the composition of the *apetairoi*, those excluded from the *hetaireiai*, politically inferior but with relatively free economic status, to the extent that they were neither bonded or enslaved.

A free man could pledge his person in payment for debt and he was then described as a *katakeimenos*, a term which could also apparently signify a slave given in pledge. A free man who was condemned for debt and handed over in bondage to his creditor was described as a *nenikamenos*.

The general Greek term for slave, *doulos*, occurs only twice in Homer, the normal Homeric term being *dmos*. Apparently cognate with *dmos* is the Cretan *mnoites* and the associated collective term *mnoia*. As was mentioned earlier, the Gortyn Code uses two terms Ϝοικεύς (*woikeus*) and δôλος (*dolos = doulos*) – to be rendered (as I think) 'serf' and 'slave' respectively. The two words are not strictly used to define two different statuses, for *dolos* is sometimes synonymous with *woikeus* and sometimes denotes a chattel slave.[69]

The word ἀπαμία (*apamia*), apparently referring to serfs or rather to the land worked by serfs was already known to us from the archaic legal fragment from Eleutherna.[70] The word is closely related to ἀφαμιῶται (*aphamiotai*), familiar in the later literature. These words, together with δôλος and Ϝοικεύς, μνοία, περίοικος and κλᾶρος, and a number of derivatives, comprise the extant vocabulary relating to Cretan servitude up to the fifth century BC. The later literary evidence on the subject is chiefly reported by Athenaios,[71] supported by two passages from Strabo[72] and one from Pollux now made familiar in contemporary writings[73] and all neatly summarized in these glosses of the lexicographer Hesychios:

(a) ἀφαμιῶται· οἰκέται, ἄγροικοι, περίοικοι.
(b) κλαρῶται· εἵλωτες, ⟨δοῦλοι⟩.
(c) μνωῖται· δοῦλοι.
and (d) μνοία· οἰκετεία.

μνοία glossed by another collective term οἰκετεία illustrates a relationship with οἶκος (household) and with the Ϝοικεύς of the Gortyn Code.

The word ἀπαμία no longer stands in such isolation, since the publication in 1969 of an important article by H. Van Effenterre and Monique Bougrat,[74] more recently consolidated by Paul Faure,[75] which fairly certainly proves the occurrence of the reading ἀφαμίαν in a treaty between the cities of Lato and Hierapytna, now available in the Museum of Ayios Nikolaos, and dated to the end of the second century BC.

In the commentary on this term in the article of 1969 the following suggestions were made: (1) that ἀπαμία territory was frontier wasteland, a masterless area of refuge, distinct from the fertile *klaros* valley areas; and (2) that the most likely root of the term is πάω, so that the *aphamiotai* would have been dispossessed peasants.[76] It was further suggested that the attested occurrence of ἀπαμία/ἀφαμία in two Cretan epigraphic contexts makes improbable the etymology generally suggested (for example by Frisk and Chantraine), based on a connection with φήμη = *réputation, dignité* (or, with Liddel-Scott-Jones = *good report*).

Frisk,[77] in his entry under ἀφαμιῶται, compares the Hesychios gloss ἀφημοῦντας· ἀγροίκους. There are, however, two more Hesychios glosses which need to be taken into account when we consider possible etymology. These are: (i) ἀφημίαστους· ἀγροικίας, where Latte suggests we might read ἀγροίκους; and (ii) ἐφημίαι· ἀγροί· καὶ βέλτιον ἀφημίαι– where Latte suggests we read ἀγροικοι.[78]

Mention has already been made of the important new evidence published in 1970[79] and revealed as a result of the acquisition by the British Museum of a semi-circular bronze plate resembling in form the 'mitra' or abdominal guard worn by Greek warriors and inscribed on both sides in an archaic Cretan script. The editors suggested a late archaic date, i.e. somewhere around 500 BC, of this earliest full record from any Greek city of the creation of a high technical office. The high position of this new office of Scribe and Recorder is clear. He gets subsistence, immunity from taxes and annual payment in kind. He does not merely attend but also participates in all meetings of the *kosmos* or board of magistrates in his capacity as secretary; and he performs the functions of priesthood (in public sacrifices) for certain cults, those which were not already managed by existing priesthoods hereditary in the local families.

Commenting on the new word ποινικάζεν (*poinikazen*), the editors argued that, since it is coupled with μναμονεῦϜεν (*mnamoneuwen*), its basic meaning must be 'to do φοινικήια, to write'. The ποινικαστάς (*poinikastas*) will then be the scribe, i.e. whoever writes and keeps records. The formation of the verb is not altogether clear. If it is built on φοίνιξ we should expect an -ίζω verb; an -άζω form may have been influenced by some other verb in which the -α- was etymologically justified, or by the substantive Φοινίκα. Also it could be argued on the evidence of ἐνεκυράζω that -άζω was a favourite suffix in Cretan, and that its distribution was wider than that of the similar suffix in Attic. In Greek -άζω rather than -ίζω is normally used to form verbs derived from colour names. Obviously this is not sufficient to prove that the original meaning of ποινικάζω was something like 'to make red' and had no direct connection with 'Phoenician'; but this possibility should be kept in mind.

In my own further provisional comments on this document in 1972, I made the point that novelty of function was here marked by the primary element of the verbal doublet ποινικάζεν κὰι μναμονεῦϜεν, meaning 'to do φοινικήια, to write', to do something more novel than be a traditional *mnamon* or 'remembrancer'; and I suggested that this could be a further reason for bearing in mind the possibility that the original meaning of ποινικάζεν was something like 'to make red' and had no direct connection with 'Phoenician'. In support I recalled that H.L. Lorimer[80] had suggested that paint would be a natural addition to inscriptions on wood and might account for the Cypriot use of ἰναλίνω (*engrave, inscribe*) = γράφω (*write*). That the characters engraved on the Idalion bronze (probably second half of the fifth century) are described in the inscription which they record as ἰναλαλισμένα at least testifies that the Cypriots had originally used a soft reed pen or a fine brush, the alternatives for a scribe who writes on parchment. Two glosses of Hesychios show that the practice continued after the Classical age.[81]

Raubitschek has rather a different view of ποινικάзεν. While the exact derivation of this verb may not be clear, he says, the editors are surely right when they translate 'to do φοινικήια'. At first glance this does not seem to be more than a confirmation of the well-known fact that the Greeks got their alphabet from the Phoenicians. A careful examination of the evidence, however, leads to a somewhat different conclusion. Herodotos (5.58) tells us how the Phoenicians who had come to Boeotia wrote Greek before anybody else did. Subsequently, the Greek neighbours of the Phoenicians – Heredotos calls them 'Ionians' and means with this term the Euboeans and Athenians – adopted the alphabet from the Phoenicians, which these had used to write Greek. Naturally, they made changes, to adjust it to their own language and dialect. They called the letters φοινικήια, not because they had derived them from the Phoenician alphabet, but because they had taken them from the Phoenicians who had used them to write Greek. This means that the Greek alphabet is a creation of the Phoenicians, and the different forms of the Greek alphabet are, at least in part, occasioned by the particular part of Greece where the Phoenicians settled, learned Greek, and tried to write it. The same process seems to have taken place in Crete. Herodotos only mentions the Phoenician settlement on the island of Thera (4.147), but linguistic, epigraphical and archaeological evidence suggests the presence of Phoenicians in Crete as well. In particular the title of the scribe, φοινικαστάς, is derived from the verb of action, φοινικάзειν, which must mean 'to write (Greek) the way the Phoenicians do'.

There also appeared in 1972 a thoroughly documented article by Chantraine in which he too discussed the ποινικάзεν of this inscription and explored the possibility that its original meaning was something like 'to make red' and had no direct connection with 'Phoenician'. Pointing out that painting inscriptions in red is a well-known practice he suggested, in the light of this practice, that the Cretan *poinikastas*, in a small community, might have fulfilled the three functions of secretary, engraver and painter – a citizen charged with the duty of transcribing official texts (in red characters) and supervising their correction.

Chantraine invoked supporting testimony from three epigraphic texts and a gloss of Hesychios. In two inscriptions of Lesbos (Mytilene)[82] there is an official called a φοινικογράφος. Perhaps he was rather like the Cretan *poinikastas*. And, since these two inscriptions are Hellenistic, when the Phoenician origin of the alphabet would have been largely forgotten, it is more likely that φοινικογράφος would signify a person who inscribed red letters rather than one who wrote Phoenician letters. The third inscription, from Teos,[83] dated about

475 BC, has the same adjective φοινικήιος which is used by Herodotos (5.58). Hesychios glosses the word ἐκφοινίξαι by ἀναγνῶσαι which, says Chantraine, can only mean 'persuade' – the gloss is corrupt. Latte boldly corrects to ἀναχρῶσαι. ἀναγνῶναι would be more cautious but is not very likely, though it would bring us back to writing. Chantraine's conclusion was that these new, remarkable terms do not relate to the borrowing by the Greeks of the Phoenician alphabet. Neither does Lesbian φοινικογράφος. If he hesitated, perhaps wrongly, about φοινικήια, this is because the word is used by Herodotos, but its use in the Tean inscription would seem strange.

Before the emergence of *poinikastas* in 1970 scholars had speculated about the use of engraved signs and red paint in early Cretan writing.[84] Some have suggested that the term φοινικήια could have been applied originally to Bronze Age syllabic writing rather than to the Phoenician alphabet. Thus G.E. Mylonas in 1966 – (though painted Linear B inscriptions are actually in various colours) – understood the legend of Kadmos as most probably referring to the introduction of letters painted in red colour and he suggested that these painted letters might be identified with the Linear B script.[85]

In their *Selection of Greek Historical Inscriptions*, published in 1969, Meiggs and Lewis included several pieces of evidence relating to paint on inscriptions which are helpful in examining a wider landscape than is provided by Cretan writing and Cypriot lexicology. Their no. 32 (p. 69), *a Halicarnassian Law concerning disputed Property* (? 465–450 BC) perhaps, they say, had the dot in its thetas coloured to distinguish it from omicron. Their three other pieces of evidence are more substantial.

Their no. 30 (p. 62) comprises two fragments of public imprecations at Teos round about 470 BC. The concluding lines of the second (B) fragment (35–41), apply a curse to anyone who breaks the stelai, cuts out the letters, or makes them unreadable. The editors comment: 'For φοινικήια (ll 37 ff) = letters, reflecting the Phoenician origin of the Greek alphabet, see Herodotos 5.58. ἀφανέας (ll 38 f): letters would be regarded as unreadable if the red paint were removed; cf. Thucydides' ἀμυδροῖς γράμμασι (6. 54.7) of the letters on the altar of Peisistratos'.

Their no. 14 (p. 25), perhaps ? late sixth century BC, an Athenian decree concerning Salamis, is the earliest Athenian decree to have survived, having to do with the status and obligations of men living on Salamis. The editors state, without further comment: 'Wilholm [Beiträge 240 n. 5] asserts that alternate lines of this text were coloured red and blue.'

Most interesting of all is their no. 11 (p. 19), the dedication of Peisistratos, son of Hippias, round about 521 BC, discussed by many scholars. There are many incidental historical problems which cannot be discussed here, but there is a matter immediately relevant to the context of the present discussion. Thucydides (6. 54.6) records that the grandson of the tyrant Peisistratos, to commemorate his archonship, dedicated the Altar of the Twelve Gods in the

Agora and of Apollo in the Pythion. Thucydides says that the Pythian inscription can still be seen, though in faded letters: ἔτι κὰι νῦν δῆλόν ἐστιν ἀμυδροῖς γράμμασι λέγον τάδε; and he quotes this version. Meiggs–Lewis comment: 'The epithet ἀμυδροῖς is surprising, since the letters are still clear; it almost certainly refers to the disappearance of the paint with which the letters had been filled.' The Gomme–Andrewes–Dover commentary on this passage says: '. . . the inscription survives – and its letters are by no means "faint" to us, as Greek inscriptions go; but no doubt the letters of any inscription a hundred years old were faint to Thucydides by contrast with the great number of much more recent inscriptions to be seen in Athens. Possibly too, they had once been painted and the paint had largely worn off. Allowance must perhaps be made for rhetorical exaggeration of the difference between old and recent inscriptions, for Thucydides is not above pride in the trouble he has taken.'

It seems fairly safe to conclude from this glance at a wider perspective (a) that any paint used in these times in written records on stone did, not surprisingly, fade; and (b) that we should be grateful, in spite of the incidental problems, for any surviving traces of paint on any surviving documents.

Those who hold that a 'red letter' explanation of *poinikastas* has plausibility or those who (like P. and R. Edwards in their *Kadmos* article) of 1974 more strongly incline to the 'Phoenician' explanation would agree that the problem is in need of further clarification and that scholarly debate is likely to continue. For the issue as posed in these terms has to do with the origin and transmission of alphabetic writing as well with the determination of the meaning of the title and function of an important official in a period when Cretan state institutions were in process of being established.

However, these two explanations which have been discussed above are not the only possibilities. It should be clear that the appearance of *poinikastas* in 1970 has generated much fruitful discussion about some fundamental social problems in archaic Crete. The most substantial and far-ranging discussion of major historical problems posed by the text since its publication has been written by A.J. Beattie.[86] He offers a quite different explanation of the meaning of the title of the new official. He proposes that noun and verb, *poinikastas* and *poinikazen* should be taken away from the sphere of writing, whether Phoenician characters or in red paint, and transferred to the vocabulary of the law-courts. The official should be regarded as a judge, not a scribe; and he should be called a 'Reeve'.

We know many things for certain about the society and government of historical Crete. However, even in documents which have been familiar to scholars for many years, there are matters which are much less certain of definition. Small wonder that, when a new document is discovered of the kind which has been considered above, with new words in new contexts, certainty about the problems they pose should be even more difficult to achieve. But even when agreement on certain points seems out of reach, the discussion provoked by the study of new documents often throws fresh light on old problems and leads to their solution, in whole or in part.

14

ARTISTIC RENAISSANCE

As the two preceding chapters have indicated, the Cretans of the archaic period were prominent in their pioneering of such indispensable components of the Classical civilization associated with the whole era of the Greek city-states as alphabetic writing and law-making. It would be surprising if these intellectual achievements had not also served as stimulating influences in a variety of contemporary artistic developments.

It has been suggested that there is a kind of continuity in structure in the line of descent from the juxtaposed complex of palace, market-place and town-hall of Mallia to the familiar complex of temple, market-place and town-hall of the city-states of the historical period.[1] The early revival of urbanization in archaic Crete gives substance to this suggestion. Pendlebury saw the eighth century BC as the beginning of the true Hellenic Period in Crete. Indications of the wealth of the island in comparison with the desperate conditions of the earlier Iron Age and the rise of its cities make us feel, he thought, that at last we are in touch with Greek literature and history.[2]

The ancient site of Prinias was set upon a natural acropolis first occupied in Late Minoan times and it was not abandoned in the archaic period. Two temples have been excavated, the earlier and more important, dated about mid-seventh century BC, being a variety of the *templum in antis* or simplest form of Greek temple, entered by a porch with two columns between the side-posts (*antae*). Some of its features (as also at Dreros) have been reminiscent not so much of an archaic Greek temple as of the little shrines of the Late Minoan III period and especially of those at Ayia Triada and at Mallia. Instead of the two columns normal in a *templum in antis*, this had only one square pier between the porch *antae*. Two wooden columns were apparently set in line with the pier, in the middle of the *cella* (9.75m. long and 5.94m. wide), on low stone bases of Minoan-Mycenaean type supporting the cross-beams for a flat roof, with a central hearth between them. The central post of the entrance from the porch to the *cella* supported a stone transom with female figures carved in low relief on the soffit. There was an animal frieze on the front of the transom, above which at each end were a pair of seated female figures helping to support the true lintel. There were fragments of low reliefs of a procession of mounted spearmen.³

The archaic site of Dreros has the same characteristic complex of temple, market-place and town-hall. This very early temple of Apollo at Dreros, dating perhaps to the second quarter of the eighth century BC, is of considerable architectural importance. Its plan is the forerunner of the Prinias temple, sub-Minoan in appearance with a central column, table of offerings and a ledge at the inner end for offerings. This rectangular temple built of small stones was 10.90m. long and 7.20m. wide, consisting of a single room with an almost north-east to south-west orientation. It had a sunken hearth, in the shape of a rectangular pit lined with stone slabs and filled with ashes. Against one wall there was an altar of horns, recalling the horned altar of Delos where Theseus was supposed to have celebrated the Crane Dance. In the west corner stood some bronze figures.⁴

Lato in the eastern part of the island conveys a good impression of the layout of an early city of the archaic period. This site probably commanded the small neighbouring plain of Lakonia by the eighth century BC, as well as the coast routes and a secondary harbour-town, Lato pros Kamara (Lato-at-the-Arch), modern Ayios Nikolaos. The city had a steep double acropolis, a market-place and a town-hall approached by a flight of steps, a temple and other buildings. Its town-hall was likened by Hutchinson to a kind of prototype of a French *hôtel-de-ville* or of an English town-hall, or, looking backwards, as the descendant of a Minoan palace approached through its 'theatral area'. He thought that the municipal architect of Lato deserves to be complimented on his economic utilization of the very small space available and also on his ingenuity in using two towers of the inner town wall to provide an imposing entrance for his town-hall.⁵

To turn from architecture to the plastic arts, as represented by sculpture, modelling, carving in varied materials such as stone, clay, bronze, gold and ivory, it is generally agreed that Cretan artists produced works of considerable merit in the course of the eighth and seventh centuries BC. These works tend to be described stylistically by the term 'Dedalic' (after Daidalos, the Cretan artist of tradition), with its marked oriental influences. It is not absolutely certain where in Greece this important new style began its development but there seems little doubt that it was in some area of Crete. Nor is the first material in which the style was practised exactly known, since early examples occur in clay, bronze, iron and wood. Clay is the cheapest and most ubiquitous of materials and so, as Higgins has suggested,⁶ is perhaps the most likely choice both for the imported models and for the local adaptations.

The Dedalic stylistic phases were defined by Jenkins as follows.⁷ A Proto-Dedalic style (680–670 BC), represented by a small group of figurines, seems to illustrate the principal features of Dedalic style in general. The head is seen from the front, the face is long and narrow, the forehead low and the chin pointed. The hair tends to be arranged like a sort of wig, in an Egyptian manner. As compared with contemporary heads from elsewhere in Greece, Cretan examples have a broader face and a treatment of the eye with firmly marked brows and two incised lines for the upper lids. Hutchinson observed that the new Dedalic style affected not only figurines of clay or bronze and jewellery, but also had a notable effect on the ancient craft of making *pithoi* or large stone jars with moulded ornaments, a craft which goes back through Minoan times into the Cretan Neolithic. While the *pithoi* of the Bronze Age or the early Iron Age had largely displayed skenomorphic patterns, such as relief imitations of the rope slings, the Dedalic artists (in Crete, as in Boeotia, the Peloponnese and the Cyclades), added friezes on the necks or shoulders of the *pithoi* with relief figures of horses, warriors, sphinxes, lions or chariots.

The Early Dedalic style (670–655 BC) modified the face to make it fuller and rounded off the pointed chin. In the seventh century, as Higgins observes (recalling that Crete was probably the centre of origin of the Dedalic style), there was a substantial output of terracottas, Dedalic plaques and other kinds of reliefs are most common, but free-standing human figures are also found. Decoration is in matt paint, rare elsewhere so early, but perhaps not surprising in Crete because of the popularity of vases in this technique. After a lull in the sixth century, the Cretan terracotta industry revived in the fifth and thereafter flourished for three or four centuries.

The Middle Dedalic (655–630 BC), divided into three sub-phases, is regarded as the culmination of the Dedalic style. The first sub-phase is characterized by improved modelling. Stone sculptures are exemplified by the horsemen procession and the goddesses from the soffit of the transom from Prinias. Assuming that it is really Cretan, the best bronze of the period is the head from Olympia in the Karlsruhe collection. The face is trapezoidal and the faintly-smiling mouth is thin-lipped, the brows up-curving. The low, flat cranium is typical of Cretan seventh-century heads. This famous work is the earliest example from Greece of hollow casting in bronze, looking as solid as if it had been actually made by solid casting.

The second sub-phase of Middle Dedalic reveals a development away from frontal emphasis towards a representation of profile. A limestone female statuette, found at Auxerre and now in the Louvre, is commonly referred to as the most characteristic product. Hutchinson shrewdly observed that the flat board like figure, with features cut out in the soft limestone by a knife, suggests the influence of wood carving. He compared, as displaying a simpler technique, some archaic funeral monuments in the form of stelai from Prinias, of some importance as the earliest figured tombstones in Greece since Mycenaean times. All details are incised in the soft stone to give an impression of low relief. The only complete example is of a woman dressed in a Doric *peplos*, spindle in hand, standing on a low base. Fragmentary examples from the district are of similar female figures or of warriors dressed as heavily-armed hoplites, with large round shields and a couple of spears.

The bronze figures of Apollo and of two attendant females found at Dreros may have belonged to this same period. These statues in the round were the result of an innovation in technique which resulted in improved methods of shaping. By this time the first large marble statues were being produced and this would have led to an imitation of the development by bronzesmiths. The 'sphyrelaton' technique involved the covering of a wooden core – a statue or statuette – with metal leaf which was fixed by rivets. This technique left its legacy in the form of chryselephantine sculpture, since gold plating could be used instead of bronze. These early statues in the round from Dreros were devised with the aesthetic qualities of their metal material in mind, with simplified masses, clear, smooth and rounded, the features intended to be viewed frontally. There are hollow cavities in the bronze for eyeballs of a different material to be inserted, a familiar refinement of technique apparently dating from this period. The eyeball is not a supplementary piece of decoration but a vivid means of adding to the animation of a statue.

The trend towards modelling in the round was further elaborated in the third sub-phase of Middle Dedalic. The Late Dedalic is dated to 630–620 BC; and a Sub-Dedalic phase to 620–600 BC.

Eight principle types of terracottas are listed by Higgins[8] for the seventh–sixth century period, subsequent to his observation that the substantial seventh century output was followed by a marked decrease in the sixth century, not only of terracottas but of other artistic products. Dedalic plaques are more common in Crete than elsewhere and hence the evolution of the Syrian Astarte plaque may have evolved into the Greek Dedalic plaque in Crete, an evolution traceable from Protodedalic, through Early, Middle and Late Dedalic to the Sub-Dedalic of about 600 BC. A naked type with hands to sides is most popular, though there are other, naked and draped, varieties. Reliefs of a man, perhaps a charioteer, in profile with Dedalic hair are common at Praisos, as are reliefs of warriors in the style of Late Geometric vase-painting, both types probably to be assigned to the early seventh century. Throughout this century rectangular relief-plaques with sphinxes and griffins were made at many sites, the faces on the sphinxes usually frontal and covering Early, Middle and Late Dedalic phases. Plaques with a winged man are rarer, with head and chest frontal, legs striding to the right, hands holding the tendrils of a plant. Narrative reliefs form another seventh-century Cretan speciality. An Athenae from Gortyn is a good example of the rare type of Dedalic heads on wheel-made bodies; and Gortyn too produced examples of the rare Dedalic heads, flat or cylindrical, on hand-made bodies.

If it can be attributed with certainty to archaic Crete, the well-known Delphi *kouros* is one of two superb examples of Cretan bronzework of the period. First of a line of archaic Apollos, there can be no doubt that this is one of the first clear statements of Greek sculptural genius, with its plastically differentiated muscle-masses and carefully designed proportions of body height seven and a half times that of the head and the division of the legs standing exactly at half the height. The other is the Berlin *kreophoros*, a man carrying a ram and wearing Cretan loincloth. This finely modelled statuette is of a more recent date, a splendid piece of work of probably late seventh century date.

What we know of the artefacts of the Late Geometric period (on Brock's dating 770–735 BC) is mainly derived from family chamber tombs excavated near Knossos and by some finds at Arkhades. Some small flasks were either imported from Cyprus or were Cretan imitations of such imports. Brock described the period from 735 to 680 BC as the Early Orientalizing period. The early Orientalizing pottery of graves around Knossos exhibits decorative motifs of Oriental origin on native vase shapes. New vase shapes were borrowed from Cyprus or the Greek mainland but (for Hutchinson)[9] the gay polychrome patterns including large cable patterns, the Oriental tree of life, lotus garlands and other stylized designs painted in the crusted technique in fugitive matt colours are reminiscent of the painted bricks of Assyria as found at Assar and, to a lesser degree, at Nineveh. This polychrome work is confined to the Knossos neighbourhood in Crete, although a few vases in a similar technique have been found near Athens.

Among the earliest and the most remarkable examples of Oriental influences on Greek art are the famous round shields found in the cave on Mount Ida, dating perhaps from the eighth and seventh centuries BC. The largest, of a diameter between 50 and 70cm., may have been used as defensive arms. A thin

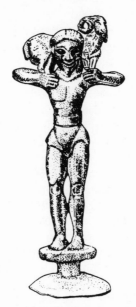

20   Kriophoros, wearing Cretan loincloth 7th century BC

sheet of decorated bronze, usually about 1mm. thick, was attached by nails or rivets to a wooden base covered with leather. The decorative technique was like that found on Cretan helmets, with relief either in repoussé or engraved, and covering the whole surface. Most shields have an animal's head in the centre, usually that of a lion. One early specimen apparently had its central boss in the shape of an eagle's head, the body with spread wings covering in low relief the larger part of the circle, among figures of sphinxes, lions and serpents. Smaller shields were used as votive offerings, perhaps used in sacred dances associated with the Cretan cult of Zeus. One type of shield is familiar all over Europe in the eighth and seventh centuries BC, in Ireland, Spain, Germany, Bohemia, Italy, Greece and Cyprus. European examples would have been related with the trade routes by which Baltic amber was distributed since, as Hutchinson pointed out,[10] Cretan graves of the period sometimes contain amber beads or jewels with inlaid amber, though the amber in them seems to be less abundant than that of many Mycenaean graves in the Peloponnese. One famous cult object found at Ida is a bronze drum with Assyrianized representation of Zeus and the Kouretes. Other objects in the find included bronze cymbals, bowls, vessels for pouring wine and basins, bronze votive animals, bulls and goats, ornamental figures like sphinxes, doves, snakes, a horse and a lion; and also groups in cast bronze, such as a warship with rowers, chariots, warriors, hounds and a man milking a cow.

A find of Cretan armour, said to be from Afrati in south central Crete, probably belonging to a period from the third quarter of the seventh century to the early sixth century BC, has been the subject of much discussion in recent years.[11] This recent evidence seems to indicate that the Cretan helmet, previously generally thought to have been a provincial offspring of the Corinthian type, had its own native evolution independently of Corinth. The *mitrai* from the find include the bronze *mitra* acquired by the British Museum with the inscription concerning Spensithios which has been earlier discussed.[12]

Cretan coinage, on present evidence, started its development in the fifth century BC, roughly about 150 years after the earliest adoption of coinage by a European Greek state on the island of Aigina. In the Classical period the usual Cretan standard was the Aiginetic, with the stater or didrachm and the drachma as chief denominations. After the time of Alexander the Great, the Attic standard gradually replaced the Aiginetic; and, after 200 BC, many cities struck imitations of the Athenian tetradrachm with their own names and symbols. Among the first cities to issue coins was Gortyn; and, in the first phase of coinage development from about 500 to 430 BC, Knossos, Phaistos, Itanos, Eleutherna, Lyttos and Praisos were other cities which issued their coinage. Their example was subsequently followed by other cities and, until autonomous issues ceased after the Roman conquest, nearly 40 cities of Crete had their coinage.

Some of these cities produced coins which have won esteem as fine examples of coin-engraving. Thus, for instance, there is featured on the earliest coins of Gortyn and Phaistos in the fifth century BC, an archaic Europa, riding on her bull;[13] and this type persisted on Gortynian coins throughout the fifth century. The pictorial character of these coins, which is even more marked in the fourth century coins both of Gortyn and Phaistos, has suggested a derivation from local frescoes. On a famous Phaistos type Europa is shown seated on a rock, welcoming with raised hand the approaching bull. From contemporary Gortyn a coin series, equally remarkable, tells the story of the marriage of Zeus and Europa.[14]

15

RELIGION

The pantheon of Olympian deities traditionally canonized by Homer and Hesiod was the framework of the official religion of the city-states for such time as these forms of social organization constituted the essential local environments of Greek civilization in the archaic and classical periods of ancient Greek history. In the most general sense this was as true of Dorian Crete as of any other part of the Greek world. However, in Crete, as in other areas, there were local differences, whose nature can be detected sometimes by the epithets attached to the Olympian deities or by the peculiarities of certain cults of these deities in particular areas. In Crete, too, the religious traditions and practices of the past, surviving from the Bronze Age and from the centuries before that epoch of enduring achievement, were bound to be there more than usually tenacious both within the fabric of official, and also in the forms of popular religion.

Olympian Zeus, as distinct from the old vegetation-god who is the specifically Cretan Zeus, was worshipped as a principal deity with many different epithets which frequently betray survival of a religious substratum earlier than the Olympian supremacy.

In his role of patron of citizens gathered in assembly at the *agora*, Zeus Agoraios ('of the market-place') is mentioned at Kantanos in the west, in the central cities of Dreros and Gortyn, and at Itanos in the east.[1] At Dreros and Gortyn Zeus Agoraios is mentioned immediately after Hera in a long list of deities, a traditional prominence presumably settled early in historical times. By contrast, in the famous Itanian oath, as late as the third century BC, the citizens significantly swear by invocation of deities in this order of precedence: Diktaian Zeus, Hera, the gods in Dikte, Athene Polias and the gods worshipped in the shrine of Athene, Zeus Agoraios and Pythian Apollo. It is in the east that we might naturally expect to find indications of old cult traditions.

In an imprecation from Phalasarna of the fourth century BC Zeus is invoked as *alekikakos* ('averter of evil'), indicating a not surprising survival of pre-Olympian superstitions.[2] Coins of Arcadia, Knossos and Aptera portray the head of Zeus Ammon and these coin-types may well indicate some quite early connexion between Olympian Zeus and Egyptian Amen-Ra.[3] A cult of Zeus

Arbios in the south is attested and this may have been quite ancient, though we do not know the meaning of the epithet.⁴ Zeus Brontaios ('of thunder') in the vicinity of Hierapytna was probably just the same as the Zeus Bronton ('he who thunders') whose cult was well established in Phrygia.⁵ No substantial knowledge can be gained from the scanty evidence concerning such Zeus epithets as *epopsios* ('overlooking') at Itanos; or Hekatombaios, the god to whom hecatombs were offered, at Gortyn (as in Arcadia); or Kroneios and Kronidas, pre-Olympian son of Kronos, at Palaikastro and Kydonia; or Makhaneus ('contriver?') in the mid-fifth century Argive draft of a treaty between Knossos and Tylissos, arranged under the auspices of Argos; or Melikhios ('the kindly one') at such places as Lato, Olous and Hierapytna; or Monnitios (of doubtful meaning), the chief deity of Malla; or Oratrios ('guardian and patron of treaties') at various places; or Skylios (also of doubtful meaning) at various places; or Soter ('the saviour') at Itanos and near Knossos; or Tallaios – associated with the legendary Talos, 'the bronze man', who was described as a bull, was also the sun, and became Zeus in Crete – at such places as Dreros and Olous.⁶

There are other epithets which firmly associate Zeus with very old cult practices and traditions. For instance, a celestial Zeus of Gortyn, called Zeus Asterios, is mentioned in Byzantine sources. He is associated with Europa; and, according to earlier writers such as Hesiod and Bakchylides, Zeus gave her in marriage to a Cretan king Asterion or Asterios or Asteros, who reared the children of Europa and Zeus. Tzetzes says that Sarpedon, Minos and Rhadamanthys were the sons of Zeus Asterios. The Minotaur was called Asterios or Asterion; and there were sacred herds of cattle of the sun-god at Gortyn. There was also at Gortyn a cult of a solar deity, Atymnos, brother of Europa, whose early death was mourned. An inscription of the early fifth century BC gives evidence of sun-worship. If the solar cycle does indeed go back into Minoan times, it could be that Gortynian Zeus Asterios, originally a Phoenician solar deity and male counterpart of Astarte, supplanted an earlier solar 'priest-king'.⁷

The young god Welkhanos is featured on coins of Phaistos from *c.*430–300 BC, sitting in the branches of a leafless tree, his right hand caressing his sacred bird, the cock; and there is a bull on reverse.⁸ A gloss of Hesychios seems to confirm his Cretan identification with Zeus; and the temple of Zeus Welkhanos was built upon the ruins of Ayia Triada. The month-name and spring festival of the god, the Welkhania, is known to us from inscriptions at Gortyn, Lyttos and Knossos.¹⁰ We are justified in supposing that Zeus Welkhanos is a form of survival of the young Minoan god of fertility, associated with a vegetation-cycle, particularly connected with Cretan Zeus, sometimes perhaps, like Hyakinthos, with Apollo. Comparing the Gortynian coin portrayals of Zeus, Europa and the eagle, we may further conjecture that the cock, like the eagle, indicates a bird-epiphany and that Welkhanos could have been partner in a sacred marriage with the Minoan goddess.[11]

We have seen[12] that the legends which centre upon the birth of Cretan Zeus were responsible for the epithet Kretagenes which appears in the epigraphic evidence of historical times; that the mythological evidence is closely associated with the Diktaian Cave; and that the epithet Diktaios derives from Dikte and the same (presumably pre-Greek) root is common to the mountain Dikte, the goddess Diktynna and to the epithet. Strabo connects the temple of Diktaian Zeus with the Eteocretans and particularly with the people of Praisos.[13]

The Hellenic temple on the site of the Minoan town of Palaikastro had been destroyed but excavation brought to light enough votive offerings near the surface to identify its position; and the location of the altar was fixed by a bed of ashes. These votive offerings, bronzes and terracottas, belonged mostly to the archaic period and indicated that the temple was most influential from the seventh to the fifth centuries BC. The discovery of the famous Hymn of the Kouretes, in honour of Zeus of Dikte, confirmed that this was undoubtedly the temple of Diktaian Zeus.[14] One verse[15] of this Hymn seems to indicate that the temple did not belong to any one city but was rather a common centre of worship for the inhabitants of several towns in eastern Crete. Though the temple was probably under the control of Praisos for some time,[16] epigraphic evidence shows that it was under the control of Hierapytna in the later half of the second century BC.[17] Even though the temple site may have been controlled by Hierapytna during its political ascendancy in eastern Crete, inhabitants of such neighbouring states as Praisos and Itanos may well have continued to frequent the temple.

The inscription of the Hymn of the Kouretes was apparently made, on the evidence of the lettering, as late as the third century AD. However, there is little doubt that the original is considerably older, since the inscription was done twice on the same stone, at first badly and then more correctly. We may then infer that it was either transmitted from one generation to another by a process of oral tradition or copied from some existing text. Any date between the sixth and fourth centuries BC might be appropriate on metrical grounds, but the end of the fourth or beginning of the third century BC is indicated for stylistic reasons. Formally, the hymn is composed of a set of stanzas, with a recurrent refrain. The text of refrain and first stanza yield this sense:

> *O hail, thou Kronian,*
> *O welcome, greatest Kouros,*
> *Almighty of Brightness,*
> *Here now present, leading thy Spirits,*
> *O come for the year to Dikte,*
> *And rejoice in this ode,*

> *Which we on the strings strike, as we*
> *Blend it with the pipes' sounds, as we*
> *Are chanting our song, standing round*
> *This thy altar, walled so well.*
>
> *O hail, etc.*

After this invocation of Zeus as son of Kronos and as 'greatest Kouros' – apparently the idealization of the most worthy of themselves by a company of youthful participants in the rite – the meaning of a damaged text becomes less certain.[18] The subject of the second stanza appears to recall the birth of Zeus and the guardianship of the Kouretes. In the later part of the hymn there are traditional fertility formulae and appeals to the god to increase cattle and flocks, corn, cities and ships, the youth of the cities and the lawful order of cities – all those essential elements of organized life that need to be renewed with the annual return of the young god to Dikte, invoked by those who have graduated by initiation into a new life themselves.

Kouretes derives from *kouros* ('boy' or 'young man') and it may well be that the Hymn of the Kouretes was sung by *epheboi*, newly-initiated citizens, as part of a festival honouring the epiphany of Zeus Kretagenes. There was an important festival in some leading cities of central and eastern Crete called the Thiodaisia, apparently associated with the annual graduation of the young men from the *agela* and with their marriages. Outside Crete the festival was associated with Dionysos, who was so little needed in Cretan religion because his cult attributes were closely attached to Cretan Zeus. The deity celebrated at the Thiodaisia could have originated in a Minoan bull-god, later allied with Zeus Kretagenes. Foot-races may have formed part of the festival which probably also included the sacrifice of a bull. Perhaps the festival at which the Hymn of the Kouretes was sung was very like the Thiodaisia.[19]

Zeus Idaios ('Zeus of Ida') is also closely involved with the indigenous cult of Zeus. This cult gained wide repute all over the Greek world and its focus was the Idaian Cave, some 20 miles distant from Knossos and connected with the city by a road where pilgrims rested in the shade of trees.[20] The cave and the surrounding meadows were sacred to Zeus and votive offerings were placed beside the entrance.[21] There was a tradition that Pythagoras had gone to the cave with Epimenides, who was both a Cretan and a Koures. Having landed in Crete, he went to the mystics of Morges, one of the Idaian Daktyloi, who purified him with the thunder-stone. He lay beside the sea at dawn and beside a river at night, with his head wrapped in the fleece of a black ram. On going down into the Idaian Cave he wore black wool and, after passing thrice nine days in accordance with custom, he offered a funeral sacrifice to Zeus, saw the throne which was spread for him every year and inscribed an epigram on his tomb entitled 'Pythagoras to Zeus' which began: 'Here Zan lies dead, whom they call Zeus'. Zan/Zeus is dead, but his return to life in the form of Zagreus is prepared for. There was a cavern ritual of death and rebirth, the initiate sharing in the death and resurrection of the god.[22]

The ritual apparently serves as background to a well-known fragment of *The Cretans* of Euripides which is quoted by Porphyrios who says that it was delivered by a chorus of inspired Cretan devotees of Zeus.[23]

> *Thou lord over Crete with her hundred*
> *Towns, O thou son of the mighty Zan*
> *And Europa, Phoenician-born.*
>
> *To thee I have come now, since I have left*
> *Those sanctified shrines which are roofed by the*
> *Native beam that was cut with Khalybian axe,*
> *Its joints of the cypress fitted*
> *Exact with the glue from a bull's hide.*
>
> *Unsullied the life I have led since*
> *I became initiate of Idaian Zeus*
> *And herdsman of Zagreus who wanders by night,*
> *Accomplished the raw-flesh feasts and held high*
> *Torches to the Mountain-mother, torches*
> *Of the Kouretes,*
> *Hallowed and named as a Bakkhos.*
>
> *All-white are the clothes I wear and I shun*
> *Human birth, touch no urn of the dead, have been*
> *On guard to avoid all taste of meat*
> *Once endowed with the breath of life.*

This is poetical description, probably not exact in all points, yet significantly evoking a mystical cult of Cretan Zeus. The Idaian Zeus of this passage is also celebrated by Kouretes just like the god who is celebrated in the Palaikastro Hymn. There can be little doubt that he is the same age-old Cretan deity whose attributes are so similar to those of Dionysos that the initiate in his mystic rites can be named as Bakkhos. He is a god who dies and is re-born, prompting renewal of life in the participants of his mysteries. A major feature of the ritual is the eating of the raw flesh of the bull, the god himself manifested in animal form, the Cretan god called by a name perhaps first Hellenized into Zagreus.[24]

Like other mountain-names, Ida means 'forest' or 'wood', and there are references to the oak-trees of Mount Ida and also to its famous cypresses. The Euripidean fragment indicates that the cypress, like the oak, had its part in the cult of Rhea and Zeus.[25] Theophrastos says that there was a fruit-bearing poplar, Pliny a willow, in the mouth of the Idaian Cave.[26] Excavation of the cave has shown that Zeus was worshipped on Mount Ida for over a millennium and well into Roman times.[27] The votive objects recovered included convex circular bronze shields, their central bosses representing a lion's head, an eagle, a hawk and the like; a bronze drum has an Assyrianized representation of Zeus and the Kouretes. There were bronze cymbals, bowls, vessels for pouring wine and basins; archaic groups in cast bronze, including a warship with rowers, chariots, warriors, hounds and a man milking a cow; bronze votive animals including bulls and goats; ornamental figures including sphinxes, doves, snakes, a horse and a lion; and objects in terracotta, iron arrow-heads and lance-heads. One tablet of terracotta has an inscription to Idaian Zeus, dated to second or third century AD; and copper coins of Crete issued by Titus and Domitian have on reverse an eagle inscribed 'Of Idaian Zeus'.[28] Other inscriptions relevant to the worship of Idaian Zeus include one from Gortyn of the first part of the fifth century BC showing that city responsible for a trieteric festival at the cave of Zeus on Mount Ida. The perioecic subjects of Gortyn, the Rhittenians, were to send to Ida for this festival 350 staters' worth of victims, or victims and money.[29]

Mythology is composed of pregnant irony and contradiction. The wife of Zeus was Hera, a name with a possible original meaning of 'lady' or 'mistress',

21   Reconstruction of bronze head-vase from the Idaian Cave

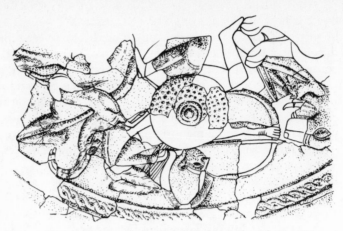

22   Detail from a bronze shield from the Idaian Cave

23   Gortyn coins

her Cretan associations suggesting that she was originally a form of the Minoan goddess. With the increasing dominance of patriarchal Zeus, she combined with him in a traditional Olympian patronage of lawful marriage, despite their repeated infidelities. This relationship was conspicuous by its absence of lawful offspring. Though Zeus fathered many children, Hera was not their mother; she was, however, the mother of rather fewer children of whom Zeus was not the father. Hesiod has it that Hebe, Ares and Eileithyia at least were children of Zeus and Hera, but this is a dubious claim. There is perhaps a more substantial possibility that Eileithyia was Hera's daughter, born as she was in a cave at the mouth of the Amnisos river near Knossos.[30]

As a goddess of marriage, Hera was worshipped in most parts of Greece in historical antiquity; but there is little doubt that her chief cult centre was the Argive area in north-east Peloponnese. Outside the Argolid other early cult locations were Euboea, Boeotia, southern Thessaly, the island of Samos and Olympia in west Peloponnese, site of the Olympic Games. On Euboea ('island of fair oxen') the myth and ritual did not much differ from the Argive. Hera had a large temple on Samos and a cult of great antiquity. According to tradition, her image arrived there from Argos, although the tradition was disputed by the Samians who believed she was born in the sanctuary under a willow tree. Her temple at Olympia was the oldest, implying links with the tradition that the games were founded by Argive Herakles – the hero 'called after Hera'. The Argive Heraion ('Our Lady's Temple') was sited on the lower slopes of a mountain named Euboea after Hera's nurse, so it was said. In the *Iliad*[31] Hera declares that Argos, Sparta and Mycenae are the three towns she loves best; and she naturally gave vigorous support to the Achaeans in the Trojan War.

Since her principal centre of cult on the mainland was the Argive Heraion, it seems plausible to suppose that Hera came from overseas to the Argolid. The oldest image of the goddess in the Heraion was made of pear wood and had been brought from Tiryns. Not far away was the fair harbour of Nauplia, a likely port of call for Minoan traders. Here there was established a cult of Hera Parthenos ('the Maiden'). There was also a good harbour at Hermione. Here too there was a cult of Hera Parthenos and a local tradition that Zeus and Hera arrived at this place on the mainland from Crete.

Evidence from the inscriptions as well as the coinage of historical times is adequate to establish Hera's continued stature in Cretan religion. At Gortyn there is epigraphic evidence from an archaic fragment of mid-seventh/mid-sixth century BC in the form of an apparent reference to victims which had to be offered to deities of the city at certain times, including Hera.[32] The Argive draft of the treaty between Knossos and Tylissos, which was arranged under the auspices of Argos, dated to roughly mid-fifth century BC, included a provision that a leg of each victim should be reserved for Hera when 60 rams were sacrificed to Makhaneus. This part of Crete had been settled by Argive colonists and, as Argos was responsible for supervising the treaty, this provision depends upon the importance of the Argive cult of Zeus Makhaneus and also of Argive Hera, principal goddess of the city. There is a further provision, moreover, that a cow should be sacrificed to Hera by the contracting parties in her sanctuary of the Heraion, which we may assume to have been a Cretan Heraion, either at Knossos or at Tylissos.[33] Knossian coins of the period roughly from 350–200 BC have a head of Hera, with a crown of floral ornaments and also a square labyrinth.[34]

A treaty of the latter second century BC between Lato and Olous includes an oath in which Hera occupies third place after Hestia and Zeus Kretagenes in a lengthy group of deities. It appears from this document that a month Heraios, named after the goddess, was in the calendar at Olous, as at Delphi.[35] An inscription from Hyrtakina, dated some time after about 170 BC, mentions a temple of Hera, apparently the most important in that city at the time.[36] The inscription from Soulia of roughly first century BC, with a dedication by a priest and his wife to Olympian Zeus and Olympian Hera records the only occurrence of this particular combination in Cretan epigraphy.[37] An inscription commemorates the restoration by Hierapytna (roughly 145–139 BC) of some statues in the temple of Zeus Diktaios, which included a head of Hera.[38] This statue was perhaps made of wood, like the old statue in the Argive Heraion.[39] In a treaty between Hierapytna and Priansos, at the beginning of the second century BC, permission is granted for the citizens to attend each other's festivals. There is special mention of the Heraia, indicating that Hera's festival was of considerable importance in both cities.[40] The goddess is invoked in Hierapytnian oaths in treaties with Lyttos (latter third/early second century BC) and with the Hierapytrian colonists (roughly second century BC).[41] A Hierapytna inscription of roughly first century AD provides important evidence that a joint cult of Zeus Melikhios and Hera Melikhia was still maintained in an Eteocretan area at a relatively late date.[42] This long-lived eminence of the cult of Hera in the area is also indicated by an invocation of Hera (second after Zeus Diktaios) in an Itanian oath of roughly early third century BC.[43]

The place-name Herais in an inscription of the third century BC offers the possibility that there was a cult of Hera at Kydonia.[44] The goddess features on coins of Tylissos (roughly 400–300 BC), her head with a crown of floral devices; on coins of Aptera (roughly 250–267 BC), her head crowned; and with her head on coins of Polyrhenia.[45]

The statues of Hera made of wood, together with the coin-types portraying the goddess wearing a crown and floral decorations, serve to remind us of those very old, traditional relationships of the Minoan goddess with sacred trees and herbal magic.[46]

There is abundant evidence, especially from the cities of the central area of the island, to demonstrate that Crete played a part of special importance in the development of the cult of Apollo.[47] There were about a dozen epithets of the god to testify to the variety of this cult in different areas.

Apollo Dekataphoros (the 'Tithe-receiver') had a temple at Hierapytna and was the principal deity of Apollonia, a city named after the god.[48] The cult of Apollo Delphinios (as 'dolphin-god') could perhaps have originated in some form in Minoan times and might have been established at Delphi itself earlier than the cult of Apollo proper.[49] The cult of Delphinios at other places outside Crete, including Miletos, Thera, Aigina, Athens and Sparta, has certain Cretan associations.[50] Apollo Delphinios continued to be of some importance at Knossos into Hellenistic times.[51] The Drerian oath of the later third or early

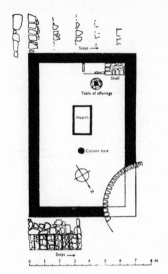

24   Temple of Apollo at Dreros

second century BC[52] indicates that the cult also flourished in that city; and the archaic temple of Delphinios in the city revealed evidence of fusion between Minoan and later Greek religion. This evidence includes an altar with many (mostly left) horns of goats, like the altar at Delos, where Theseus danced the Crane-dance.[53] Three statuettes were found on the altar, one of a male representing Apollo, the other two perhaps Artemis and Lato. A sacrificial pit points to archaic Greek custom, but the ledge for idols and an offering table indicate a Minoan origin.[54] There was a month Delphinios in the Olountian calendar.[55] At Hyrtakina, the city's 'common hearth', normally placed in a town-hall, was still within the temple of Delphinios even in the second century BC. The inference is that no town-hall had yet been built; and also that the cult of Delphinios was not only of some importance still but had once been more important than the cult of Hera.[56] For an inscription survives from Hyrtakina, dated some time after about 170 BC, which does make mention of a temple of Hera, apparently at the time the most important in the city.[57]

In the historical period the month-name Karneios appears in inscriptions at Knossos and Gortyn.[58] This evidence suggests a cult of Apollo Karneios, better known in the Peloponnese than in Crete, but with characteristics familiar in Cretan religious tradition. The epithet, deriving from *karnos* (a horned sheep), suggests an ancient ram-god and there are legendary associations which support this antiquity.[59] At Sparta the festival of the Karneia was held at full moon in the month of Karneios.[60] It was supervised by young bachelors called Karneatai,[61] perhaps five from each tribe, who held office for four years. At the festival there was a race of *staphylodromoi*, a name derived from the vine-branches they carried. One of them, garlanded and perhaps disguised in the skin of a beast, prayed, as he ran, for blessing on the city. The others ran in pursuit. Good luck followed if he was caught, the reverse if he was not. The vines associate the ritual with the fruit-harvest, the name of the festival recalls the flocks; and we seem to have a familiar pattern deriving from a vegetation cycle. For the Kouretes, who came from Crete to Olympia, ran a race like the Karneatai, crowning the victor with wild olive. Cretan and Spartan *epheboi* were initiates; and the race of the *staphylodromoi* can be compared with the Athenian festival of the *Oskhophoria* ('carrying of vine-shoots laden with grapes'), its essentials derived from Minoan Crete.[62]

The Delphic and Cretan cults of Pythian Apollo have a common background, perhaps actually deriving from Crete.[63] It is at least not surprising that the temple of Pythian Apollo, a principal monument at Gortyn, reveals evidence of early origin.[64] Just as state documents were published in the Pythion of the cities of Lyttos and of Itanos,[65] so the most important state documents of the city of Gortyn were published in the Pythion there, from about the seventh century until mid-fifth century BC, and also continuously from the third century BC.[66] A Gortynian decree regarding the island of Kaudos indicates the high status of the Pythion in the early second century BC; and likewise shows that it performed the service of a state treasury, receiving tithes from the citizens of Gortyn and its perioecic subjects.[67] The tithe imposed on all products of Kaudos by land and sea, excluding flocks, vegetables and harbour-dues, was dedicated to the Pythian Apollo at Gortyn. This god was invoked in Gortynian oaths in several treaties, one of which also mentions the festival of a Pythia in the city.[68]

Pythian Apollo had a cult in other central and eastern areas of Crete in addition to Gortyn, Lyttos and Itanos, such as Dreros[69] and Hierapytna;[70] and he was invoked in oaths of Dreros, Lato, Lyttos, Olous, Malla, Hierapytna, Itanos and Praisos, in Hellenistic times.[71]

25 Praisos (Hellenistic)

The important cult of Apollo Amyklaios has already been discussed in detail within the wider context of relations with the Peloponnese and Cyprus.[72]

To turn now from Apollo to Artemis, it is clear that, apart from her links with Lato and Apollo, with Britomartis and Diktynna, this goddess had independent cults in various cities in the historical period. Her cult in the city of Aptera is particularly interesting in the sense that the city not merely took its name from the deity, as others also derived their names from deities, but was named after a specific local epithet of the goddess. This seems to imply that Aptera actually preceded Artemis, with resulting fusion of cults of a similar character, perhaps connected with the Minoan origin of Artemis as Mistress of Animals.[73] Equally interesting, as we have seen, is the possibility that there was some cult of Artemis and of her Mother-goddess prototype as a bear-goddess, guardian of the young, in a cave on the peninsula of Akrotiri, north-east of Khania, the ancient Kydonia.[74] Actual finds in this cave included several heads of Artemis, both Classical and Hellenistic; and this indicates a cult of Artemis in historical times, among other deities, one of whom was apparently Apollo. The possibility of a bear-goddess cult with such associations could correlate with traditions elsewhere. Before the investigations on Akrotiri were announced, the argument had been advanced[75] that such a bear-goddess was brought by the Pelasgians ultimately from the Black Sea into the Aegean via the Propontis, into Attica from Lemnos, from Attica to Arcadia; and perhaps she was first identified with Artemis in the Troad, under the influence of the Ephesian goddess. In Attica, there was a temple of Artemis Brauronia (at Brauron) where young girls, dressed in saffron, performed their bear-dance before marriage.[76]

The name of Athene (after whom various cities took the name of Athenai) seems to be originally pre-Greek, as indeed is consistent with her familiar links with the olive and the owl, with snake-cult, tree-cult and bird epiphanies. She features in the epigraphic and the numismatic evidence from a number of Cretan cities in historical times; and various special epithets were applied to her. As Athene Oleria, for example, her cult was prominent in the city of Oleros, which became subject to Hierapytna by the Hellenistic period. The people of Hierapytna published treaties in the temple of Athene Oleria, invoked her in oaths and also seem to have had a festival of the goddess.[77] There is epigraphic evidence from Oleros (end of the second or early first century BC) suggesting that officials of Hierapytna took charge of repairs to the temple of Athene Oleria.[78]

It is likely that Aphrodite originated as an Oriental fertility goddess, with characteristic magical attributes such as the dove, the apple, myrtle, poppy and rose. There is evidence of her cult in several cities, including Hierapytna, Knossos, Dreros, Lato and Phaistos. At Knossos, the epithet Antheia ('flower-goddess') was applied to Aphrodite.[79] At Phaistos she was called Skotia ('dark' or 'secret'), patron of youths due to be initiated into adult status and marriage, and who, in Crete, were known as *skotioi* ('secret ones'), their transition to manhood involving seclusion from the city for a period of two months.[80] Recalling the cult of Lato Phytia and the festival of the Ekdysia, we can be sure that the city of Phaistos firmly maintained the survival of a complex of ritual which involved traditional patterns of fertility, initiation and marriage.

16

CONFLICT AND SUBJECTION

The Greeks of Classical times had become accustomed to the inevitability of warfare as a component of everyday life in the relations between city-states. In Aristotle's view,[1] for instance, the proper purpose of military training was not the enslavement of those undeserving of this fate but, in the first instance, that a people might avoid enslavement to others; secondly, so as to seek leadership in bestowing benefit on behalf of subjects, but not in pursuit of despotic power over all and sundry; and thirdly to wield such despotic power over those who deserve to be in servitude. In his previous discussion of the Cretan political system, however, Aristotle makes clear his opinion that the relative stability of this system had been due to the self-contained geographical situation of the island. Compared with the ephors of Sparta, he points out,[2] the *kosmoi* of Crete were not in a position to profit from their office, because they lived in an island removed from people who might corrupt them. He acknowledged a familiar situation of creating factional divisions which led to strife among the people and an end of lawful government.

Such a situation implied a temporary collapse of the state and a dissolution of civil bonds. When this sort of thing could happen, a city was imperilled by the possibility that those who had a motive could also be strong enough to make an attack. However – harking back to his earlier remark – he emphasizes that its geographical position had been Crete's salvation and that distance had produced the same results as alien acts. This also brought about the consequence that Crete's servile population was not disaffected, whereas the Spartan helots frequently revolted. The Cretans, moreover, had no foreign dominions; and the island had only lately been invaded by warfare from abroad, an event which had revealed the frailty of existing laws.

It is obvious that Aristotle regarded the breakdown of isolation from the wider world of contagious conflict as an ominous portent. We are unable to specify the precise time and nature of the incursion of warfare from abroad to which he refers. The event may perhaps have occurred in 343 BC when Phalaikos the Phocian came with a mercenary force to serve with Knossos against Lyttos; or the reference may be to a war in 333 BC.[3] Inconclusive as the reference is, we may fairly safely infer from its context that, although strife and conflict were no novelty, within or between cities, the social system as a whole had remained relatively stable. The novelty now threatening their relative stability was the involvement of Crete with the external world and the consequent frailty of constitutional safeguards. Reference has already been made to the indications of internal change and stress which the Gortyn Code reveals of the situation in one of the major cities in the previous century. The intervening period must surely have witnessed the influence of a monetary economy, the growth of private property, and modifications in family life and other social relationships.

These remarks of Aristotle take on a kind of prophetic significance when we examine the records of Cretan history after the decade to which he is presumably alluding, not only in terms of the ensuing incessant warfare which beset the cities of the island, but also as applying to the related subjects of piracy and mercenary recruitment. We may be short of population statistics and other demographic information, but these records of chronic malaise tell a plain tale of the withdrawal of a surplus of able-bodied men from peaceful pursuits into more hazardous enterprises. In his brief survey of the Hellenistic period, Pendlebury observed that, in spite of the wars which racked the island, the confusing changes of sides reminiscent of the Wars of the Roses and the deliberate destruction of cities such as Lyttos, the population as a whole had increased and more open sites were being chosen.

The information in ancient sources[4] about the employment of Cretan mercenaries during this period by such foreign powers as Egypt, Syria, Sparta, the Achaean League, Pergamon, Macedon, Syracuse and Rome certainly supports the possibility of an increased population. Cretans were much in demand as archers and guerilla fighters. If we bear in mind the relatively small size of the cities and of their free population the numbers of men cited in our sources are remarkable in themselves and also an indirect testimony of the stable serf-system in the midst of strife. A treaty between the city of Hierapytna and the Rhodians (200–197 BC)[5] contains a guarantee that the Cretan city should, if necessary, send two hundred men to the assistance of Rhodes. Of these not less than half were to be citizens, the remainder mercenaries; a stipulation which indicates that trained Cretans were so much in demand for foreign service that the Cretan cities had sometimes to employ mercenary troops to make good the drain on manpower caused by their willingness to allow their own citizens to be recruited by others.

In 219 BC the Polyrhenians sent 500 Cretans to Philip's army, while Knossos sent a thousand to the Aetolians, in two detachments of 500, one of which was definitely a mercenary force.[6] A mercenary force in Alexandria in 221 BC included 1000 Cretans, and at the battle of Raphia in 217 BC there were 3000 Cretans with the Egyptian army and 2500 (perhaps mercenaries) in the opposing army of Antiochos III.[7] Comparable figures on other occasions illustrate how the Cretan mercenaries were drawn into the maelstrom of conflicts between the major powers, sometimes to be engaged as enemies on the same battlefields.[8] A visit to Knossos by one Dorylaos[9] is probably but one example of regular recruiting campaigns in Cretan cities by foreign powers which were sanctioned by the authorities. It is also significant that the mercenaries recruited from Crete were citizens who were able to provide their own arms.[10]

Cretan piracy had a Homeric ancestry[11] and, in Hellenistic times, became an occupation as lucrative, as dangerous, and sometimes as much a part of contemporary conflict between the powers as mercenary service. The harbours of Crete were assembly stations for pirate fleets and centres of involvement in the disposal of captives for ransom or the slave trade.

A gloomy and sustained chapter of Cretan political history, whose opening was announced by Aristotle in his reference to a recent invasion of warfare from abroad, was abruptly terminated by Roman conquest in 67 BC. The closing of the chapter has a kind of inevitability. It was, however, but a chapter in a tenacious record.

Crete was the last remaining area of Greek independence when, accused of supporting Mithridates, it became a target for Roman conquest. A first attempt encountered such virile resistance that Rome was obliged to make an unfavourable peace in 71 BC. This peace was soon to be repudiated with renewed provocation; and the Romans under Quintus Metellus (thereafter called Creticus) ruthlessly subdued the island, which was then amalgamated with Cyrene in North Africa to form a single Roman province, with its capital at Gortyn. It was to serve as a granary for Rome. St Paul and his disciple Titus began to convert Crete to Christianity. After the division of the Roman Empire, Crete became a part of the Eastern or Byzantine Empire and was of considerable strategic and commercial importance.

The Byzantine period of Cretan history was interrupted for more than a century when, about the year 823, during the reign of Michael II, a band of Arab invaders who had emigrated from Spain to Egypt, sailed from Alexandria and occupied the island. Once again, as had not infrequently been the case since Homeric times, Crete became a base for piratical assaults upon the islands and coastal regions of the Aegean. Most existing Cretan cities were destroyed, but a new city was built named Chandax (since 1822 the modern Iraklion), after the ditch which surrounded it for fortification. This city was re-named by the Venetians Candia, the name also by which the whole of Crete was known for a long time. In the year 961, after various unsuccessful attempts to liberate the island, Crete was recovered for the Byzantines by the General (later Emperor) Nikephoros Phokas. With a considerable force under his command, he sailed for Crete in the summer of 960 and laid siege to the capital throughout the whole winter. Chandax was stormed by his troops in March 961. The recovery of Crete after nearly a century and a half removed the most important base of Arab sea power in the eastern Mediterranean.

After this major victory of Nikephoros, 'the white death of the Saracens', the Mohammedan religion, imposed under the Saracen occupation, was suppressed, and few traces now remain of this particular phase of foreign domination.

The fourth crusade was diverted against the capital of Byzantium and, on 13 April 1204, Constantinople, inviolate since the time of Constantine against assault by Persians, Arabs, Avars and Bulgars, was entered by conquering crusaders and Venetians and subjected for three days to pillage and massacre. Compared with these Latins, bearing the cross of Christ upon their shoulders, wrote the eyewitness Niketas Khoniates, even the Saracens were more merciful and kind to Christians after the capture of Jerusalem. The Byzantine Empire was divided up into a great number of states, partly Frankish, partly Greek. The leader of the crusade, Marquis Boniface of Montferrat, sold Crete to Venice for 1000 marks of silver. A Venetian governor was appointed by 1210; but, although Italian colonists began to arrive within two years, local resistance was such that most of Crete was not in complete Venetian control until 1343. Thereafter it became for several centuries a bastion of Venetian sovereignty in the eastern Mediterranean. Great fortresses were built at such places as Iraklion, Spinalonga, Gramvoussa, Souda, Rethymno, Khania, Ierapetra and Frangokastello.

The Venetian occupation of Crete had been promptly challenged by the Genoese but, when Venetian rule was established in 1212, the island was apportioned to Venetian nobles and colonists in the form of 132 knight's fiefs and 48 sergeant's or footsoldier's fiefs. Venetian rule endured in Crete for 465 years, a rule frequently challenged by internal revolt. The central government comprised two councils of the colonists, two Councillors who represented the Doge, and the Duke. The Venetians exploited the island to the detriment especially of the peasant serfs, though the unhappy internal situation was eventually improved through the administrative reforms of Giacomo Foscarini who was sent to Crete in 1574. There were then 479 fiefs, mostly in possession of Venetian knights, others belonging to a few Cretan notables, the Latin Church and the Venetian government.

Venice became much dependent upon Cretan commerce and resources. Pursuing their own designs of expansion as well as to damage Venetian power, the Turks made a series of incursions against Crete in the course of the sixteenth century, which were eventually to culminate in the Turkish conquest of the island. The process of Turkish conquest began in earnest in 1645 when the fortress of Ayioi Theodoroi was invested by an army of 50,000 men. Failing there, the Turkish troops then landed in the bay of Khania. Khania itself was captured and so was Rethimno in 1646. Within two years, except for Iraklion and the fortified coastal islands, the Venetians had lost control of the major part of Crete. The great siege of Iraklion began in 1648 and lasted for more than twenty years, ending in 1669 with the whole of Crete now in

Turkish hands, except for three fortified islands which also eventually fell.

During the period of Turkish rule from 1670, there were constant revolts against bad government and further exploitation by foreign masters. With the outbreak of the Greek War of Independence in 1821, there was a vigorous fresh stimulus to insurrection, which was to be constantly renewed throughout the nineteenth century.

Eventually in 1898 Turkish troops were obliged to abandon Crete, after the principal ports had been occupied by British, Russian, French and Italian forces. In December of that year Prince George of Greece became High Commissioner of an independent Crete. A period of autonomy now ensued, marked by the prominence of the statesman Eleutherios Venizelos, the leader of the Cretan Liberal Party. Venizelos became Prime Minister of Greece in 1910; and the movement for the union of Crete with Greece eventually succeeded when, a few days before war broke out between Greece and Turkey in October 1912, Venizelos admitted Cretan deputies to the Greek Parliament. This union was formally acknowledged by Turkey in the Treaty of London on 30 May 1913.

During the Second World War, the Germans, after occupying the mainland of Greece, decided upon an airborne invasion of Crete. The Battle of Crete lasted for ten days, 20–29 May 1941, and the Cretans, true to tradition, distinguished themselves by their resistance alongside the Greek, British and New Zealand forces. Cretan independence was recovered with the defeat of Germany.

Appendix

TRANSLATION OF THE
LAW CODE OF GORTYN

COLUMN
I

Gods!

Whosoever may be likely to contend about a free man or a slave is not to seize him before trial. But if he make seizure, let (the judge) condemn him to (a fine of) ten staters for a free man, five for a slave of whomsoever he does seize and let him give judgment that he release him within three days; but if he do not release him, let (the judge) condemn him to (a fine of) a stater for a free man and a drachma for a slave, for each day until he do release him; and the judge is to decide on oath as to the time; but if he should deny the seizure, unless a witness should testify, the judge is to decide on oath. And if one party contend that he is a free man, the other party that he is a slave, whichever persons testify that he is a free man are to prevail. And if they contend about a slave, each declaring that he is his, the judge is to give judgment according to the witness if a witness testify, but he is to decide on oath if they testify either for both or for neither. After the one in possession has been defeated, he is to release the free man within five days and give back the slave in hand; but if he should not release or give back, let (the judge) give judgment that the (successful party) be entitled, in the case of the free man to fifty staters and a stater for each day until he releases him, in the case of the slave ten staters and a drachma for each day until he gives him back in hand; but at a year's end after the judge has pronounced judgment, the threefold fines are to be exacted, or less, but not more. As to the time the judge shall decide under oath; but if the slave on whose account a man has been defeated take sanctuary in a temple (the defeated party), summoning (the successful party) in the presence of two free adult witnesses, shall point him out at the temple where he takes refuge, either himself or another for him; and if he do not summon or point out, let him pay what is written; but if he should not give him back at all within the yearly period, he shall in addition pay the single penalties. If he (the defeated party) die while the suit is being tried, he shall pay the single penalty. And if one who is *kosmos* make a seizure of another (seize the slave) of one who is *kosmos*, they are to contend after he resigns, and, if defeated, he shall pay what is written from the day he made the seizure. But one who seizes a man condemned (for

216

debt) or who has mortgaged his person shall be immune from punishment. COLUMN
If a person commits rape on the free man or the free woman, he shall pay II
one hundred staters; and if on account of an *apetairos*, ten; and if the slave
on the free man or the free woman, he shall pay double; and if a free man
on a male serf or female serf, five drachmas; and if a male serf on a male
serf or female serf, five staters. If a person should forcibly seduce a slave
belonging to the home, he shall pay two staters; but if she has already been
seduced, one obol by day, but if in the night, two obols; and the slave shall
have preference in the oath. If someone attempt to have intercourse with a
free woman who is under the guardianship of a relative, he shall pay ten staters
if a witness should testify. If someone be taken in adultery with a free woman
in a father's, brother's or the husband's house, he shall pay a hundred staters;
but if in another's, fifty; and if with the wife of an *apetairos*, ten; but if a slave
with a free woman, he shall pay double; and if a slave with a slave, five. Let
(the captor) proclaim in the presence of three witnesses to the relatives of the
one caught in (the house) that he is to be ransomed within five days; and to
the master of the slave in the presence of two witnesses; but if he should not be
ransomed himself, it is to be within the power of the captors to deal with him
as they may wish; but if anyone should declare that he has been taken by
subterfuge, the captor is to swear, in a case involving fifty staters or more, with
four others, each calling down solemn curses upon himself, and in the case of
an *apetairos* with two others, and in the case of a serf the master and one other,
that he took him in adultery and not by subterfuge. And if a husband and wife
should be divorced, she is to have her own property which she came with to
her husband and half of the produce, if there be any from her own property,
and half of whatever she has woven within, whatever there may be, plus five
staters if the husband be the cause of the divorce; but if the husband should
declare that he is not the cause, the judge is to decide on oath. And if she COLUMN
should carry away anything else belonging to the husband, she shall pay III
five staters and whatever she may carry away; and let her restore whatever
she may have filched; but as regards things which she denies (the judge) shall
decree that the woman take an oath of denial by Artemis, before the statue of
the Archeress in the Amyklaian temple. And whatever anyone may take away
from her after she has made her oath of denial, he shall pay the thing itself plus
five staters. If a stranger should help her in packing off, he shall pay ten staters
and double the value of whatever the judge swears he helped to pack off. If a
man die leaving children, should the wife so desire, she may marry, holding
her own property and whatever her husband might have given her according
to what is written, in the presence of three adult free witnesses; but if she
should take away anything belonging to the children, that becomes a matter
for trial. And if he should leave her childless, she is to have her own property
and half of whatever she has woven within and obtain her portion of the
produce that is in the house along with the lawful heirs as well as whatever her

husband may have given her as is written; but if she should take away anything else, that becomes a matter for trial. And if a wife should die childless (the husband), is to return her property to the lawful heirs and the half of whatever she has woven within and the half of the produce, if it be from her own property. If the husband or wife wish to make payments for porterage (these should be) either clothing or twelve staters or something of the value of twelve staters, but not more. If a female serf be separated from a serf while he is alive or in case of his death, she is to have her own property; but if she should carry away anything else, that becomes a matter for trial. If a wife who is separated (by divorce) should bear a child, (they) are to bring it to the husband at his house in the presence of three witnesses; and if he should not receive it, the child shall be in the mother's power either to rear or expose; and the relatives and the witnesses shall have preference in the oath as to whether they brought it. And if a female serf should bear a child while separated, (they) are to bring it to the master of the man who married her in the presence of two witnesses.

COLUMN IV

And if he do not receive it, the child shall be in the power of the master of the female serf; but if she should marry the same man again before the end of the year, the child shall be in the power of the master of the male serf, and the one who brought it and the witnesses shall have preference in the oath. If a woman separated (by divorce) should expose her child before presenting it as is written, if she is convicted, she shall pay, for a free child, fifty staters, for a slave, twenty-five. And if the man should have no house to which she shall bring it or she do not see him, there is to be no penalty if she should expose the child. If a female serf who is unmarried should conceive and bear, the child shall be in the power of the master of her father; but in case the father should not be living, it shall be in the power of the masters of her brothers. The father shall be in control of the children and the division of the property and the mother of her own property. So long as they are living there is no necessity to make a division; but if any one should be fined, the one fined shall have his share apportioned to him as is written. And in case (the father) should die, the city houses and whatever there is in those houses in which a serf living in the country does not reside, and the cattle, small and large, which do not belong to a serf, shall belong to the sons; but all the rest of the property shall be fairly divided and the sons, no matter how many, shall each receive two parts, while the daughters, no matter how many, shall each receive one part. The mother's property too, in case she dies, shall be divided in the same way as is prescribed for the father's; but if there should be no property except the house, the daughters shall receive their share as is prescribed. And if the father, while living, should wish to give to the married daughter, let him give according to what is prescribed, but not more. Any (daughter) to whom he

COLUMN V

gave or pledged before shall have these things, but shall obtain nothing besides from the paternal property. Whatever woman has no property either by gift from father or brother or by pledge or by inheritance as (enacted) when the Aithalian *startos*, Kyllos and his colleagues, formed the *kosmos*, such women are to obtain their portion; but there shall be no ground for action against previous female beneficiaries. When a man or a woman dies, if there be children or children's children or children's children's children, they are to have the property. And if there be none of these, but brothers of the deceased and brothers' children or brothers' children's children, they are to have the property. And if there be none of these, but sisters of the deceased and sisters' children or sisters' children's children, they are to have the property. And if there be none of these, they are to take it up, to whom it may fall as source of the property. And if there should be no kinsmen, those of the household composing the *klaros* are to have the property. And if some of the next-of-kin wish to divide the property while others do not, the judge shall decree that all the property shall be in the power of those who wish to divide until they divide it. And if anyone enters in by force or drives or carries off anything once the judge has made his decision, he shall pay ten staters and double the value of the piece of property. So far as livestock, produce, clothing, ornaments and movable property are concerned, if they do not wish to make a division, the judge shall decide under oath with reference to the pleas. And if, when dividing the property, they cannot agree about the division, they shall offer the property for sale; and, having sold it to him who offers most, let each of them take his share of the values. And when they are dividing the property, three or more COLUMN adult free witnesses are to be present. Should he give to a daughter, the VI same procedure is to be followed. As long as the father lives, no one shall offer to purchase any of the paternal property from a son nor take out a mortgage on it; but whatever (the son) himself may have acquired or inherited, let him sell, if he wishes. Nor shall the father sell or mortgage the possessions of his children, whatever they have themselves acquired or inherited. Nor shall the husband sell or pledge those of his wife, nor the son those of his mother. And if anyone should purchase or take on mortgage or accept a promise otherwise than is written in these writings, the property shall be in the power of the mother and the wife, and the one who sold or mortgaged or promised shall pay two-fold to the one who bought or accepted the mortgage or the promise and, if there be any other damage besides, the simple value; but in matters of previous date there shall be no ground for action. If, however, the defendant should maintain, with reference to the matter about which they contend, that it is not in the power of the mother or the wife, the action shall be brought where it belongs, before the judge where it is prescribed for each case. If a mother die leaving children, the father is to be in control of the mother's property, but he shall not sell or mortgage unless the children consent and are of age; but if anyone should otherwise purchase or take on mortgage, the property shall be in the power of the children and the seller or mortgagor shall pay twofold the value to the purchaser or mortgagee and, if there be any other damage besides, the simple value. And, if he should marry another woman, the children are to be in control of the mother's property. If anyone, bound by necessity, should get a man gone away to a strange place set free from a foreign city at his own request, he shall be in the power of the one who ransomed him until he pay what is due; but if they do not agree about the amount or on the ground that he did not request to be set free, the judge is to decide on oath with

COLUMN VII reference to the pleas . . . . (If the slave) goes to a free woman and marries her, their children shall be free; but if the free woman goes to the slave, their children shall be slaves. And if free and slave children should be born of the same mother, in a case where the mother dies, if there is property, the free children are to have it; but if there should be no free children born of her, the heirs are to take it over. If someone has bought a slave from the market-place and has not terminated the agreement within sixty days, the one who has acquired him shall be liable, if (the slave) has done any wrong before or after (the purchase). The heiress is to be married to the brother of her father, the oldest of those living. And, if there be more heiresses and brothers of the father, they are to be married to the next oldest. And if there should be no brothers, they are to be married to the next after the son of the oldest. The (who is the son) of the oldest. And if there should be more heiresses and sons of brothers, they are to be married to the next after the sons of the oldest. The groom-elect is to have one heiress and not more. As long as the groom-elect or the heiress is too young to marry, the heiress is to have the house, if there is one, and the groom-elect is to obtain half the revenue from everything; but if the groom-elect should not wish to marry the heiress, though they are both of an age to marry, on the grounds that he is still a minor, all the property and the produce shall be at the disposal of the heiress until he does marry her; but if the groom-elect, now an adult, should not wish to marry the heiress who is of an age and willing to be married to him, the relatives of the heiress are to bring the matter to court and the judge is to order the marriage to take place within two months. And if he should not marry her as is written, the heiress, holding all the property, is to marry the next in succession, if there be another; but if there be no groom-elect, she is to be married to whomsoever she wishes of those who ask from the tribe. And if the heiress, though of an age to marry, should not wish to be married to the groom-elect, or the groom-elect be too young and

COLUMN VIII the heiress be unwilling to wait, the heiress is to have a house, if there be one in the city, besides whatever may be in that house, and, obtaining half a share of the rest, she is to be married to another, whomsoever she may wish of those who ask from the tribe; but she is to give a share of the property to that one (i.e. to the rejected groom-elect). And if there should not be kinsmen of the heiress as is defined, she may hold all of the property and be married to whomsoever she may wish from the tribe. And if no one from the tribe should wish to marry her, the relatives of the heiress are to proclaim throughout the tribe: 'Does no one wish to marry her?' And if anyone should marry her (it should be) within thirty days from the time they made the proclamation; but if not, she is to be married to another, whomsoever she can. And if a woman becomes an heiress after her father or brother has given her (in marriage), if she should not wish to remain married to the one to whom they gave her, although he be willing, if she has borne children, she may be married to another of the tribe, dividing the property as is prescribed; but if there should be no children, she is to be married to the groom-elect, if there be one, and take all the property; and if there is not, as is prescribed. If a husband should die leaving children to an heiress, let her be married to whomsoever of the tribe she can, if she should so wish, but without any compulsion; but if the deceased should leave no children behind, she is to be married to the groom-elect as is prescribed. And if the man who has the right to marry the heiress should not be at home, and the heiress should be of marriageable age, let her be married to the (next) groom-elect as is prescribed. Now an heiress is one who has no father or brother from the same father. And as long as she is not of an age to marry, her father's brothers are to be responsible for the administration of the property, while she takes half a share of the produce; but if there should be no groom-elect while she is not of an age to marry, the heiress is to have charge of the property and the produce and is to be brought up with her mother as long as she is not of an age to marry; and if there should be no mother, she is to be brought up with her mother's brothers. Now if anyone should marry the heiress otherwise than is prescribed, the lawful heirs are to lay information COLUMN before a magistrate. If someone owing money should leave behind an heiress, IX she either personally or through her paternal and maternal relatives shall mortgage or sell to the value of the debt, and the purchase and mortgage shall be legal. And if anyone should otherwise buy or take on mortgage the property of the heiress, the property shall be at the disposal of the heiress, and the seller or mortgagor, if he be convicted, shall pay double to the buyer or mortgagee, and if there is any other damage he shall pay the simple value in addition, since the inscription of this law, but there shall be no liability in matters of previous date; but if the defendant should maintain, with reference to the matter about which they contend, that it does not belong to the heiress, let the judge decide under oath. And if he should win his case that it does not belong to the heiress, action should be brought where it is prescribed for each case. If one dies who has gone surety or has lost a suit or owes money given as security or has been involved in fraud (?) or has made a promise (?) or another (be in like relationship) to him, one must bring suit against that person before the end of the year; and let the judge give his decision according to the testimony. If the suit be with reference to a judgment won, the judge and the recorder, if alive and a citizen, and the heirs as witnesses (shall testify), but in the case of surety and money given as securities and fraud (?) and promise (?), the heirs as witnesses shall testify. And after they have testified, let (the judge) decree that (the plaintiff), when he has taken oath himself along with the witnesses, have judgment for the simple amount. If a son has gone surety, while his father is living, he and the property which he possesses shall be subject to fine. If one has formed a partnership with another for a mercantile venture, in case he does not pay back the one who has contributed to the venture, if witnesses who are of age should testify – three in a case of a hundred staters or more, two in a case of less down to ten staters, one for still less – let (the judge) decide according to testimony. But if witnesses should not testify, in case the contracting party comes, whichever course the complainant demands, either to deny on oath or

COLUMN ... (14 lines damaged). A son may give to a mother or a husband to a wife one
X hundred staters or less, but not more. And if he should give more, the heirs are to keep the property if they wish, once they have handed over the money. If anyone owing money or being the loser in a suit or while a suit is being tried should give anything away, the gift shall be invalid, if the rest of the property should not be equal to the obligation. No one shall offer to buy a man while pledged until the mortgagor release him, nor one who is the subject of legal process nor accept him (in payment) nor accept him (in pledge) nor take him in mortgage. And if anyone does any of these things, it shall be invalid, if two witnesses should testify. Adoption may be made from whatever source anyone wishes. And the declaration of adoption shall be made in the place of assembly when the citizens are gathered, from the stone from which proclamations are made. And let the adopter give to his *hetaireia* a sacrificial victim and a measure of wine. And if he (the adopted person) should receive all the property and there should be no legitimate children besides, he must fulfil all the obligations of the adopter towards gods and men and receive as is written for legitimate children; but if he should not be willing to fulfil these obligations as is written, the next-of-kin shall have the property. And if there should be legitimate children of the adopter, the adopted son shall receive with the males just as

COLUMN females receive from their brothers; and if there should be no males, but
XI females, the adopted son is to have an equal share and it shall not be incum-bent upon him to pay the obligations of the adopter and accept the property which the adopter leaves; for the adopted son is not to take possession of more (than the females); but if the adopted son should die without leaving legitimate children, the property is to revert to the heirs of the adopter. And if the adopter wishes, he may renounce (the adopted son) in the place of assembly when the citizens are gathered, from the stone from which proclamations are made; and he shall deposit ten staters with the court, and the secretary (of the magistrate) who is concerned with strangers shall pay it to the person re-nounced; but a woman shall not adopt nor a person under puberty. And these regulations shall be followed from the time of the inscription of this law; but as regards matters of previous date, in whatever way one holds (property), whether by adoption or from an adopted son, there shall still be no liability. Anyone may at any time receive a man if any person seize him before trial. Whatever it is written that he shall give judgment upon, either according to witnesses or under oath of denial, the judge is to give judgment as is written;

but in other matters he shall decide under oath according to the pleas. If a person should die owing money or having lost a suit, if those to whom it falls to receive the property should wish to pay the fine on his behalf and the money to those to whom he may owe it, they are to have the property; but if they do not so wish, the property shall belong to those who won the suit or those to whom he owes money, and the heirs shall not be liable to any further fine; and the paternal property shall be laid under obligation for the father's debts, the maternal for the mother's. If a judge has decreed an oath in a case where a wife is divorced from her husband, let her take the oath of denial of whatever one charges within twenty days in the presence of the judge; and let the initiator of the suit make his denunciation to the woman and the judge and the secretary (of the court) on the fourth day beforehand in the presence of a witness who has been adult for fifteen years or more. If a son has given property to his mother or a husband to his wife in the way prescribed before these regulations, there shall be no liability; but henceforth gifts shall be made as here prescribed. If there are no judges in the affairs of orphans, the heiresses shall be treated according to these regulations so long as they are not of marriageable age. And where the heiress, in default of a groom-elect or of judges in the affairs of orphans, is brought up with her mother, the paternal and maternal relatives, those who have been nominated, shall administer the property and the income to the best of their ability until she is married. And she is to be married when twelve years of age or older.

COLUMN
XII

BIBLIOGRAPHY

Åberg, N. *Bronzezeitliche und Früheisenzeitliche Chronologie IV*, Stockholm, 1933

Alexiou, S. Ἡ μινωϊκὴ θεὰ μεθ' ὑψωσμένων χειρῶν, KK (1958)

———— *Minoan Civilisation*, Iraklion, 1969

Allen, T.W., Halliday, W.R., and Sikes, E.E. *Homeric Hymns*, 2 ed., Oxford, 1936

Allen, W.S. *Vox Graeca*, Cambridge, 1968, 2 ed. 1974

Aly, W. *Der kretische Apollonkult*, Leipzig, 1908

Anderson, K.J. *Ancient Greek Horsemanship*, Berkeley, 1961

Andrewes, A. *The Greek Tyrants*, London, 1956

———— *The Greeks*, London, 1967

Autran, C. *La préhistoire du Christianisme*, Paris, 1941

Bachofen, J.J. *Das Mutterrecht*, Stuttgart, 1861

Bachtin, N. *Introduction to the Study of Modern Greek*, Cambridge, 1935

Banti, L. *Myth in Pre-Classical Art*, AJA 58

Barnett, R.D. *The Epic of Kumarbi and the Theogony of Hesiod*, JHS 65

Baudissin, W.W. *Kyrios als Gottesname im Judentum und seine Stelle in der Religions-geschichte*, Giessen, 1929

Baunack, J. and T. *Die Inschrift von Gortyn*, Leipzig, 1885

Baur, P.V.C. *Eileithyia: The University of Missouri Studies* I:4, 1902

Beattie, A.J. *A Plain Guide to the Ventris Decipherment of the Linear B Script. Mitteil-ungen des Instituts für Orientforschung*, 6.1 (1958)

———— *Mr. Ventris' Decipherment of the Minoan Linear B Script*, JHS 76

———— *The 'Spice' Tablets of Cnossos, Pylos and Mycenae* in *Minoica*, 6–34

———— *Some Notes on the Spensitheos Decree*, Kad. 14.1, 8–47

Bechtel, F. *Die griechischen Dialekte*, Berlin, 1921–4

Beloch, K.J. *Griechische Geschichte*, 2 ed., Strasbourg, 1912–27

Belon, P. *Observations sur plusieurs singularitez*, Paris, 1553

Bérard, J. *Les Hyksos et la légende d'Io*, S 29

Bernhöft, F. *Die Inschrift von Gortyn*, Stuttgart, 1886

Biesantz, H. *Kretisch-mykenische Siegelbilder*, Marburg, 1954

Bischoff, H. RE s.v. *Kalender*

Bittel, K. *Die Ruinen von Bogazköy der Haupstadt des Hethiterreichs*, Berlin/Leipzig, 1937

Blass, F. *Die kretischen Inschriften*, in SGDI III.2.3, 227–423, Göttingen, 1905

Blegen, C.W. *The Coming of the Greeks*, AJA 32

———— *Troy and the Trojans*, New York, 1963

Blinkenberg, C. *The Thunder-weapon in Religion and Folklore*, Cambridge, 1911
Boardman, J. *The Cretan Collection in Oxford*, Oxford, 1961
————— *Greek Gems and Finger Rings*, London, 1970
————— *Greek Art*, London/New York, 1964
————— *The Greeks Overseas*, 2 ed., Harmondsworth, 1973
————— *Island Gems*, London, 1963
Boisacq, E. *Dictionnaire étymologique de la langue grecque*, 4 ed., Heidelberg, 1950
Bonner, R.J., and Smith, G. *The Administration of Justice from Homer to Aristotle*, Chicago, 1930–8
Bosanquet, R.C. *The Palaikastro Hymn of the Kouretes*, ABSA 15
Bossert, H.T. *Die Beschwörung einer Krankheit in der Sprache von Kreta*, OL 34
————— *The Art of Ancient Crete*, London, 1937
Bowra, C.M. *Greek Lyric Poetry*, 2 ed., Oxford, 1961
————— *Heroic Poetry*, London, 1952
————— *Homer and his Forerunners*, Edinburgh, 1955
————— *Homer*, London, 1972
Brandenstein, W. *Bermerkungen zur Völkertafel in der Genesis, Festschrift Debrunner*, Bern, 1954, 66–70
Branigan, K. *Copper and Bronzework in Early Bronze Age Crete*, Lund, 1968
————— *The Foundations of Palatial Crete*, London, 1970
————— *The Tombs of Mesara*, London, 1970
Brause, J. *Lautlebre der kretischen Dialekte*, Halle, 1909
Brice, W.C. (ed.). *Europa: Festschrift für Ernst Grumach*, Berlin, 1967
————— *Inscriptions in the Minoan Linear Script of Class A*, Oxford, 1961
Brock, J.K. *Fortetsa*, Cambridge, 1957
Bucholz, Hans-Günter and Karageorghis, V. *Prehistoric Greece and Cyprus*, London, 1973
Buck, C.D. *Comparative Grammar of Greek and Latin*, Chicago, 1933
————— *The Greek Dialects*, Chicago, 1955
Budge, E.A.W. *The Gods of the Egyptians*, London, 1904
Burford, A. *Craftsmen in Greek and Roman Society*, London, 1972
Burn, A.R. *The Lyric Age of Greece*, London, 1960
————— *The Pelican History of Greece*, Harmondsworth, 1966
————— *Persia and the Greeks*, London, 1962
Bury, J.B. *History of Greece*, 4 ed. by R. Meiggs, London, 1975
Busolt, G. *Griechische Staatskunde*, in I. von Müller's *Handbuch der klassischen Altertums-Wissenschaft*, IV. 1.1. 3 ed., Munich, 1920–6
Cambridge Ancient History, Vols. 1 and 2 (3 ed., Cambridge), 1970–2
Carpenter, R. *Discontinuity in Greek Civilization*, Cambridge, 1966
Cary, M. *Geographic Background of Greek and Roman History*, Oxford, 1949
Chadwick, H.M. *The Growth of Literature*, Cambridge, 1925–39
————— *The Heroic Age*, Cambridge, 1912
Chadwick, J. *The Greek Dialects and Greek Pre-History*, GR 3.1
————— *The Decipherment of Linear B*, Cambridge, 1967
————— *The Mycenaean World*, Cambridge, 1976
Chamoux, F. *Cyrène sous la monarchie des Battiades*, Paris, 1953
Chantraine, P. *Grammaire homérique*, Paris, 1942

———————— *Études sur le vocabulaire grec*, Paris, 1956

———————— *Morphologie historique du grec*, Paris, 1945

Chapouthier, F. (and others). *Fouilles exécutées à Mallia (Rapports 1, 2, 3)*, Paris, 1928–42

Charbonneaux, J. *Greek Bronzes*, London, 1961

————————, Martin, R., Villaid, F. *Archaic Greek Art 620–480 B.C.*, London, 1971

Childe, V.G. *The Aryans*, London, 1926

———————— *The Bronze Age*, Cambridge, 1930

———————— *The Bronze Age*, PP 12

———————— *The Date and Origin of Minyan Ware*, JHS 35

———————— *The Dawn of Europeen Civilization*, 6 ed., London, 1957

———————— *History*, London, 1947

———————— *Piecing Together the Past*, London, 1956

———————— *The Prehistory of European Society*, London, 1958

———————— *Progress and Archaeology*, London, 1944

Chishull, E. *Antiquitates Asiaticae*, London, 1728

Chrimes, K.M.T. *Ancient Sparta*, Manchester, 1949

Christopoulos, G.A. (and others). *History of the Hellenic World* 1. *Prehistory and Protohistory*, London, 1974. 2. *The Archaic Period*, London, 1975

Clark, G. *From Savagery to Civilisation*, London, 1946

Clark, R.T. Rundle. *Myth and Symbol in Ancient Egypt*, London, 1959

Cohen, R. *La Grèce et l'hellénisation du monde antique*, 2 ed., Paris, 1939

Coldstream, J.N. *Greek Geometric Pottery*, London, 1968

———————— and Huxley, G.L. *Kythera*, London, 1972

———————— *Knossos: The Sanctuary of Demeter*, London, 1973

Collingwood, R.G. *The Idea of History*, Oxford, 1946

Comparetti, D. *Le leggi di Gortyna e le altre iscrizioni arcaiche cretesi edite ed illustrate*, MA 3

Cook, A.B. *Zeus*, Cambridge, 1914–40

———————— *Who was the Wife of Zeus?*, CR 20

———————— *Zeus, Jupiter and the Oak*, CR 17

Cook, J.M. *The Greeks in Ionia and the East*, London, 1962

Cook, S.A. *The Religion of Ancient Palestine in the Light of Archaeology*, London, 1930

Cornford, F.M. *The Ἀπαρχαί and the Eleusinian Mysteries*, in Quiggin 153

———————— *The Origin of the Olympic Games*, in Harrison, T. 212

———————— *Principium Sapientiae*, Cambridge, 1952

Cortsen, S.P. *Die Lemnische Inschrift*, Gl. 18

Croiset, A. and M. *Histoire de la littérature grecque*, 3 ed., Paris, 1901–21

Crossland, R.A. and Birchall, A. (ed.). *Bronze Age Migrations in the Aegean*, London, 1974

Daremberg, C. and Saglio, E. *Dictionnaire des antiquités grecques et romaines*, Paris, 1877–1919

Davaras, C. *Die Statue aus Astritsi*, Bern, 1972.

———————— *Guide to Cretan Antiquities*, New Jersey, 1976

Davis, S. *Decipherment of the Minoan Linear A*, Johannesburg, 1967

Dawkins, R.M. *The Sanctuary of Artemis Orthia at Sparta*, London, 1929

Bibliography

De Sanctis, G. *Storia dei Greci dalle origini alla fine del secolo V*, Florence, 1939

Deiters, P. *De Cretensium titulis publicis quaestiones epigraphicae*, Diss. Jena, 1904

Demargne, P. *La Crète dédalique*, Paris, 1947

———— *Aegean Art. The Origins of Greek Art*, London, 1964

Demetrakos, D. Μέγα λεξικὸν τῆς ἑλληνικῆς γλώσσης, Athens, 1936–

Desborough, V.R. D'A. *Protogeometric Pottery*, Oxford, 1952

———— *The Last Mycenaeans and their Successors*, Oxford, 1964

———— *The Greek Dark Ages*, London, 1972

Diamond, A.S. *Primitive Law*, 2 ed., London, 1950

———— *The Evolution of Law and Order*, London, 1951

———— *Primitive Law, Past and Present*, London, 1971

Deiterich, A. *Mutter Erde*, Leipzig/Berlin, 1905

Dikaios, P. *The Excavations at Vounous-Bellapais in Cyprus, 1931–2*, Arc. 88

Dodds, E.R. *The Greeks and the Irrational*, Oxford, 1951

———— *The Ancient Concept of Progress*, Oxford, 1973

Dunbabin, T.J. *The Greeks and their Eastern Neighbours*, London, 1957

Durkheim, E. *Les formes élémentaires de la vie religieuse*, 2 ed., Paris, 1912

Egger, A.E. *Études historiques sur les traités publics*, 2 ed., Paris, 1866

Ehrenberg, V. *The Greek State*, Oxford, 1960

———— *From Solon to Socrates*, London, 1968

———— *The Greek State*, 2 ed., London, 1969

———— *The People of Aristophanes*, 2 ed., Oxford, 1951

Elderkin, G.W. *The Marriage of Zeus and Hera*, AJA 41

Engnell, I. *Studies in Divine Kingship in the Ancient Near East*, Uppsala, 1943

Evans, A.J. *Knossos Excavations, 1903*, ABSA 9

———— *The Mycenaean Tree and Pillar Cult*, JHS 21

———— *The Palace of Minos*, London, 1921–35

———— *Scripta Minoa* I and II, Oxford, 1909 and 1952

———— *Shaft Graves and Beehive Tombs of Mycenae*, London, 1929

———— *The Prehistoric Tombs of Knossos*, London, 1906

———— *The Ring of Nestor*, JHS 45

Farnell, L.R. *Cults of the Greek States*, Oxford, 1896–1909

———— *Greek Hero Cults*, Oxford, 1921

Faure, P. *Grottes crétoises*, BCH 80

———— *Nouvelles recherches de spéléologie et de topographie crétoises*, BCH 84

———— *Spéléologie et topographie crétoises*, BCH 82

———— *Fonctions des cavernes crétoises*, Paris, 1964

———— *La vie quotidienne en Crète au temps de Minos*, Paris, 1973

———— *La vie quotidienne en Grèce au temps de la guerre de Troie*, Paris, 1975

———— *Les minerais de la Crète antique*, RA 1966

Fick, A. *Hattiden und Danubier in Griechenland*, Göttingen, 1909

———— *Vorgriechische Ortsnamen als Quelle für die Vorgeschichte Griechenlands*, Göttingen, 1905

Finley, M.I. *Aspects of Antiquity*, London, 1968

———— *Democracy Ancient and Modern*, London, 1973

———— *Early Greece: The Bronze and Archaic Ages*, London, 1970

———— *The Ancient Economy*, Berkeley/Los Angeles, 1975

Bibliography

——— *The World of Odysseus*, London, 1956
Fontenrose, J. *Python*, Berkeley/Los Angeles, 1959
Forman, W. and B., and Poulík, J. *Prehistoric Art*, London, 1955
Forrest, G. *The First Sacred War*, BCH 80
——— *A History of Sparta*, London, 1968
——— *The Emergence of Greek Democracy*, London, 1966
Forsdyke, J. *Greece before Homer*, London, 1956
——— *Minos of Crete*, JWCI 15
——— *The Pottery called Minyan Ware*, JHS 34
——— *The Chieftain Vase*, JWCI 15 (1952), 13–19
——— *The Harvester Vase, ibid.* 17 (1954), 1–9
Fotheringham, J.K. *Cleostratus*, JHS 39
Frankfort, H. *Cylinder Seals*, London, 1939
——— *Kingship and the Gods*, Chicago, 1948
Frazer, J.G. *Apollodorus*, London, 1921
——— *Folklore and the Old Testament*, London, 1919
——— *Lectures on the Early History of the Kingship*, London, 1905
——— *Pausanias's Description of Greece*, London, 1898
——— *The Golden Bough*, London, 1923–7
——— *The Prytaneum, The Temple of Vesta, The Vestals, Perpetual Fires*, JP 14
——— *Totemica*, London, 1937
——— *Totemism and Exogamy*, London, 1910
Frödin, O., and Persson, A.W. *Asine*, Stockholm, 1938
Frost, K.T. *The Critias and Minoan Crete*, JHS 33
Furtwängler, A. *Aegina. Das Heiligtum der Aphaia*, Munich, 1906
Galanopoulos, A.G. and Bacon, E. *Atlantis*, London, 1969
Gardner, P. *The Types of Greek Coins*, Cambridge, 1883
Gemoll, A. *Das Recht von Gortyn*, Striegau, 1889
Glotz, G. *La civilisation égéenne*, Paris, 1923. *Aegean Civilisation*, London, 1926
——— *La cité grecque*, Paris, 1928
Gordon, C.H. *Evidence for the Minoan Language*, Ventor, 1966
——— *Ugaritic Handbook*, Rome, 1947
——— *Ugaritic Literature*, Rome, 1949
——— *Ugaritic Manual*, Rome, 1955
Graham, A.J. *Colony and Mother City in Ancient Greece*, Manchester, 1964
Groenewegen-Frankfort, H.A. *Arrest and Movement*, Chicago, 1951
Grumach, E. *Bemerkungen zu M. Ventris-J. Chadwick, Evidence for Greek Dialect in the Mycenaean Archives*, OL 52 7/8
——— (ed.) *Minoica*, Berlin, 1958
Gruppe, O. *Griechische Mythologie und Religionsgeschichte*, Munich, 1906
Guarducci, M. *Note sul calendario cretese, Epigraphica*, 7.72
Gurney, O.R. *The Hittites*, London, 1952
Guthrie, W.K.C. *Early Greek Religion in the Light of the Decipherment of Linear B*, BICS 6
——— *Orpheus and Greek Religion*, 2 ed., London, 1952
——— *The Greeks and their Gods*, London, 1950
——— *A History of Greek Philosophy*, Cambridge, 1962–
Halbherr, F. *Cretan Expedition*, AJA 9 (1894), 11 (1896), i (1897), 2 (1898), 5 (1901)

228

——————— *Iscrizioni cretesi*, Mus. It. 3

——————— and Comparetti, D. *Epigrafi arcaiche di varie città cretesi*, Mus. It. 2

——————— and Fabricius, E. *Leggi antiche della città di Gortyna*, Florence, 1885

Haley, J.B. *The Coming of the Greeks*, AJA 32

Hall, H.R. *The Civilisation of Greece in the Bronze Age*, London, 1928

Hammond, N.G.L. *A History of Greece*, Oxford, 1959

Hansen, H.D. *Early Civilisation in Thessaly*, Baltimore, 1933

Harris, J.R. *Boanerges*, Cambridge, 1913

——————— *The Origin of the Cult of Hermes*, Manchester, 1929

Harrison, J.E. *Myths of the Odyssey*, London, 1882

——————— *Prolegomena to the Study of Greek Religion*, 3 ed., Cambridge, 1922

——————— *Primitive Hero Worship*, CR 6.474, 7.74

——————— *Sophocles' Ichneutae and the Dromena of Kyllene and the Satyrs*, Quiggin, 136

——————— *The Kouretes and Zeus Kouros*, ABSA 15

——————— *Themis*, 2 ed., Cambridge, 1927

Hartland, E.S. *Primitive Paternity*, London, 1909–10

Hasebroek, J. *Staat und Handel in alten Griechenland*, Tübingen, 1928. *Trade and Politics in Ancient Greece*, London, 1933

Hastings, J. *Encyclopaedia of Ethics and Religion*, Edinburgh, 1908–18

Hawes, Mrs H.A. (Boyd). *Excavations at Gournia, Crete* (By. Harriet A. Boyd), Washington, 1908

Hawkes, C.F.C. *The Prehistoric Foundations of Europe*, London, 1940

Hawkes, J. *Dawn of the Gods*, London, 1968

Hazzidakis, J. *Tylissos à l'époque minoenne*, Paris, 1921

——————— *Les Villas minoennes de Tylissos*, Paris, 1934

Head, B.V. *Historia Numorum*, 2 ed., Oxford, 1911

Heichelheim, F. *Wirtschaftgeschichte des Altertums*, Leiden, 1939. *An Ancient Economic History I*, 1958, Vol. 2, 1964; Vol. 3, 1970, Leiden

Heurtley, W.A. *Prehistoric Macedonia*, Cambridge, 1939

Higgins, R.A. *Greek and Roman Jewellery*, London, 1961

——————— *Greek Terracottas*, London, 1967

——————— *Minoan and Mycenaean Art*, London/New York, 1967

Hobhouse, L.T. *The Simplest Peoples*, BJS 7.2

———————, Wheeler, G.C., and Ginsberg, T. *Material Culture and Social Institutions of the Simpler Peoples*, London, 1930

Hocart, A.M. *Kingship*, Oxford, 1927

Hodges, H. *Technology in the Ancient World*, Harmondsworth, 1971

Hoeck, K. *Kreta*, Göttingen, 1823–9

Homolle, T. *Comptes des hiéropes du temple d'Apollon délien*, BCH 6

Hood, S. *The Home of the Heroes: the Aegean before the Greeks*, London, 1967

——————— *The Minoans: Crete in the Bronze Age*, London, 1971

Hooke, S.H. (editor). *The Labyrinth*, London, 1935

——————— *Myth and Ritual*, Oxford, 1933

——————— *Myth, Ritual and Kingship*, Oxford, 1958

Hooker, J. T. *Mycenaean Greece*, London, 1976

Hope Simpson, R. and Lazenby *The Catalogue of the Ships in Homer's Iliad*, Oxford, 1970

How, W.W. and Wells, J. *A Commentary on Herodotus*, 2 ed., Oxford, 1928

Hutchinson, R.W. *Prehistoric Crete*, Harmondsworth, 1962
Huxley, G.L. *Crete and the Luwians*, Oxford, 1961
————— *Early Sparta*, 2 ed., Shannon, 1970
————— *The Early Ionians*, London, 1966
Jardé, A. *Les céréales dans l'antiquité grecque I*, Paris, 1925
Jeanmaire, H. *Couroi et Courètes*, Lille, 1939
————— *Dionysos*, Paris, 1951
————— *La Cryptie lacédémonienne*, REG 26
Jeffery, L.H. *The Local Scripts of Archaic Greece*, Oxford, 1961
Jenkins, R.J.H. *Dedalica*, Cambridge, 1936
Jones, A.H.M. *Sparta*, Oxford, 1967
Kahrstedt, U. *Griechisches Staatsrecht I*. Göttingen, 1922
Kantor, H.J. *The Aegean and the Orient in the Second Millennium B.C.*, Bloomington, 1947
Kazamanova, L.N. *Rabovladenie na Krite v VI–IV vv.do n.e.*, VDI 3 (40)
Kenna, V.E.G. *Cretan Seals*, Oxford, 1960
Kirchhoff, A. *Studien zur Geschichte des griechischen Alphabets*, 4 ed., Gütersloh, 1887
Kirk, G.S. Heraclitus. *The Cosmic Fragments*, Cambridge, 1962
————— (ed.) *The Language and Background of Homer*, Cambridge, 1964
————— and Raven, J.E. *The Presocratic Philosophers*, Cambridge, 1957
————— *The Songs of Homer*, Cambridge, 1962
Kirsten, E. *Die Insel Kreta im fünften und vierten Jahrhundert*, Diss. Leipzig, 1936
Klingender, F.D. *Palaeolithic Religion and the Principle of Social Evolution*, BJS 5.2
Kohler, J., and Ziebarth, E. *Das Stadtrecht von Gortyn*, Göttingen, 1912
Kovalevsky, M.M. *Tableau des origines de l'évolution de la famille et de la propriété*, Stockholm, 1890
Kraay, C.M. *Greek Coins and History*, London, 1969
————— and Hirmer, M. *Greek Coins*, London/New York, 1966
Kretschmer, P. *Einleitung zur Geschichte der griechischen Sprache*, Göttingen, 1896
————— *Die Stellung der lykischen Sprache*, Gl. 27.256, 28.101
————— *Mythische Namen*, Gl.8
Kubitschek, W. *Grundriss der Antiken Zeitrechnung: Handb. der Altertumswissenschaft*, I, t. VII München, 1927
————— *Die Kalenderbücher von Florenz, Rom und Leyden, Wiener Denkschr.* Bd. 57. Abh. 2
Kunze, E. *Kretische Bronzereliefs*, Stuttgart, 1931
Kurtz, D.C. and Boardman, J. *Greek Burial Customs*, London, 1971
Lacey, W.K. *The Family in Classical Greece*, London, 1968
Landtman, G. *Origin of the Inequality of the Social Classes*, London, 1938
Langdon, S. *The Babylonian Epic of Creation*, Oxford, 1923
————— *Babylonian Menologies and Semetic Calendars*, London, 1935
Larsen, J.A.O. *Perioeci in Crete*, CP 31
Leaf, W. *Homer and History*, London, 1915
Legrand, E. *Descriptions des îles de l'Archipel par Christophe Buondelmonti*, Paris, 1897
Lejeune, M. *Traité de phonétique grecque*, Paris, 1947
Lekatsas, P. Ἡ Ψυχή, Athens, 1957
————— Διόνυσος, Athens, 1971

Bibliography

Lethaby, W.R. *The Earlier Temple of Artemis at Ephesus*, JHS 37
Levi, D. *Gli scavi del 1954 sull'acropoli di Gortina, Annuario*, 1955–6
────── *Gleanings from Crete*, AJA 49
Levi, P. *Pausanias: Guide to Greece*, Harmondsworth, 1971.
Lilley, S. *Men, Machines and History*, 2 ed., London, 1965
Lloyd, S. *Early Anatolia*, London, 1956
Lloyd-Jones, H. *The Justice of Zeus*, Berkeley, 1971
Lorimer, H.L. *Homer and the Monuments*, London, 1950
Lowie, R.H. *Primitive Society*, New York, 1929
Luce, J.V. *The End of Atlantis*, London, 1969
Maine, H.J.S. *Dissertations on Early Law and Custom*, London, 1883
Maiuri, A. *Il calendario cretese*, RL 19
────── *Studi sull' onomastica cretese*, RL 19–20
Marinatos, S. *Excavations at Thera I–VI*, Athens, 1968–74
────── *The Cult of the Cretan Caves*, RR 5
────── and Hirmer, M. *Crete and Mycenae*, London, 1960
Mason, O.T. *Woman's Share in Primitive Culture*, London, 1895
Matz, F. and Biesantz, H. (eds.). *Corpus der Minoischen und Mykenischen Siegel*, Berlin, 1964
────── (ed.). *Forschungen auf Kreta 1942*, Berlin, 1951
────── *Frühkretische Siegel*, Berlin, 1928
────── *Kreta, Mykene, Troja*, Stuttgart, 1956
Meillet, A. *Aperçu d'une histoire de la langue grecque*, 4 ed., Paris, 1935
────── *Introduction à l'étude comparative des langues indoeuropéenes*, 8 ed., Paris, 1937
────── and Vendryes, J. *Grammaire comparée des langues classiques*, 2 ed., Paris, 1927
Meister, K. *Der syntakitsche Gebrauch des Genetivs in den Kretischen Dialektinschriften*, Indogerman. Forsch. 18
Mellaart, J. *Catal Hüyük*, London, 1967
Mendelsohn, I. *Slavery in the Ancient Near East*, New York, 1949
Merriam, A.C. *Law Code of the Kretan Gortyna*, AJA I (1885) and 2 (1886)
Meyer, E. *Geschichte des Altertums*, 2 ed., Stuttgart, 1937
Michell, H. *Economics of Ancient Greece*, 2 ed., Cambridge, 1957
────── *Sparta*, Cambridge, 1952
Morgan, L.H. *Ancient Society*, 2 ed., Chicago, 1910
Morrow, G.R. *Plato's Cretan City*, Princeton, 1960
Müller, K. *Frühmykenische Reliefs in* Jahrb., 30 (1915)
Müller, K.O. *Die Dorier*, 2 ed., Breslau, 1844. *The History and Antiquities of the Doric Race*, Oxford, 1830
────── *Orchomenos und die Minyer*, 2 ed., Breslau, 1844
────── *Prolegomena zu einer wissenschaftlichen Mythologie*, Göttingen, 1825
Murray, G. *The Hymn of the Kouretes*, ABSA 15
────── *The Rise of the Greek Epic*, 3 ed., Oxford, 1924
Muttelsee, M. *Zur Verfassungsgeschichte Kretas im Zeitalter des Hellenismus*, Diss. Hamburg, 1925
Mylonas, G.E. *Ancient Mycenae*, London, 1957
Myres, J.L. *Homer and his Critics*, London, 1958
────── *Who were the Greeks?*, Berkeley, 1930

Bibliography

Neugebauer, O. *The Exact Sciences in Antiquity*, Princeton, 1952

Nilsson, M.P. *Das frühe Griechenland von innen gesehen*, Hist. 3.3

——————— *Die Entstehung und Religiöse Bedeutung des griechischen Kalenders*, Lunds Universitets Arsskrift. N.F. Aud. 1, 14.21, Lund, 1918

——————— *Die Grundlagen des spartanischen Lebens*, K.12

——————— *Geschichte der griechischen Religion*, Munich, 1941–50

——————— *Greek Piety*, Oxford, 1948

——————— *Greek Popular Religion*, New York, 1940

——————— *Griechische Feste von religiöser Bedeutung mit Ausschluss der attischen*, Darmstadt, 1957

——————— *History of Greek Religion*, 2 ed., Oxford, 1949

——————— *Homer and Mycenae*, London, 1933

——————— *Minoan-Mycenaean Religion*, 2 ed., Lund, 1950

——————— *Minoan-Mycenaean Origin of Greek Mythology*, London, 1932

——————— *Opuscula Selecta 1–2*, Lund, 1951–2

——————— *Primitive Time Reckoning*, Lund/Oxford, 1920

——————— *Sonnenkalendar und Sonnenreligion*, Arch. f. Religionswiss. 30

——————— *Studia de Dionysiis Atticis*, Lund, 1900

——————— *The New Inscriptions of the Salaminioi*, AJP 59

Oliva, P. *Sparta and her Social Problems*, Amsterdam/Prague, 1971

Overbeck, J. *Die antiken Schriftquellen z: Geschichte d. bildunden Künste bei d. Griechen*, Leipzig, 1868

Page, D.L. *History and the Homeric Iliad*, Berkeley/Los Angeles, 1959

——————— *The Santorini Volcano and the Desolation of Minoan Crete*, London, 1970

Palmer, L.R. *Archaeans and Indo-Europeans*, Oxford, 1955

——————— *A New Guide to the Palace of Knossos*, London, 1969

——————— *Mycenaeans and Minoans*, 2 ed., London, 1965

——————— *The Penultimate Palace of Knossos*, Rome, 1969

——————— and Boardman, J. *On the Knossos Tablets*, Oxford, 1963

Parke, H.W., and Wormell, D.E.W. *The Delphic Oracle*, Oxford, 1956

Parker, R.A. *The Calendars of Ancient Egypt*, Chicago, 1953

Pashley, R. *Travels in Crete*, Cambridge/London, 1837

Pauly, A., Wissowa, G., and Kroll, W. *Realencyclopädie der classischen Altertumswissenschaft*, Stuttgart, 1894–

Pendlebury, J.D.S. *Archaeology of Crete*, London, 1939

Pernier, L., and Banti, L. *Il palazzo minoico di Festos*, Rome, 1935–51

Persson, A.W. *Der Ursprung der eleusinschen Mysterien*, Arc. f. Religionswiss. 21

——————— *The Religion of Greece in Prehistoric Times*, Berkeley/Los Angeles, 1942

Pfuhl, E. *Malerei und Zeichnung der Griechen*, Munich, 1923

Picard, C. *Ephèse et Claros*, Paris, 1922

——————— *Les Origines du Polythéisme Hellénique*, Paris, 1930

——————— *Les Religions Préhelléniques*, Paris, 1948

——————— *Sur la patrie et les pérégrinations de Déméter*, REG 40

Pickard-Cambridge, A. *Dithyramb, Tragedy and Comedy*, Oxford, 1927

——————— *The Dramatic Festivals of Athens*, Oxford, 1953

Pomerance, L. *The Final Collapse of Santorini (Thera) 1400 B.C. or 1200 B.C.?*,

Göteburg, 1970

Popham, M.R. *The Last Days of the Palace at Knossos*, Lund, 1964

———————— *The Destruction of the Palace at Knossos and its Pottery*, Ant. 40 (1966), 24ff

Preller, L. von. *Griechische Mythologie*, 4 ed., by C. Robert, Berlin, 1887–1926

Pritchard, J.B. (ed.). *Ancient Near Eastern Texts*, Princeton, 1950

Proceedings of the Second International Congress of Classical Studies, Copenhagen, 1958

Quiggin, E.C. *Essays and Studies Presented to William Ridgeway*, Cambridge, 1913

Ransome, H.M. *The Sacred Bee*, London, 1937

Reichel, A. *Die Stierspiele in der kretisch-mykenischen Cultur*, AM.34

Renfrew, C. *The Emergence of Civilisation: The Cyclades and the Aegean in the Third Millennium B.C.*, London, 1972

Richter, G.M.A. *A Handbook of Greek Art*, London, 1959

———————— *Kouroi: Archaic Greek Youths*, 2 ed., London, 1960

———————— *Korai: Archaic Greek Maidens*, London, 1968

Ridgeway, W. *The Early Age of Greece*, Cambridge, 1901–31

Rivers, W.H.R. *Kinship and Social Organisation*, London, 1932

Robert, C. *Sosipolis in Olympia*, AM 18

Robert, L. *Les Asklepieis de l'Archipel*, REG 46

Robertson Smith, W. *Religion of the Semites*, 3 ed., London, 1927

Rodenwaldt, G. *Tiryns*, Athens, 1912

Rohde, E. *Psyche: Seelencult und Unsterblichkeitsglaube der Griechen*, Freiburg, 1898

Roscher, W.H. *Ausführliches Lexicon der griechischen und römischen Mythologie*, Leipzig, 1884–1937

———————— *Selene und Verwandtes*, Leipzig, 1890

Rose, H.J. *Primitive Culture in Greece*, London, 1925

———————— *Handbook of Greek Mythology*, 5 ed., London, 1953

Rostovtzeff, M. *A History of the Ancient World I*, 2 ed., Oxford, 1930

———————— *The Social and Economic History of the Hellenistic World*, 2 ed., Oxford, 1957

Rouse, W.H.D. *Greek Votive Offerings*, Cambridge, 1902

Saggs, W.H.F. *Everyday Life in Babylonia and Assyria*, London, 1965

Sapouna-Sakellaraki, Effie. *Eastern Crete*, Athens, 1975

Schaeffer, C.F.A. *Cuneiform Texts of Ras Shamra*, London, 1939

Seager, R.B. *Excavations on the Island of Pseira, Crete*, Boston/New York, 1912

———————— *Explorations in the Island of Mochlos*, Philadelphia, 1910

———————— *Excavations at Vasiliki, 1904*, University of Pennsylvania. Transactions of the Department of Archaeology I (1905), 207–21

———————— *Report of Excavations at Vasiliki, Crete, in 1906*, University of Pennsylvania. Transactions of the Department of Archaeology II (1907), 111–32

Seebohm, H.E. *The Structure of Greek Tribal Society*, London, 1895

Seltman, C. *Greek Coins*, 2 ed., London, 1955

———————— *Masterpieces of Greek Coinage*, Oxford, 1949

Semenoff, A. *Antiquitates iuris publici Cretensium*, Petrograd, 1893

Shipp, G.P. *Studies in the Language of Homer*, 2 ed., Cambridge, 1972

Shrewsbury, J.F.D. *The Plague of the Philistines*, JH 47

Singer, C., Holmyard, E.J., Hall, A.R., and Williams, T.I. (editors). *A History of*

Bibliography

Technology, 1–2, Oxford, 1954–6

Snodgrass, A.M. *Arms and Armour of the Greeks*, London, 1967

———————— *Early Greek Armour and Weapons*, Edinburgh, 1964

———————— *The Dark Age of Greece*, Edinburgh, 1971

Spratt, T.A.B. *Travels and Researches in Crete*, London, 1865

Starr, C.G. *The Origins of Greek Civilisation, 1100–650 B.C.*, London, 1962

Stubbings, F.H. *Mycenaean Pottery from the Levant*, Cambridge, 1951

———————— *Prehistoric Greece*, London, 1972

Svoronos, J.N. *Numismatique de la Crète ancienne*, Macon, 1890

Swindler, M.H. *Cretan elements in the Cults and Ritual of Apollo*, Bryn Mawr, 1913

Swoboda, H. *Lehrbuch der griechischen Staatsaltertümer*, 6 ed., Tübingen, 1913

Tarn, W.W. and Griffith, G.T. *Hellenistic Civilisation*, 3 ed., London, 1952

Taylor, A.E. *The Laws of Plato*, London, 1934

Taylour, W. *The Mycenaeans*, London, 1964

Thiel, J.H. *De Feminarum apud Dores condicione*, M. 57

Thomson, G. *Aeschylus and Athens*, 2 ed., London, 1946

———————— *Aeschylus, Oresteia*, Cambridge, 1938; Prague, 1966

———————— *Aeschylus, Prometheus Bound*, Cambridge, 1932

———————— *From Religion to Philosophy*, JHS 73

———————— *Studies in Ancient Greek Society. 1: The Prehistoric Aegean*, 2 ed., London, 1954

———————— *Studies in Ancient Greek Society. 2: The First Philosophers*, London, 1955

———————— *The Greek Calendar*, JHS 63

———————— *The Greek Language*, Cambridge, 1960

———————— *The Wheel and the Crown*, CR 59

Thomson, J.A.K. *Studies in the Odyssey*, Oxford, 1914

Thomson, J.O. *History of Ancient Geography*, Cambridge, 1948

Thumb, A. *Handbuch der griechischen Dialekte*, 2te Auflage von E. Kieckers, Heidelberg, 1932

Thurnwald, R. *Economics in Primitive Communities*, London, 1932

Tod, M.N. *Teams of Ball-Players at Sparta*, ABSA 10

Tomlinson, R.A. *Greek Sanctuaries*, London, 1976

Trevor-Battye, A. *Camping in Crete*, London, 1913

Ucko, P.J. and Dimbleby, G.W. (ed.). *The Domestication and Exploitation of Plants and Animals*, London, 1969

Van Der Mijnsbrugge, M. *The Cretan Koinon*, New York, 1931

Van Effentèrre, H. *A propos du serment des Drériens*, BCH 61

———————— *Inscriptions archaïques crétoises*, BCH 70

———————— *La Crète et le monde grec de Platon à Polybe*, Paris, 1948

Van Gennep, A. *L'état actuel du problème totémique*, Paris, 1920

———————— *Les rites de passage*, Paris, 1909

Ventris, M., and Chadwick, J. *Documents in Mycenaean Greek*, Cambridge, 1956

———————— *Evidence for Greek Dialect in the Mycenaean Archives*, JHS 73

Vermeule, E. *Greece in the Bronze Age*, Chicago, 1964

Vollgraff, W. *Inscription d'Argos (Traité entre Knossos et Tylissos)*, BCH 37

Wace, A.J.B. *A Cretan Statuette in the Fitzwilliam Museum*, Cambridge, 1927

——————— *Chamber Tombs of Mycenae*, Arc. 82
——————— *Excavations at Mycenae*, ABSA 25
——————— *Mycenae*, Princeton, 1949
——————— *Mycenae*, Ant. 10
——————— *Mycenae 1939*, JHS 59
——————— *The Treasury of Atreus*, Ant. 14
Wackernagel, J. *Sprachliche Untersuchungen zu Homer*, Gl. 7
Webster, H. *Primitive Secret Societies*, 2 ed., New York, 1932
Welcker, F.G. *Kleine schriften*, Bonn, 1844–67
——————— *Griechische Götterlehre*, Göttingen, 1857–63
Westermarck, E.A. *Origin and Development of Moral Ideas*, London, 1906–8
——————— *The History of Human Marriage*, 5 ed., London, 1921
Wide, S. *Lakonische Kulte*, Leipzig, 1893
Widengren, G. *The King and the Tree of Life in Ancient Near Eastern Religion*, Uppsala Universitets Arsskrift, 1951–4
Wilamowitz-Moellendorff, U. von. *Der Glaube der Hellenen*, Berlin, 1931–2
Willetts, R.F. *Ancient Crete: A Social History*, London/Toronto, 1965, 2 ed., 1974
——————— *Aristocratic Society in Ancient Crete*, London, 1955
——————— *A Neotas at Dreros?*, H 85.3
——————— *Cretan Cults and Festivals*, London/New York, 1962
——————— *Cretan Eileithyia*, CQ 8.3–4
——————— *Everyday Life in Ancient Crete*, London, 1969
——————— *Europa*, E 1
——————— καρποδαῖσται, Philol. 105.1/2
——————— *Some Elements of Continuity in the Social Life of Ancient Crete*, IRSH, 2.3
——————— *The Law Code of Gortyn*, Berlin, 1967
——————— *The Myth of Glaukos and the Cycle of Birth and Death*, K. 37
——————— *The Neodamodeis*, CP 49
——————— *The Servile Interregnum at Argos*, H 87.4
Winter, F.E. *Greek Fortifications*, Toronto/London, 1971
Woodhead, A.G. *The Greeks in the West*, London, 1962
——————— *The Study of Greek Inscriptions*, Cambridge, 1959
Woolley, L. *A Forgotten Kingdom*, London, 1953
Xanthoudides, S.A. *The Vaulted Tombs of Mesara*, London, 1924
Xenaki-Sekallariou, A. *Les cachets minoens de la collection Giamalakis*, Paris, 1958
Zanotti-Bianco, U. *Archaeological Discoveries in Sicily and Magna Graecia*, JHS 57
Zervos, C. *L'Art de la Crète*, Paris, 1956

EPIGRAPHICAL PUBLICATIONS

CIG   A. Bockh, *Corpus Inscriptionum Graecarum*, Berlin, 1827–77
Delphinion   A. Rehm, *Das Delphinion in Milet*, in *Milet: Ergebnisse der Ausgrabungen und Untersuchungen seit dem Jahre 1899*, III 362–406, Berlin, 1914
DHR   R. Dareste, B. Haussoullier, T. Reinach, *Recueil des inscriptions juridiques grecques*, 1 série, Paris, 1891–5; 2 série, Paris, 1898–1904
Die Inschriften von Magnesia am Maeander, ed. O. Kern, Berlin, 1900

Bibliography

F. Durrbach   *Choix d'Inscriptions de Délos*, Paris, 1921

Heikel   I.A. Heikel, *Griechische Inschriften sprachlich erklärt*, Helsingsfors, 1924

Hicks-Hill   E.L. Hicks and G.F. Hill, *A Manual of Greek Historical Inscriptions*, Oxford, 1901

IC   *Inscriptiones Creticae opera et consilio Friderici Halbherr collectae. 1. Tituli Cretae mediae praeter Gortynios*, Rome, 1935. *2. Tituli Cretae Occidentalis*, Rome, 1939. *3. Tituli Cretae Orientalis*, Rome, 1942. *4. Tituli Gortynii*, Rome, 1950. *Curavit Margarita Guarducci*

IG   *Inscriptiones Graecae*, Berlin, 1873–

IGA   H. Roehl, *Inscriptiones Graecae antiquissimae praeter Atticas in Attica repertas*, Berlin, 1882

IGR   *Inscriptiones Graecae ad res Romanas pertinentes*, Paris, 1911–27

IIGA   H. Roehl, *Imagines inscriptionum Graecarum antiquissimarum*, 3 ed., Berlin, 1907

IPE   *Inscriptiones orae septentrionalis Ponti Euxini*, ed. B. Latyshev, Petersburg, 1885–1901: I^2 = vol. i, 2 ed., 1916

Inscr.Cos.   *The Inscriptions of Cos*, ed. W.R. Paton and E.L. Hicks, Oxford, 1891

Inscr.Perg.   *Die Inschriften von Pergamon, in Altertümer von Pergamon viii*, ed. M. Fraenkel, Berlin, 1890–5

MAMA   *Monumenta Asiae Minoris Antiqua*, Manchester/London, 1928–

Meiggs-Lewis, Russell Meiggs and David Lewis, *A Selection of Greek Historical Inscriptions to the end of the Fifth Century B.C.*, Oxford, 1969

Michel   C. Michel, *Recueil d'inscriptions grecques*, Paris/Brussels, 1900–27

OGI   *Orientis Graeci Inscriptiones Selectae*, ed. W. Dittenberger, Leipzig, 1903–5

Roberts   E.S. Roberts, *An Introduction to Greek Epigraphy, I*, Cambridge, 1887

Schwyzer   E. Schwyzer, *Dialectorum Graecarum exempla epigraphica potiora* (3 ed. of P. Cauer's *Delectus inscriptionum Graecarum propter dialectum memorabilium*), Leipzig, 1923

SGDI   *Sammlung der griechischen Dialekt-Inschriften*, ed. H. Collitz, F. Bechtel, O. Hoffmann, Göttingen, 1884–1915

SIG   *Sylloge Inscriptionum Graecarum*, ed. W. Dittenberger, 3 ed., Leipzig, 1915–24

Solmsen   F. Solmsen, *Inscriptiones Graecae ad inlustrandas dialectos selectae* (4 ed. by E. Fraenkel), Leipzig, 1930

Tod   M.N. Tod, *Greek Historical Inscriptions, I.*, to the end of the fifth century B.C., 2 ed., Oxford, 1946. II, from 403 to 323 B.C., Oxford, 1948

PERIODICALS

ABSA   *Annual of the British School at Athens*, London, 1894–

AJA   *American Journal of Archaeology*, v.p. 1885–

AM   *Mitteilungen des deutschen archäologischen Instituts, Athenische Abteilung*, 1876–

Ann.Ép.   *L'Année épigraphique*, published in *Revue Archéologique*

Bibliography

Annuario   *Annuario della regia Scuola Archeologica di Atene*, 1914–
Ant.   *Antiquity*, London, 1926–
Arc.   *Archaeologia*, London, 1770–
               Archaeologia Homerica, Göttingen, 1967–
Arch.Anz.   *Archaologischer Anzeiger*, in *Jahrbuch des (kaiserlich) deutschen archaologischen Instituts*, 1886–
Ἀρχ.Δελτ.   *Ἀρχαιολογικὸν Δελτίον*, Athens, 1915–
Ἀρχ.Ἐφ.   *Ἀρχαιολογικὴ Ἐφημερίς*, Athens, 1910–
Arch.f.   *Archiv für Religionswissenschaft*, Freiburg im Breisgau, 1898–
Religionswiss.
Archiv   Prague, 1929–
Orientálni
Ausonia   *Ausonia, Rivista della Società italiana di archeologia e storia dell'arte*, 1906–
BCH   *Bulletin de correspondance héllenique*, Paris, 1877–
Berl.Sitzb.   = *Sitzungersberichte der Preussischen Akademie der Wissenschaften*, Berlin, 1882–
BICS   *Bulletin of the Institute of Classical Studies*, London, 1954–
BJS   *British Journal of Sociology*, London, 1950–
BSLP   *Bulletin de la société de linguistique de Paris*, Paris, 1869–
CP   *Classical Philology*, Chicago, 1906–
CQ   *Classical Quarterly*, London, 1907–
CR   *Classical Review*, London, 1887–
CRA   *Comptes rendus de l'Académie des Inscriptions et Belles-Lettres*, 1857–
E   *Eirene. Studia Graeca et Latina*, Prague, 1960–
Epigraphica   *Epigraphica. Rivista italiana di epigrafia*, Milan, 1938–
Ἐφ. Ἀρχ.   *Ἐφημερίς Ἀρχαιολογική*, περίοδος τρίτη, Athens, 1893–1909
Etudes   Paris, 1928–
Crétoises
GL.   *Glotta*, Göttingen, 1907–
GR   *Greece and Rome*, Oxford, 1931–
H   *Hermes*, Berlin-Wiesbaden, 1866–
Hesperia   *Hesperia: Journal of the American School of Classical Studies at Athens*, Cambridge, Mass., 1932–
Hist.   *Historia, studi storici per l'antichità classica*, Milan/Rome, 1927–
Indogerman   *Indogermanische Forschungen*, Strassburg/Berlin, 1891–
Forsch.
Iraq   London, 1934–
IRSH   *International Review of Social History*, Assen/Netherlands, 1956–
Jahrb.   *Jahrbuch des (kaiserlich) deutschen archäologischen Instituts*, 1886–
Jahresh.   *Jahreshefte des österreichischen archäologischen Institutes*, Vienna, 1898–
JAOS   *Journal of the American Oriental Society*, New Haven, 1843–
JCP   *Jahrbücher für classische Philologie*, Leipzig, 1855–
JH   *The Journal of Hygiene*, Cambridge, 1901–
JHS   *Journal of Hellenic Studies*, London, 1880–
JP   *Journal of Philology*, London, 1868–1920
JRAS   *Journal of the Royal Asiatic Society*, London, 1834–
JWCI   *Journal of the Warburg and Courtauld Institutes*, London, 1937–

Bibliography

K   Klio, Beiträge zur alten Geschichte, Leipzig, 1901–
Kad.   Kadmos, Berlin, 1962–
Kerameikos   Kerameikos: ergebnisse der ausgrabungen, Berlin, 1939–
KK   KPHTIKA XPONIKA, Iraklion, 1946–
M   Mnemosyne, Leiden, 1852–
MA   Monumenti antichi pubblicati per cura della Reale Accademia dei Lincei, Rome–Milan, 1890–
Mus.It.   Museo italiano di antichità classica, Florence, 1885–90
OL   Orientalistische Literaturzeitung, Leipzig, 1897–
PAE   πρακτικὰ τῆς ἐν ᾿Αθήναις ἀρχαιολογικῆς ἑτειρείας, Athens, 1872–
Philol   Philologus, 1846
PP   Past and Present, London, 1951–
RA   Revue Archéologique, Paris, 1844–
REA   Revue des études anciennes, Bordeaux, 1930–
REG   Revue des études grecques, Paris, 1888–
Rev.Phil.   Revue de Philologie, Paris, 1877–
RF   Rivista di filologia e di istruzione classica, Turin, 1873–
RHR   Revue de l'histoire des religions, Paris, 1880–
RIA   Rivista del R. Instituto d'Archeologia e Storia dell' Arte, Rome, 1929–
Rivista di storia antica, Padua/Messina, 1895–1910
RL   Rendiconti della Reale Accademia nazionale dei Lincei, Rome, 1873–
RM   Rheinisches Museum für Philologie, Frankfurt, 1842–
RR   Review of Religion, New York, 1936–
S   Syria, Paris, 1919–
SK   The Sacral Kingship. (Studies in the History of Religions IV). Contributions to the Central Theme of the 8th International Congress for the History of Religions, Leiden, 1959
Wiener   Denkschriften der Akademie der Wissenschaften in Wien, Phil.-Hist.
Denkschr.   Klasse, 1850–
Wien-Sitz.   Sitzungsberichte der (kaiserlichen) Akademie der Wissenschaften in Wien, Phil.-hist. Klasse, 1849–
WS   Wiener Studien, 1879–

REFERENCES AND NOTES

I GEOGRAPHY

1   Hood M17 and 151 n. 2.
2   Davaras in 'Αρχ. 'Εφ. (1967) 84–90. Cf., for oscillations in sea-level at Mallia since Roman times, *Etudes Crétoises* 13 (1963) 29–31.
3   Hood *ib.* 17–18; Davaras in ABSA 69 (1974) 91 n. 18.
4   As Nausicaa explains to Odysseus: *Od.* 6. 262–9.
5   Spratt 2. 135 ff., 241 ff.; Hood 18. Hood observes (*ib.* 151 n. 3) that there is no evidence for a sudden and cataclysmic rise as suggested by Pendlebury AC 3.
6   *Acts* 27.14.
7   Warren MSV 124–5, 132; Hutchinson 33–4; Hood M 15.
8   Warren *ib.* 138 ff.; Evans JHS 17 (1897) 327–95; cf. also Boardman IG 15–16.
9   Porph. *Antr.* 20; Ps. Luc. *Am.* 34; Willetts CCF 141 ff.
10 Branigan FPC 152.
11 FCC *passim*.
12 Pendlebury AC 6; Hutchinson 42–3; Warren KK (1972) 70, 73.
13 The 'Kydonian' quince has an early and continuous place in literature: Stesich. 29, cf. Alcm. 143; Canthar. 6; Phylarch. 10 J; Ibyc. 1.1; Dsc. 1.115.
14 IC 1.XVII. 17–19.
15 Hood, M 88, comments: 'The occupants of these chariots may be divine; but there is no reason why goats should not have been trained as draught animals!'
16 See Chapter 2.
17 Pendlebury (*ib.* 6), stated: 'In the Lasithi plain, for instance, there is an extraordinary depth of soil due entirely to the fact that the surrounding hills have been denuded.'
18 Warren KK (1972) 77–8 n. 19.
19 Pashley 2. 326.
20 Raulin 203–4.
21 Raulin 41, 204, 206.
22 Pococke 265.
23 Raulin 207–8.
24 Allbaugh 466.

2   NEIGHBOURS

1   AC 7–16.
2   Cf. Bachtin 6 ff. '. . . nothing perhaps is more illuminating for the understanding of Greek prehistory and early history than the study of the geographical distribution and modes of life of the present populations of that country. . . .'
3   Reports in Hesperia 42 (1973) 45 ff.; 253 ff.
4   Hood M 27, citing ABSA 60 (1965) 225–7, 239.
5   Hodges 32 fig. 27, with the further comment: 'An Egyptian wall painting of a much later date shows how the process was carried out. Mud was puddled with water and packed down into the moulds, which were then lifted away, leaving the newly formed brick sitting in the full sun to dry. The process is still used in exactly the same manner throughout the large part of the Near East to-day.'
6   Mellaart 15.
7   Mellaart 11.
8   Mellaart 67, 78.
9   B.C. Dietrich in *Hist.* Bd. 16. Ht. 4 (1967), 392.
10 Mellaart 22.
11 Branigan FPC 1.
12 Lilley 16; Hodges 79.
13 Branigan FPC 1–3.
14 Lilley 1–24.
15 Saggs ch. 3, citing Dossin, Jean and Kupper: *Archives Royales de Mari*, vols. 1–4, Paris, 1950–2.
16 Lilley 17–18.
17 FK 108–9; cf. *ib.* 76–7, 156–7, 158–9.
18 Margaret Drower in CAH 2. 21(b)iv, *passim*.
19 An ornate battle-axe of Mitannian origin (of about 1300 BC) was wrought from three metals, with an iron blade and socket of copper with gold inlays. The iron of the blade has a high percentage of nickel, a treatment involving considerable technical skill and metallurgical knowledge. The copper socket, produced by the *cireperdue* method, was cast round the blade; and the contraction of the copper on cooling was adequate to secure the blade without rivets. See H.H. Coghlan in Singer: pp. 618–19 and fig. 418.
20 See Gordon UL 122–6.
21 Drower *ib.* 7–8.
22 S.H. Hooke in Singer 762–3.
23 Drower *ib.* 19.
24 Evans PM 1. 1–7.
25 See e.g. Hood M 35–6, Branigan FPC 17–22. Both prefer the retention of the Evans system as basically valid, despite the difficulties.

3   EARLY SETTLERS AND EARLY ACHIEVEMENTS

1   ABSA 38 (1937–8) 50, fig. 21; Hood M 22; cf. Hutchinson PC 45 who remarks: 'It must be admitted, however, that the average archaeologist who works in

Crete would not recognize the less obvious type of Palaeolithic tool, and is not a good enough geologist to look in the right places. One or two palaeontologists, however, have examined some early cave deposits, and so far have discovered no artefacts associated with the fossils contemporary with the Old Stone Age.'

2 Cf. Hood M 17 f.

3 Hood M 22.

4 Cf. Hutchinson PC 45 f. for some remarks on palaeontological evidence.

5 Hood M 28 and n. 9. Cf. Evans PM 1.14: 'Neolithic Crete may be regarded as an insular offshoot of an extensive Anatolian province'; and also Pendlebury AC 37. Cf. J.D. Evans in ABSA 63 (1968) 273 ff. for the Anatolian links.

6 Apparently an unusual feature among the Neolithic peoples of Greece: Hood M 27.

7 As was usual in later times in Crete.

8 Weinburg in CAH 1. 51–61; J.D. Evans in ABSA 59 (1964) 132–240, 63 (1968) 239–76; Hood M 22 ff.; PPS 38.2 (1971). Cf. Evans PM 1. 32–55, 2.1–21.

9 On these early settlers see Hood M Ch. 2; and cf., for a detailed discussion of the Neolithic problems, Branigan FPC pp. 9 ff. Also PPS 38.2 (1971) 117.

10 J.D. Evans in BSA 59 (1964) 174–6 fig. 16; Hood M 24 fig. 6.

11 Hawkes 126, 130, 172–3, 261, 309; Childe DEC *passim*; Nilsson MMR 53; Faure BCH 80 *passim*.

12 Nilsson *ibid.* n. 1. Cf. BSA 6.77; Pl. *Min.* 315 d.

13 FPC 37 f.; cf. Evans PM 2. 1–21; J.D. Evans in PPS (1971), Warren and Tzedhakis in ABSA 69 (1974).

14 See my fuller discussion, with refs., in CCF 4–8.

15 M 27.

16 *Ibid.* 16 n. 8. Cf. ABSA 63 (1968) 271–2.

17 Cf., on the advanced nature of the earliest pottery at Knossos, Branigan FPC 9 f. Also J.D. Evans *loc. cit.*

18 Branigan *ib.* 196.

19 M 29. Cf. Warren and Tzedhakis in ABSA 69 (1974).

20 Branigan *ibid.*

21 For summary of details and bibliography see Buchholz–Karageorghis 17–19 *et passim.*

22 Xanthoudides VTM.

23 Branigan TM.

24 *Ib.* 3, adding: 'Unsatisfactory by modern standards of excavation and publication, its production was nevertheless a superb achievement on the part of Xanthoudides. Here we find, described in quite considerable detail, excavations which had been conducted as much as twenty years previously. Many items are given a remarkably precise provenance, disturbed areas are noted, details of stratification recorded, and the text is abundantly illustrated with a series of fine drawings and photographic plates. Not a definitive account by current standards perhaps, but a miracle for its time and an object lesson to some of Xanthoudides' successors.'

25 *Ib.* 5.

26 *Ib.* 24.

27 *Ib.* 25. Cf. also FPC 48–9.

28 *Ib.* 27.

29 As Branigan notes, *ib.* 178. Cf. Caskey in *Proc. Am. Phil. Soc.* 113 no. 6 (1969) 433 ff.

30 Seager *Vasilike* I, II, and in *Gournia* 49–50. Cf. now Alexiou in 'Αρχ. Δελτ, 19 (1964), Sinos in *Arch. Anz.* (1970) 1–24.

31 Hutchinson PC 145.

32 Cf. also Branigan FPC 44. Hood (M 156) is doubtful about this possibility.

33 Warren *Myrtos.*

34 Warren points out that, since textile production was a main activity, a hill-top location with good winds for drying cloth may have been appreciated, and the siting of the Hellenistic dyeworks on the Rachmi at Isthmia near Corinth provides a close parallel. However, he grants that other factors could have determined the choice of site: *ib.* 268 cf. 263 n. 3.

35 *Ib.* 255–6. Cf. also Warren's conclusions about early Bronze Age agriculture in Western Crete on the evidence from the EM settlement of Debla in Ant. 48 (1974) 130–2.

36 *Ib.* 267.

37 *Ibid.* n. 2. Cf. p. 48.

38 *Ibid.*

39 *Ib.* 265–6.

40 *Ib.* 265.

41 *Ibid.*, citing Banti *Annuario* 3–5 (1941–3) 28–50; Nilsson, MMR 77–116.

42 In consequence, Warren notes (*ibid.*): 'the interesting discussions of Dietrich (*Hist.* 16 (1967) 402; 18 (1969) 263–4; and Branigan (*Studi Micenei ed Egeo-Anatolici* 8 (1969) 34–8 on cult development need considerable revision'.

43 *Ibid.*, citing Pernier, *Festós* I 195–208, Nilsson MMR 94–6.

44 *Ib.* 266, citing for Koumasa, Xanthoudides VTM 12, 39, Plates 2 and 19, 4137 (cf. also 4138–9, 4993); for Mallia, Demargne *Et. Crét.* 7 (1945) Plates 31–2; for Mochlos, Seager *Mochlos* 64 and fig. 32, Marinatos and Hirmer, *Crete and Mycenae* (1960) Plate 10; for Trapeza, H.W. and J.D.S. Pendlebury and M.B. Money-Coutts in ABSA 36 (1935–6) 94–5 and Plate 13. Cf. also Zervos Plates 116 (Mallia), 186–7 (Mochlos), 222 (Koumasa 4137). Warren expresses full agreement with Branigan's interpretation of the Koumasa figure, 4137, as a snake goddess and of the other figures as probably representing a different divinity or divinities (Branigan *op. cit.* 34–5).

45 *Ib.* 266, citing RE 6.1. 428–30 *s.v.* Ergane and Farnell CGS 1.265–70.

46 *Ibid.* citing Nilsson MMR 122–30.

47 *Ib.* 258–9.

48 *Ib.* 266.

49 Cf. p. 35 f. Study of the plasters and mural decoration has evoked similar comparisons. M.A.S. Cameron (in Warren M 311) writes: 'Seen against this background-picture of considerable artistic progress in wall-painting among the older civilizations bordering the East Mediterranean, the achievements of EM II wall-painting in Crete are modest. With no sure evidence for patterned or pictorial ornamentation, Crete's greatest achievement in the field lay in a certain technical mastery of materials, notably in the use of a lime-plaster such

as was rarely employed elsewhere at the time. Only, it seems, at Catal Hüyük some three or four thousand years earlier and perhaps at Khafaje in Mesopotamia (where a lime-kiln dating at latest to 2500 BC has been found), were somewhat similar lime-plasters manufactured.' Cameron, however, adds that the idea of mural decoration in Early Minoan Crete, if inspired or brought in from outside, would appear to have originated from an area where only the most elementary form of wall-painting was known; but the simplicity of EM II wall-painting and its slow development as an art thereafter are equally consistent with a local invention of the craft on the island itself – quite independently of progress elsewhere; in that case, Knossos probably has the best claim to its invention in view of its long history in wall-plastering.

50   *Ib.* 260–1.

4   PALACES AND PALACE ECONOMY

1   PM.
2   Matz FK 27 ff.; Hood M 154 n. 6.
3   O. Pelon in BCH 90 (1966) 552–85; Hood M 63–4.
4   See pp. 128 ff.
5   Hazzidakis VMT; Hood M 64–5.
6   Hood *ib.* 65.
7   Childe WHH 146; cf. 53 and 85; Saggs ELBA *passim*; Willetts CCF 21 ff.
8   Cf. e.g. Woolley FK 108–9, Evans PM *passim*, Lorimer HM *passim*, Bittel DRBHH fig. 38.
9   See Graham PC.
10   Willetts CCF 22, citing ABSA 11.270; 14.365; Pendlebury AC 63–5; Mallowan in *Iraq* 2 (1935) 28; Seton Lloyd in Singer 484–5.
11   Willetts *ibid*; cf. now Platon in Christopoulos HHW 1. 143; 'Evans held the view that the very first palace grew up out of a number of isolated blocks of buildings, with rounded corners, grouped around a central courtyard with broad open passages between them. He believed that these blocks, which he called *insulae* or islands, were joined together by the process of roofing over the open spaces between them to form the first unified palatial building. To the west there was a paved courtyard, which fulfilled a double function as the principal forecourt giving access to the palace building and as an assembly place for the discussion of political and social matters. Each "island" contained deep basement rooms with no outside entrance; these rooms would obviously have been reached from above through trapdoors. In these basements, which when seen from above look like deep, sunless dungeons, were found quantities of household utensils dating from the time of the first palace. However, if the basements were so deep, while other rooms were at a higher level, this would simply mean that the general ground level grew higher later on. This was confirmed by the evidence of other sections of the west wing, where there was a long row of storage magazines, each fitted with built-in chests beneath the floor, not very different from those that were a feature of the later palace. There is good reason to believe that the western façade did not follow the same line as

the façade of the later palace, as Evans thought it did. At Phaistos and Mallia, it was further to the west and fronted onto the paving of the west court. At Mallia, only its foundations can be seen; they join on to the foundations of rooms that occupied the whole northwestern section of the palace. At Phaistos, however, the excavations have laid bare the whole solid base of the façade with its frontage of *orthostates* (flagstones standing on edge) and a narrow *podium* (low ledge) round the bottom. Behind the façade, whole sets of rooms were unearthed: some of these were used as store-rooms, some as workshops, and others for cult purposes.'

12 A similar arrangement was adopted by the Hittites: Bittel DRBHH fig. 38.
13 Faure FCC 63.
14 Graham PC; cf. Hood M 51 and n. 9.
15 Hood M 65.
16 *Ib.* 67.
17 See p. 53; cf. Childe WHH 146.
18 Cf. my comments in CCF 24.
19 Cf. Platon in Christopoulos HHW 1.146 and further at pp. 74 f.
20 Platon *ib.* 177.
21 Hood M 67 and n. 6.
22 Platon *ibid.*
23 See Platon KK 8.428, 480.
24 Pp. 111 ff.
25 In Christopoulos HHW 1.149.
26 *Ib.* 180–2.
27 Pendlebury AC 212.
28 All weights until *c.*1450 are of stone or lead. See Skinner in Singer 779 and cf., for Crete, Pendlebury AC 213; Renfrew 408 ff.
29 See further pp. 91 ff.
30 Hood M. 123 ff.; Platon in Christopoulos HHW 1.150, 202.
31 Platon in Christopoulous HHW 1.193–5.
32 *Ibid*; also Hood M.83. For country houses see Cadogan in BICS 18 (1971) 105 ff.
33 Cf. Hood *ibid.* and n. 2, citing work along these lines already done at Mallia, as reported in *Etudes Crétoises* 13 (1963) Ch. 3.
34 See pp. 177 ff.

5 TECHNOLOGY AND THE ARTS

1 In Christopoulos 1.208.
2 *Ibid.*; see further pp. 106–109 and Willetts CCF 23 and n. 68.
3 *Ib.* 209; cf. p. 40 f. and Willetts CCF *passim.*
4 See also generally Graham PC.
5 See further Platon in Christopoulos 1.146; Hood M 65, 70, 71, 77.
6 See further pp. 111 ff.
7 Platon in Christopoulos 1.146. Cisterns at Tylissos, Pyrgos and Arkhanes.
8 Discussed by Platon *ib.* 146–8.
9 See further Platon in Christopoulos 1.209–10; Marinatos *ib.* 220–26; Hood M.78–81 *et passim*; Marinatos ET *passim.*

10 Plaster relief frescoes appear to have been made at Knossos during the time before the disasters of *c*.1450 BC, but not later: Hood M 79 and n. 16.

11 Levi *Archaeology* 9 (1956) 192–9; Hood M 80 and n. 17.

12 Hood M 80, who continues: 'This treatment, very different from Egyptian conventions, may reflect the hilly character of the Cretan countryside which affords a background to almost every view. In spite of their conventional character the landscapes painted on Cretan walls during the flourishing period of the Minoan civilization before the disasters of *c*.1450 BC were remarkably life-like. The artists may have found inspiration in the beautiful flowers that carpet the island in the spring. But the flowers and plants, although they look so real, are often imaginary or highly stylized versions. Thus a rock rose is made symmetrical with six petals instead of the natural five. A favourite plant depicted in a variety of ways, sometimes hybridized with other flowers, was the papyrus native to Egypt and, if grown in Crete, exotic there.'

13 As Platon rightly emphasizes (Christopoulos 1.209).

14 Hood notes (M.80) that the white figures engaged in bull-leaping on a fresco from Knossos appear to be women dressed as men, as Evans assumed.

15 In contrast with Eastern and Egyptian art, though Hood (M.80) observes that it looks as if figures in the same picture might vary in size according to their importance.

16 Platon in KK (1947) 505–24, (1960) 504; later dating suggested by M. Cameron; discussion in Hood M.78 and n. 14.

17 Cf. Platon in Christopoulos 1.206; Hood M. Plate 52 and n. 52 p. 223.

18 See Willetts CCF *passim*. On bull-leaping see now Younger in AJA 80.2 (1976) 125 ff.

19 Willetts ELAC 131; Hood M.79, Plate 29 and n. 29 p. 220.

20 Cf. Willetts *ib*. 132.

21 Cameron BICS 17 (1970) 163 ff.

22 Hood M.220 n. 32.

23 Helen Waterhouse (London Mycenaean Seminar Minutes January 1974) who also wondered whether Evans' first impression, that there were at least three figures, might not have something to commend it. See further pp. 111 ff.

24 Willetts ELAC 133.

25 Hood 221 n. 34. Cf. n. 15.

26 Willetts ELAC 134.

27 Hood M.220–21 n. 33, who observes that negro soldiers from the Sudan served in Egyptian armies, and these might be Sudanese mercenaries, serving as Palace Guards, as Evans suggested.

28 Willetts ELAC 134–5.

29 Evans PM 3.31 ff.; cf. Willetts *ib*. 135–6.

30 Cf. Hood M 224 nn. 59 and 60; Willetts *ib*. 136–7.

31 Marinatos ET *passim*; also in Christopoulos 1.218–226. See further pp. 140 ff.

32 Branigan (FPC 74), noting the wide agreement with the view that specialization (by male potters) coincides with the introduction of the wheel.

33 Warren (M.261), pointing to the evidence of a turn-table, with a small hole to receive a spindle, which was being re-used as a pot stand by the time of the destruction of the site.

34 *Ibid.*
35 Hood M.39, cf. Hodges 59–61. Hood (*ib.* 83) points out that a pottery workshop appears to have been attached to the villa at Vathipetro, where several clay disks, weights from potters' wheels, were found, along with traces of a large kiln, implying manufacture of vases on a scale beyond the necessity of household needs.
36 On the vital topic of pottery and chronology, see Hood M. Ch. IV 35–48.
37 Hodges 79.
38 Branigan CBEBAC 49–53, cf. FPC 78 ff., Faure RA 1966.
39 Branigan FPC 79–81.
40 See further pp. 194 ff.
41 Cf. p. 191 ff.
42 Platon (in Christopoulous 1.215) comments: 'Many of the tools in everyday use – for wood and stone cutting, metal-work and farming – were themselves works of art. The craftsmen evidently liked to use tools in which they could take both pride and pleasure.' Cf. also Branigan FPC 84–7.
43 Warren MSV. This monograph repays careful study. The hope is that it will be followed in other fields. As the author observes (p. 1): 'Individual excavations and their publication will continue to enrich our knowledge of particular sites in particular periods, but for an understanding of the civilization as a whole we cannot hope to have elicited the maximum information from the discoveries until we can examine in detail the history and development of the various classes of material. The present work is an attempt to examine one such class.'
44 Serpentine is an altered basic rock, called steatite in Minoan publications, used for about 47 per cent of all Minoan stone vessels. There are 70 vases of steatite, almost all from the EM–MM I period: Warren *ib.* 138–40; cf. also Boardman IG 15–16.
45 As a material for vases obsidian is either black (grey/black translucent against the light) or black with white spots. The latter probably came from the islet of Gyali off Nisyros in the Dodecanese. The former (rarely used for vases) may have come from a south Anatolian source: Warren *ib.* 135–6.
46 Warren *ib.* 157–165.
47 Platon in Christopoulos 1.210, 212; Hawkes, J. DG 71.
48 Warren *ib.* 162, adding that, for workmanship of this quality to be repeated the world had to wait three thousand years until the great vase-makers of Venice, Prague, France and Germany adorned the tables of the courts of Europe with their products.
49 Warren *ib.* 89; Hood M 223 and Pl. 53; Willetts ELAC 119.
50 Hood *ibid.* and Pl. 54; Warren *ib.* 90.
51 P. 85.
52 Forsdyke HV; Warren *ib.* 174–9 cf. 88; Hood *ib.* 221 and Pl. 18; cf. Willetts ELAC 121.
53 Hood *ib.* 229 and Pl. 96.
54 Warren *ib.* 174–6, 178–80, cf. 37; Hood *ib.* 229–30 Pl. 97; Forsdyke CV, cf. Evans PM 2.792.
55 Warren *ib.* 174–5, 178–80, cf. 87; Hood *ib.* 136, 231 and Pl. 114.
56 Hood M.110, citing H.C. Beck on Early Magnifying Glasses in *Antiquaries*

Journal 8 (1928) 327–30. For detailed surveys of the whole fascinating subject see further Evans PM *passim*, Kenna, Matz and Biesantz, Xenaki-Sakellariou.

57 PM 1.477; cf. Hood M.122, 230 and Pl. 99; Willetts ELAC 129.
58 Willetts *ib.* 126–7; Platon in Christopoulous 1.216.
59 On the Aigina treasure, recognized to be Minoan by R.A. Higgins in ABSA 52 (1957) 42–57, see Hood M.101–2.

6 CRETAN WRITING IN THE BRONZE AGE

1   JHS 14 (1894) 270–372.
2   Cf. p. 41.
3   SM 1.7.
4   JHS 17 (1897) 327–95.
5   Hood M 111 and n. 10.
6   In Brice *Europa* 179 and n. 23.
7   So Platon in Christopoulos 1.157. Cf. Hood M 111: 'Sign-like marks on clay vases suggest that writing may have been known in Crete in Early Minoan times. But the earliest certain examples of Cretan writing are on seal impressions from Middle Minoan 1A deposits at Knossos. The signs on these are realistic pictures of actual things (a fish, a double axe, a human leg) after the manner of Egyptian hieroglyphs.'
8   Hood M 111.
9   M. Cameron in Kad. 4 (1965) 7–15.
10 In SM 1.234–5.
11 *Ib.* 243–4.
12 Cf. Evans *ib.* 273–93; Platon in Christopoulos 1.161–2; Hood M 112.
13 SM 1.6–7.
14 On the researches and reports *ib.* 6 n. 5.
15 *The Tartaria Tablets* in Ant. 41 (1967) 99–113, with detailed documentation.
16 Hood *ib.* 112 n. 15.
17 Ant. 1. (1927) 83 and 88e.
18 I.e. in *The Danube* (1929) 31 and 33.
19 Cf. Evans SM 1.144.
20 Citing R. Braidwood, *Excavations in the Plain of Antioch*, 1 (1960), 63.
21 Citing M.J. Mellink in Kad. 3 (1964) 1–7.
22 Cf. Hood M 111.
23 A reason which, with commendable caution, Hoods perhaps understates.
24 So Platon in Christopoulos 1.217.
25 So Karageorghis *ib.* 357.
26 Hood M 113, suggesting that such changes may have been inspired by considerations of convenience; and further that the Linear B script seems to have evolved, probably at Knossos itself after the disaster of *c.*1450 BC, from some variety of script used earlier at Knossos.
27 See further pp. 139–40.
28 Cf. Hood M 113–115 on the subject of decipherment and doubt, with its conclusion: 'The controversy about the decipherment may be incapable of resolution without long consecutive texts or bilinguals like the Rosetta stone.

But even if this particular decipherment is false, it does not necessarily follow that the language of the Linear B tablets is not Greek; moreover, even if the language proves to be non-Greek, it is always possible that rulers of Greek speech controlled Knossos at the time, retaining an alien written language for administrative purposes.' See further pp. 145 ff.

29 Davis DMLA, Gordon EML.

7 MYTHS AND LEGENDS

1 Str. 10.476, 478. See further pp. 154 ff.
2 *Il.* 2.645–52.
3 *Ibid.* 575, 602, 587, 637, 557.
4 . .Cf. Lorimer 47 and, on the further implications, pp. 136–7.
5 13.449–52.
6 *Ib.* 14.321–2.
7 See p. 126.
8 Apollod. 3.1.1, 3.4.1.
9 1.1–2.
10 4.45. Europe first appears as a geographical name in Homer *h. Ap.* 251, *Pi. N.* 4.70 (perhaps as an adjective), *A.fr.* 191. In Hes. *Th.* 357, she is a daughter of Ocean.
11 Head 287 cf. 525, 728, 797–8, 801.
12 Seltman GC 169; cf. Head 465, 467, 472; Guarducci IC 4 p. 37. Svoronos 153.
13 See further pp. 196–7.
14 Seltman GC 170–1.
15 *Od.* 17.523.
16 *Il.* 18.590–606.
17 D.S. 1.61 and 97, Plin. *NH* 36.84 ff.
18 Rather than the palace itself as Evans argued. Cf. Cook Z.1.473 and Willetts CCF 102–3, 123–4.
19 Apollod. 3.1.1. ff.; cf. D.S. 4.77, Tz. *H.* 1.473 ff.
20 Sch. A.B. *Il.* 18.590, cited by Cook Z. 1.481, noting that Eust. (*ad Il.* 1166.17 ff.) adds that this was the first occasion on which men and women danced together, that Sophocles had referred to the 'dances of Knossos' (*Aj.* 700) and that old-fashioned people in his own time, especially sailors, performed a dance with many twists and turns which was designed to recall the windings of the Labyrinth.
21 Plu. *Thes.* 21; Poll. 4.101; Call. *Del.* 312 ff.; Willetts CCF 124–6.
22 Plu. *Thes.* 15, 21; Call. *Del.* 307–13; *Il.* 18.590–606; Hsch. Θαργήλια; D.L. 2.44; Anon. *VPlat.* 6 Cobet; Plu. *M.* 717d; X. *Mem.* 4.8.2; Pl. *Phd.* 58a–b; Phot. *Lex.* φαρμακός; Phot. *Bibl.* 534; Suda φαρμακούς.
23 *Od.* 11.568–72.
24 *Od.* 11.321–5.
25 PM 1.1–7.
26 *Pol.* 1329a 40–1329b 5.
27 JHS (1912) 111 ff.; ABSA 18.37 ff.

28 Fick VOQVG 26–7; Kretschmer EGGS 401; Haley in AJA 32.141; Nilsson HM 64–5; Meillet AHLG 40; Wackernagel 212.

29 MMR 486.

30 Arist. *Pol.* 1322b 20.

31 Arist. *Ath.* 57.

32 Nilsson *ib.* 485 and n. 1. Cf. Thomson SAGS 1.392; 518–26.

33 CCF 82–92 *et passim.*

34 *Ib.* 83.

35 In PM 1.159; 224, 270–7, 447; 2.792–5; 4.397–9, 4.412–13.

36 Paribeni in RL 12, Evans PM 2.790 ff.; cf. Hood M Pl. 97 and p. 229; see pp. 86–7.

37 PM 2.353, 427, 644, 774–95, frontispiece, Pl. xiv; 4.6, 323, 400; cf. Hood M Pl. 32 and p. 220: see p. 78.

38 Forsdyke MC; cf. Groenewegen-Frankfort AM 207; Willetts CCF 85 ff.

39 Forsdyke *ib.* 17; cf. Thomson SAGS 1.370–1, Hall CGBA 265–6.

40 Hdt. 1.171.

41 As I pointed out in CCF 88 n. 149.

42 Th. 1.4.

43 *Marmor Parium* 11, 19; cf. Plu. *Thes.* 20, D.S. 4.60.

44 Forsdyke *ib.* 18.

45 *Ibid.*, adding (and citing Homer *Od.* 14.256–72) that if he got as far as Egypt it was only to be driven off by the seamen of Ramses or Merneptah. It was in the fifth year of Merneptah, about 1230, that the great attack on Egypt of the Libyans and the Peoples of the Sea, among whom the Achaeans are specified, was defeated at Piari in the Western Delta. Cf. Thomson SAGS 1.170, 370.

46 *Ibid.*

47 In *Minoica* 334 ff.

48 Hood M 220 n. 27.

49 In KK 15/16, 335.

50 In *Proceedings of the Second International Cretological Congress* (1968) 274 ff.

51 In *Proceedings of the Third International Cretological Congress.*

52 Summary in *Minutes of the Mycenaean Seminar* (University of London Institute of Classical Studies) 23 January 1974.

53 See Ch. 9. pp. 128 ff.

54 Cf. also Hood in BICS 20 (1973) 151–3.

55 Specifically, the MM Knossos sealings (PM 1.272, fig. 201) with heads of 'king' and 'boy prince', the 'Priest-King' relief fresco (discussed and dismembered by Cameron in BICS 17 (1970, 163 ff.), the Ayia Triada Chieftain vase and painted sarcophagus (see p. 79).

56 PM 2.276, 3.56 f., 227, 457.

57 In ABSA 6 (1899–1901) 42 n. 1. Cf. H. Reusch in *Minoica* 334 ff.

58 F. Matz, *Göttererscheinung und Kultbild, passim.* (Mainz, Abh. der geistes und socialwissenschaflichen Klasse, 1958, 385 ff.

59 Even in Classical times, it is rightly noted, women were the primary vehicles of oracular response: cf. the opening speech of Aeschylus *Eumenides.*

60 JHS 22.78 nos. 12 and 13; *Annuario* 8/9.123, no. 114.

61 Starr in Hist. 3.282 ff.; Renfrew EC 367, 473; Buck in Hist. 11.129 ff.

62 In AAA 5.445.

63 *Mallia, Maisons* ii (*Et. Crét.* 11) 84.

64 J. Sakellarakis, *Archaeology* 20.276 ff., *Proceedings of the Second International Cretological Congress* (1968) 239 ff.

65 In CCF *passim*. Cf. further, the conclusion reached by Paul Faure at the end of his study *Le sens des cachets et des scellés crétois* (Bulletin de l'association Guillaume Budé. Tome XXXII. Quatrième série, no. 4. Dec. 1973): '. . . il faut appeler *sanctuarire de Rhéa* ce que les archéologues ont abusivement appelé le *palais de Minos à Knosos.*'

8 CULTS

1 In an essay on *The Religion of the Ordinary Man in Classical Greece* in his ACP 144. As an instance of the timelessness of ritual usage Dodds cites the vessel used at harvest festivals in the Greek Church today, consisting of a set of little cups and candle-holders attached to a common base like a modern cruet, the cups being filled with corn, wine, olive oil, and other country produce. The same vessel, used for the same purpose of containing harvest offerings, had been described in the Hellenistic age by the antiquarian Polemon, who called it a *kernos* (cited by Ath. 11.476 f.). Now actual examples of *kernoi* had been dug up, not only in the *agora* at Athens and elsewhere in mainland Greece, but in Cretan graves some of which date back to the Early Minoan age.

2 A general thesis maintained in my CCF, where the detailed evidence is elaborated for the summary treatment of this chapter.

3 See Ch. 15.

4 2.53.2.

5 Guthrie OGR 112–13, cf. *id.* GG 45.

6 Hood M 131–2.

7 Willetts CCF 177, 179, 250–1. See further pp. 106, 197.

8 Argued by Hood M 138–9.

9 Cf. my discussion in CCF 60–7 *et passim*.

10 Hood M 139.

11 *Ibid.*

12 *Ibid.*; cf. p. 79.

13 Evans PM 4.962 ff.; Hood M 145.

14 Hood *ibid.*

15 Hood M 140, adding that, in some parts of Anatolia, for instance, cremation appears to have been general by this time.

16 Hutchinson PC 232. Cf., generally, Xanthoudides VTM, Branigan TM, Hood M 31 ff., 140 ff. and in Ant. 34 (1960) 166–76.

17 A. Lebesis in PAE (1967) 195–209.

18 J.A. Sakellarakis in *Archaeology* 20 (1967), 276–81.

19 A revolution in burial custom which, though already under way, was accelerated by the events of *c.* 1450 BC, in the opinion of Hood (M 147). He also considers that it may have been first stimulated by the increasing wealth and complexity of Cretan society with a consequent loosening of clan ties. As the gap between

rich and poor became wider during the flourishing period of the later palaces from 1700 BC onwards, and the force of custom became weaker, the rich would probably want to furnish their burials more expensively and lavishly.

20 Hutchinson in ABSA 51 (1956) 74–80, cf. Cadogan *ib*. (1967) 257–65; Evans PTK; Hood M 146.
21 Pp. 89–90; Hood M 145.
22 See p. 46.
23 PM 1.43–55; cf. Nilsson MMR 290.
24 Cf. Evans *ib*. 45, 51–2; Nilsson MMR 290, Hawkes 84 and 89.
25 PM 1.52.
26 Pendlebury AC 274; Nilsson MMR 226; Willetts CCF 70.
27 Willetts CCF 78–9.
28 Hsch. βριτύ· γλυκύ· Κρῆτες. Cf. *EM* 214.29 *s.v.* βρίτου; Solin. 11.8.
29 Hsch. Βριτόμαρτις· ἐν Κρήτη ἡ ᾽Αρτεμις D.S. 5.76; Paus. 3.14.2; Willetts CCF 179 ff.
30 Ant. Lib. 40, cf. Paus. 2.30.3; Hsch. *s.v.* ᾽Αφαιά.
31 Call. *Dian*. 189–203.
32 Willetts CCF 179 ff.
33 MMR 527. Ariadne was thought to have hanged herself when she was deserted by Theseus. When he had carried her off and abandoned her, she came to Naxos, accompanied by a nurse called Korkyne, whose tomb was at Naxos, where Ariadne also died (Plu. *Thes*. 20). According to Pausanias (2.37.7) she was buried in the temple of the Cretan Dionysos at Argos. Again, she was supposed to have died in childbirth at Amathos in Cyprus, during the absence of Theseus, who then returned and ordered a sacrifice to Ariadne; and her tomb was in a grove named after Ariadne Aphrodite (Plu. *Thes*. 20). According to Homer, Artemis killed Ariadne on the island of Dia (modern Standia) at the instigation of Dionysos (*Od*. 11.324).
34 Plu. *Thes*. 20; Nilsson MMR 525.
35 MMR 527–8.
36 Hsch. *s.v.* ἀδνόν; Willetts CCF 193 n. 390.
37 Willetts CCF 193 and n. 391.
38 Hood M 117, citing H. Reusch in *Minoica* 334–58, adds: 'But this would not imply that Crete was ruled by queens. Tradition and analogy suggest that power was in the hands of kings, although it is always possible that succession to the throne was through the female line by marriage to the king's daughter.'
39 Faure FCC; Willetts CCF 275–7.
40 *Il*. 11.270, 16.187, 19.103, h.Ap. 115–22.
41 *Od*. 19.188, Nilsson MMR 73.
42 Willetts CCF 168–172.
43 Nilsson MMR 516.
44 Willetts CCF 175 ff., with detailed references.
45 *H.Cer*. 123; *Od*. 5. 125–8 cf. D.S. 5.49, Hes. *Th*. 969 ff.
46 Persson RGPT *passim*; Nilsson MMR 403.
47 Harrison PSGR 273; cf. Paus. 8.4.1.
48 Willetts CCF 20.
49 Willetts *ib*. 148 ff.

50 Coldstream KSD.
51 *Ib.* 180 ff.
52 *Ib.* 131–3, 180, 182.
53 IC 1.VII. 21.
54 *Ib.* 3 p. 23 and III. 12.
55 Ib. 1 p. 55, 291; 2 p. 114; cf. Head 461, 464, 477.
56 Willetts CCF 150–1.
57 Cornford AEM 157–91.
58 D.S. 5.77.3–5.
59 Coldstream KSD 186.
60 Thomson SAGS 1.235 and n. 191.
61 Willetts CCF 79–81.
62 *Ib.* 200 ff.
63 *Ib.* 183, 210; Fick VO 32; Haley 145.
64 Willetts CCF 218, cf. 59–67, 71–4.
65 Ath. 9.375f–376a.
66 Cf. pp. 154 ff.
67 Willetts CCF 98–9 *et passim.* See further pp. 200–201.
68 *Ib.* 219 with detailed references.
69 *Ib.* 167.
70 Od. 19.178–9.
71 Details described Willetts CCF 95 n. 185.
72 Thomson SAGS 2.127–30.
73 Willetts CCF 92–103.

9 CLIMAX AND TRANSITION

1 Hood M 51; Platon in Christopoulos 1.167. Cf., on Luwians, Huxley CL, Palmer MM, and criticisms by Mylonas in *Hesperia* 31 (1962) 284–309, Schachermeyr in *Kad.* 1 (1962) 27–39.
2 Cf. Hood *ibid.*
3 Matz in CCAH 2.IV (b) 21.
4 Cf. Matz *ib.* 25.
5 Ch. 7 pp. 111–14 and n. 52.
6 Cf. *ibid.*, and Matz CAH 2.XII 39.
7 PM 3.56.
8 *Ibid.* 227.
9 *Ibid.* 457.
10 Cf. e.g. *ib.* 1.224; 2.394 f., 602; 3.56.
11 Particularly Thomson SAGS 1.177–8, 249–93; cf. J. Hawkes DG 37–160; Hood M 117–18.
12 Cf. my argument in CCF 74 ff.
13 *Ib.* 32–3.
14 CAH 2.IV (b) 20 ff.
15 *Ib.* XII 37 ff.

16 P. 111.
17 Matz *ib.* 39 ff.
18 Cf. also Hood M 129–30, 162, 231; Willetts CCF 34–5.
19 Cf. also Hood M 89, 121; Willetts CCF 34, citing Evans PM 3, 308, 313 ff., Lorimer HM 137–8.
20 Cf. Lorimer *ib.* 254 ff., 261 ff.; Hood M 118 ff.
21 Cf. Rutkowski in Proc. Third Internat. Cret. Congress I, 290 ff.
22 M 58 ff.
23 *Od.* 19.172–9.
24 PM 1.10–12.
25 *Il.* 2.645–52.
26 *Origini Cretesi, Ausonia* 4 (1910) 220–1.
27 Lorimer 47.
28 I.e. *Od.* 19.175–6.
29 As I pointed out in CCF 133.
30 AC 228–31. These views and arguments are worth recalling against the background of succeeding (and inconclusive) discussion.
31 Citing Evans PM 4.942 ff.
32 Hood M 149–50.
33 Marinatos ET is essential. For theory and speculation up to 1970 see especially Luce EA, Galanopoulos-Bacon A, Page SVDMC, Hood HH, Pomerance FCS. Further discussions in Ant. since 1972. See now Luce in AJA 80.1 (1976) 9 ff.; for renewed discussion and detailed refs.
34 See the careful and thorough discussion of Pomerance's views by Warren in *Gnomon* 45 (1973) 173–8.
35 See Hood M 54–60.

10 PRELUDE TO THE IRON AGE

1 In particular Desborough LMS and GDA; Snodgrass DAG; Coldstream GGP.
2 As Snodgrass remarks DAG viii: 'A casual glance at the preliminary notices of archaeological discoveries, particularly in Greek periodicals of the last few years, will show that new evidence on this period is coming to light at a bewildering speed. Modern building-operations have very often been responsible for these discoveries; but since we may expect (and, up to a point, hope) that they will continue at the same pace, there is no real ground for thinking that the future will bring an opportune lull in which to take stock of the situation.'
3 *Some Late Minoan III Pottery from Crete* in ABSA 60 (1965) 316–42.
4 *Ib.* 334 f. But Popham points out (*ib.* 316 n. 1) that Pendlebury's observation (in AC 253) that one of the greatest necessities for Minoan archaeology is the excavation of a stratified LM III site remains as true as when it was written.
5 Cf. pp. 154 ff.
6 EGBAA 54–6.
7 Bowra H20, with the comment: 'Greaves were, it seems, a uniquely Greek accoutrement, and called for emphatic notice.' It is of some interest that the earliest actual examples of the bronze greave known in the Aegean after the

Bronze Age are from Crete: see Snodgrass EGAW 56.

8   *Il.* 4.285, 12.354, 13.255.

9   *Il.* 2.645–52; see further pp. 136–7.

10 Buck GD 7; cf. Nilsson HM 86–7.

11 As I argued in more detail in my CCF 129 ff.

12 *Od.* 14.199–359.

13 *Ib.* 15.403–84.

14 *Ib.* 19.164–348.

15 Cf. pp. 154 ff.

16 As argued in my CCF 131–7; see further pp. 136–7.

17 *Ibid.* Cf. also Hammond in CAH 2.36 p. 30 f. : '. . . they may have come to Crete when the Heraclids came to the Dodecanese, or they may have come earlier in the thirteenth century from Thessaly as some traditions suggest and received the name later (FGH 10 F 16 Andron, 269 F 12 Staphylus; Hdt. 7.171.1; D.S. 4.60.1 and 5.80.2). It is probable that there were Dorians not only in Crete but also in Rhodes. For the system of three tribes which made up the Dorian group offers the best explanation for Homer's epithet τριχάϊκες for the Dorians in Crete and for his description of Tlepolemus' followers settling in Rhodes τριχθὰ καταφυλαδόκ "in three parts by tribe". As Hesiod, fr. 191 implies, members of the three tribes probably took their parcels of land in tribal groups in Crete and Rhodes.'

18 Hdt. 7.170–1.

19 As maintained in my ACSH 31.

20 Pendlebury AC 303; AJA 5 (1901) 125 ff.; ABSA 38.57 ff., 55.1 ff. Desborough GDA *passim*.

21 Pendlebury AC *passim*; Willetts ACSH 57–8.

22 Forbes in Singer, 595; Pendlebury, AC 336; Desborough, PG 288, 301–2 cf. 252, 255; Willetts CCF 38.

23 GDA 314 ff.

24 DAG 237 ff.

II LANGUAGE AND THE ALPHABET

1   *Od.* 19.172–9; cf. p. 149.

2   10.475.

3   *Inscr. Cret.* 3, VI. 1–6; cf. *Rev. Phil.* (1946) 131–8.

4   7.170; cf. p. 126.

5   Cf. my CCF 133; and, for comments on the Kydonians, and Pelasgians *ib.* 133–6.

6   Boardman GO 61 ff.; Bury–Meiggs 521.

7   *Ib.* 58–9.

8   *Ib.* 59–60.

9   Meiggs–Lewis GHI 1.

10 R. Young in *Hesperia* 38 (1969) 252–96.

11 See p. 168 cf. 189.

12 GO 35 f. *et passim*.

13 *Iliad* 2.645–52; cf. Lorimer HM 47.
14 Willetts CCF 250–1.
15 Nilsson MMR 464, 550.
16 *Inscr. Cret.* 4.3.1 (a–c), an archaic inscription from the Pythion, and *ibid.* 184.3, early second century BC; *ib.* 1.XVIII.11.2, second–third century AD; *ibid.* XVI.3.2, *c*.120–116/115 BC.
17 SGDI 86; Cook Z 2.948.
18 Paus. 1.3.2, Pi. *P.* 2.15–17.
19 *Iliad* 11.19–28, *Odyssey* 8.362–3.
20 Tac. *H* 2.3, Paus. 2.29.4, Ptol. Meg. 1 = FHG 3.66, SEG 6.820.
21 Willetts CCF 284–6.
22 Cf. Guarducci *Inscr. Cret.* 2 pp. 47, 114, 220.
23 *Inscr. Cret.* 3.III 3 B 14, 20 f.; 5.14.
24 *Ib.* 1.VIII 4b 14, and Guarducci *ad loc.* (Antheia was an epithet of Aphrodite at Knossos: Hsch. *s.v.*); *ib.* IX.1 A 27.
25 *Ib.* XIV 2.3 (if belonging to Istron and not to Lato: Guarducci (*ad loc.*).
26 *Ib.* XVI.5.70, cf. 75, second century BC; 18.7, second century BC; *ib.* 24, 25, second century BC; perhaps also *ib.* 27.
27 *Ib.* 4.174.59 f., 75; cf. also perhaps *ib.* 189.2, *c.* second century BC.
28 EM *s.v.* κυθερέια; see further Willetts CCF 285–6.
29 References and discussion in Thomson SAGS 1.386–7, cf. 399, 401.
30 Str. 416 (cf. 129, 496; FHG 3.639; Amm. Marc. 22.8.25; D.H. 1.89.4; Kretschmer in Gl.21.213.
31 Ath. 360e; Str. 671.
32 Hdt. 7.91; Kretschmer in Gl.21.213, 24.203.
33 *Iliad* 6.396–7, 415–16, cf. 1.366.
34 Str. 672, 682 (cf. Hdt. 7.90), Isoc. 9.17–18.
35 Cf. Thomson GL 32, SAGS 1.515–26; Beattie in Wace-Stubbings CH 311–24, Palmer *ib.* 89–94; Chadwick in CAH 2.39.
36 *Inscr. Cret.* 2 V (Axos) 1 (sixth–fifth century BC), 20 A (third century BC); *ib.* XII (Eleutherna) 3, 11, 16Ab (sixth–fifth century BC), 22A, B, C (third or second century BC); Buck GD 23, 100, 144–7; Bechtel GD 1.358, 429, 2.766–7, 771.
37 Buck *ib.* 23.
38 *Inscr. Cret.* 2.V.1.
39 *Ib.* 2.XII.9, 4.78; Willetts ASAC 40 ff.
40 *Ib.* 2.XII.16 Ab 2; Willetts *ib.* 46–7; see further pp. 185–6.
41 *Inscr. Cret.* 2.XII 22B.
42 *Ib.* 4.58, 78, perhaps also 79, 144.
43 *Ibid.* p. 30.
44 *Iliad* 2.584.
45 Hope–Simpson–Lazenby CSHI 79.
46 *Ibid.* 78 (cf. 74) with refs.
47 Hdt. 1.69.
48 Paus. 3.10.8.
49 Paus. 3.19.2. Levi PGG 2.67 n. 169, observes that the statue seems to be represented on the Lakonian coinage of Commodus.

50 Paus. 3.19.3.
51 Nilsson MMR 471; Levi *ib*. 67; ABSA 55 (1960) 74–6 and plate 17c, 1; Desborough LMS 234.
52 Plb. 8.30.
53 Huxley ES 37.
54 *Ibid.* 115 n. 214. Cf. Willetts ASAC 35, 185.
55 Paus. 3.19.3.
56 Willetts CCF 222. Cf. Nilsson MMR 557 and Perrson RGPT 137 on Artemis Hyakinthotrophos at Knidos.
57 *Inscr. Cret.* 1.XVI (Lato) 3.3; *ibid.* XIX (Malla), 3A.40 (second century BC). For the associated festival see Willetts CCF 222–3.
58 St. Byz. s.v. Γόρτυν. Detailed discussion in Willetts *ib*. 152–68.
59 *Inscr. Cret.* 4.252.
60 *Ib.* 1.17.21.
61 Pl. *Lg.* 4.708a; Paus. 8.53.4.
62 Konon *Narrat.* 36, cf. 47.
63 Paus. 3.2.6.
64 *Iliad* 2.646; cf. Eust *ad loc*.
65 Haley in AJA 32.145; Fick VO 91, 113.
66 See further Guarducci *Inscr. Cret.* 4 p. 14.
67 Kedrenos *Hist. Comp.* in Migne 121, 65 D; Eust. *ad* D.P. 88.
68 See n. 58 above; Hope–Simpson–Lazenby *op. cit.* 111; Desborough LMS 167, 183. Occupation of the acropolis goes back to neolithic times: JHS 76 (Sup.) p. 31.
69 *S.v.* ʼΑμύκλαι. Cf. Eust. *ad Iliad* 2.584.
70 *Leg. Gort.* III.5–9.
71 Willetts LCG 41, 61; Guarducci *Inscr. Cret.* 4.72 (*ad loc.*); cf. Paus. 3.19.1f.
72 *Inscr. Cret.* 4.182.23.
73 *Ibid.* 173.12 f. and Guarducci *ad loc.*
74 *Inscr. Cret.* 4.172; Guarducci *ad loc*; Larsen CP 31. p. 31; Willetts ASAC 119.
75 See e.g. Guarducci *Inscr. Cret.* 4 p. 32 and Huxley ES 100 n. 31.
76 See Swindler 35 ff.; and cf. Guarducci *Inscr. Cret.* 4. *ibid.*
77 Masson *Les inscriptions chypriotes syllabiques* Paris, (1961) p. 7, no. 220 pp. 246–8, with bibliography; cf. Dussaud in Schaeffer *Enkomi-Alasia* Paris, 1952, p. 7; and, more recently, Hemmerdinger in *Gl.* 48, 1–2 (1970) p. 43 *s.v.*

12 LAW AND CUSTOM

1 In the general sense intended by A.R. Burn in his LAG.
2 See my ASAC, ACSH and LCG for more detailed study of the many aspects and implications.
3 Guarducci has argued for 480–460 BC in *RF* 66 (1938) 264–73; others prefer a somewhat later date.
4 Bibliography in my LCG; cf. also Meiggs–Lewis 94.
5 *De An.* 434 a 10.
6 Diamond PLPP 22, citing (*ibid.* n. 3), J.W. Jones, *The Law and Legal Theory of*

the Greeks and, for a systematic account of the family and property law of Athens in the period of the orators, A.R.W. Harrison, *The Law of Athens*, vol. I.

7   *Ib.* 23.

8   In *Whole Formulaic Verses in Greek and Southslavic Heroic Song*, first published in *TAPA* 64 (1933), 179–97, reprinted in *The Making of Homeric Verse*, ed. Adam Parry 376–90: see *ib.* 377. In a Harvard address delivered in 1934 on *The Historical Method in Literary Criticism*, Parry cited Ernest Renan with approval (*ib.* 409): 'How can we seize the physiognomy and the originality of early literatures if we do not enter into the moral and intimate life of a people, if we do not place ourselves at the very point in humanity which it occupied, in order to see and to feel with it, if we do not watch it live, or rather if we do not live for a while with it?'

9   P. 165 f.

10 PLPP vii–viii.

11 *Ib.* 4.

12 *Ib.* 82.

13 PL 54.

14 PLPP 22.

15 Willetts LCG 74; cf. Diamond PL 365.

16 Lilian H. Jeffery and Anna Morpurgo Davies: ΠΟΙΝΙΚΑΣΤΑΣ and ΠΟΙΝΙΚΑΖΕΝ: *BM 1969. 4–2.1, A New Archaic Inscription from Crete* in *Kadmos* IX.2 (1970) 118–54. See further A.E. Raubitschek *ib.* 155–6 and in Hoffmann, *Early Cretan Armourers* (Mainz, 1972) 47–9; Willetts in *Kadmos* XI.1 (1972) 96–8; R. Merkelbach in ZPE 9 (1972) 102–3; P. Chantraine in *Studii Clasice* XIV (1972) 7–15; H. Van Effenterre in BCH 97 (1973) 31 ff.; G. and R. Edwards in Kadmos XIII.1 (1974) 48–57; F. Gschnitzer in ZPE 13 (1974) 265–75; and (with a different view of *poinikastas* as a kind of judge) A.J. Beattie in *Kadmos* 14.1 (1975) 8–47.

17 Bonner and Smith AJHA 67–71.

18 *Ib.* 75.

19 Pl. *Lg.* 624.

20 Pol. 1271 b: διὸ καὶ νῦν οἱ περίοικοι τὸν αὐτὸν τρόπον χρῶνται αὐτοῖς ὡς κατασκευάσαντος Μίνω πρώτου τὴν τάξιν τῶν νόμων. See my discussion of the passage in LCG 12.

21 See G. Thomson, *Aeschylus, Oresteia* (Cambridge, 1938) 2.352: 'The view that the custom of purification for homicide developed in the eighth and seventh centuries does not of course preclude the possibility that it had been practised during the Minoan period in Crete and perhaps in parts of the Greek mainland as well; and certainly Minoan society had advanced beyond the point at which it normally appears. Roman law, though older, was less primitive than the law of the Franks and Burgundians; and in the same way traditions of a Minoan law of homicide, like other memories of the advanced institutions of Minoan society, for example the *lex talionis* . . . may have survived the collapse of the Minoan empire'; and *id., ib.* 2 ed. (Prague, 1966) 2.141, on A. *Ch.* 312–14 δρασάντι παθεῖν (cf. *Ag.* 533, 1535–6, 1562–4, *Supp.* 432–7, S. *fr.* 877, Pl. *N.* 4.32, *AP* 16.199 and Pl. *Lg.* 872 d–e, Arist. *EN* 5.5): 'It seems probable that the Greeks inherited the proverb from the society of Minoan Crete, which long remained famous for its legal institutions and no doubt had some influence on

the advanced system partially preserved in the Laws of Gortyn; and this conclusion is confirmed when we find that the proverb in question, like the institution of the ordeal by oath, was traditionally ascribed to Rhadamanthys.'

22 *Leg. Gort.* Cols. III–IV.
23 *Ib.* Col. VII 1–10.
24 Willetts LGC 15 and commentary *ad loc.*
25 Str. 6.260; Plu. *Lyc.* 4.
26 See Chapter 13 pp. 180–2.
27 *Ap.* Str. 10.484; Arist. *Pol.* 1272a.
28 *Inscr. Cret.* 3.III.9.
29 See my comments in *Aristocratic Society in Ancient Crete 137–8,* regarding *Inscr. Cret.* 4.259.
30 On dating and the purpose of the legislation see my discussion in LCG 8 f.
31 Plb. 6.45. 1–47.6.
32 ASAC *passim.*
33 Implied in *Leg. Gort.* Col. IV 31–6.
34 *Pol.* 1264a.
35 Col. V. 25–8. See my discussion in LCG 15 and 66.
36 Cf. also Dosiad. *ap.* Ath. 4.143a–b.
37 Col. VII.10–15; LCG 14 and n. 73.
38 3.59.
39 Col. V 44–51.
40 Col. VII 52–VIII 8.
41 Survey of the evidence in ASAC 40–41.
42 Col. II 11–16.
43 Col. II 2–16.
44 LCG 16 and nn. 113–114.
45 *Ap.* Ath. 6.263e–f.
46 *Ibid.*; Eust. 1024.35; Str. 15.1.34; Hsch. *sv.*
47 *Inscr. Cret.* 2 XII.16A b.2. See further Ch. 13 185–6.
48 Willetts LCG 15.
49 *Ib.* 10–22; cf. my ASAC 59–96; ACSH *passim.*
50 Cols. VII.15–IX.24, XII 6–19.
51 *Inscr. Cret.* 3.III.4.15.
52 Str. 10 482; Willetts LCG 18 and n. 3.
53 Col. V 9 ff.
54 LCG 18–22.
55 *Ib.* 24.
56 Col. XII 6–19.
57 Col. VIII 42–53.
58 A modification of considerable interest and importance which is discussed in detail in LCG 27.

13 SOCIETY AND GOVERNMENT

1 In ACP 97 f.

2 Dodds *ib.* 98, citing Ar. *Av.* 1035 ff., X. *Mem.* 4.4.14 and S. *Ant.* 454 f.

3 1271b 20–33.

4 1272a 40–1272b 23.

5 Willetts ASAC 160 nn. 2 and 3.

6 DK 22 B 114; cf. Dodds *op. cit.* 98.

7 To the eleven inscriptions listed by Muttelsee in ZVK and Van der Mijnsbrugge in CK, two others (viz. *Inscr. Cret.* 2 XVI 9, from Lappa, and ’Αρχ.’Εφ. 1925–6, 9 ff., no. 129.3, from Oropos, were added by Van Effenterre in his list in CMG 128–9. Cf. also Willetts ASAC 227 f.

8 *Inscr. Cret.* 2.XVI.2 (Lappa) lines 15 f. and 17 f. (= IG XII.5.868A, line 11).

9 SIG 560, lines 10–12.

10 *Inscr. Magn.* 16 no. 20.

11 *Inscr. Cret.* 2.XVI.9 (Lappa).

12 *Inscr. Cret.* 2.V.22 (Axos).

13 SIG 653A.

14 Durrbach, *Choix d’inscrs. de Délos* 1517 lines 2 and 31–2.

15 SIG 654A, line 5.

16 ’Αρχ.’Εφ. 1925–6, 9 ff., no. 129.3.

17 Either Attalos I, 241–197 BC (Dittenberger, Guarducci, Van Effenterre) or Attalos II, 159–138 BC (Haussoullier, Michel, Blass, Scrinzi) is intended.

18 *Inscr. Cret.* 3.IV.9 (Itanos) lines 107–8.

19 *Inscr. Cret.* 4.197 (Gortyn) = IG XII 3.254.

20 *Inscr. Cret.* 1.XXIV.2 (Priansos) lines 24–5.

21 See also Muttelsee *op. cit.* 42 and Van Effenterre *op. cit.* 130.

22 SIG 535, line 12.

23 SGDI 5157–5164.

24 Deiters, *Rh. Mus.* 59, (1904) 565 ff., line 13.

25 Plb. 7.11.9 and 14.4.

26 Plb. 29.10.6.

27 *Inscr. Cret.* 2.III.10A, line 4.

28 Durrbach, *Choix d’inscrs. de Délos* 1517, line 19.

29 *Inscr. Cret.* 3.IV.9 (Itanos) line 23.

30 By Van Effenterre, *op. cit.* 130.

31 Livy 43.7.

32 Plb. 33.16.1.

33 D.S. 40.1.

34 Van der Mijnsbrugge *op. cit. passim*; Van Effenterre *op. cit.* 131 f.

35 See further Van der Mijnsbrugge *ib.* 28, Van Effenterre *ib.* 132, Willetts ASAC 229 n. 2.

36 See nn. 14 and 28.

37 SIG 627.

38 Plb. 29.10.6.

39 Plu. 2.490b. Cf. ref. συγκρητίζω, EM 732.55.

40 Relying on Plb. 4.53.4.

41 *Gött. gel. Anz.* (1900) 453.

42 *Op. cit.* 43 ff. and 63.

43 *Op. cit.* 132–8, arguing on the basis of the evidence of SIG 535–7 and IG XII.5.

867 f., cf. IG XII suppl. 304.

44 ASAC 225–34.

45 *Pol.* 1272b 23. (See n. 57.) The exact meaning is disputed. Aristotle could have had in mind the events of 343 BC when the Phocian Phalaikos crossed into Crete with a mercenary force and took service with Knossos against Lyttos; or the war in the time of Agis in 333 BC. See further Willetts ASAC 160 nn. 2 and 3 for refs.

46 *Inscr. Cret.* 3.III.4 = SGDI 5040 (Hierapytna), early second century BC: *ib.* 4.197b = IG 12 (3).254 (Anaphe), second century BC; Plb. 22.15.4. Cf. *Inscr. Perg.* 1.163A, col. II 3 f. The *Koinodikion* has been generally agreed to be a common or federal tribunal: see Van der Mijnsbrugge *op. cit.* Ch. IV, Guarducci *Epigraphica* 2 (1940) 162, Van Effenterre *op. cit.* 145–50. Guarducci and Van Effenterre reject Van der Mijnsbrugge's view of it as a contract of arbitration, a condition of membership of the Koinon. Others have seen it as a Cretan federal law, a sort of *ius commune*: Caillemer in Daremberg-Saglio *s.v.* Cretensium res publica, cf. Perrot *ib. s.v.* Cretarcha, Van Effenterre *op. cit.* 148.

47 Cf. Van der Mijnsbrugge *op. cit.* 40 and n. 2.

48 *Inscr. Cret.* 1.XVI.1, cf. 4 [169].

49 *Inscr. Cret.* 3.III.4.

50 *Inscr. Cret.* 4.174.

51 *Inscr. Cret.* 4.197, cf. n. 46 above.

52 Van der Mijnsbrugge *op. cit.* 53; cf. Van Effenterre *op. cit.* 143 and Guarducci *Epigraphica* 2 (1940) 166.

53 *Inscr. Cret.* 1.VIII.4; and, more recently, Meiggs–Lewis SGHI no. 42.

54 Argos had close ties with Crete and was linked with Knossos and Tylissos by bonds of tradition, cult and language. On the interesting federal structure involving Argos, Knossos, Tylissos and perhaps other cities, see Meiggs–Lewis *op. cit.* 104.

55 See my survey of the evidence in ASAC 152–91.

56 Pl. *R.* 9.575d; also Plu. 2.792e; cf. Pherecr. 220. I am grateful to Helen Waterhouse for drawing my attention to the Platonic passage.

57 See my discussion of *Pol.* 1272b 20 in ASAC 160.

58 Polybios was to comment upon the consequences and express his surprise that the most learned of the ancient writers – Ephoros, Xenophon, Kallisthenes and Plato – could say that Crete was one and the same as Sparta and declare it to be worthy of praise: 6.45.1–47.6.

59 *Lg.* 776c–d.

60 *Pol.* 1269a 29–1269b 12.

61 *Pol.* 1328b 32–1330a 32.

62 *Reflexions sur l'historiographie grecque de l'esclavage* in *Actes du colloque 1971 sur l'esclavage* (Annales littéraires de l'Université de Besançon, Paris, 1973) pp. 25–44.

63 FGrH 115 *fr.* 122, *ap.* Ath. 265 b–c. The translation, with trifling modifications, is from Gulick (Loeb).

64 *Historia* 8 (1959) 164 = *Slavery in Classical Antiquity* (1968) 72.

65 I have considered this social terminology in detail elsewhere more than once, have several times changed my mind about specific meanings and (I trust) made

my reasons clear. See further the Introduction and Commentary in my LCG.

66 See my LCG 15–16. Cf. p. 174 and n. 45.

67 Eust. 727.18, 1592.55 ff.

68 *Pol.* 1272a 28–35.

69 See pp. 173–4.

70 *Inscr. Cret.* 2.XII.16 Ab 2, p. 159.

71 6.263e–264a.

72 12.542, 15.701.

73 3.83 : μεταξὺ δὲ ἐλευθέρων καὶ δούλων οἱ Λακεδαιμονίων εἵλωτες καὶ Θετταλῶν πενέσται καὶ Κρητῶν κλαρῶται καὶ μνωῖται καὶ Μαριανδυνῶν δωροφόροι καὶ Ἀργείων γυμνῆτες καὶ Σικυωνίων κορυνηφόροι.

74 *Les frontières de Lato* in KK (1969).

75 In *Amaltheia* (1972).

76 '– qui ont essayé de se tailler des "champs francs" dans les maquis où subsistait encore un peu de liberté.'

77 H. Frist, *Griechisches Etymologisches Wörterbuch.*

78 A further tentative suggestion has been made to me by A.J. Beattie, worthy of serious consideration, namely that we might perhaps read under ἐφημίαί, ἀγροικίαι· βελτίον ἀφημίαι which would suggest a possible original sense of 'voicelessness', 'inability to discuss', hence both 'without a political voice' and 'boorishness'.

79 P. 168 and n. 16 for bibliography.

80 HM 126 n. 1.

81 Viz. (i) διφθεραλοίφος· γραμματοδιδάσκαλος παρὰ τοῖς Κυπρίοις and (ii) ἀλειπτήριον· γραφεῖον. Κύπριοι. Buck (GD *s.v.* ἰναλίνω) adds another: ἀλίνειν· ἀλείφειν.

82 IG XII 2.96 a d 97.

83 SIG 38.

84 My examination of the evidence so far as the Gortyn Code is concerned obliged me to conclude that while the few engraved signs there employed on the stone do help to identify sections, the painted signs normally do not. See my LCG 4.

85 *Mycenae and the Mycenaean Age* (1966) 204. The same scholar had shown his interest in the subject in a long article published in the *Proceedings of the Athenian Academy* in 1959.

86 *Comments on the Spensithios Inscription* in *Kadmos* 14.1.

14 ARTISTIC RENAISSANCE

1 By Van Effenterre in BCH 87.

2 AC 327.

3 Hutchinson PC 333.

4 Pendlebury AC 318; Hutchinson PC 332.

5 Hutchinson PC 330–32; cf. Pendlebury AC 329–31.

6 GT 26.

7 R.J.H. Jenkins, *Dedalica*, 1936. Cf. Pendlebury AC 338–9; Hutchinson PC 341–9; Higgins GT 26 and his comment: 'The Dedalic face has been studied in detail by Jenkins in a series of perceptive articles. We may accept his conclusions

with two reservations. The style was not, as he believed, restricted to Dorian communities, but was almost universal throughout the Greek world in the greater part of the seventh century. And secondly, in his stylistic sequence and in his absolute chronology he attempts considerably greater precision than is warranted by our knowledge of seventh century Greek art.' Also, more recently, *Dädalische Kunst auf Kreta im 7. Jahrhyndert* (Museum für Kunst und Gewerbe Hamburg) 1970; Robertson.

8 GT 28 and plates 10A–F.
9 PC 335.
10 *Ib.*, 335.
11 See S. Alexiou and A. Lembesis in *Arch.Delt* 24 (1969) 415–18, fig. 1, plates 425–6; and Hoffman ECA, with bibliography.
12 Pp.
13 Willetts CCF 152 and n. 39.
14 See p. 106 and n. 14.

15 RELIGION

1 IC 2.VI.1 *circa* 2nd C. BC (a most plausible restoration); ICI. IX.1.A17 of 3rd/2nd C. BC and IC4.171.13 of 3rd C. BC; IC3.IV.8.1–9 of 3rd C. BC.
2 IC2.XIX.7; Willetts CCF 234 f.
3 IC I. V p. 7, Head 458; IC2 III p. 13, Head 458; IC I VIII p. 55, Head 462; Willetts CCF 235.
4 St. Byz. s.v. Ἄρβις·, Guarducci IC I IV p. 5, Cook Z 2.945, Jassen in RE s.v. Arbios, Evans PM1.630 f., cf. JHS 14.285; on the etymological conjectures, Willetts CCF 236.
5 Halbherr *Mus.It.* 3.621 n. 38, IC 3 III 13, Willetts CCF 237.
6 Detailed survey of the evidence with refs. in Willetts CCF 238 ff.
7 See the argument and detailed refs. in Willetts *ib.* 166–7; cf. IC 4.65 and Guarducci *ib.* pp. 33–4.
8 Head 473; Cook Z.2.946; Guarducci IC 1 p. 270.
9 Hsch. s.v. Γελχάνος; RL 14.381; Guarducci *ad* ICI XXIII 4 f.; Nilsson MMR 464, 550.
10 IC 4.3.1 (a–c), *ib.* 1.XVIII.11.2, XVI.3.2.
11 As I argued in CCF 250–1.
12 Pp. 125 ff.
13 10.475, cf. 10.478.
14 Bosanquet in ABSA 15.339, cf. *ib.* 8.286, 9.280, 10.246, 11.298.
15 L.29. Cf. Guarducci IC 3 p. 6.
16 Str. 10.475; Guarducci *ibid.*
17 IC 3.II.1. On the association of the temple with Hierapytna see Willetts ASAC 143.
18 See the text, with conjectural restorations, in IC 3 III.2. Kouretes derives from *Kouros* ('boy', 'young man').
19 See the argument in my CCF Ch. 7 *et passim*.
20 Lact. Plac. in Stat. *Theb.* 4.105; Pl. *Lg.* 625a–b.

21 D.S. 5.70; Thphr. *HP.* 3.3–4.
22 D.L. 8.3; Porph. *VP* 17; Cook Z.1.646 f.; Willetts CCF 219 and n. 138.
23 Porph. *Abst.* 4.19; E. *Cret.* fr. 472 Nauck; Willetts CCF 238 n. 67.
24 As suggested by Guthrie OGR 112–13, cf. *id.* GG 45.
25 Willetts CCF 241 f. with refs.
26 Thphr. *HP.* 3.3.4; Plin. *NH* 16.110. The iron-coloured stones found in Crete which were shaped like a human thumb and called *Idaei dactyli* were perhaps thought to be thunderbolts; see refs. in Willetts CCF 242 n. 78.
27 See Willets CCF 144 *et passim.*
28 IC I. XII.1; Head 479; Cook Z.2.933.
29 IC 4 80; Willetts ASAC 110–14.
30 Paus. 1.18.5.
31 4.50–2.
32 IC 4.3.3 (a–c).
33 IC I.VIII.4b 9; Willetts CCF 244, 253 and n. 12.
34 Head 461.
35 IC I. XVI 5.73, 88; cf. *ib.* XVIII 9c 5(111–110 BC).
36 IC 2.XV.2.10.
37 IC 2.XXV.3 and Guarducci *ad loc.*
38 IC 3.II 1.10.
39 Willetts CCF 254 and n. 19.
40 IC 3.III 4.
41 *Ib.* 3B 14, 20; 5, 12.
42 IC 3.III.14.
43 *Ib.* IV.8.
44 IC 2.X.1.16.
45 Head 478; Guarducci IC 2 p. 13; *ib.* p. 241.
46 Willetts CCF 255 and n. 32.
47 Detailed review of the evidence in Willetts CCF 256–71.
48 IC 3.III.9 cf. 10 and *ib.* 3 B 11, 12; IC I. III.1.9.
49 Willetts CCF 262–4.
50 Swindler 24–6.
51 IC I.VIII.8.12 f., 12–45 f.; *ib.* XVI 3.17, 4A 12 f.; 5.49.
52 *Ib.* IX.A21, C 117.
53 Cf. p. 107.
54 Nilsson MMR 455–6; Willetts CCF 264 n. 72.
55 IC I XVI.4A 22.
56 IC I 2.XV.2.18; Guarducci *ad loc.*
57 IC 2.XV.2.10.
58 IC 4.181.5 (early second century BC); *ib.* 172.21 (third–second century BC), 197.8 (second century BC), 235.7 f. (early second century BC).
59 Willetts CCF 265; cf. Paus. 3.13.1.
60 E. *Alc.* 445–51.
61 Hsch s.v.
62 Willetts CCF 195–7, 266.
63 Swindler 14–22.
64 Guarducci IC 4. pp. 5, 33.

65 IC I.XVIII.8.9 f.; *ib.* 3.IV.7.14 f.; 29 f.
66 Guarducci IC 4. p. 6 and *ib.* 182.19.
67 IC 4.184; Willetts ASAC 138–40; cf. Guarducci *ad* IC 4 p. 33.
68 Viz. IC 4.171 (third century BC); also *ib.* 174 (second century BC) and *ib.* 183 (*c.* second century BC).
69 BCH 70.603 f. n. 6. Guarducci *ad* IC4 p. 33 (seventh century BC).
70 If Hierapytnian Dekataphoros was synonymous with Pythios; Willetts CCF 261, 269.
71 IC 1, 3 *passim.*
72 Pp. 159 ff.
73 Willetts CCF 188–91.
74 P. Faure in BCH 84.209–15 and also in FCC. See also pp. 121 ff.
75 Thomson SAGS 1.276–80.
76 Ar. *Lys.* 645 sch., Harp. ἀρκτεῦσαι; cf. Lys. *fr.* 82, E. *Hyps. fr.* 57.
77 IC 3.III.3 B11, 13, 19, *ib.* 4.174, 58 f., 74 (early second century BC); *ib.* 3.III.58; 12 (later second century BC); Xenion *ap.* St.Byz. s.v. Oleros, cf. Eust. *ad.* Il. 2.639.
78 IC 3.V.1; Willetts ASAC 144.
79 Hsch. s.v.
80 Willetts ASAC 14, 121–2, CCF 116–17. 285–6, cf. 293–4.

16 CONFLICT AND SUBJECTION

1   *Pol.* 1333b 39–1334a2.
2   1272a 40 ff.
3   Willetts ASAC 160.
4   Griffith MHW 234–5, 245; Willetts ASAC 246 n. 7.
5   IC 3.III.3A.
6   Plb. 4.55.5, cf. 53.8.
7   Plb. 5.36, 5.65.7, 5.79.10, 82.10.
8   Refs. in Willetts ASAC 247–8.
9   Str. 10.477.
10 Willetts ASAC 248 and nn. 7–9.
11 *Ibid.* 244 ff.

INDEX

I SUBJECT INDEX

Achaean League 180
Acropolis 151, 158, 191, 192
Administration 17, 38, 41, 60,
  67, 69, 91, 132, 133, 176, 214
Adoption 164
Age-grades 175, 184
Agela 175, 176, 184, 201
Agora 111, 151, 189, 198
Agriculture 27, 29, 30, 34, 35,
  37, 38, 44, 57, 67, 94, 120,
  123, 127, 132, 152, 171
Agrimi 28, 87
Akkadian 39, 92
Alabaster 40, 64, 71, 85
Alien-acts 178, 211
Alloy 36, 82
Almonds 16, 26, 27, 88
Alphabet 41, 91, 92, 100,
  154–163, 164, 171, 187, 188,
  189, 191
Altars 27, 64, 79, 86, 87, 95,
  98, 107, 108, 111, 117, 160,
  188, 192, 200, 201, 207
Altitudes 28
Amber 196
Amethyst 88
Ancestors 45
Anchorage 23
Andreion 172, 184
Anebos 184
Animals 27, 28, 34, 36, 44, 45,
  76–79, 81, 84, 85, 88, 90, 92,
  94, 95, 98, 101, 116, 117, 119,
  120, 124, 161, 165, 191, 196,
  202, 203
Anoros 184
Antelopes 80, 81
Anthropology 166, 167, 177
Antiquity 11, 12, 17, 26–30,
  32, 34, 93, 106, 108, 110, 116,
  126, 127, 138, 158, 160, 162,
  164, 167, 171, 172, 177, 182,
  205, 207
Apamia 185
Apetairoi 172, 174, 184, 185
Aphamiotai 159, 174, 185, 186

Apiaries 27
Apodromos 176, 184
Apparel 35
Apples 27, 209
Apricots 27
Aqueducts 72, 75
Arbutus 27
Archaeologists 18, 19, 115,
  141, 142, 145
Archaeology 11, 18, 26, 30, 45,
  47, 48, 51, 59, 71, 91, 100,
  102, 104, 108, 110, 119, 126,
  128, 136, 137, 139, 141,
  145–7, 162, 166, 171, 181,
  187
Archaic period 43, 151, 154,
  164, 169, 177, 178, 186, 189,
  191–4, 198, 200
Archers 16, 84, 212
Architecture 15, 35, 36, 39, 45,
  47–9, 52, 53, 59, 63, 64, 73,
  74, 80, 119, 135, 192
Archives 39, 41, 68, 69, 91, 133
Aristocracy 143–215
Armour 112, 148, 196
Arms 112, 134, 172, 182, 193,
  195, 213
Army 16, 37, 38, 147, 180,
  212, 214
Arrows 16, 113, 148
Arrow-heads 44, 203
Artefacts 19, 30, 36, 85, 145,
  147, 153, 195
Artisans 37, 41, 63, 158, 159
Arts 15, 34, 35, 46, 60, 73–90,
  99, 108, 112, 113, 123, 126,
  128, 129, 133–5, 151, 157,
  171, 191–7
Ashes 27, 141, 192, 200
Asparagus 27
Assembly 179, 180, 198
Asylia 179, 180
Athletes 77
Authorities 17
Authors 12
Autobiography 15

Autonomy 67
Awls 36, 83, 85
Axes 36, 44, 52, 67, 69, 83,
  116, 120, 152, 202

Babylonian 39, 92
Barbarians 14
Barberry 27
Barges 38
Barley 16, 27, 34, 38, 51, 95
Barracks 38
Barrier 24
Barter 171
Basileus 109
Basins 23, 41, 61, 69, 70, 72,
  196, 203
Bathrooms 41, 61, 64, 67
Baths 37
Battles 81, 113, 134, 135, 148,
  212, 213, 215
Bays 24, 29, 33, 141, 214
Beads 36, 86, 89, 90, 196
Beams 64, 85, 139, 191, 202
Beans 27
Bear 122, 209
Bees 89, 90, 94, 125
Berth 24
Bellows 37
Benches 36, 52, 108
Beowulf 166
Beverages 27
Biography 15
Birds 28, 76, 77, 79–81, 84, 85,
  88, 106, 116, 118–20, 125,
  135, 157, 196, 197, 199, 203,
  209
Blades 34, 44, 135
Blocks 24, 25, 38, 45, 108, 138,
  141
Blood relations 45
Boar 28, 135
Boatmen 38
Boats 79, 81, 117, 118
Bone 33, 34, 44, 88
Books 12, 17, 30
Boots 16

265

Index

Index

Temples 24, 37, 38, 41, 61, 63, 64, 67, 69, 92, 108, 109, 112, 118, 120, 121, 123, 124, 129, 134, 151, 154, 157, 162, 191, 192, 199, 200, 205, 206, 207, 208, 209
Terebinth 26
Terraces 64, 73
Terracotta 75, 119, 193, 194, 200, 203
Testimony 14
Textiles 35, 51, 72
Texts 39, 92, 99, 101, 115, 149, 154, 162, 165, 168, 169, 185, 187, 188, 189, 200, 201
Thalassocracy 111, 113
Theatre 165
Theocracy 69, 112
Theogonies 116
Thiodaisia 201
Tholoi 47, 118, 133, 135, 160
Throne 68, 75, 77, 108, 111, 201
Throne Room 61, 68, 69, 75, 77, 108, 109, 111, 122, 139
Thunder 199
Thunder-stone 201
Thyme 27
Timber 39, 40, 64, 71, 73, 80, 85, 120
Tin 36, 39, 71, 82, 83
Tinstone 83
Tithes 206, 208
Tobacco 27
Tomatoes 27
Tombs 18, 25, 47, 51, 52, 79, 83, 88–90, 103, 115, 117–19, 126, 134–6, 157, 160, 193, 195, 201
Tongs 37
Tools 34, 35, 36, 37, 59, 82, 83, 85, 86, 94, 95, 100, 151, 153
Topography 32
Totem 45, 117, 119, 120, 125
Town-hall 151, 191, 192, 207
Towns 23, 35, 38, 39, 47, 48, 60, 61, 64, 72, 76, 81, 109, 112, 122, 123, 129, 137, 141, 142, 146, 147, 150, 154, 157, 158, 159, 173, 192, 200, 202, 205
Townsmen 38
Tracks 32
Trade 16, 27, 30, 35, 39, 40, 47, 48, 67, 71, 85, 113, 139, 147, 154, 157, 171, 172, 173, 184, 196, 213
Traders 16, 39, 205
Tradition 14, 15, 26, 39, 40, 46, 48, 63, 67, 72, 82, 83, 88, 104, 105, 107, 108, 109, 110, 111, 113, 116, 120, 122, 125, 126, 127, 129, 149, 150, 151, 154, 155, 157, 158, 161, 162,

167, 168, 170–2, 177, 178, 180–2, 192, 198–201, 204–7, 209, 210, 215
Traffic 32, 139
Transition 15, 18, 46, 128–41, 164, 210
Travellers 16, 17, 23, 30, 33, 39
Treasures 36, 90, 94, 119
Treasury 53, 68, 71, 121, 133, 208
Treaties 40, 158, 175, 179, 180, 181, 185, 199, 205, 206, 208, 209, 212
Treatment 15
Trees 26, 27, 28, 30, 51, 77, 79, 81, 94, 95, 106, 115–17, 120, 124, 126, 195, 197, 199, 201, 202, 203, 205, 206, 209
Trial 167
Tribal system 40, 45, 51, 118, 119, 126, 129, 137, 149, 154, 166, 167, 169, 174, 175, 180, 181, 184, 207
Tribesmen 38
Tribute 16, 72, 107, 110, 113, 132, 139, 159
Trinkets 36
Trojan War 141, 148, 149, 150, 158, 205
Troops 38, 40, 78, 81, 84, 105, 132, 134, 135, 147, 148, 179, 180, 182, 186, 193, 194, 196, 203, 212–15
Troughs 71
Tsunamis 142
Tub 67
Tubes 36
Turkish period 215
Tundra 34
Turn-tables 81
Tweezers 83
Twelve Tables 167
Tyrant 69, 181, 188

Ugaritic 39
Ulcer 28
Urbanization 191

Valleys 25, 34, 39, 96, 128, 185
Vases 25, 48, 71, 75, 77, 79, 82, 84, 85, 86, 87, 94, 96, 97, 101, 109, 117, 118, 136, 140, 156, 157, 193, 194, 195
Vassals 133
Vats 69, 71
Vaults 41, 133
Vegetables 16, 27, 87, 208
Vegetation 26, 27, 76, 77, 116, 120, 121, 123, 161, 198, 199, 208
Venetian period 214
Vessels 25, 40, 52, 69, 79, 81–3, 86, 96, 100, 133, 139, 196, 203

Vetch 61
Villages 16, 35, 45, 47, 48, 61, 64, 67, 72, 119, 141, 150, 152, 159
Villagers 38
Villas 60, 63, 71, 72, 75, 85, 134
Vine 51, 207, 208
Vineyard 40
Viticulture 51
Votaries 70
Voyage 16, 118, 139

Wainwrights 40
Wall-paintings 35, 36, 75, 76, 77, 82, 108
Walls 29, 35–7, 41, 44, 48, 50, 52, 61, 63–5, 67, 68, 74–6, 78–82, 87, 94, 123, 128, 136, 141, 161, 164, 165, 192, 201
War 48, 102, 110, 128, 134, 136, 139, 142, 148, 171, 178–82, 211–15
Warehouses 38, 67
Warriors (see Troops)
Warships 23, 81
Wasp 89
Water 23, 24, 27–9, 33, 38, 41, 43, 50, 52, 61, 68, 74–7, 79, 81, 85, 117, 141, 142, 164
Waves 24, 76, 142
Wax 16, 37
Wax-pitch 28
Weapons 35, 40, 82, 83, 95, 132, 134, 135, 148, 151, 153, 160, 162, 193
Weather 32
Weavers 38
Weaving 34, 35, 37, 44, 52, 53, 72
Weights 27, 44, 61, 70, 72, 100
Welkhania 157, 199
Wells 28, 29, 61, 63, 64, 67, 73, 75
Wheat 16, 34, 51
Wheels 32, 37, 82, 83, 86, 88, 99, 107, 194
Willow 26, 87, 106, 197, 203, 205
Windmills 29
Windows 61, 80
Winds 11, 14, 23, 29, 139
Wine 16, 27, 30, 40, 71, 133, 196, 203
Winter 24, 28
Wire 12, 86, 89
Withies 34
Witnesses 14, 167, 184
Woikeus 185
Women 27, 35, 38, 61, 72, 76, 77, 79, 80, 81, 95, 107, 112, 117, 120, 129, 149, 160, 169, 175, 184, 193

273

II INDEX OF DEITIES, PERSONS, PLACES

274

Index

Index

Index

Index

Spratt, T.A.B. 17, 24, 31
Staphylos 154
Starr, Chester 113
Stephanos 161
Strabo 105, 126, 154, 175, 185, 200
Suez Canal 141
Sumatra 141
Sumer 63
Syracuse 168 212
Syria 34, 37, 39, 44, 47, 71, 83, 88, 97, 98, 99, 100, 113, 128, 135, 139, 146, 152, 155, 156, 212
Syrians 46

Talos 199
Tammuz 123, 126
Taramelli, Antonio 18
Taras 160
Tarsus 36
Tartaria 96, 97, 99, 103
Tegeans 161
Tegeates 161
Telesterion 125
Tell Hariri 37
Tenos 179
Teos 187, 188
Terpander 94
Tersa (or Terzi) 25
Teukroi 158
Teukros 157, 158
Thales 33
Thasos 105
Thebes 101, 105, 136, 139, 140, 147
Thenon 164
Theopompos 183
Theophrastos 202
Theotokopoulos (El Greco) 16
Thera (Santorini) 80, 113, 129, 137, 140, 141, 142, 187, 206
Therasia 141
Thermi 36
Theseus 107, 108, 113, 121, 139, 192, 207
Thesprotia 149
Thessaly 34, 98, 147, 154, 182, 205
Thessalians 182, 183
Thucydides 14, 15, 110, 188, 189

Thevet 16
Thornax 160
Thothmes 110
Thrace 124
Thriphte Mountains 24
Tigris 34
Tiryns 18, 101, 109, 140, 147, 205
Tisza 96
Titans 125
Titus 203
Tordos 96, 97, 98
Tournefort 17
Trajan 121
Transcaucasia 152
Transylvania 95, 96, 99
Trapeza Cave 52
Triptolemos 123
Tritsch, F.J. 111
Troad 47, 209
Troy 18, 36, 48, 85, 96, 98, 99, 105, 139, 147, 148, 149, 150, 158
Tsangli 98
Tsoutsouros 32
Turkey 17, 30, 35, 63, 215
Turks 16, 30, 32, 214, 215
Twelve Gods 188
Tylissos 18, 61, 70, 75, 83, 134, 138, 181, 199, 205
Tyre 39, 40, 106
Tzetzes 199

Ugarit (Ras Shamra) 37, 39, 40, 41, 42, 74, 100, 134
Ur 37
Uruk 97

Van der Mijnsbrugge 180
Van Effenterre, Henri 19, 111, 180, 185
Vaphio 160
Varro 126
Vasiliki 18, 48, 51, 53, 57, 76
Vathypetro 71, 75, 134
Venetians 32, 214
Venice 214
Venizelos 215
Ventris, Michael 101, 102
Vesuvius 141
Vidal-Naquet, Pierre 183

Vinča 96
Vitsilia 71
Vlassa, Dr N. 96, 97
Vrokastro 146, 150
Vulcan 116

Wace 138
Warren 19, 25, 30, 50, 51, 52, 53
Waterhouse, Helen 111
Welkhanos 116
White Mountains 24, 25, 29
Woolley 39

Xanthoudides, Stephanos 18, 47

Yiali 71
Yarim-Lim 39

Zagreus 116, 202
Zakro 18, 28, 59, 61, 64, 66, 67, 68, 71, 74, 86, 87, 101, 137, 138, 142
Zaleukos 168, 170
Zan 126, 201
Zeus 105, 106, 107, 109, 116, 121, 122, 125, 126, 127, 136, 168, 169, 196, 197, 198, 199, 201, 202, 203, 204, 205, 206
Zeus Cretan (Kretagenes) 116, 122, 125, 126, 157, 161, 169, 178, 196, 198, 199, 200, 201, 202, 206
Zeus Agoraios 198; Alexikakos 198; Ammon 198; Arbios 199; Asterios 107, 199; Brontaios 199; Bronton 199; Diktaios 154, 198, 200, 206; Epopsios 200; Hekatombaios 199; Idaios 201, 202, 203; Kroneios (Kronidas) 199, 200; Makhaneus 199, 205; Melikhios (Meilikhios) 199, 206; Monnitios 199; Olympios 198; Oratrios 199; Skylios 199; Soter 199; Tallaios 199; Welkhanos 157, 199
Zou 71
Zygioi 158